Along the River During the Qingming Festival

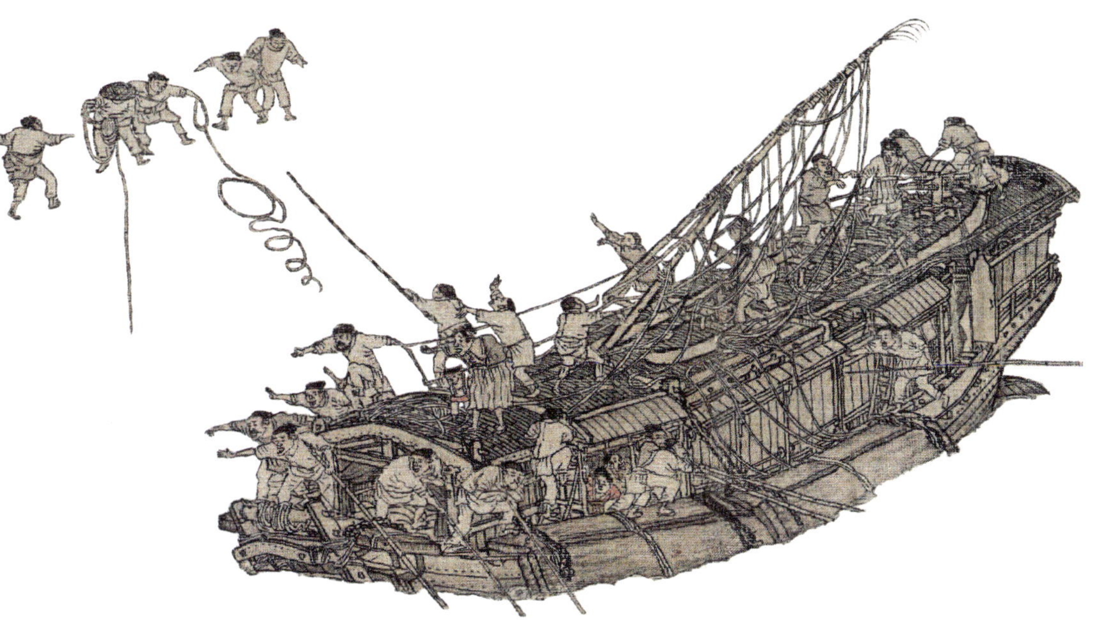

Along the River During the Qingming Festival

One Day in the Song Dynasty

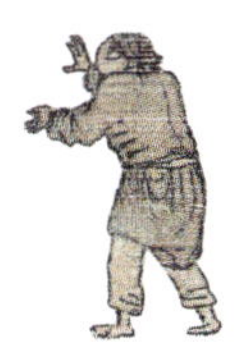

Tian Yubin

Translated by Ning Jing

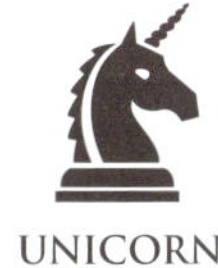

UNICORN

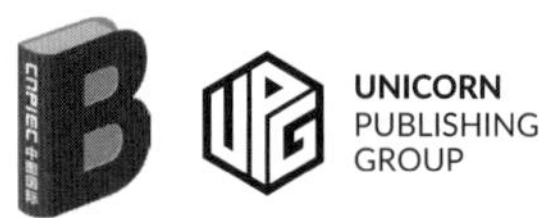

Published in association with CNPIEC by Unicorn
an imprint of Unicorn Publishing Group, 2024
Charleston Studio
Meadow Business Centre
Lewes, BN8 5RW

www.unicornpublishing.org

Cataloging-in-Publication (CIP) Data
Along the River During the Qingming Festival: One Day in the Song Dynasty/
Tian Yubin, Translated by Ning Jing. — Zhengzhou: Henan
Fine Arts Publishing House, 2022.1 (Reprinted in November 2023)
(Series of Comprehend Chinese Painting)
ISBN 978-7-5401-5630-5
1. ① Qing... 2. ① Tian... 3. ① Along the River During the Qingming
Festival — Painting Critique IV. ① J212.05
National Library of China CIP Data C-2021-235609

Translated by Ning Jing, Xijing University

10 9 8 7 6 5 4 3 2 1

ISBN: 978-1-916846-48-7

Printed in the UK by Short Run Press, Exeter

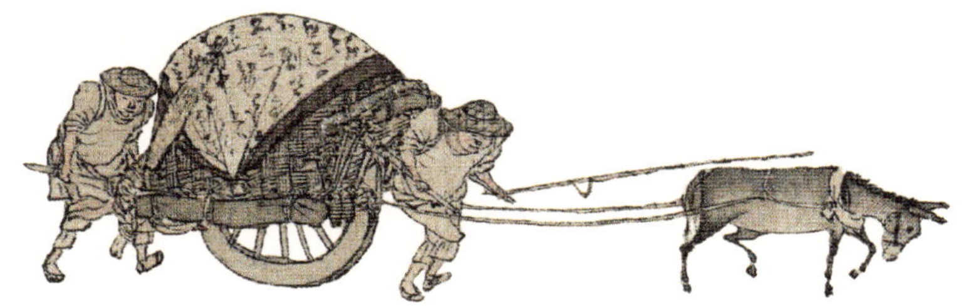

Contents

Preface

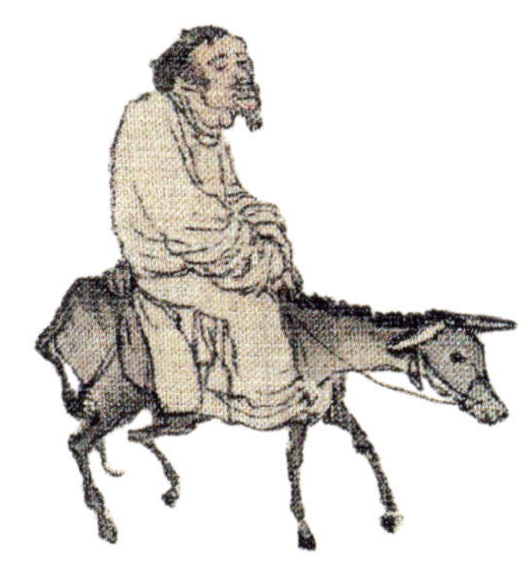

COMPREHEND CHINESE PAINTING

Bring the beauty of Chinese arts to everyone

I am so excited that Henan Fine Arts Publishing House has planned and published a series of books on 'Comprehend Chinese Painting', which is an important initiative to strengthen aesthetic education and disseminate fine traditional Chinese culture. This series reflects the distinctive positioning of the times and creativity in book planning and publishing.

Aesthetic education has become a buzzword in recent years in academic circles. Both the economic and material development of our society have made people aspire to a richer spiritual world. In their pursuit of a better life, there is a growing demand for beauty. Therefore, it is necessary to adopt a comprehensive approach and to open up a new path to shape aesthetic education in schools, society and at home. The publication of books with aesthetic significance, especially those outstanding books, is an action in the right direction to put aesthetic education into practise. This series of books is designed for our general readers, rooted in traditional culture and centred on the spirit of aesthetic education. It leads us to the mysteries of the art of Chinese painting and the depths of classic Chinese paintings, so that we can realise the creation of beauty, feel the charm of that beauty, and understand the cultivation of beauty in the process of appreciating the arts. This is an effective way to shape, cultivate and construct masculinity within aesthetic education.

The idea of aesthetic education has been in the blood of Chinese culture for 5,000 years. At the end of the Han Dynasty and the beginning of the Wei Dynasty, Xu Gan, one of the 'Seven Scholars of Jian'an', wrote about *Artistic Discipline (Yiji)* in his book *The Theory* (*Zhonglun*): 'To educate a student is just like teaching him an art.' Although there is a difference in the meaning of 'education' here and the spirit of modern aesthetic education, the ancients integrated 'art' into self-cultivation, a well-managed family and the ability to administer the state and bring peace to the nation. It can be said this combines aesthetic education with the shaping of a 'gentleman's' perfect personality, which is inseparable from modern aesthetic education in the deeper connotations.

Turning this rich and profound traditional culture into aesthetic education is also an important task in realising the creative transformation and innovative development of fine traditional Chinese culture. Ancient Chinese paintings are the essence of Chinese traditional culture, and the masterpieces of this culture can be regarded as the richest heritage of aesthetic education resources.

How to explore such heritage? It is extremely important to enjoy and appreciate ancient works of art. Famous paintings such as *Along the River During the Qingming Festival, A Thousand Li of Rivers and Mountains* and *Five Oxen,* are well known to the world. However, in the past, many Chinese people had only heard about these paintings but had never had the chance to appreciate them. Fortunately, in recent years, we can see more of these ancient paintings through museums, the Internet and in various publications. However, we still have a lot of work to do in terms of understanding Chinese paintings in detail.

Along the River During the Qingming Festival: One Day in the Song Dynasty is one of the *Comprehend Chinese Paintings* series, and I was touched while reading it. The book provides a detailed analysis of the painting, allowing readers to appreciate its intricacies and meaning. Secondly, the illustrations of the paintings are of high quality and the presentation is well laid out. The details are clear and easy to understand, with a proper interpretation alongside, eliminating the need for readers to search for it elsewhere. This enhances the reading experience and makes it more enjoyable. In ancient China, reading paintings was like a cultural pilgrimage ritual. When the weather was fine, people would sit at a clean table by a bright window, burn incense, and unfold the scroll to 'appreciate' and 'taste' the artwork with respect. They would view the painting from afar, then move closer to examine the details. Through these times of 'viewing and reading', they would gain a deeper understanding and appreciation.

Today, publications serve as a medium for reading paintings. Although not as ceremonial as in ancient times, they offer a wider range of knowledge and allow for a detailed interpretation. This enables our readers to engage in in-depth reading and immerse themselves in the world of paintings. This book is not only a sample of the

Comprehend Chinese Painting series but also a valuable resource for contemporary readers seeking to fully understand Chinese painting. The next publication of this series is highly anticipated.

The value of aesthetic education lies in its subtle impact. With interesting and clear words, the book interprets the details that are usually hard to read or understand, starting with the curiosity of our general readers. It embodies idealism, humanity and practicability, truly reflecting the characteristics of aesthetic education in the new era. This makes it appealing to students at various stages and adult readers alike. We hope that more books like this will be published to enhance the public's aesthetic and humanistic qualities. May the seeds of beauty be sown throughout China.

范迪安

Chairman of the China Artists Association
Former President of the Central Academy of Fine Arts

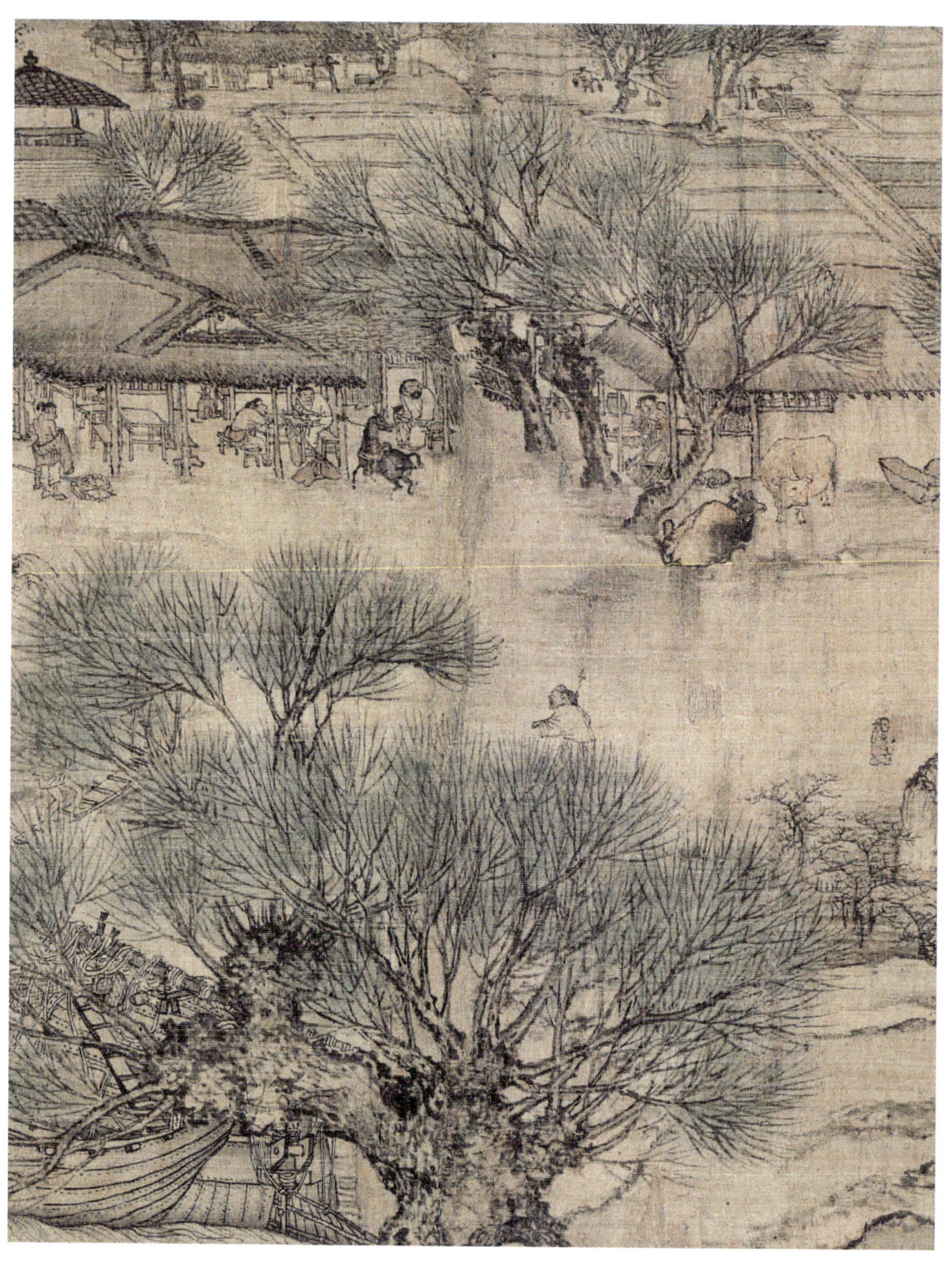

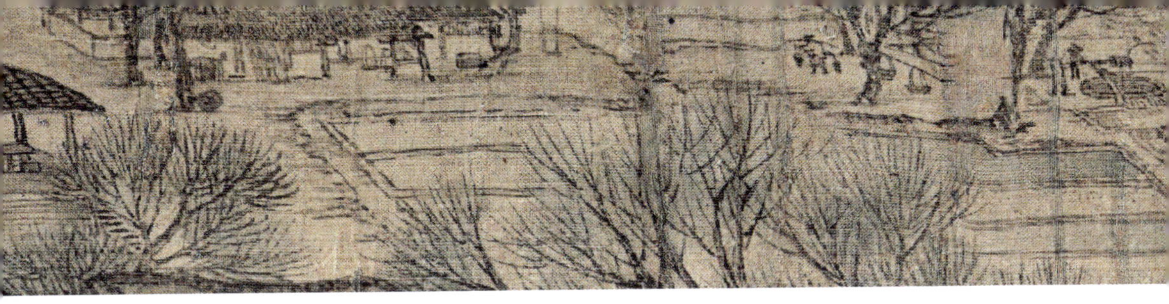

I Love Chinese Paintings

This book series is entitled *Comprehend Chinese Painting*. The 'Chinese paintings' here specifically refer to ancient Chinese paintings (Chinese paintings for short). I have a profound appreciation for Chinese paintings. My sentiment is not that of a painter or an expert, but rather than of a fellow Chinese, like you, my dear readers, who are driven by a natural curiosity and appreciation for the ancient Chinese paintings.

One thing is certain, there are different levels of love. Initially, its beauty arouses our fondness for it. Gradually, the deeper understanding and more interactions we have, the more profound our love becomes. Eventually, love becomes so captivating that we are addicted to it, making it inseparable. At this stage, passion blossoms.

Well, it is fair to say that my love is for the Chinese painting.

The Good-looking Chinese Pictures, my first 'fruit' of love for Chinese paintings, has been published. Through this book, I have connected with many readers who have the same passion as I do. One of these readers is Kang Hua, Editor-in-Chief at Henan Fine Arts Publishing House. She and her team have invited me to participate in the *Comprehend Chinese Painting* series and I am delighted to have been invited and eager to contribute.

In *The Good-looking Chinese Pictures*, I wrote nearly eighty pages about *Along the River During the Qingming Festival*. However, this is not sufficient to fully appreciate its greatness, as it is one of the most celebrated paintings in China. It is a painting that evokes strong emotions in me and compels me to keep writing.

However, my dear friends, sometimes I feel frustrated for loving it. I studied the picture many times but still discovered new information upon subsequent viewings. For example, I recently noticed a swing (marked by the red arrow in the image above) hanging beside the wall of a farmhouse at the end of a wheat field. It was just there in the picture but I failed to notice it before. I know, my kind readers, you will forgive me, as it is drawn at the edge, in such an obscure place. I still blame myself even now for not noticing it before. Scholars have debated the meaning of 'Qingming' in *Along the River During the Qingming Festival.* Some argue it refers to 'peaceful and orderly', while others suggest it refers to 'Qingming Square'. Additionally, there is debate over whether the season depicted in the painting is autumn rather than spring, which is close to the Qingming Festival. However, focusing on the swing, it has hung there for almost a thousand years, silently witnessing the custom of swinging during the Qingming Festival in the Song Dynasty.

How can he overlook such details while making arguments? It is essential to delve deeper and uncover more details beyond just the swing.

Besides, I observed a man fetching water at the well while wearing his *Kai dang ku* (开裆裤), which translates literally as 'split-crotch-pants'. *Kai dang ku*! An adult in *Kai dang ku*! That's funny! It is worth noting that both men and women wear this type of clothing. In another part of the scroll, the woman on a boat is pouring out water used for washing. There is a pair of *Kai dang ku* hanging amongst her washed clothes. *Kai dang ku*! Both men and women! That's so ridiculous! The details of my observations may seem unconventional but they are entertaining to me. What a skilled painter he is! He showed us the man's buttocks, but the woman's *Kai dang ku*. The portrayal perfectly demonstrates his unparalleled mastery of nuance.

My dear readers, what I'm eager to unveil about *Along the River During the Qingming Festival* are some of the most captivating and overlooked intricacies. I can even imagine your gasps from time to time, like I did whilst reading: 'Wow, who would've thought this was from the Song Dynasty!' 'Oh, I see!' 'Ah, I can't believe it!' and so on.

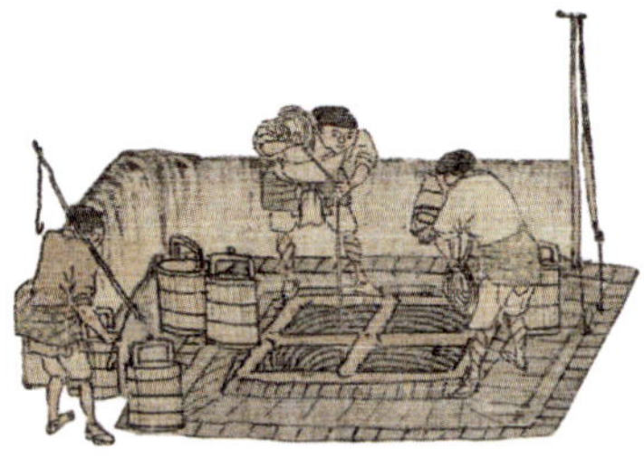

My dear friends, I reiterate, I love Chinese painting. My adoration for Chinese painting burns with fervour, tinted with a trace of frustration and a hint of resentment. Yes, there's resentment – I lament my inability to vividly capture and articulate its essence. In the first scene of *Along the River During the Qingming Festival*, there is a *liu zhou* (碌碡), a cylindrical farming instrument used as a roller to crush or press, in the courtyard. Some say it is a *Nian zi* (碾子), which is a roller used to make things flat. *Liu zhou* and *Nian zi* are similar in shape, but they are completely different farming tools. Definitely different! But more often than not, I feel frustrated with myself for the inaccurate interpretations I made before. For example, emerging from the shadows, there is a figure of mystique, with his cascading braids. I used to interpret him as a spy from the Jin Dynasty, but I don't think so now, since shreds of evidence were discovered in the printing.

The desire for accuracy and the fear of uncertainty are both due to love. Love, as it deepens, evolves into philosophy: to some extent ambiguity is a form of precision. For example, who is this mysterious person? We can't be sure. If you're not sure, just say so. That's accurate too. On the other hand, it is also wrong to abuse vagueness to avoid arguments. Striking a balance between inaccuracy and precision is not much different from taking shortcuts. For example, how many figures are there in *Along the River During the Qingming Festival*? This seemingly simple question is surprisingly controversial. Some say more than 500 people, while others say more than 1,000. My God, what a big difference that is! Of course, there are some serious people who used the 'rice counting method' and counted the rice several times to get 815 people. That's right and I respect those serious people. But to be more rigorous, statistics are meaningless without clear criteria. The standard I set is that as long as a little bit of the body is exposed, even a sleeve or a foot, it can be counted as one person. With the help of computer software, my answer is 806 people[1]. Once serious statistics have been compiled, what is the point of saying 'maybe', 'probably' or 'possibly' about the number of people?

All right, let's draw a close to my opening words. I invite you to join me in unravelling the mysteries of this masterpiece with the same curiosity as if you were listening to a friend sharing tales of a painting.

All right, let's draw a close to my opening words. I invite you to join me in unravelling the mysteries of this masterpiece with the same curiosity as if you were listening to a friend sharing tales of a painting.

[1] Counted again with my readers. The latest number is 835 people (2 are still in question).

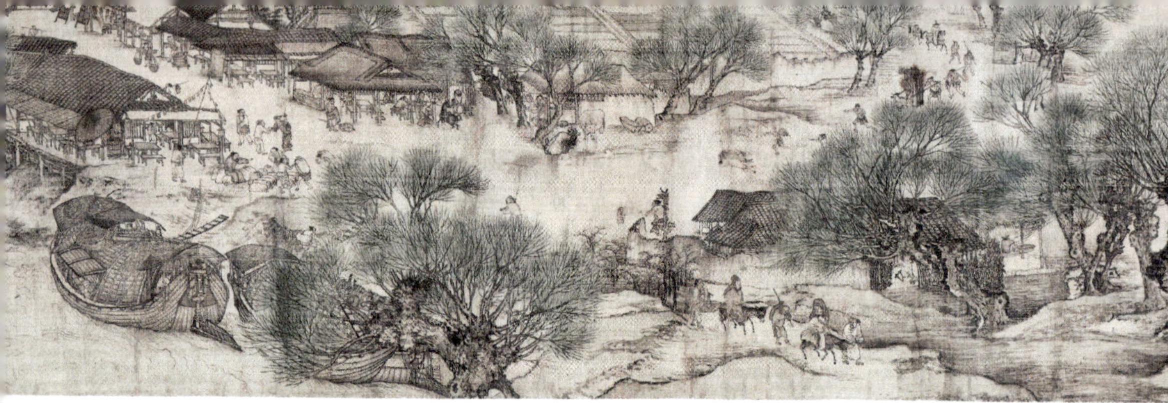

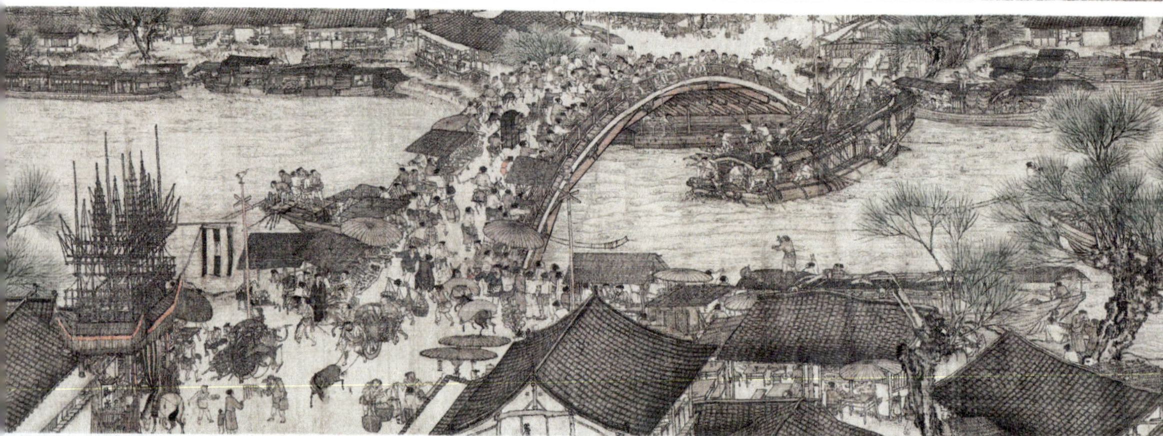

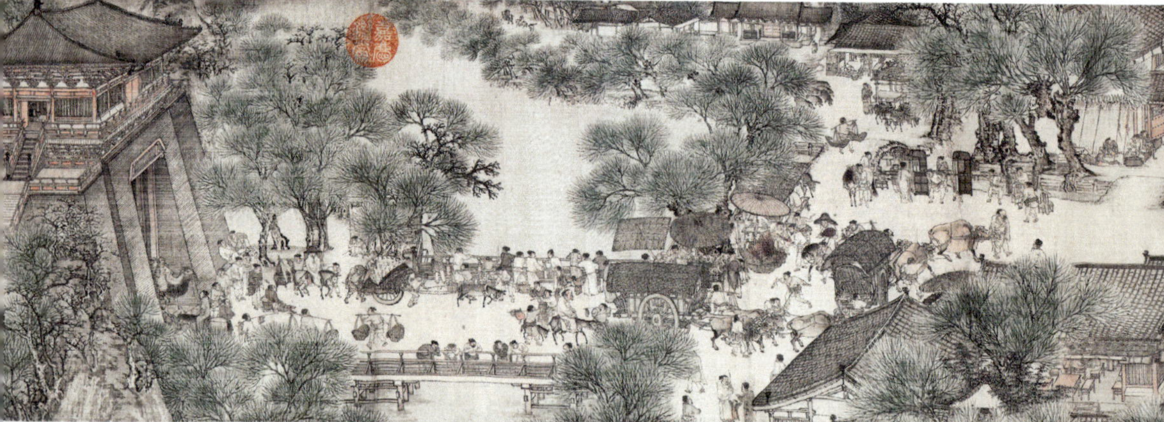

Full Preview of *Along the River During the Qingming Festival* (from right to left)

Part I
Part II
Part III
Part IV

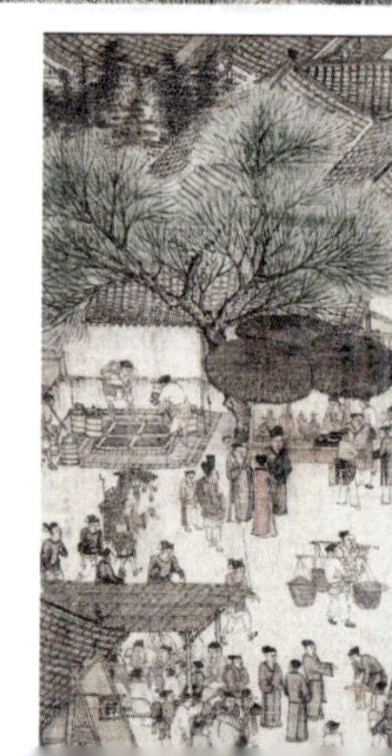

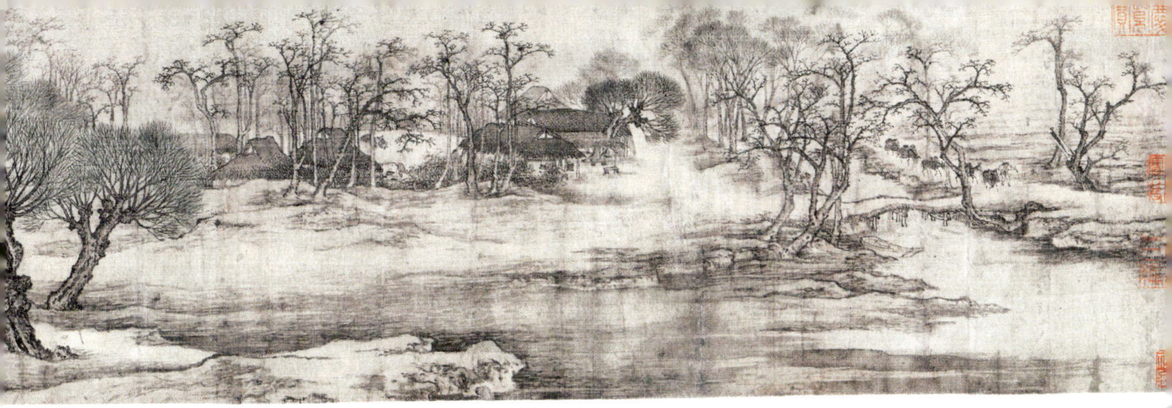

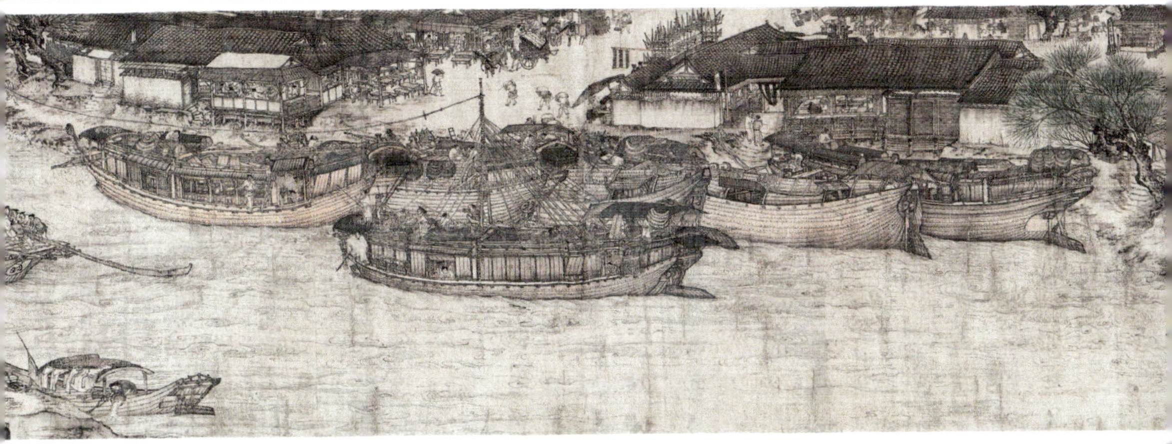

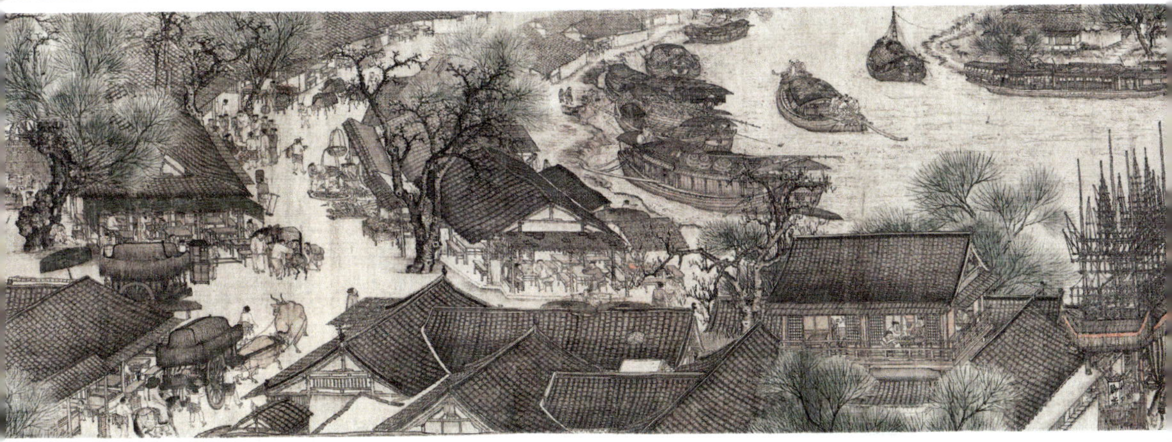

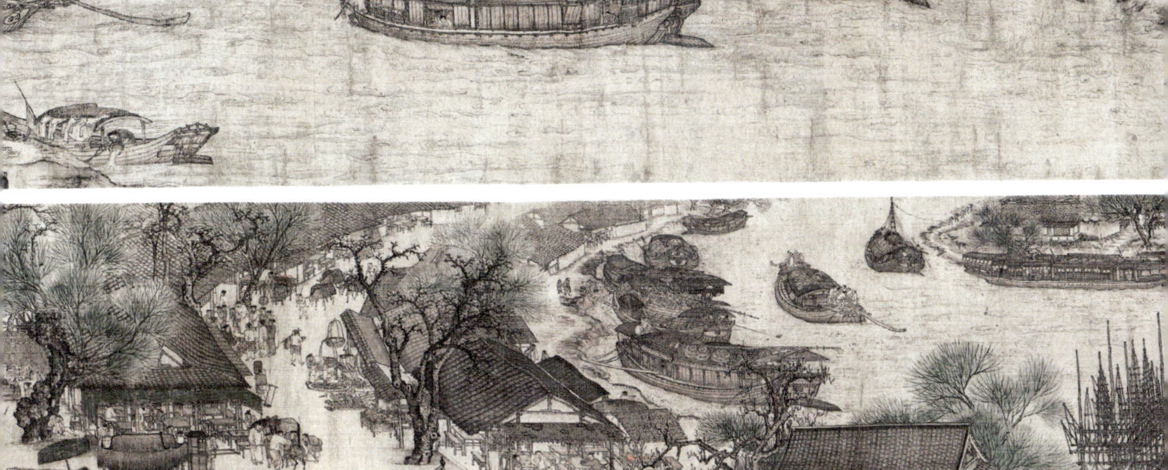

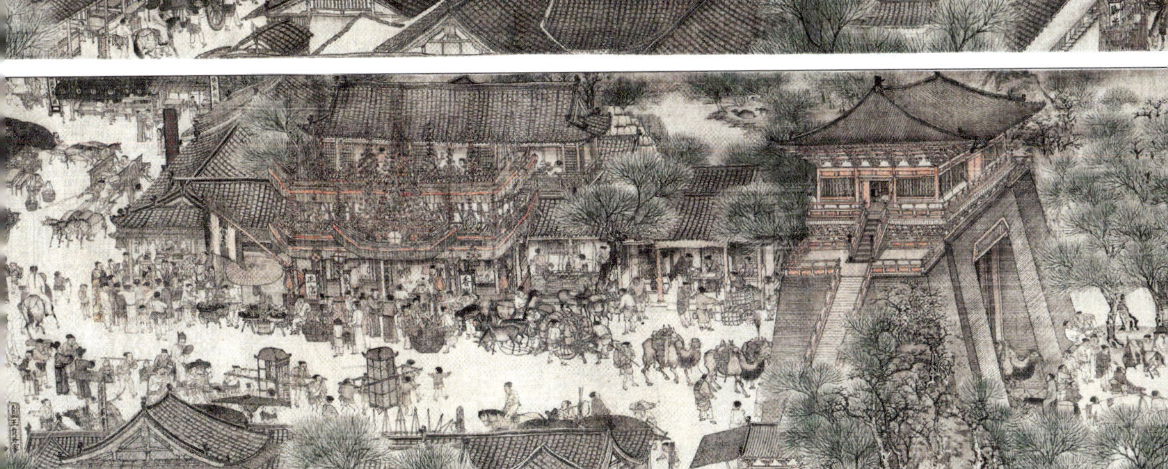

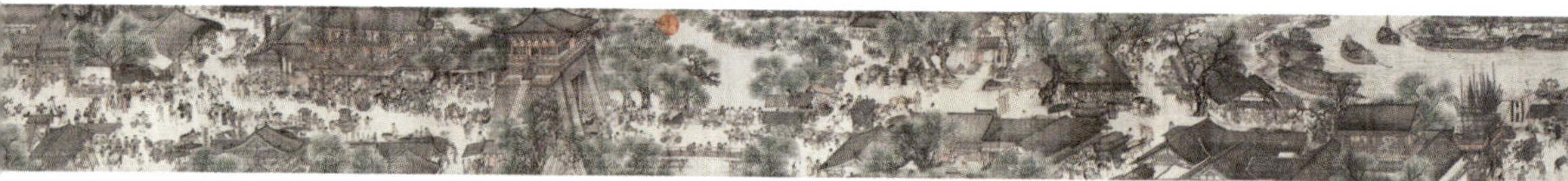

Hua xin (original image) of *Along the River During the Qingming Festival*

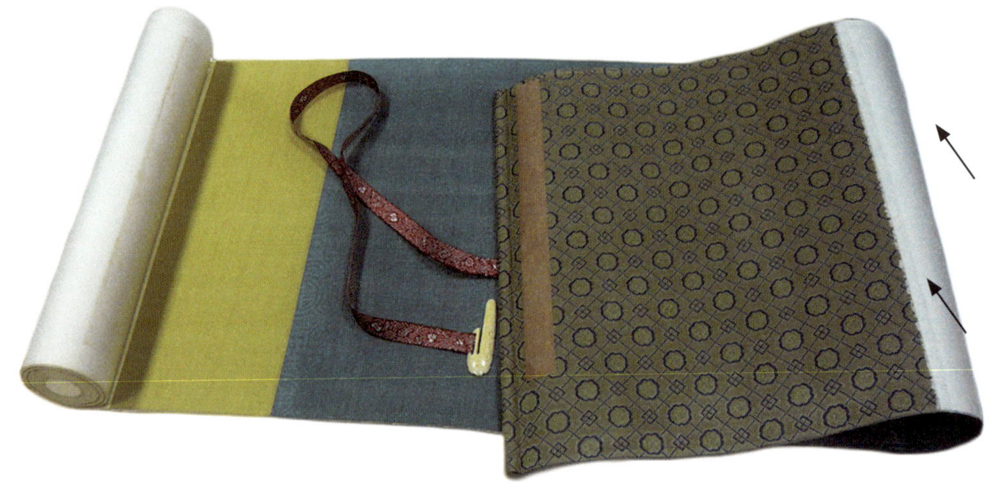

Above: Handscroll

Below: Diagram of handscroll mounting format

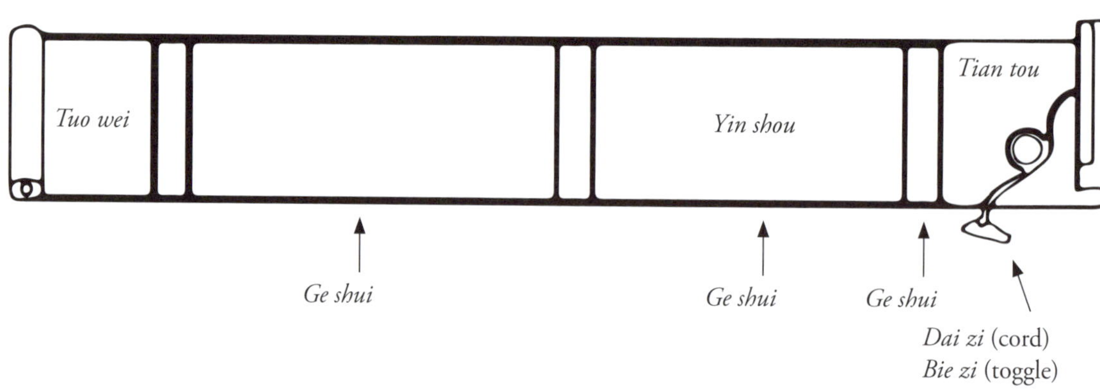

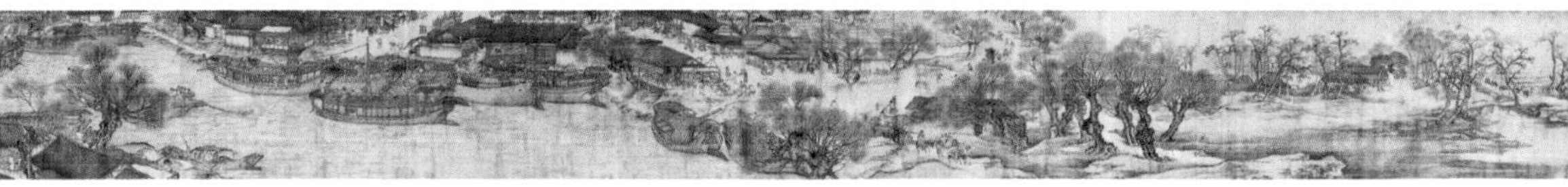

Along the River During the Qingming Festival is mounted on a 'scroll' ①. The scroll is one of the oldest mounting formats for paintings and calligraphy in China and has since evolved into the vertical scroll and the booklet ②. One of the main reasons why the 'scroll' is also called a 'handscroll' is that, when reading a handscroll, one would advance the scroll from right to left, pausing to admire and study it, shoulder-width section by section, rerolling a section before proceeding to the next one. Now, following my words, please imagine how an ancient Chinese person would read a handscroll.

The ancient Chinese man is reading the handscroll. He lightly holds one side in his left hand and the other in his right. Unrolling it from the right to a shoulder-width section, he pauses to read. When he is ready to move on from a scene, his right hand moves the scroll back towards the left. Then his left hand lightly loosens its grip, allowing the scroll to shift towards the left while the right hand follows. In this manner, he unfurls and reads the handscroll section by section until reaching the end.

The term 'handscroll' owes its origins not solely to the act of unrolling by hand for viewing, but also profoundly to the nuances of the experience itself. In contrast to being hung upon walls for public display, or the full unfurling of scrolls by museums for public exhibition, reading a handscroll is an intimate affair. It invites you to take your time, unveiling it gradually and patiently, savouring it in tranquil solitude or, at most, in the company of one or two close companions. The experience of the ancients reading a handscroll is somewhat akin to modern people reading a book or watching a movie: reading a book involves holding it in one's hands and turning the pages one by one; watching a movie involves viewing a sequence of scenes followed one after another. It is just that the turning of the pages and the changing of the camera are not as random or self-paced as in the case of a handscroll: an adult can unfold it wider, while a child would unfold it more narrowly. Therefore, what you can read depends on how far you unfold it.

① The origins of the scroll can be traced back to the *Jian ce* (简策) from the Spring and Autumn period to the Han Dynasty. *Jian ce* refers to the practice of stringing together bamboo or wooden slips inscribed with text using cords, forming elongated horizontal strips that could be easily rolled up for storage. After the Eastern Han Dynasty, even though the use of silk paper gradually became widespread, *Jian ce* was still the main method of mounting, allowing paintings and calligraphy works to be rolled up. Before the Tang Dynasty, handscrolls remained the primary format for mounting paintings and calligraphy.

② When readers see the names of ancient paintings, they often find these names followed by *Juan* (卷, scroll), *Zhou* (轴, hanging scroll), or *Ce ye* (册页, album of paintings), as in *Along the River During the Qingming Festival juan* (《清明上河图》卷), *Listening to the Qin zhou* (《听琴图》轴), and *Bird Attracted to Ripe Fruit or Bird and Fruits ce ye* (《果熟来禽》图). These words indicate the mounting formats. However, some may mistakenly include the mounting format in the title brackets, such as *Along the River During the Qingming Festival Juan*. This mixes up the painting's name with its format, which is incorrect.

Handscrolls are generally not very wide, often around 30 centimetres (if they are wider than 50 centimetres they would be considered 'large scrolls'). But they can be very long, with some extending several metres or even over 10 metres long. Of course, there are exceptions: some handscrolls are very short, only a few tens of centimetres, which can be referred to as 'pocket-sized scrolls'; some are both wide and long, such as *Emperor Shizong's Majestic Return from the Mausoleum by Water* (《入跸bi图》) in the Ming Dynasty, which is nearly 1 metre wide and over 30 metres long, and can only be described as an 'extra-large scroll'.

The mounting of ancient Chinese calligraphy and painting has evolved through generations, forming a common format. However, it is not entirely unchanging. For instance, handscrolls in the Song Dynasty consist of the *Tian tou* ①, *Ge shui* ②, *Hua xin* ③, *Ge shui*, and *Tuo wei* ④, arranged from right to left. In the Ming Dynasty, an additional section called *Yin shou* ⑤ was added to handscrolls, forming a format such as *Tian tou*, *Ge shui*, Yin *shou*, *Ge shui*, *Hua xin*, *Ge shui* and *Tuo wei*.

① *Tian tou* (天头，frontispiece): The *Tian tou* of a handscroll refers to the mounted material at the beginning of the scroll. It was quite short before the Yuan and Ming dynasties. However, the inscriptions and labels, which were mostly mounted inside the scroll, gradually moved from the interior to the exterior. Consequently, the *Tian tou* inside the scroll was extended, leading to the development of the *Yin shou* (引首，preface), which first appeared in the early Ming Dynasty. Hanging scrolls feature not only a *Tian tou* (upper) but also a *Di tou* (地头，bottom).

② *Ge shui* (隔水，border), also known as *Ge jie* (隔界) ,refers to a strip of silk mounted between the *Tian tou*, *Yin shou*, *Hua xin* and *Tuo wei* of a handscroll. It serves two purposes: firstly, it is a divider separating the different sections of the scroll; secondly, it enhances the overall aesthetics. *Ge shui* located in front of the main painting area is called the *Qian* ge *shui* (前隔水，front border), while the one placed at back is *Hou* ge *shui* (后隔水，back border).

③ *Hua xin* (画心，original painting): The *Hua xin* refers to the original painting or calligraphy mounted in the handscroll.

④ *Tuo wei* (拖尾，blank portion for inscriptions), or *Wei zhi* （尾纸）, is an integral part after the *Hou ge shui*. It serves two primary functions: firstly, it helps protect the main painting area, or *Hua xin*; secondly, it provides space for inscriptions. You will not read this part until you have fully unrolled the handscroll to the end. That's why it is called *Tuo wei*.

⑤ *Yin shou* (引首，preface) refers to the blank paper left in front of the main painting area, or *Hua xin*, in a handscroll. It is generally used for colophons or commentary. The *Yin shou* is separated from the *Hua xin* by the *Qian ge shui*. The moment you unroll the handscroll, you can see the *Yin shou*, which literally means preface.

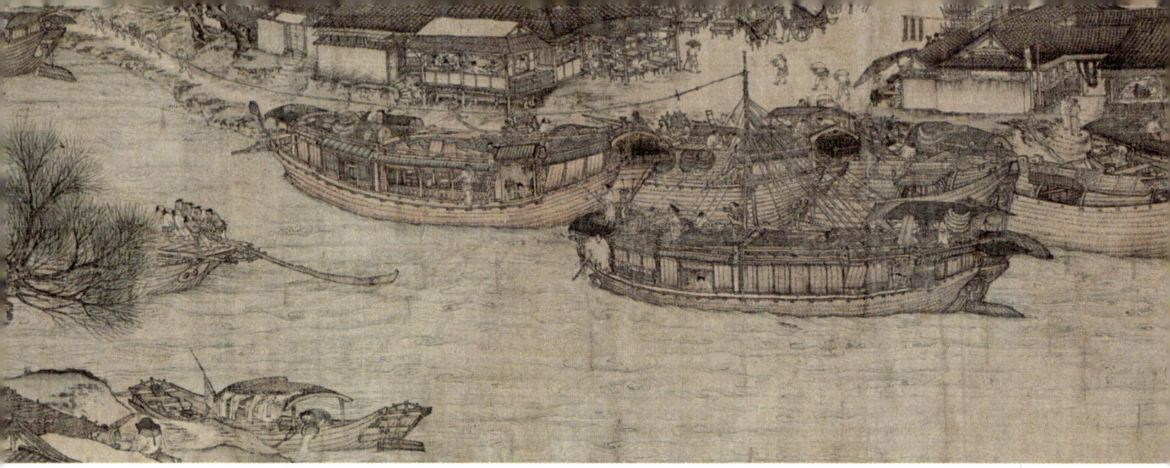

CHAPTER I

Introduction: What We Should Know Before Reading

Along the River During the Qingming Festival **juan,**
the Song Dynasty artist Zhang Zeduan (张择端, 1085–1145)
lightly inked and colour on silk, 25.5 cm × 525 cm (10.0 in × 207 in),
in the collection of the Palace Museum, Beijing

We have taken a look at the *Along the River During the Qingming Festival* and gained some knowledge about 'handscrolls'. Now, please turn your attention to the four lines in a small font below the title on this page, which provide the basic information about the *Along the River During the Qingming Festival*, including the dynasty, the artist, the mounting format, the material, the colour, the dimensions and the collection place. Among these details, '*She se* (设色)' indicates that this painting is in colour. '*Dan she se* (淡设色)' means that the painting is lightly inked and coloured.

Before we delve into the painting itself, I'm sure you're curious about more than just the basic information. You might be wondering about the subject, the artist and the fascinating stories attached to it. In the following sections, let me unveil these intriguing details one by one, allowing you to fully appreciate the significance and allure of this remarkable work of art.

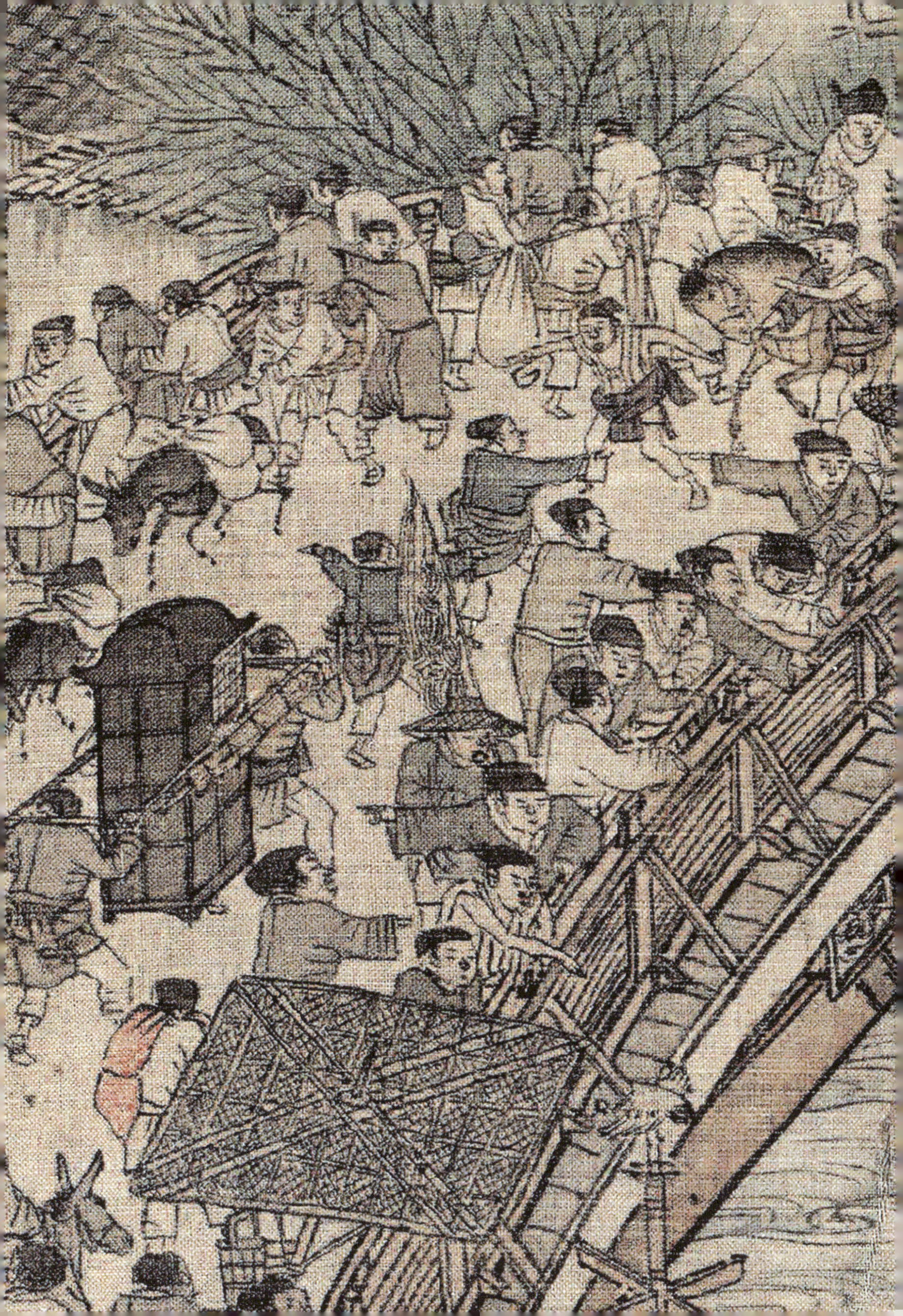

1. Scenes of *Along the River During the Qingming Festival*

Along the River During the Qingming Festival captures the hustling and bustling street life in rural areas and the city of Bianjing (present-day Kaifeng, Henan Province), the capital of the Northern Song Dynasty during the Qingming Festival. Rather than presenting a panoramic view of the entire city, the artist has chosen to focus on a specific route that guides the viewer's eye from the outskirts to the heart of the city. The journey begins at a small bridge in the suburbs, from which the path meanders through the countryside to the bustling docks along the Bian River. Here, the painting shifts its focus from the road to the river, following the waterway as it winds its way towards the city gate. At the centre of the scroll, the river passes beneath the great bridge, called the Rainbow Bridge (*Hong qiao,* 虹桥), a focal point that draws the viewer's attention. Not far from the bridge the river takes a sharp turn, prompting the artist to once again shift the focus back to the road. The path now leads the viewer towards the city gate, passing through the imposing entrance and into the heart of Bianjing. The painting concludes with a final stretch of road within the city walls, bringing the visual journey to a close.

As you might have guessed, *Along the River During the Qingming Festival* is not a mere roadmap or waterways of Bianjing (how dull would that be?). Instead, the artist captured the lively scenes of the street markets and the bustling riverside bazaars, particularly near the Rainbow Bridge and along the banks of the Bian River. In essence, the painting is a vivid portrayal of the daily life and lifestyle of all levels of society from rich to poor in Bianjing. Now, that's where things get interesting, don't you think? The scroll features over 800 figures, each with their own unique story to tell, from government officials and their servants, to merchants, sedan chair bearers, labourers, storytellers, fortune-tellers, wandering monks, barbers, doctors and even beggars. Although women and children make fewer appearances, each of their portrayals is equally fascinating. For instance, there is a little boy on the left who stretches out his arms, desperately seeking attention, while the two adults beside him remain engrossed in their conversation. It reminds me of my childhood when my mother took me to the market only to stop and chat endlessly with acquaintances, leaving me feeling ignored and frustrated. Seeing the poor little boy from the Song Dynasty here strikes a chord with me, filling me with a sense of righteous indignation. As you read the painting, you'll find yourself marvelling at the artist's extraordinary ability to bring each of the hundreds of figures to life with stunning vividness and individuality. This is no easy feat, not only because of the exquisite painting skills required but also due to the limited size of the scroll. *Along the River During the Qingming Festival* is only 24.8 centimetres in height, which means that in order to depict both the grand scenes and the numerous characters, the figures had to be painted on a remarkably small scale. How small could that be? On average, the figures in the painting are a mere 2 to 3 centimetres tall.① Go ahead, grab a ruler and see for yourself just how tiny they are! It's incredibly challenging to imbue such small figures with a sense of emotion and vitality, don't you think?

Despite the difficulty, the artist refused to resort to generic and formulaic representations. Instead, he went to great lengths to ensure that each person in the painting is distinct and unique. That's why we are treated to a captivating array of the Song Dynasty characters, each with their own emotions, personalities and even stories. Speaking of stories, I can't help but wonder about the mysterious figure I mentioned earlier (pictured below right). He's completely wrapped up, revealing only his back to the viewer, making him stand out from the crowd. Sometimes, I wish I could call out to him and ask him to turn around, just so we could catch a glimpse of his face. As you lose yourself in the painting, you'll realise that not a single person is idle. Everyone is engaged in their own activity, each with their own emotion and intriguing detail. Before you know it, half the day will have slipped by as you find yourself utterly absorbed in the mesmerising world of *Along the River During the Qingming Festival*.

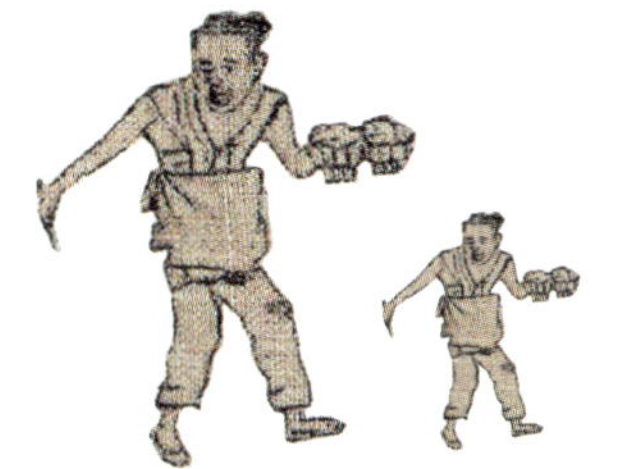

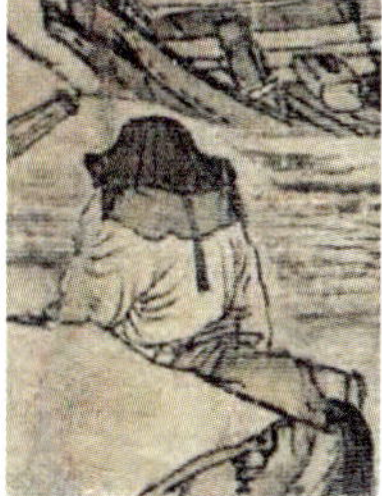

① In this book, I've enlarged certain sections of the painting to help our readers appreciate the intricate details more easily. As a result, the figures in the book often appear larger than they are in the original painting. The image on the left side above is an enlarged view, while the one on the right shows the figures at approximately their actual size in the scroll.

In addition to the people, the artist has also meticulously depicted large ships that were considered 'high-tech' compared to other vessels around the world during the time of the Song Dynasty. The details are remarkable, allowing us to clearly see, for example, how the rudder blades of the large ships are constructed using vertically joined wooden planks, reinforced with horizontal timbers. In addition to the ships on the river, the streets of Bianjing are filled with a variety of carts and carriages. Some of the large carts have wheels that stand taller than a person, with the entire vehicle reaching a height of two men! Can you imagine what it would feel like to stand next to one of these massive carts?

As you'd expect from a painting that captures the hustle and bustle of street life, *Along the River During the Qingming Festival* is filled with a wide variety of merchants and their trades. For instance, you'll spot street vendors selling '*Yin zi* (饮子)', a kind of secret-recipe beverage that's somewhat similar to today's herbal tea. You'll also find sugarcane sellers, which is particularly noteworthy because sugarcane wasn't grown north of the *Yangtze* River during the Northern Song Dynasty. The fact that it was available in Bianjing is a testament to the advanced state of transportation and trade at that time. Flowers were another popular commodity, and people in the Song Dynasty had an immense love for them, especially the men! In the painting, you can even spot a bearded gentleman purchasing flowers from a vendor. But it's not just goods that are being sold on the streets of Bianjing, there are also skilled artisans offering their services, such as barbers shaving their customers. Amidst the buyers and sellers, you'll also notice intermediaries who promote transactions. Keep an eye out for the man walking along the street, his long sleeves swinging at his sides. At any moment, he's ready to discreetly grasp a customer's hand under the cover of his sleeve, sealing a deal.

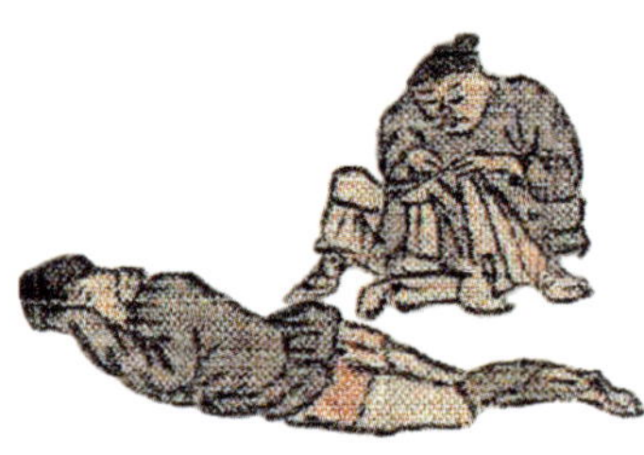

Exploring the painting further, you'll come across some rather puzzling and unexpected details that go beyond the ordinary scenes of its people, vehicles and trades. For example, the two figures on the left. They appear to be government couriers, but for some inexplicable reason one of them is mending his clothes while the other is sleeping on his stomach. However, that's not even the most perplexing part. What's truly baffling is that just across from them is a bustling and crowded street.

How is this man not embarrassed to be caught napping in such a public place? What's more, he even exposed his red underpants for all to see!

If you delve deeper into the painting, you'll notice that the artist has depicted a wealth of trees, buildings, furniture and animals. At first glance, these elements might seem less captivating than the human subjects. But each detail holds its own peculiar charm and intrigue. For instance, the old willow tree. Upon closer inspection, you'll realise that its trunk is completely severed, yet somehow it remains suspended in the air as if by magic. Isn't that strange and wondrous? In front of some of the buildings, you'll spot a type of lantern called a *Zhi zi* (栀子) in the shape of a gardenia fruit. Imagine how enchanting these lanterns must look when illuminated at night, casting a warm glow? And then there are the animals: just outside the city gate, a group of pigs roam freely, unsupervised and unattended.

Well, that's all I have to say about the scenes of *Along the River During the Qingming Festival* for now. Let me tell you stories about the artist who created this masterpiece.

2. The Fate of the Artist and the Painting

Zhang Zeduan (张择端, 1085–1145), courtesy name Zhengdao, is the artist behind the masterpiece *Along the River During the Qingming Festival*. From his name, we can speculate that his parents hoped he would grow up to be a person of integrity, following the righteous path. Zhang Zeduan was born in Dongwu (present-day Zhucheng, Shandong Province), a region steeped in Confucian culture, which emphasised benevolence and humanity. The area also boasted a strong artistic tradition that focused on realism. It undoubtedly had a subtle but profound influence on young Zhang Zeduan. As he grew older, Zhang Zeduan left his hometown for Bianjing, the capital city, to take the Imperial examinations. However, for reasons unknown (possibly due to changing policies, academic failure or family misfortune that left him unable to continue his studies), he abandoned his scholarly pursuits and turned to painting instead. He eventually earned a place in the Imperial Painting Academy, known as the Hanlin Academy.

At the Hanlin Academy during the Song Dynasty, a group of exceptionally talented artists gathered, each with their own unique specialities. So, what was Zhang Zeduan's forte? He excelled in the art of *Jie hua* (界画), a painting technique that draws precise lines by a *Jie bi* (界笔)① and a straight-edge ruler. However, as you can see, Zhang Zeduan's artistic skills demonstrate *Jian gong dai xie* (兼工带写), which refers to a style that combines highly detailed brushwork (工笔, *Gong bi*) with looser, more expressive strokes (写意, *Xie yi*). Not only was he a master of *Jie hua*, but he was also incredibly skilled at figure painting, capturing his subjects with both accuracy and soul. Moreover, because Zhang Zeduan had first pursued a scholarly education before turning to painting, the characters he depicted from everyday life were devoid of any coarseness or vulgarity. Instead, they exuded an air of refinement and gentleness. The earliest commentator on *Along the River During the Qingming Festiva*l, Zhang Zhu from the Jin Dynasty, praised the painting's unique style, describing it as '*bie cheng jia shu*' (别成家数), meaning 'forming a school of his own'.

① The *Jie bi* (界笔) is a rather unusual paintbrush. It features a circular brush holder that encases the brush during the painting, exposing only the tip of the bristles. To draw lines, the artist places the brush holder against a straight-edge ruler and moves it along, resulting in perfectly even and straight ink lines. If the artist wants to draw thicker lines, they simply expose more of the bristle tip; conversely, for thinner lines, they expose less. But why use a *Jie bi* for painting? The purpose is to achieve greater precision and realism when depicting the intricate details of architectural structures, furniture, boats and other objects that require clean, straight lines.

In addition to *Along the River During the Qingming Festival*, Zhang Zeduan also drew another masterpiece entitled *Dragon Boat Racing on the West Lake* (《西湖争标图》). Both of these two handscrolls are highly acclaimed and regarded as '*Shen pin*', which refers to masterpieces. Sadly, *Dragon Boat Racing on the West Lake* has long since been lost.

In 1127, the Northern Song Dynasty was conquered by the Jin Dynasty. More than half a century later, in 1186 (the 25th year of *Dading*, ruled by Emperor Shizong of Jin), the day after the Qingming Festival, a scholar in the Jin Dynasty named Zhang Zhu wrote an eighty-five-character epilogue for the *Along the River During the Qingming Festival.* This short epilogue is the primary source of information about the life of the painter, Zhang Zeduan. Beyond this, many of the questions that still intrigue people can only be answered through speculation. For instance, when exactly did Zhang Zeduan paint *Along the River During the Qingming Festival*? Some scholars believe it was painted in the early years of Emperor Huizong's reign (between 1101 and 1110), when Zhang Zeduan was around forty years old. However, others argue that it was painted during the reign of Emperor Shenzong of Song (1068–1085). Emperor Shenzong was the one who appointed Wang Anshi to implement reforms, and he passed away at the age of thirty-eight, passing the throne to his sixth son, Zhao Xu. Zhao Xu, also known as Emperor Zhezong of Song, ascended to the throne at the age of ten, but died at twenty-five. Then, with the strong support of Emperor Shenzong's empress, Shenzong's eleventh son, Zhao Ji, became the emperor. Zhao Ji later became known as Emperor Huizong of Song.

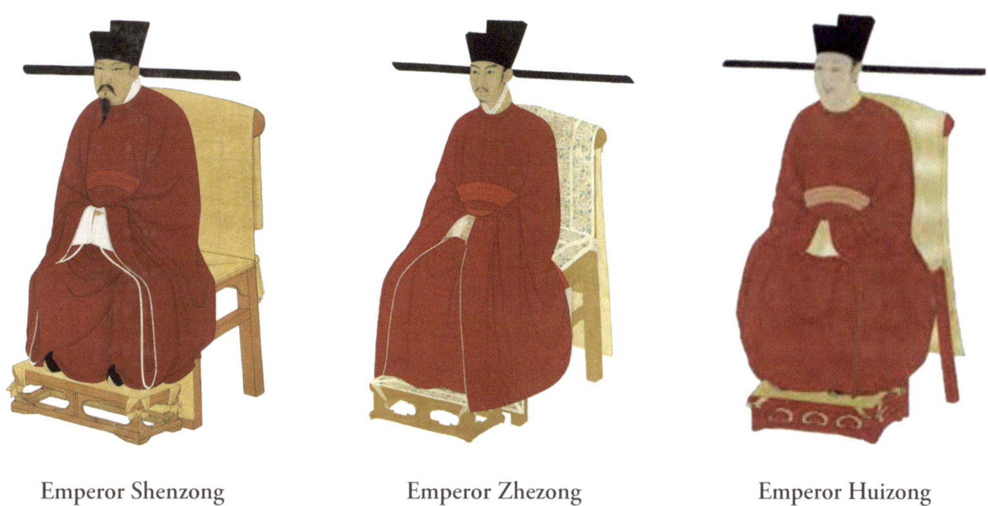

Emperor Shenzong **Emperor Zhezong** **Emperor Huizong**

Emperor Huizong of the Song Dynasty once viewed the painting *Along the River During the Qingming Festival*. He inscribed the title of the painting at the beginning of the scroll and stamped it with his 'Double Dragon Seal'. Huizong's inscription and imperial seal were highly treasured and were still seen as late as the Ming Dynasty. Unfortunately, his inscription and seal on *Along the River During the Qingming Festival* were removed by a mounter in the late Ming period. It is said that the same scroll mounter also painted a donkey in a spot not far from the beginning of the scroll (more details of this will be discussed in the next chapter).

What happened to Zhang Zeduan afterwards? After the fall of the Northern Song Dynasty, some of these court painters like Zhang Zeduan, fled to the south and eventually became court painters in the early Southern Song Dynasty. A small number escaped to Shu, present-day Sichuan Province. Others were left stranded in the conquered areas or were captured by the Jin army and taken to the north, where most of them had to fend for themselves. It is highly likely that Zhang Zeduan stayed in the northern region under the rule of Jin. As for how he spent the rest of his life, what caused his death, or when he passed away, we have no way of knowing.

Now, what is the story behind *Along the River During the Qingming Festival*? This takes us to Empress Xiang, whose life is deeply intertwined with the painting. After the death of Emperor Shenzong, his son Zhao Xu (Emperor Zhezong) ascended to the throne and Empress Xiang became Empress Dowager Xiang. When Emperor Zhezong passed away, Empress Dowager Xiang favoured Zhao Ji and orchestrated his succession to the throne. Ascending as Emperor Huizong, he showed great respect to Empress Dowager Xiang and bestowed many benefits upon her brothers, that is to say, his imperial uncles, as a show of gratitude. Among these gifts was the painting *Along the River During the Qingming Festival*, which he presented to his uncle Xiang Zonghui. The scroll later passed down to the descendants of the Xiang family, coming into the possession of Xiang Zishao.

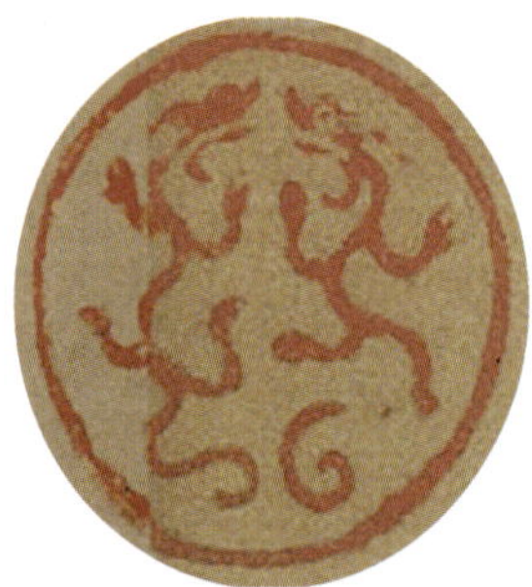

One of Emperor Huizong's 'Double Dragon Seal' *Zhang hao hao shi* juan, Du Mu, Tang Dynasty in the collection of the Palace Museum, Beijing

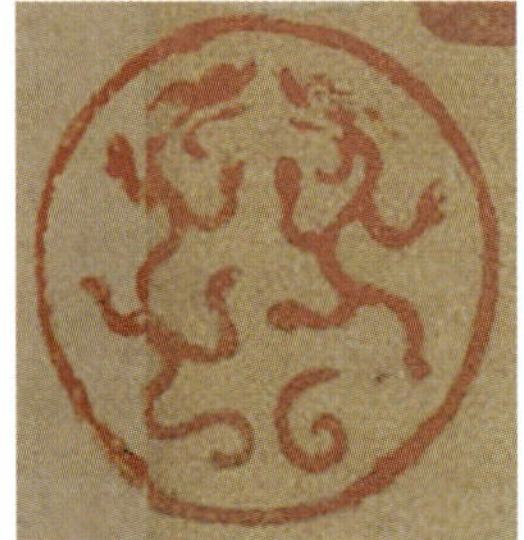

One of Emperor Huizong's 'Double Dragon Seal' (remained to be verified) Printing: *Journey of the King of Dong Dan* in the collection of the Museum of Fine Arts, Boston

Some say that while Emperor Huizong of the Song Dynasty was not a tyrant, he was certainly incompetent. His interests were simply too numerous and diverse – painting, calligraphy, music and collecting rare stones and unusual woods. Having diverse interests is not inherently wrong, but neglecting his primary duties was a serious problem. After all, the higher one's position, the greater one's responsibilities. Shouldn't this be taken seriously? Alas, Emperor Huizong was like a distracted student, his mind constantly wandering to thoughts of play and leisure, resulting in him making a complete mess of his studies. In the end, the Northern Song Dynasty collapsed. It is often said that the fall of the Northern Song was due to Emperor Huizong, but could it not also be laid at the feet of Empress Dowager Xiang? Of course, such emotive commentary holds little true meaning. Instead of engaging in conjecture about alternative scenarios, we should focus on introspecting and understanding history.

Let us now return to the story of the *Along the River During the Qingming Festival.* Xiang Zishao, who we mentioned earlier, was the grandnephew ① of Empress Dowager Xiang. Xiang Zishao was determined to resist the Jin invasion. In the second year of the Jianyan era (1128), the Jin invaders launched a relentless assault on the city, day and night. Even after the city fell, Xiang Zishao continued to lead his remaining troops and citizens into a fierce street battle against the Jin invaders until he himself was captured. The Jin invaders attempted to coerce Xiang Zishao into surrendering, with soldiers on either side of him forcefully pinning him down to make him kneel, but Xiang steadfastly refused to yield. Instead, he defiantly pointed his finger ② (as a halberd) at the Jin invaders and cursed them furiously. And, consequently, he was executed. Later, his entire family was massacred, with only one six-year-old child surviving. All of his family's possessions, including the *Along the River During the Qingming Festival,* were looted. For over half a century, after the fall of the Northern Song, this great work of art was caught up in the turbulent tides of history, undoubtedly

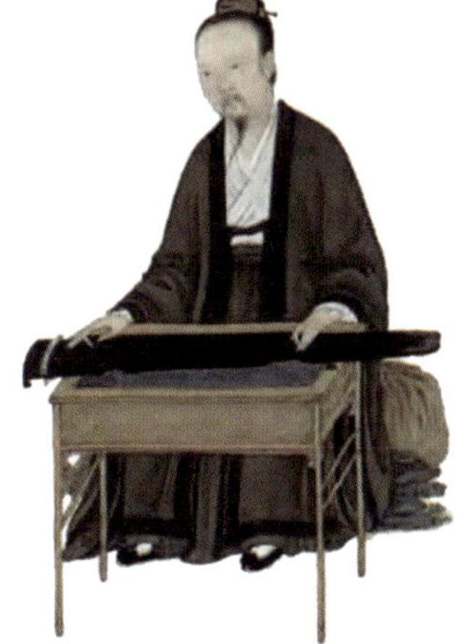

Emperor Huizong playing a qin zither from *Listening to a Zither*, Zhao Ji, Northern Song Dynasty in the collection of the Museum of Fine Arts, Boston

experiencing countless harrowing moments. Then, one day, it was finally recognised by Zhang Zhu, and from that point on its chronicled journey began.

① A grandnephew is the grandson of one's grandfather's biological brothers.

② The act of extending one's index and middle fingers, and pointing at someone in a manner resembling a halberd, is called *Ji zhi* or halberd pointing. This gesture is used to express anger or a display of valour and prowess. A halberd is an ancient Chinese weapon, as shown in the image below. It consists of a long shaft with a spear point at one end, flanked by crescent-shaped blades.

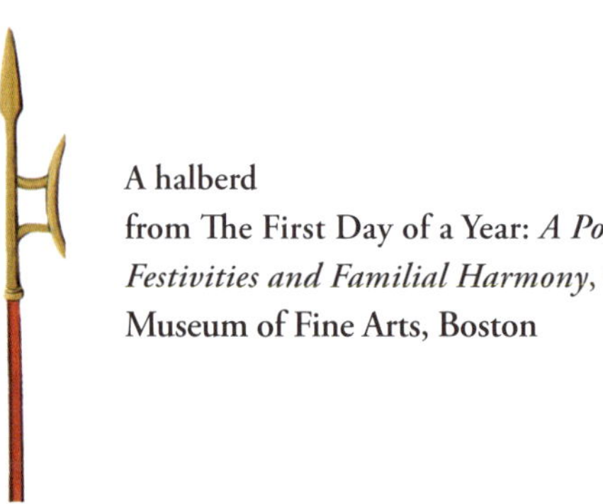

A halberd
from The First Day of a Year: *A Portrait of Qianlong Emperor's Imperial Festivities and Familial Harmony*, Qing Dynasty in the collection of the Museum of Fine Arts, Boston

3. 'The Forbidden City Run'

Within the ceaseless flow of history, a pivotal moment arose in 2015 when the *Along the River During the Qingming Festival* was unfurled in its entirety for public exhibition at the Hall of Martial Valor (*Wuying Dian*) at the Palace Museum in Beijing. This exhibition caused a tremendous sensation and even spawned a new term: 'The Forbidden City Run'. According to news reports at the time, people queued up overnight, with some 'waiting for seven hours just to catch a glimpse of this national treasure'. As soon as the Meridian Gate (*Wu men*) opened in the morning, the crowds dashed towards the Hall of Martial Valor (*Wuying Dian*), a scene that was humorously dubbed 'The Forbidden City Run' by netizens.

In the race from the Meridian Gate to the Hall of Martial Valor, the young had an obvious advantage, swiftly claiming spots at the front of the exhibit, leaving some of the elderly and children who had arrived early to queue to fall behind and having to view the

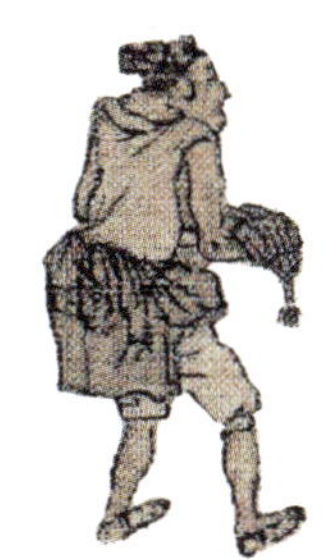

exhibit from further back. Nevertheless, an octogenarian remarked, 'To see this national treasure in my lifetime is truly exhilarating!' A little child declared that he must see 'the most beautiful Chinese painting'. Indeed, works of art cannot always be judged solely on the criterion of 'beauty'. In my opinion, *Along the River During the Qingming Festival* transcends the question of aesthetics – it is the most mundane yet most grandiose of all the Chinese paintings, deserving our meticulous appreciation inch by inch, rather than just a hurried glance. So, let's begin our appreciation of this masterpiece!

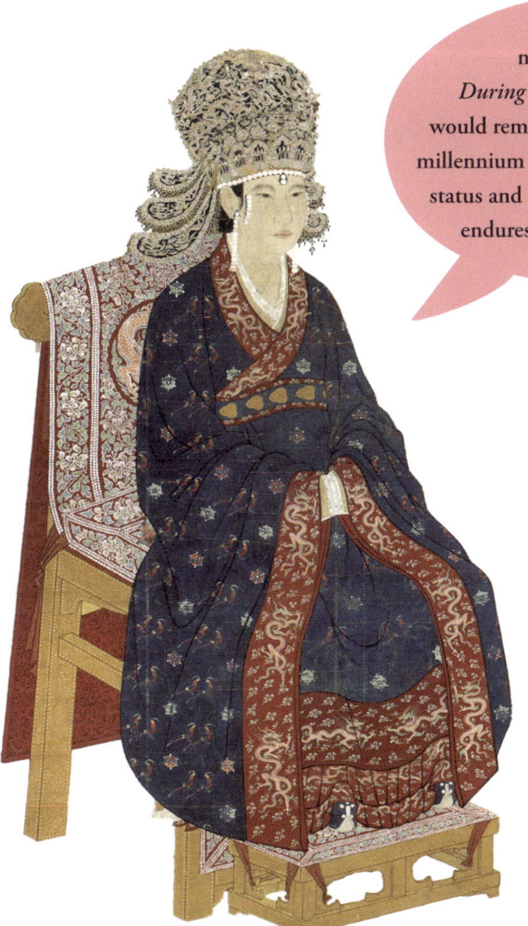

Portrait of Empress Dowager Gao of the Song Dynasty zhou in the collection of National Palace Museum, Taipei

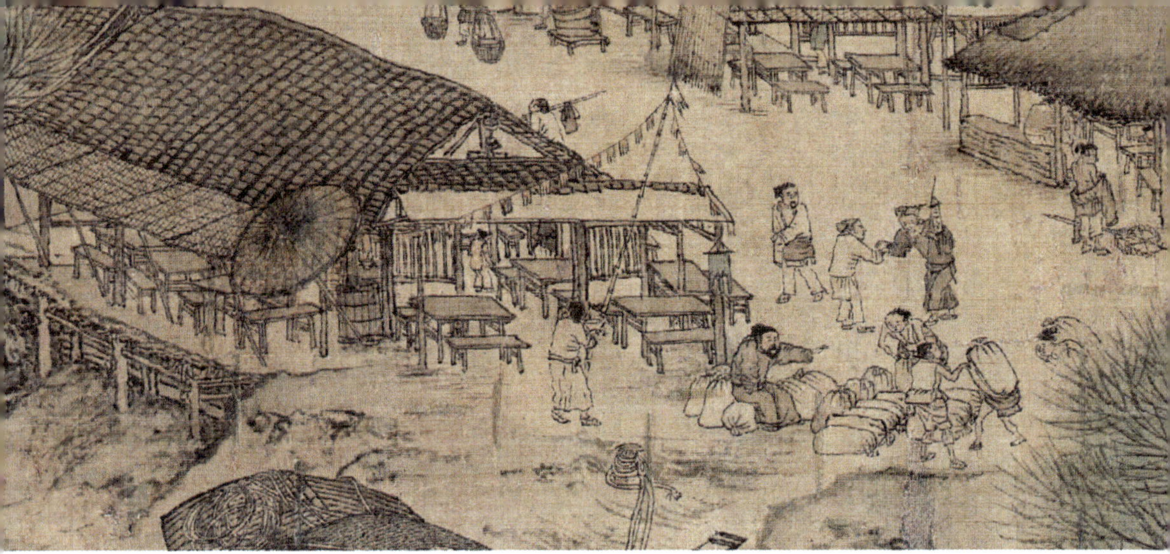

CHAPTER II

In-depth Reading: 36 Detailed Interpretations of Street Life in the Song Dynasty

In this chapter, let's take on a journey to read and appreciate the intricate details of *Along the River During the Qingming Festival.*

Some may wonder why the word 'read' is preferred over 'look' when it comes to appreciating ancient paintings. The reason is that our ancient Chinese paintings demand more than mere viewing – they are to be read. To 'look' is just to see, but to 'read' emphasises understanding. Take *Along the River During the Qingming Festival*, for example, its value lies not merely in its aesthetic appeal but in its rich connotations. In other words, ancient paintings carry a wealth of information. Thus, it is insufficient to merely 'look'; we must also employ certain methods and knowledge to interpret them, enabling us to thoroughly observe the details and 'read' between the lines.

Of course, emphasising the act of reading does not devalue the importance of looking – the two are inextricably intertwined. I often remark that to truly grasp the essence of ancient Chinese paintings, we must embark on a threefold journey. First and foremost, we must observe meticulously, as this is the cornerstone of interpreting the work. That's why

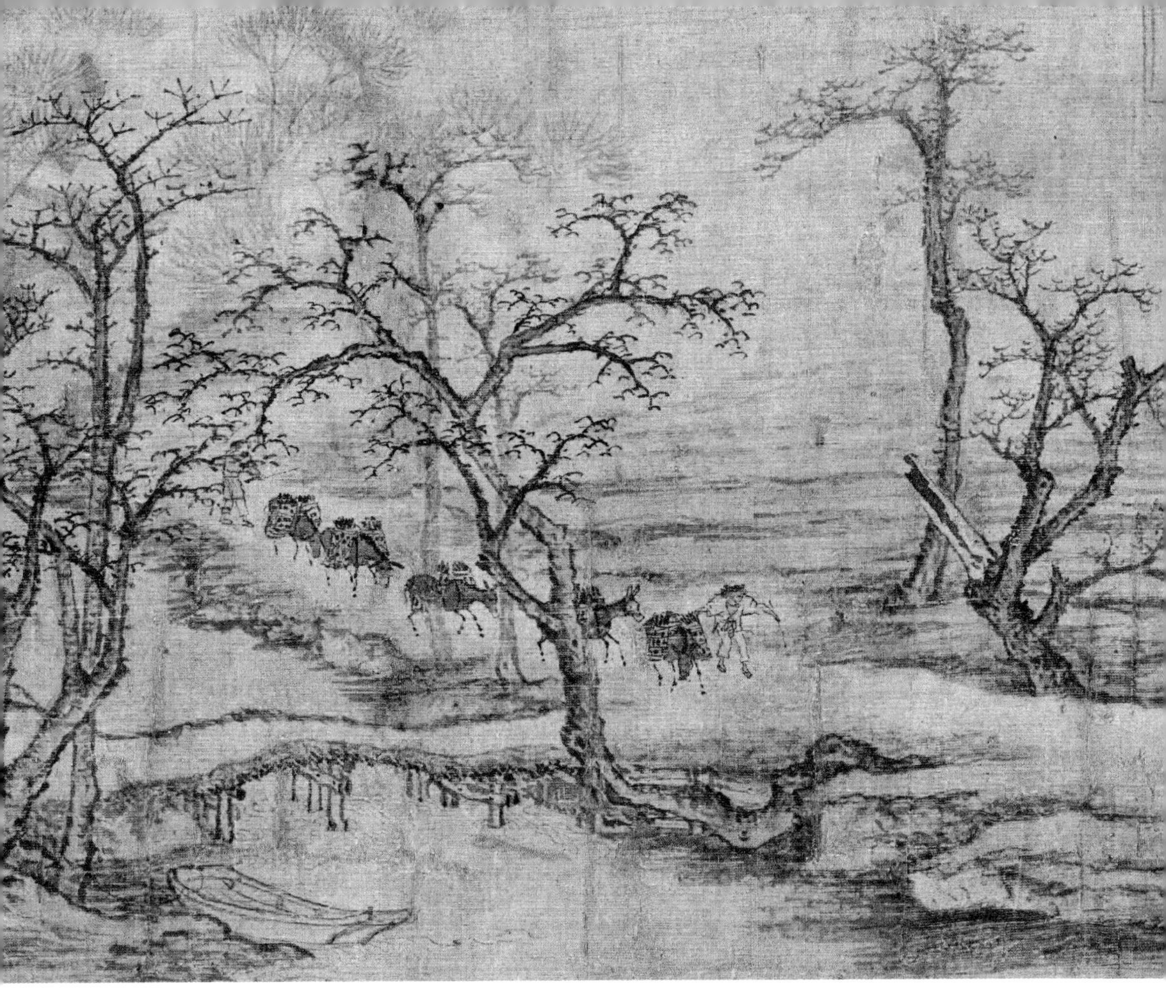

I always illustrate the minutiae in each section to ensure that my dear readers can perceive every aspect distinctly. Subsequently, it is invaluable to consider the insights of ancient commentators and modern scholars. Finally, I encourage every reader to confidently venture into their own interpretations. Only when we develop our own interpretations can ancient Chinese paintings be imbued with renewed vitality.

1. What are the donkeys carrying?

Chinese handscrolls are viewed from right to left, with the painting gradually unfolding section by section. Thus, as we begin to explore *Along the River During the Qingming Festival*, the first scene is a donkey caravan wending its way out of the misty dawn. The paths and fields are empty, accentuated only by this unhurried procession of donkeys; not another soul is in sight. Undoubtedly, it heralds a tranquil morning.

This donkey caravan has five small donkeys and two men. Each donkey carries two baskets filled with black, rod-like objects. What might these be? They bear a striking resemblance to charcoal. According to historical notes from Song Dynasty scholars in *Ji le bian* (《鸡肋编》), by the time Zhang Zeduan painted *Along the River During the Qingming Festival*, the majority of households in Bianjing had already burned coal instead of charcoal for their daily fuel needs ①. As a result, some speculate that the charcoal carried by this donkey caravan was likely intended for warming wine. This theory makes some sense, considering the Song people's fondness for alcohol (to the extent that even relief supplies sometimes included wine) and a demand for warm wine. Others suggest that the charcoal might have been burned by wealthy households in the capital for warmth, as the climate in China entered the 'Little Ice Age' during the late Northern Song Dynasty, making the Qingming Festival period much colder than it is today.

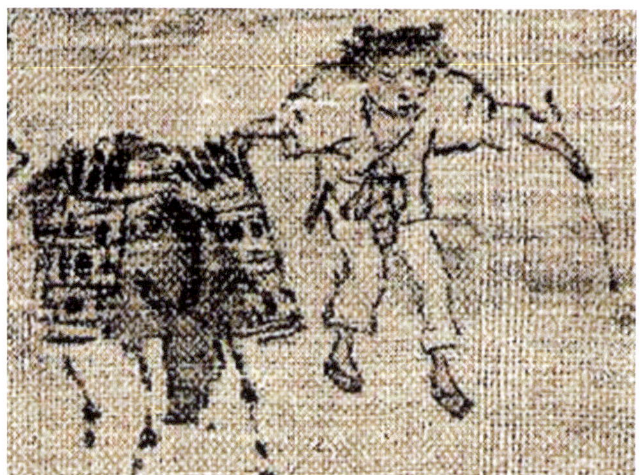

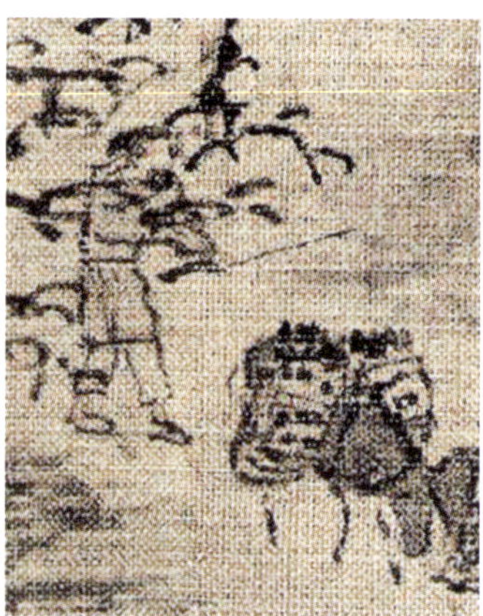

The old man at the rear of the caravan

① *Ji le bian* (《鸡肋编》), Volume 2: Zhuang Chuo from the Southern Song Dynasty writes: 'In the past, the millions of households in Bianjing relied entirely on coal and not a single household burned wood. Bianjing, a metropolis of the world at the time with a population exceeding one million and a density beyond later generations' imagination, once faced a severe shortage of wood. But this problem was eventually resolved when coal replaced charcoal as the primary fuel source in the capital.'

Leading the caravan is a young boy. Upon closer inspection, we can see that his hair is styled in a distinctive fashion known as *Zong jiao* (总角). In ancient China, boys aged eight or nine to thirteen or fourteen would part their hair into two halves, tying each into a knot atop their heads, resembling the horns of a ram – hence the name *Zong jiao.* Bringing up the rear of the caravan is an old man with a bushy beard, likely his father. It is plausible that they set out before daybreak, making their way to the capital to sell charcoal. Please take a closer look at the boy and the leading donkey. As they approach a small bridge, the boy continues forward, yet the donkey has already instinctively angled its head towards the bridge, indicating a turn. This behaviour tells us that the donkey has travelled this route many times before – so familiar with the route that it knows to turn without any guidance.

On this note, let me reveal a scholarly assertion that most people are unaware of. Some scholars speculate that the current beginning of the scroll may not be the original one. After five centuries, the beginning of *Along the River During the Qingming Festival* had suffered deterioration (estimated to be about one foot). Consequently, during the late Ming Dynasty, the scroll mounters trimmed off the damaged portion and remounted the painting. What might be depicted in this missing section? It probably featured mountains and trees. While it remains uncertain whether these speculations are accurate, I believe that the current beginning is perfect as it is. A masterpiece does not necessarily need to start with a grandiose scene. Rather, it is often the subtle, nuanced details that endow a masterpiece with a profound and understated elegance. *Along the River During the Qingming Festival* with just a boy and a donkey turning their heads captures this essence, providing a perfect

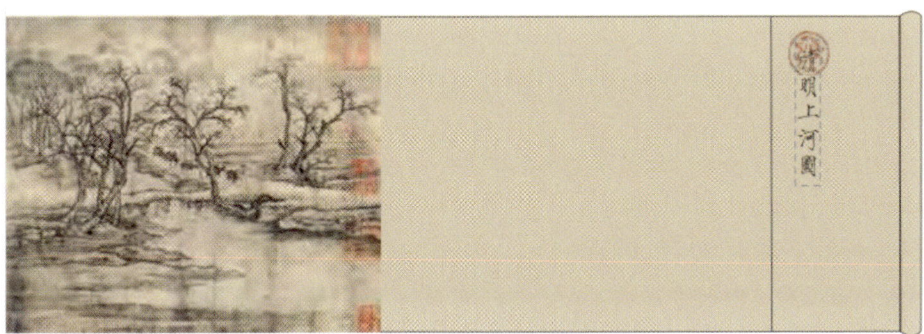

The deteriorated section trimmed from the beginning of the scroll

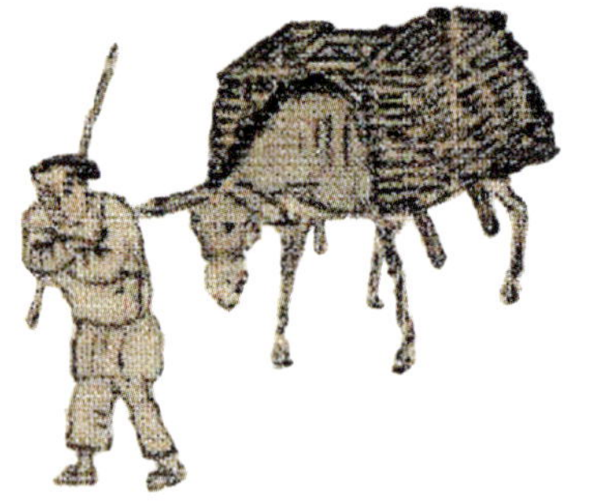

entry into the world of the painting – and I couldn't imagine a more fitting beginning.

The image on the left is taken from the donkey caravan after selling charcoal in the latter part of the scroll. Please excuse my imperfect cutout of the donkey legs.

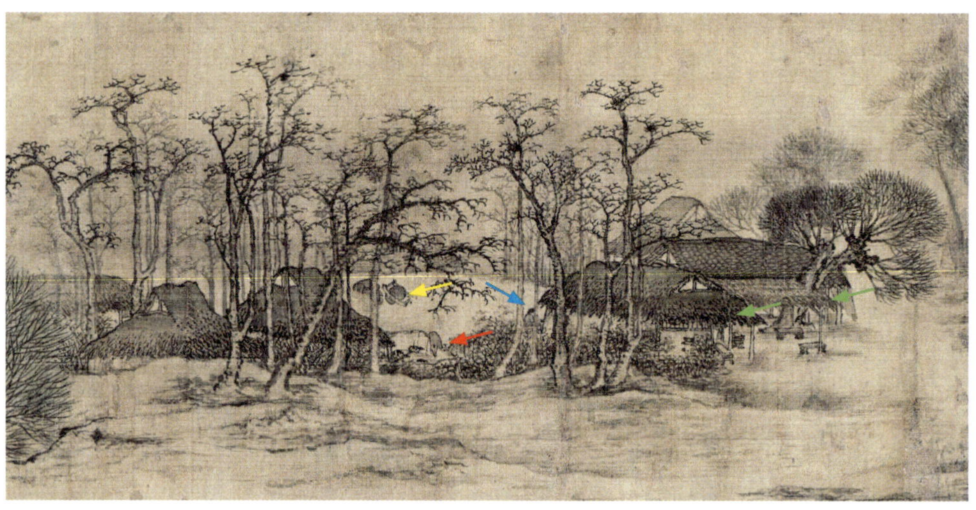

2. What are the tools found in the farmyard on the outskirts of the capital?

'A small bridge, flowing river and a household' is a classic combination of imagery in Chinese art. At the beginning of the painting, we see the small bridge and the flowing river, but do you see a household? Looking further ahead, Zhang Zeduan has indeed painted a household (as shown in the picture on previous page). At first glance, it appears utterly tranquil, seemingly devoid of any inhabitants. But is that true? No one living there? Let's take a closer look.

Now let's look at the right side of the painting, where several houses appear. Upon closer inspection, we notice an arbour outside the houses (indicated by the green arrows), with a few benches beneath it. It seems that this household, situated alongside the path leading to the capital, also earns a living: offering a resting spot for passing vendors.

However, in the early morning, there are not many vendors yet, so the owner is not around at the moment.

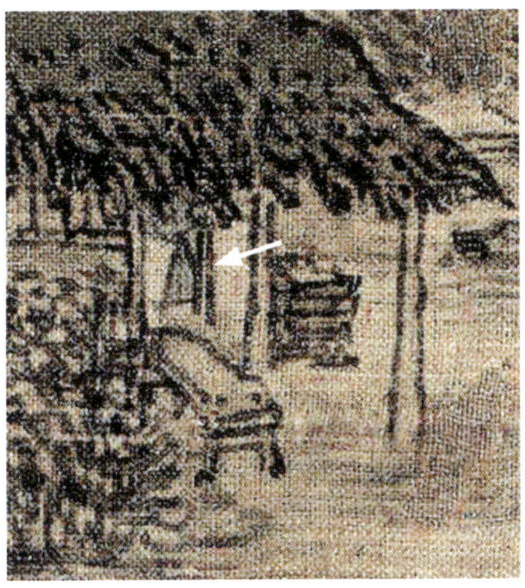

The picture above shows the doorway of the house. What do you think the object indicated by the white arrow is? While counting the number of people throughout the scroll, I noticed that its colour is similar to that of the housewife's top garment. However, upon further examination, I concluded that it is a cyan cloth door curtain, tied up in the middle to allow for ventilation.

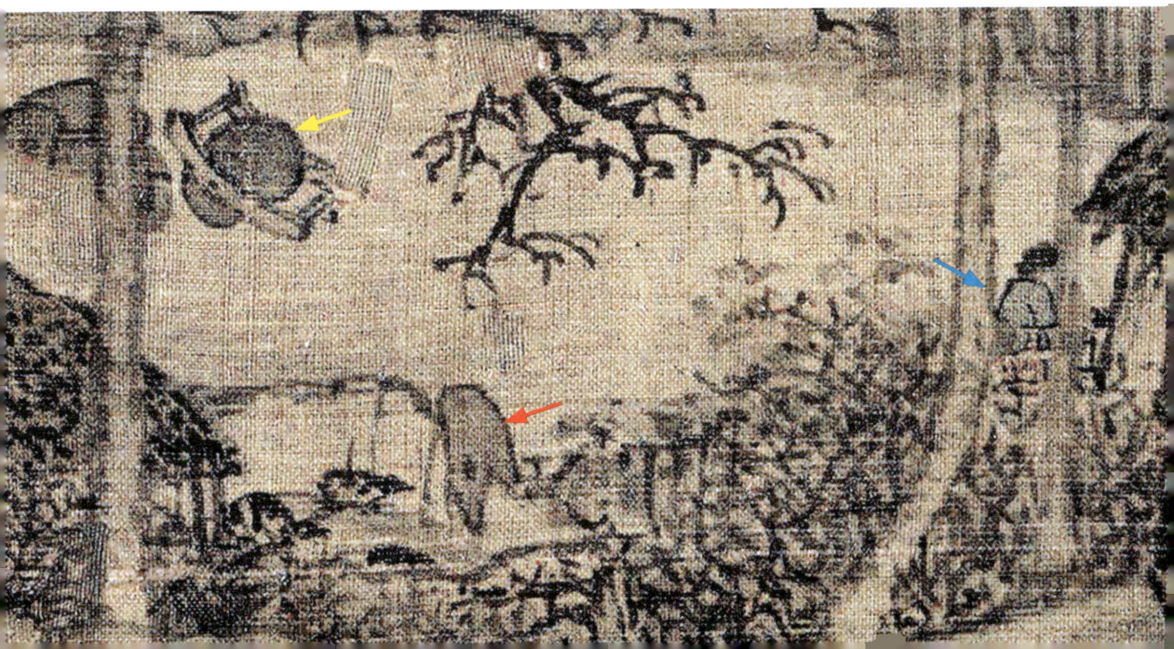

Where has the owner gone? Let's take a look towards the back of the house. The position indicated by the red arrow is a low earthen wall, and it seems that something is crouching beside it. I believe it is a pig. I guess the owner has just poured out its feed and it runs to eat it. The blue arrow points to the figure of the homeowner. It seems to be a woman, who, after feeding the pig, is heading back into the house.

Behind her house lies a threshing floor where a round, bulky farming tool rests. Some say it is *Nian zi,* but how could that be? A *Nian zi* consists of a grinding plate and a rolling stone. By spreading grains like wheat or corn on the plate and then pushing the rolling stone across, the grains are crushed.

In *Along the River During the Qingming Festival*, the farming tool depicted is a *liu zhou*. Even a thousand years later, this tool is still sometimes used to compact soil and crush grains.

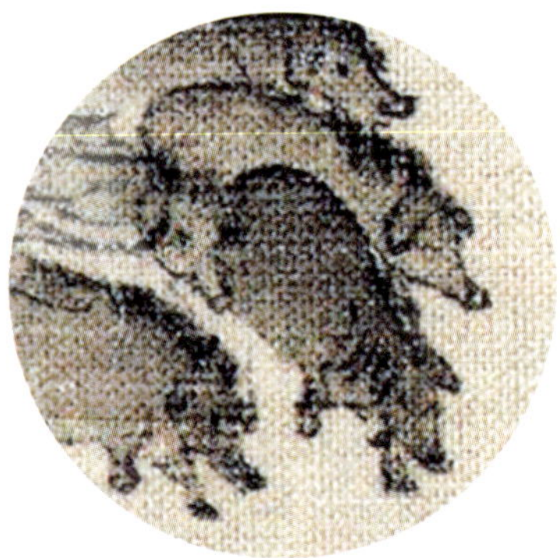

Turning this page, we will see old photos of people pushing a *Nian zi* and pulling a *liu zhou*. No further explanation is needed; a single glance will make the difference clear.

A sounder of pigs outside the gates of Bianjing

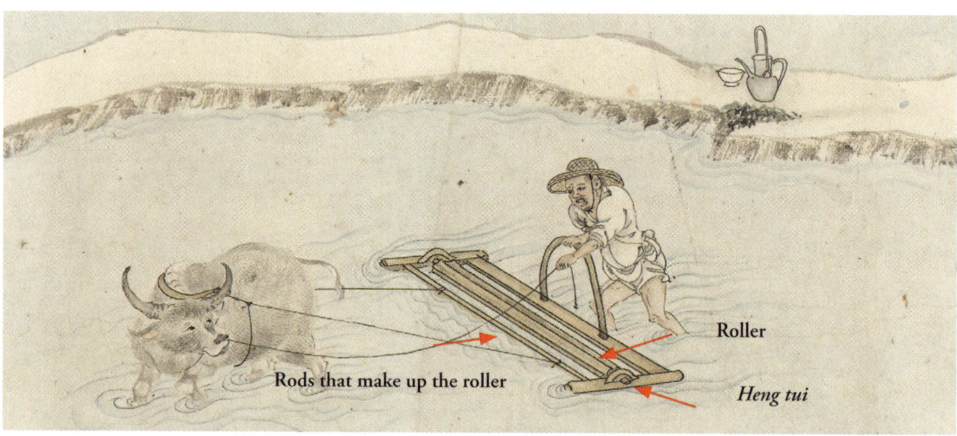

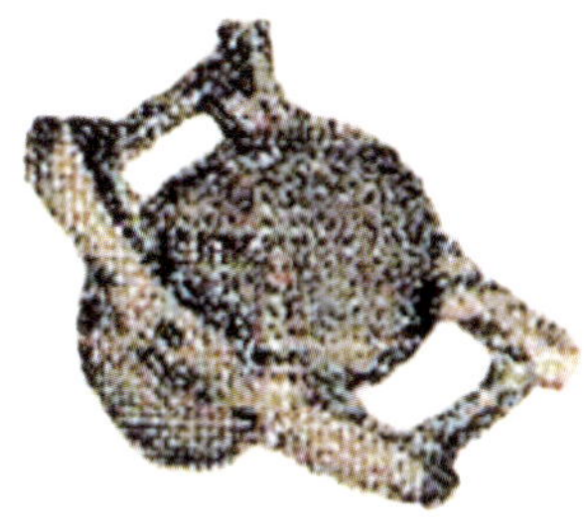

The *liu zhou* in *Along the River During the Qingming Festival*

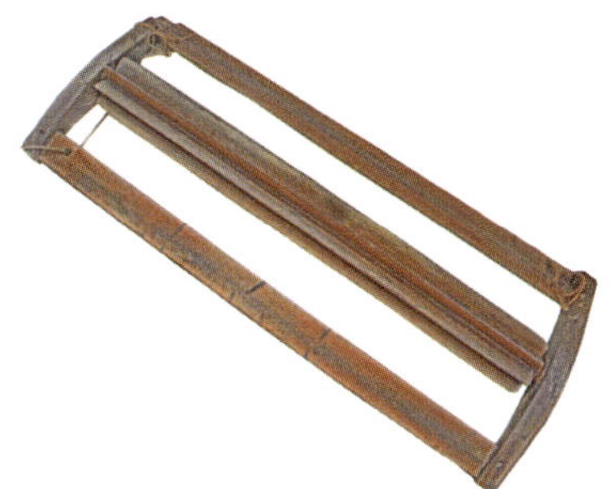

Photo of a southern *liu zhou* used to level paddy fields (photo by Lin Gaozhi)

Look on the page 38, we will find old photos of the *Nian zi* and the *liu zhou*. Due to regional variations, the *liu zhou* that southern readers are familiar with may differ from the one depicted in *Along the River During the Qingming Festival*. The northern *liu zhou*, also known as a stone roller, is a stone-made rolling farm tool. In contrast, the southern *liu zhou* is a wooden tool used for levelling paddy fields, consisting of a roller and a sleeve (a rectangular crude wooden frame surrounding the roller). The long wooden planks that make up the roller are called rods, which are hard and durable. As the *liu zhou* rolls forward, the rods create a crisp, rhythmic 'clack-clack' sound.

At the top of this page, the picture depicts a southern *liu zhou* from the *Pictures of Tilling and Weaving* (《耕织图》) from the Song Dynasty (a copy made by Cheng Qi during the Yuan Dynasty). Does it look quite different from the northern *liu zhou*? On the right, there is a photo of a modern southern *liu zhou*. We can see that the modern *liu zhou* has undergone little change.

All right, let's take our time to appreciate 'A small bridge, flowing river and a household'. With that, the prologue to *Along the River During the Qingming Festival* gradually unfolds. Then, we will witness the grand spectacle.

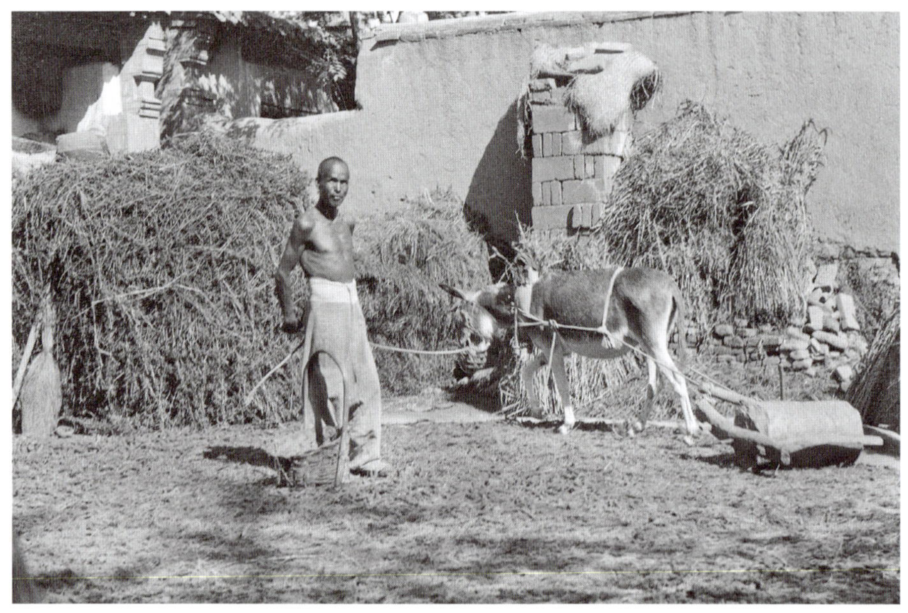

A donkey pulling *liu zhou*, from the *Gan bo Photography, 1931–1932*, in Ding County, Hebei Province

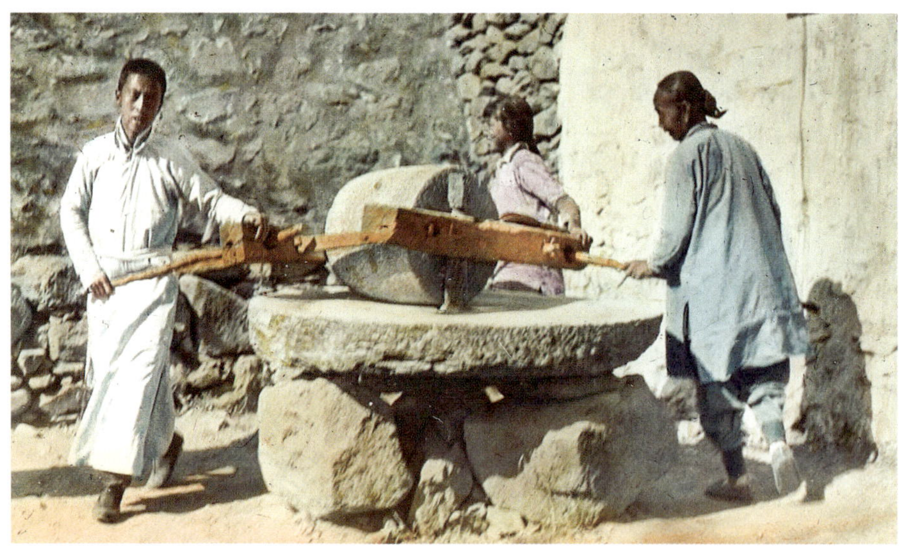

Pushing *Nian zi*, from the *Gan bo Photography*, 1917–1919, in Shifang Pujue Temple, Beijing

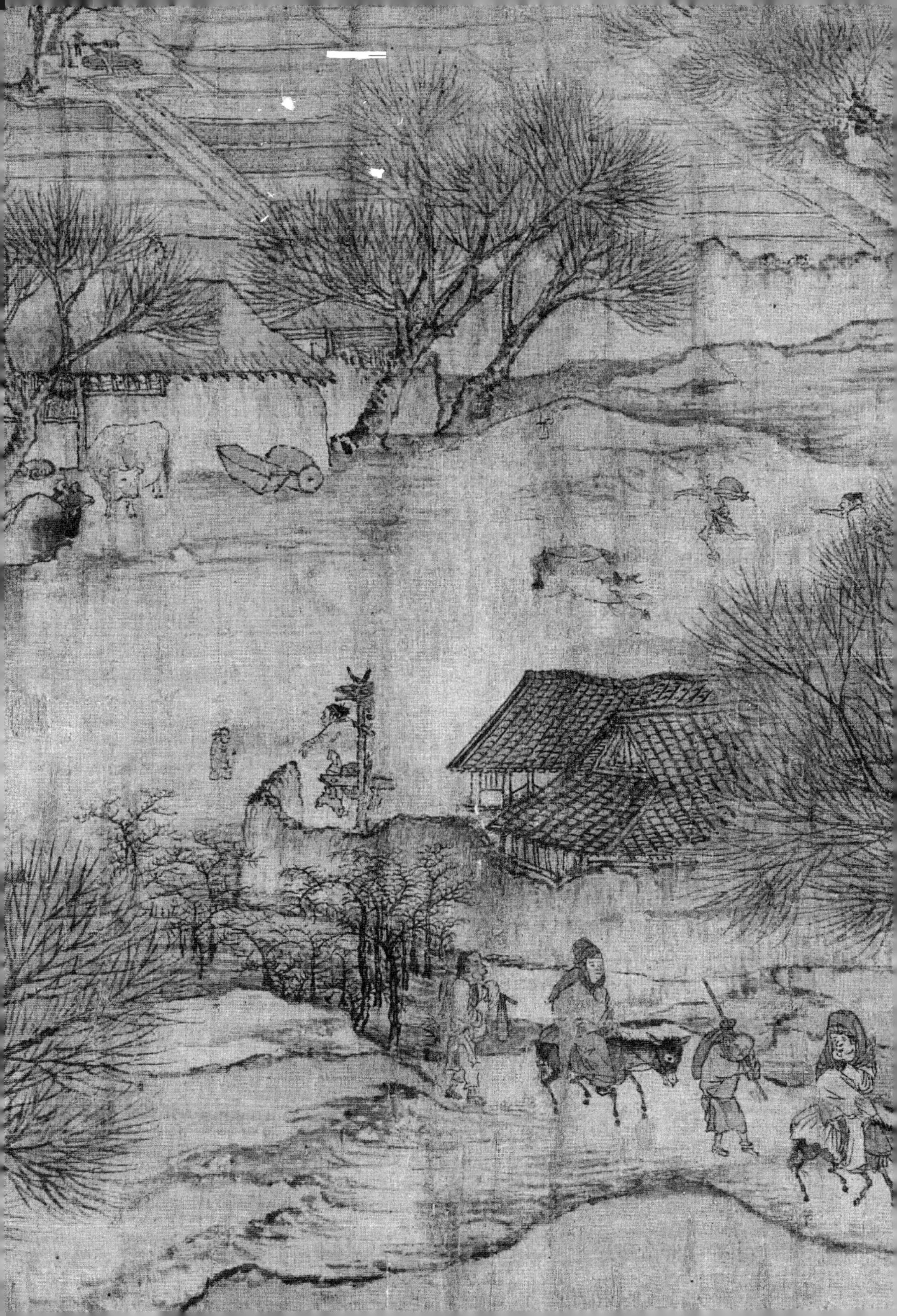

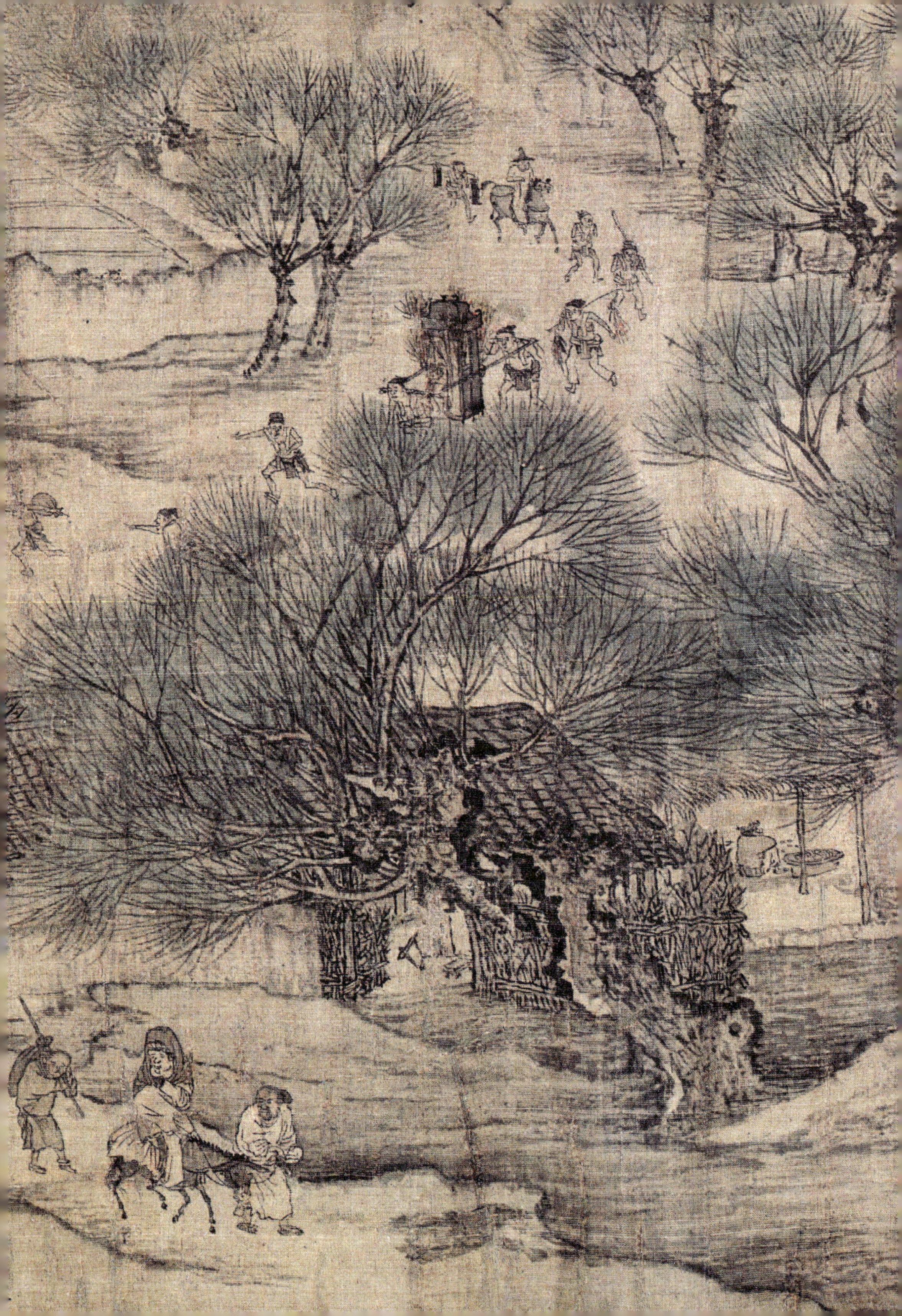

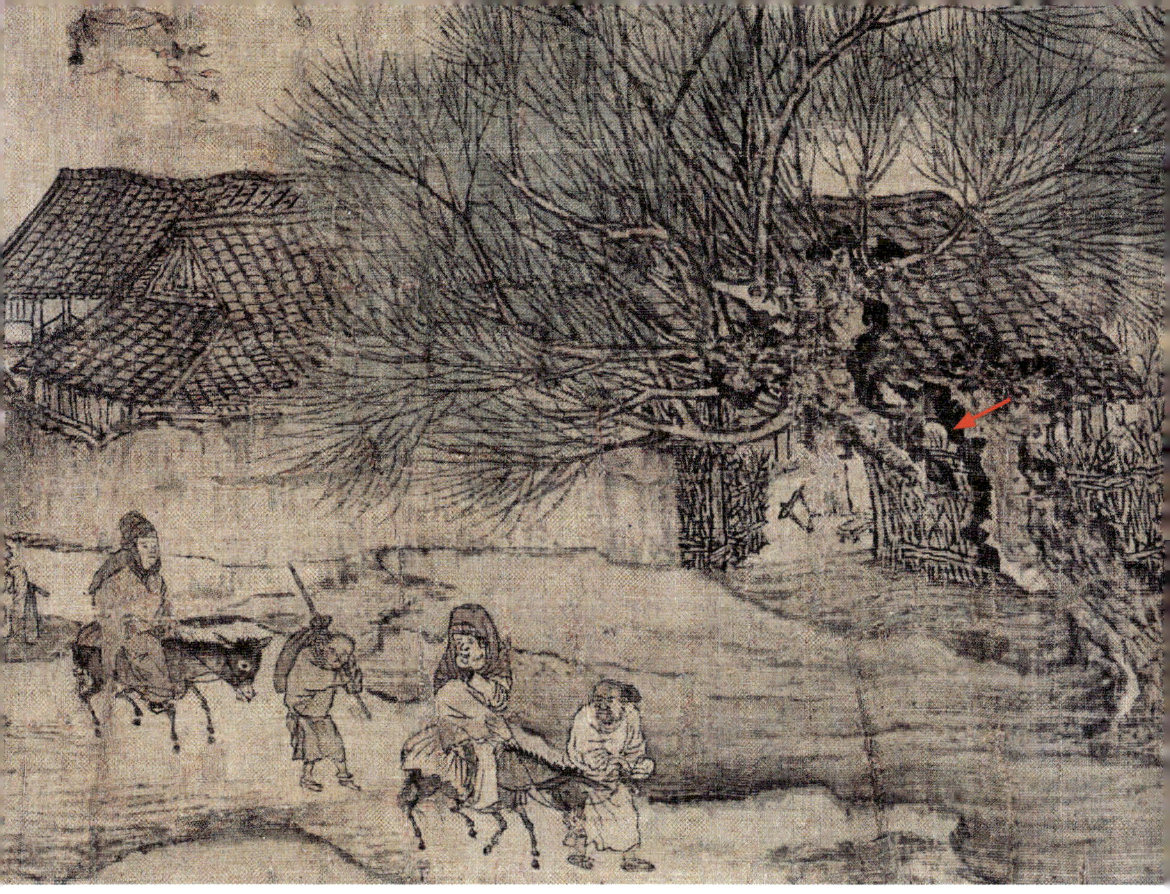

3. Why is the willow broken?

On the previous page, we saw the first major scene in *Along the River During the Qingming Festival,* which occurs just past the 'A small bridge, flowing river and a household', after walking through a grove of willows. At this point, readers are typically first captivated by the 'startled horse' scene. However, there are several mysteries here. Let's unravel them one by one.

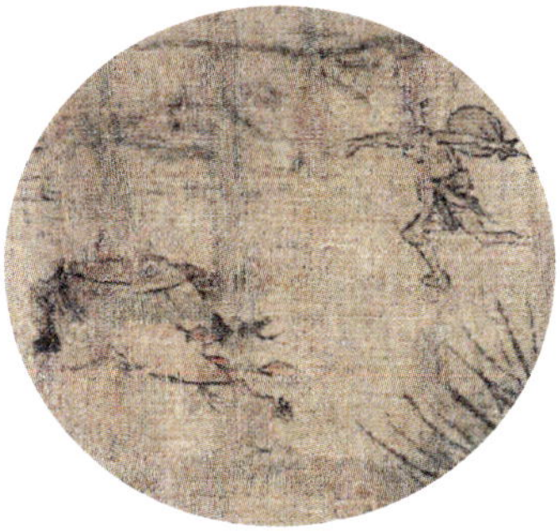

'Startled horse' and the man chasing after it

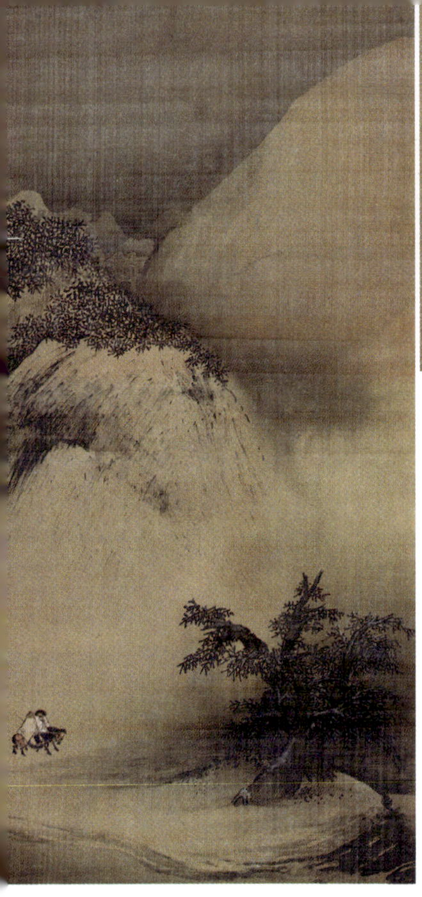

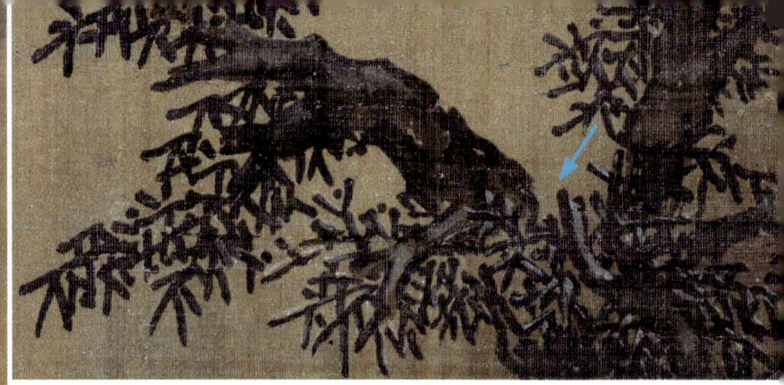

LEFT: *Snowy Landscape* by Liang Kai in Southern Song Dynasty in the collection of Tokyo National Museum

Let's start with this willow tree. It grows beside a household, with a large crown and an aged trunk. Please take a closer look at the position indicated by the blue arrow in the picture above. Do you notice anything unusual? The trunk is broken! It's not just a partial fracture, but a complete break. Through the gap we can see the fence and roof tiles behind the tree. How could this be? Logically speaking, if the trunk is broken, the crown shouldn't be able to stay in place, right? Moreover, it's hard to imagine how the tree could still be lush and green. Yet, there it hangs, eerily suspended.

Unfortunately, I have not come across any researchers providing a reasonable explanation for this phenomenon. However, the lack of an explanation might be a good thing, as we can gather a wealth of information simply through our intuition and careful observation. First, the broken willow evokes a sense of unease, discomfort and tension, which can be felt without any need for theoretical analysis. Second, let's consider the potential consequences brought by the broken willow. The tree leans towards a small path beside it, just as a group of travellers passes underneath. They are completely unaware of the

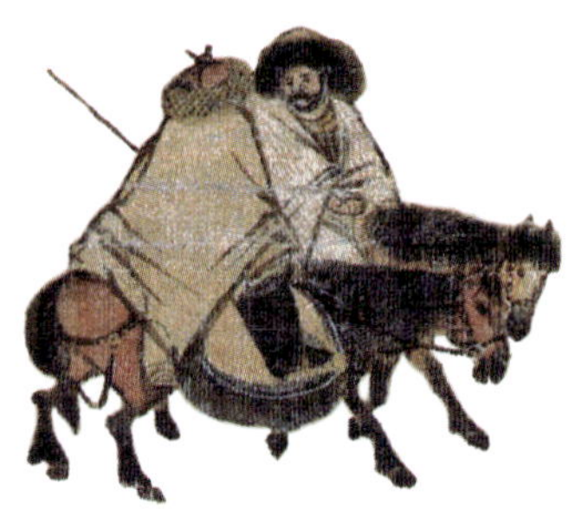

broken willow, especially the two people at the front of the group, who are distracted by something in the opposite direction to the willow. This experience is reminiscent of watching a horror movie: danger is imminent, but the protagonists are oblivious, leaving the audience on the edge of their seats. Therefore, the 'broken willow' scene is definitely not intended to make people feel pleasant or amused; rather, it is a clear reminder to our readers to pay attention to its underlying meaning.

So, what might this meaning be? My thoughts turn to *Snowy Landscape* (《雪景山水图》) by Liang Kai, a Southern Song Dynasty painter. Although the painting is titled *Landscape*, it features a peculiar tree. The trunk appears to be decayed and hollow, and moreover, if we look at the spot indicated by the blue arrow – it is completely broken there as well! In both the *Snowy Landscape* and *Along the River During the Qingming Festival*, there are seemingly carefree and leisurely travellers near the broken willows. The presence of these broken willows reminds us of the calm before the storm. In fact, when danger exists, and we remain unperturbed, then immense peril may descend at any moment.

Some may wonder, wasn't the scene of 'A small bridge, flowing river and a household' perfectly tranquil just a moment ago? Why has the style suddenly shifted, leaving us with a sense of unease? In fact, throughout the entire scroll of *Along the River During the Qingming Festival*, this is not the only subtle warning of impending danger. As we delve deeper into the painting, we will naturally come to understand Zhang Zeduan's underlying message – he is not merely depicting a world of peace and prosperity.

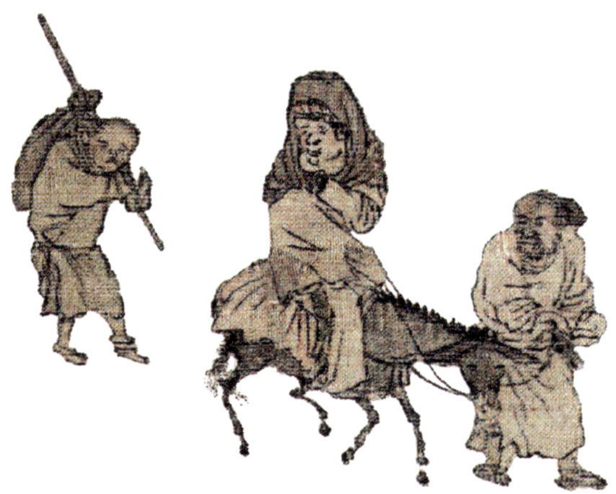

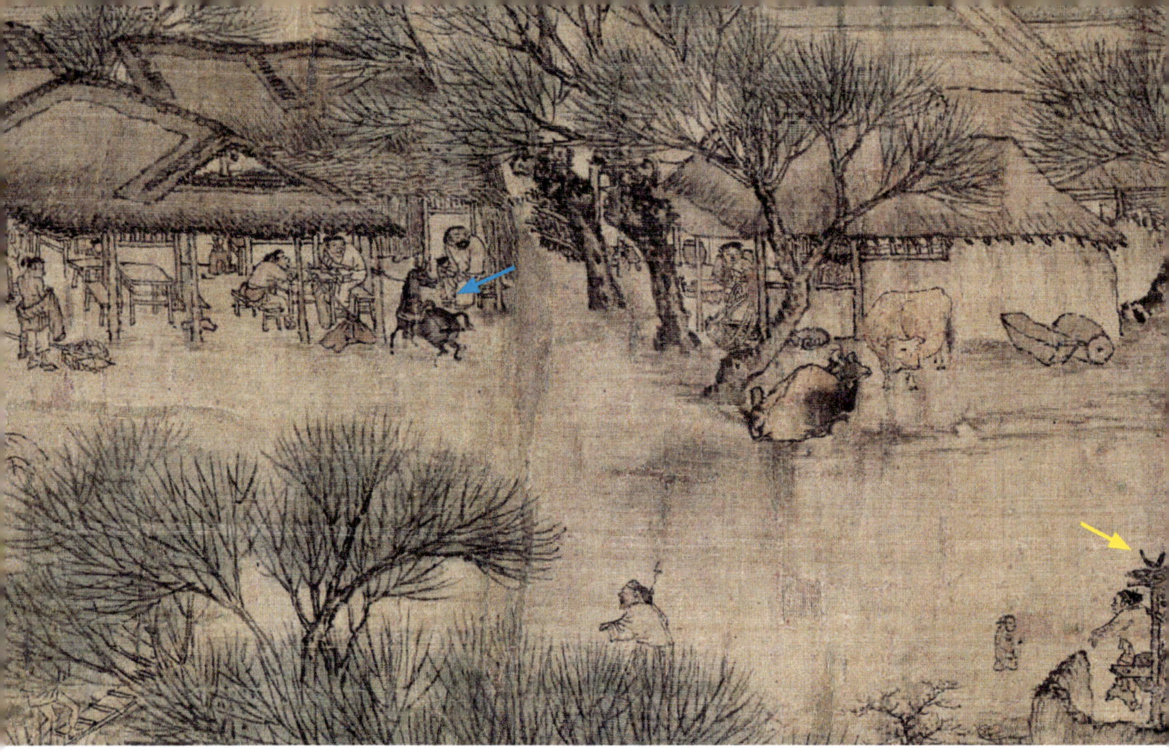

4. What startled the horse?

The red arrow in the picture above points to the 'startled horse'. I wonder if we have ever witnessed a frightened horse in real life. Once spooked, a horse will not listen to anyone and will gallop wildly, bursting with an energy that seems to say, 'I'm not even afraid of a tiger'. In the painting, a child is playing in the street when the startled horse charges towards him. An adult hurriedly stands up and calls the child back.

I said 'the so-called' because the painting is damaged in this area, making it uncertain whether the figure is indeed a startled horse. Some believe it might be a male donkey. It is a female donkey in heat that causes this male donkey's frenzied galloping. The female donkey was originally painted where the yellow arrow points, but it is no longer visible. During the restoration work at the Forbidden City in 1973, the donkey's body was removed, leaving only the female donkey's gaping mouth. Now, the wildly galloping male donkey has become the focal point of the scene, with some people chasing after it and even more anxiously watching. Nearby, two cows remain undisturbed, glancing at the commotion but seemingly somewhat indifferent. However, further away from the cows, where the blue arrow points, there is an agitated donkey looking back, with its front hooves in the air, tail raised, seemingly trying to break free from its reins.

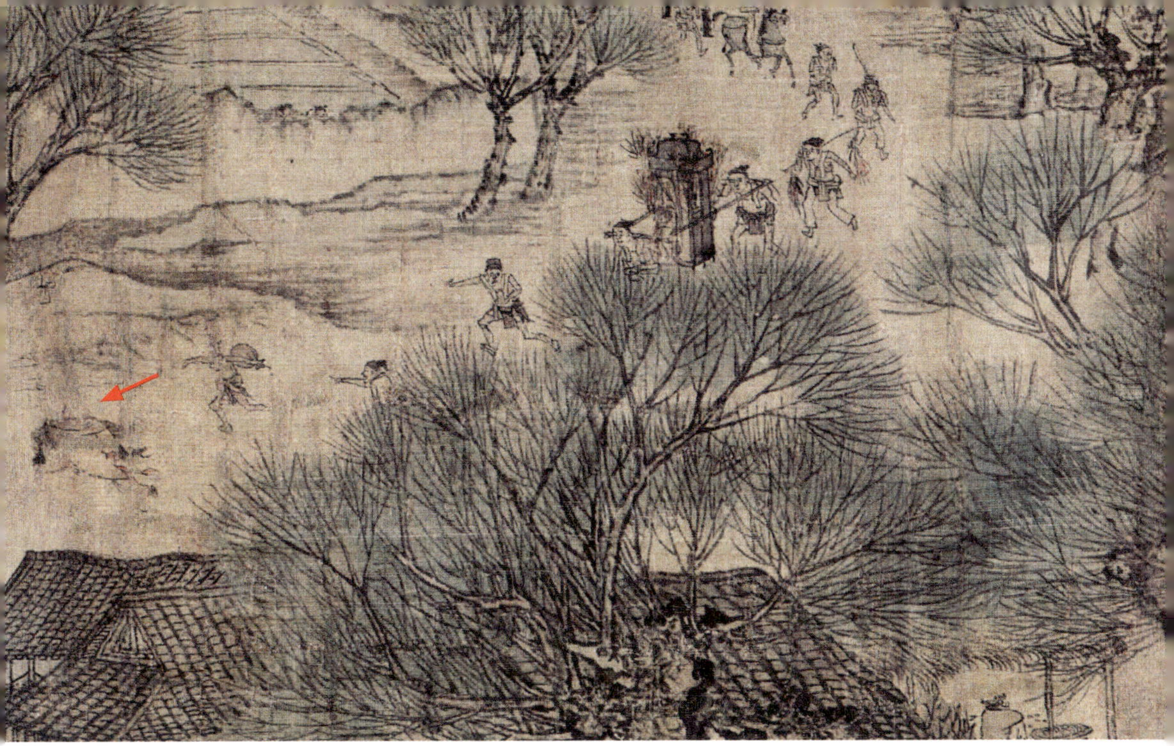

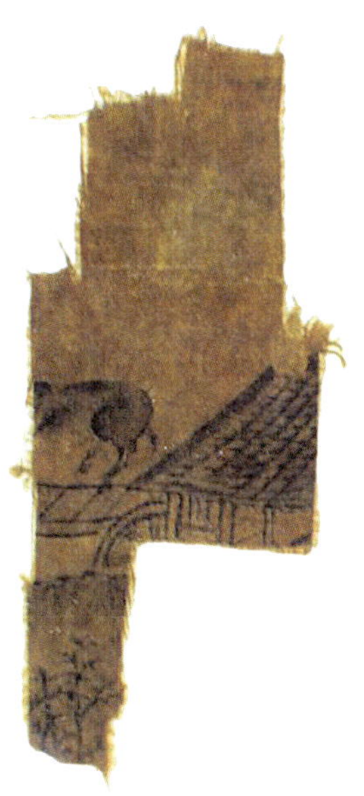

Fragments of the donkey's body removed during the 1973 restoration

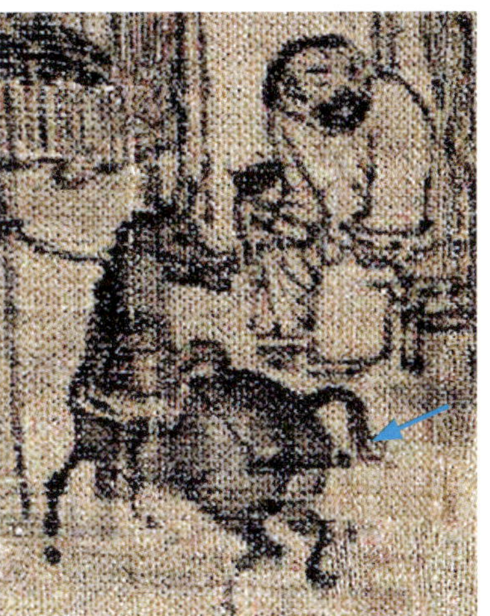

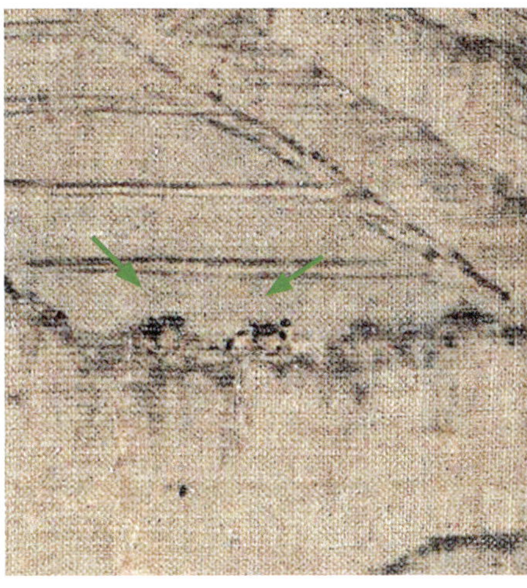

The running, neighing and cries aroused the curiosity of two young boys. They climb atop a wall to see what is happening on the street. However, whether it is the startled horse or donkey, it runs too fast. By the time they peek their heads out, all they see is a sedan chair heading back to the city.

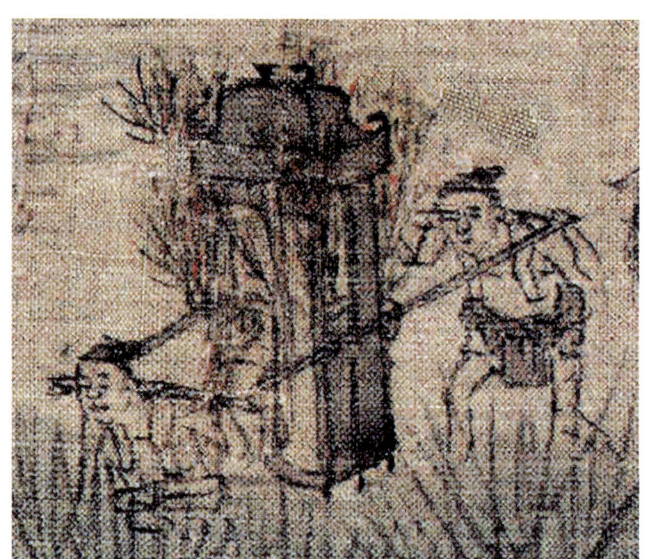
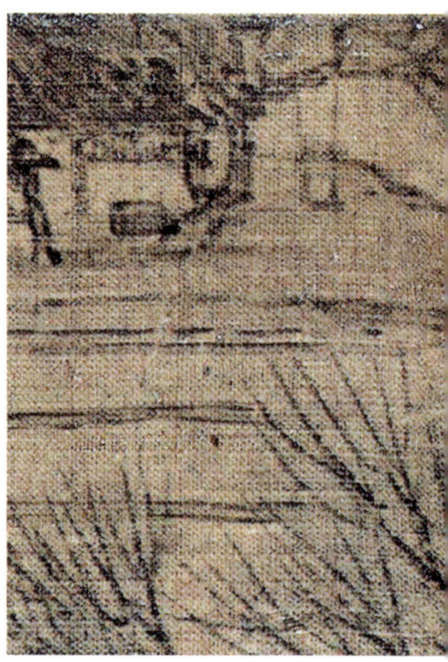

This is a small sedan chair carried by two people. The chair is peculiarly decorated, with branches and what appear to be red flowers (some say they are Chinese redbud flowers), giving it a fiery look at first glance. However, according to the records in the *Dongjing Meng Hua Lu* (《东京梦华录》, *The Eastern Capital: A Dream of Splendor*) ①, filling the sedan chair with willow branches and assorted flowers is a custom during the Qingming Festival. Affected by the 'startled horse', the bearers are carrying the chair unsteadily and it seems that a woman inside is lifting the curtain to peek out.

① *Dongjing Meng Hua Lu* (《东京梦华录》, *The Eastern Capital: A Dream of Splendor* 《东京梦华录》) is a book written by Meng Yuanlao, describing the customs and life in Bianjing during the Northern Song Dynasty. Most of the records document events from the reign of Emperor Huizong, spanning the years from Chongning to Xuanhe (1102–1125). It serves as an important historical document for studying the urban social life, economy and culture of the Northern Song Dynasty. The creation of this book is close to the time when *Along the River During the Qingming Festival* was painted. If viewed together, the two works complement each other with vivid illustrations and detailed descriptions.

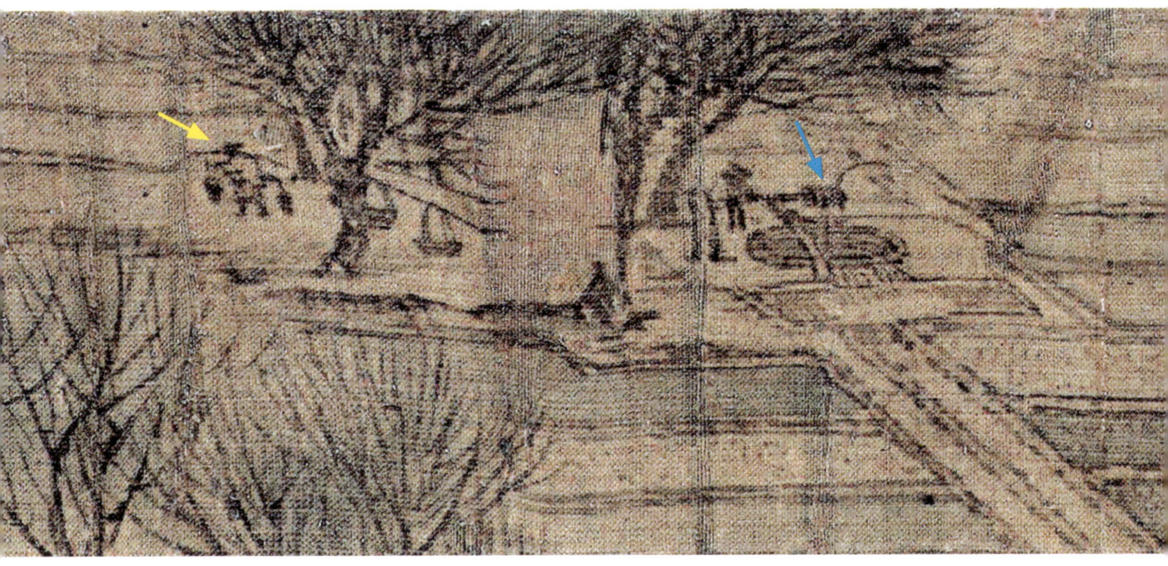

5. The fields and temperature during the Qingming Festival in the Northern Song Dynasty

Accidents often draw our attention, leaving the vast fields behind the earthen walls less noticed. In the picture on the right page, where the yellow arrow points, there is a person carrying a shoulder pole. Some say he is carrying manure, while others say water... Well, both interpretations make sense. Looking at where the blue arrow points, there appears to be a well, with an oval-shaped mouth. Above it seems to be a *Lulu* (辘轳), which is a windlass. Young readers might not be familiar with a *Lulu*, so I thoughtfully provided a clear picture for my dear readers (on the right). Now, look at where the red arrow points at the top of thispage. What do you think that is? That's right, a swing! Swinging is one of the customs during the Qingming Festival in ancient China. Do you remember the two young boys on top of the wall? It is the swing that tells

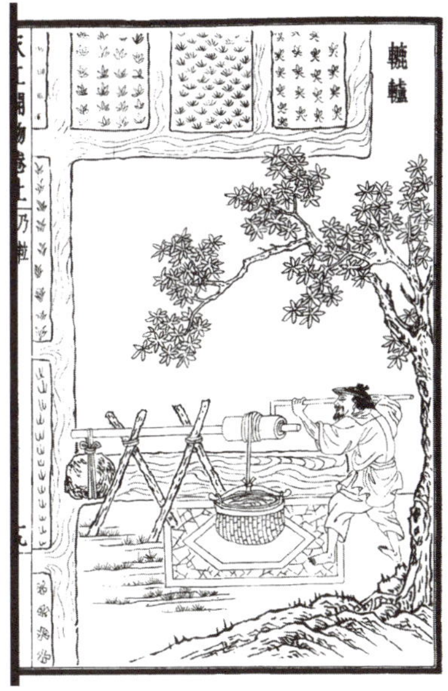

Lulu*, from *Tian Gong Kai Wu* (《天工开物》): *Heyday of Agriculture and Handicraft Industry in Ancient China

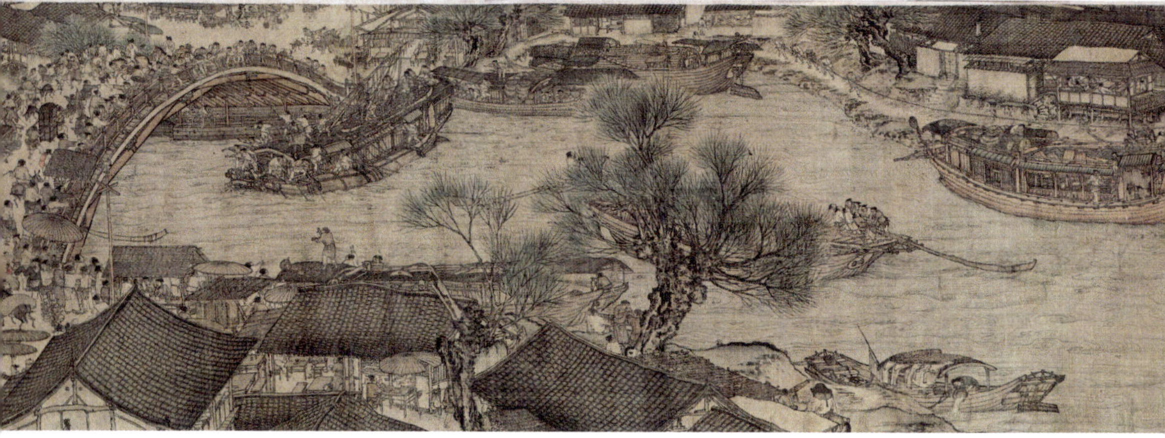

us that their home is likely right here. Seeing this, I am truly touched! Trivial details like the person carrying water, the swing and the *Lulu* are incredibly important for us to understand the daily lives of people during the Song Dynasty. Zhang Zeduan, what a meticulous person he is!

The fields in this area are neatly arranged, with some parts glistening in shades of green. Some believe these are vegetable patches, while others argue that they are wheat fields, as the Qingming Festival coincides with the time when winter wheat turns green and requires irrigation.

Along the River During the Qingming Festival was painted during the late Northern Song Dynasty when the climate was quite different from what it is now. At that time, China entered a cold climatic period (also known as the 'Little Ice Age'), which began during the reign of Emperor Huizong of the Northern Song Dynasty and lasted until mid-Southern Song Dynasty (from 1110 to the 1290s), enduring nearly a century. It wasn't until after 1200 that the climate warmed up again. The abnormally low temperatures brought about frequent natural disasters and extreme weather events, indirectly leading to wars and dynastic changes.

During the Qingming Festival in the late Northern Song Dynasty, the average daily temperature in Bianjing was around 12°C (54°F). It was a time when it was 'warming yet still chilly'. The lower-class labourers, who were engaged in physical work, wore thin

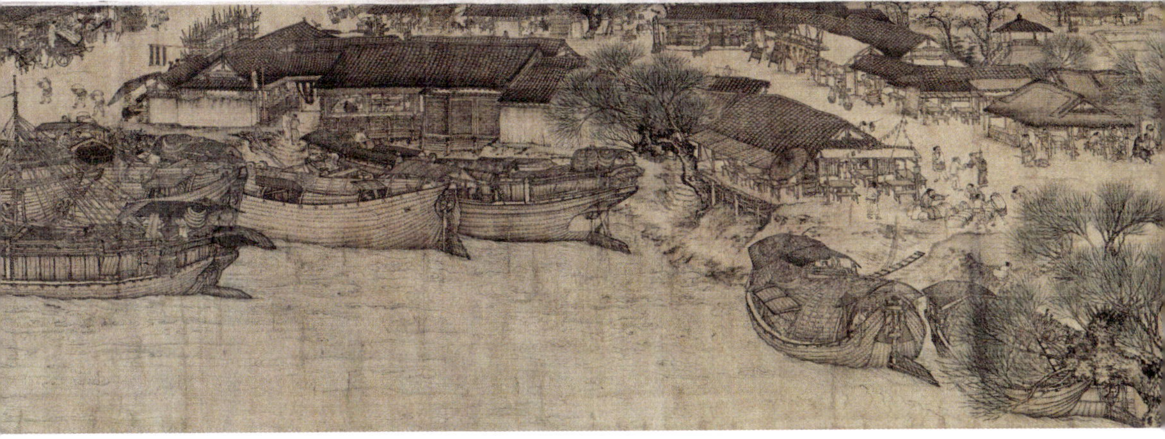

clothes, often bare-chested and bare legs, but seemingly unfazed by the cold. In contrast, people who were less active or travellers on long journeys wore thick clothes and still appeared to be shivering.

6. The Bian River! The Bian River!

Passing through the startled horse scene, we arrive at the Bian River. Why am I so excited to see the Bian River? Because it is incredibly important. In June of the second year of the Chunhua era (991), a section of embankment on the Bian River collapsed. Emperor Taizong of the Song Dynasty went to inspect the damage in person. His *Bu nian* (步辇),

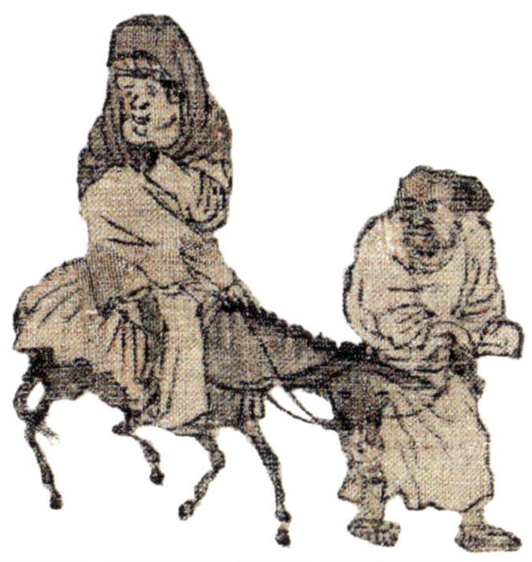

Travellers in thick clothes

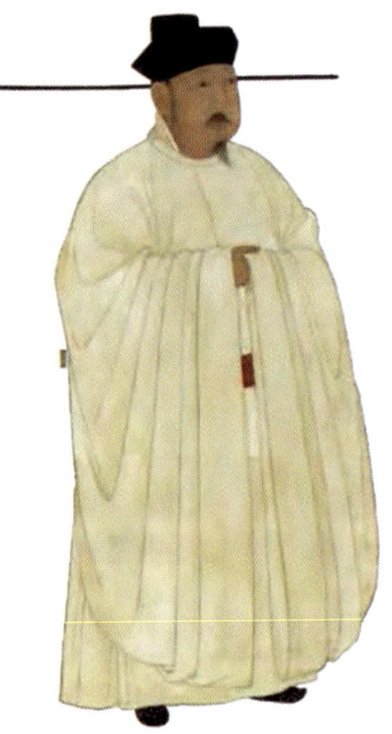

Portrait of Emperor Taizong of Song, **Anonymous, Song Dynasty, in the collection of the National Palace Museum, Taipei**

a kind of palanquin, moved through the muddy ground and his ministers hurriedly advised him to return to the palace. However, Taizong insisted on proceeding. He said, 'In the Eastern capital (Bianjing), hundreds of thousands of soldiers are stationed, and there are a million households. The entire country relies on this single canal for grain transportation and provisions. How can I afford not to care about it?'

During the Northern Song Dynasty, a four-capital system was implemented: the Eastern, Southern, Western and Northern Capitals. The Eastern Capital was located in the area of ancient Bianzhou, thus it was also called Bianjing. *Zhuan cao* (转漕) refers to the transportation of grain and provisions. In ancient times, land transportation was called *zhuan* (转), while water transportation was called *cao* (漕). *Yang ji* (仰给) means relying on others for supplies. Emperor Taizong's statement implied that with so many people living in the Eastern Capital, the transportation of grain and supplies depended entirely on the Bian River. How could he not be concerned about it?

Despite its importance and significance, the Bian River was still notoriously difficult to manage. But why? The Bian River was an artificial waterway that diverted the waters of the Yellow River. Utilising the Yellow River had its advantages: its large water volume and rapid currents. However, there were drawbacks as well. Firstly, the river carried an immense load of silt, necessitating extensive dredging each year from winter to early spring to ensure smooth water flow for the coming year. Secondly, the Yellow River would freeze, and in early spring ice floes would rush down from the upstream not only destroying the river embankments but also blocking the channel and causing floods. To protect the areas along the Bian River from floods, the Northern Song government resorted to an extraordinary measure: they would construct a dam each winter at the confluence where the Bian River met the Yellow River. This dam would then be dismantled on the first day of the Qingming Festival the following year. Although it was troublesome and affected the volume of water transport, it was considered a relatively effective solution given the conditions at that time.

After a dormant and lifeless winter, the Bian River finally heralded its inaugural voyage of the year on the first day of the Qingming Festival. The dam built in winter was dismantled, and soon water from the Yellow River filled the Bian River. Various boats that had been waiting for a whole winter, loaded with grain and passengers, sailed through villages and fields, heading towards Bianjing. The Bian River, like being resurrected from the dead, revived in a single day to a bustling scene of hundreds of ships vying for passage. The people of Bianjing naturally wouldn't miss the opportunity to enjoy the lively atmosphere on the first day. They flocked to the riverbanks, which is called *Shang he* (上河), and thus, year after year, *Shang he* has become a custom.

Once the custom of *Shang he* during the Qingming Festival was established, it would last for generations. Therefore, Emperor Shenzong of the Song Dynasty changed the water source of the Bian River from the Yellow River to the clear and non-freezing Luo River, eliminating the need for seasonal closures and openings, the tradition of *Shang he* persisted. On the day of the Qingming Festival, the waterway was busy, the markets were lively and everything seemed to be renewed, making it the ideal time to depict the transportation on the Bian River and the local customs along its banks.

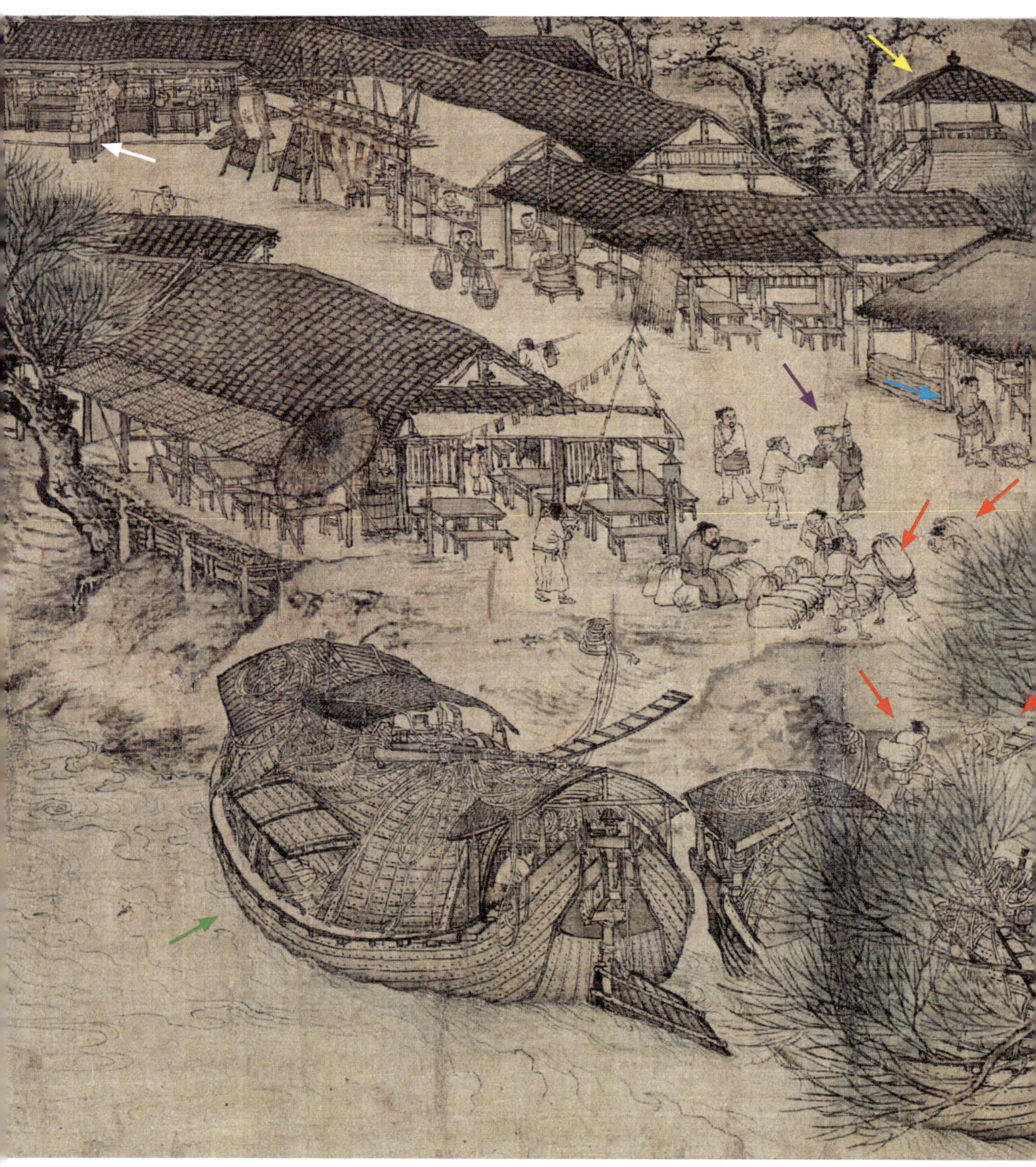

7. The Bian River dock and little diagonal street

There are quite a few attractions at the Bian River dock waiting for us to explore.

Firstly, two large boats are moored at the riverbank, with people busy unloading cargo onto the shore. We can see four porters (indicated by the red arrows on the opposite page, with one of the porters partially obscured by branches and leaves). The goods are packed in burlap sacks, and judging from the porters' postures and the shape of the sacks, they likely contain grain. These sacks of grain are quite heavy, so two more helpers are needed to unload and stack the goods. The person indicated by the black arrow is likely the boss, sitting on the sacks and supervising the work. The boat sits deep in the water (indicated by the green arrow), suggesting that the unloading has just begun. At the beginning of the scroll, the artist shows us donkey caravan carrying charcoal. Now, right after arriving at the banks of the Bian River, we see boats transporting grain. Charcoal and grain are the daily necessities for life in Bianjing, indicating that the artist elaborately considered what to depict and the sequence in which to present the scenes.

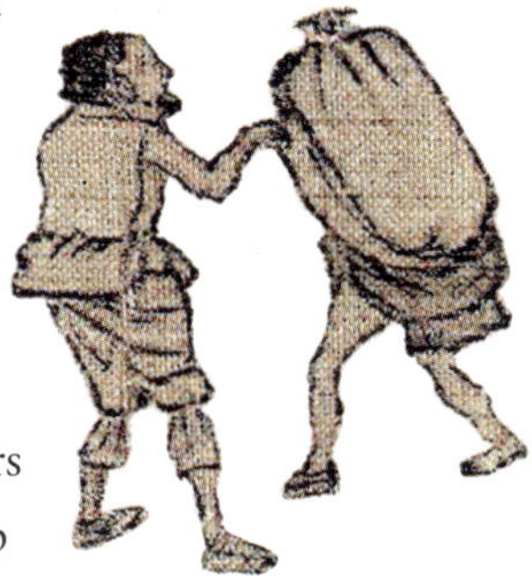

Adjacent to the unloading area, a fortune teller (indicated by the purple arrow on the opposite page) is telling his customer's fortune. People in the Song Dynasty held a keen interest in fortune-telling, resulting in a plethora of fortune tellers of varying social ranks. High-ranking fortune tellers would set up fixed stalls, while those of lower rank, like the one we see now, wandered around the docks catering primarily to labourers and shop servers. Such fortune tellers' own fates are rather bleak.

Behind the fortune teller, there is a man (indicated by the blue arrow on the opposite page) who is bare-chested, with his upper garment either just taken off or about to be put on. The question is, why did he take off his shirt? I have been puzzled by this for a long time. Some people say he is searching for lice – what an enlightening idea! There are some objects at his feet. Some say these are tools used during the Qingming Festival but I cannot agree. Those seem like a carrying pole and a coil of rope, which are the tools of his work. He might be a porter who hasn't found any work yet.

From this poor porter to the shop at the white arrow on the opposite page, there lies a 'dock diagonal street'. This narrow street is primarily lined with small food stalls catering mainly to vendors and labourers. The shop highlighted by the white arrow is an exception. It does not sell foods but items for commemorating the deceased, such as paper figures, paper horses, paper buildings and paper money. The shopkeeper has stacked these goods in several layers right on the street, which aligns perfectly with the descriptions found in *Dongjing Meng Hua Lu* (《东京梦华录》, *The Eastern Capital: A Dream of Splendor*) : During the Qingming Festival, all shops selling paper horses along the streets fold paper into the shapes of buildings and pavilions and stack them outside their doors.

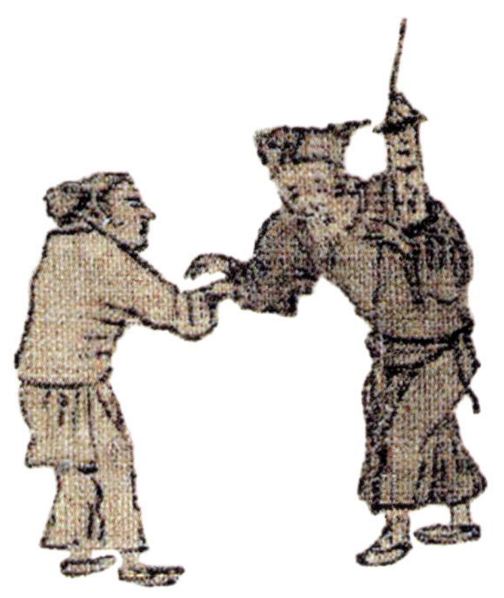

There is one more yellow arrow in the picture. It points to a brick-built platform with staircases on both sides. Atop the platform is a pavilion, containing a table and seating. There is a popular explanation about this structure, claiming that it is a 'fire lookout tower' used to observe from a high vantage point and promptly identify fire emergencies as part of the firefighting and alert system.

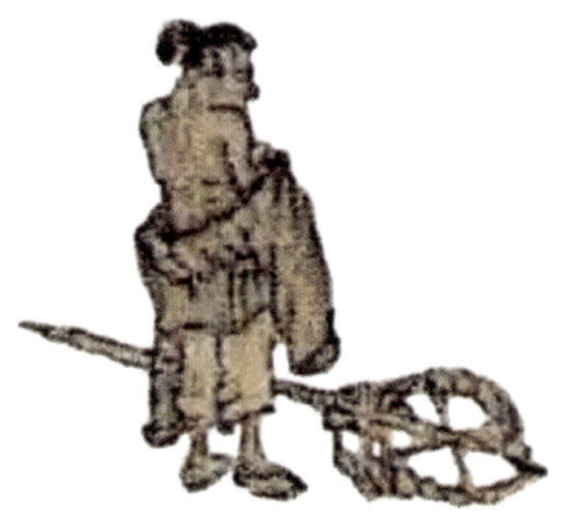

Indeed, the Song Dynasty government took fire prevention very seriously, maintaining dedicated firefighting teams and facilities. As recorded in *Dongjing Meng Hua Lu* (《东京梦华录》, *The Eastern Capital: A Dream of Splendor*): 'Moreover, fire lookout towers built with bricks were erected at high places, with people stationed to keep watch. Below were several official rooms, garrisoning over hundreds of soldiers and firefighting equipment, ready for firefighting...' Therefore, the base of this pavilion is

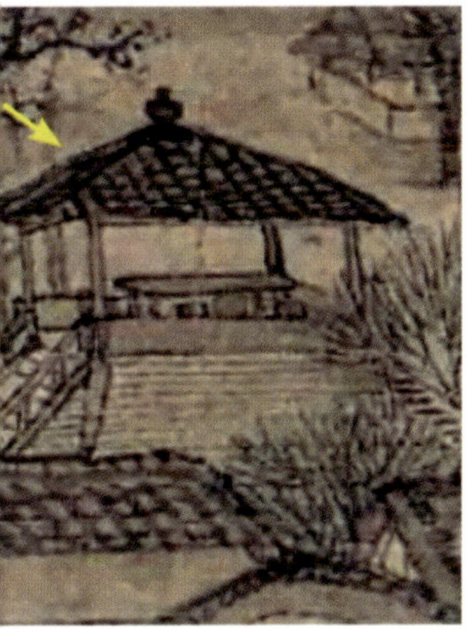

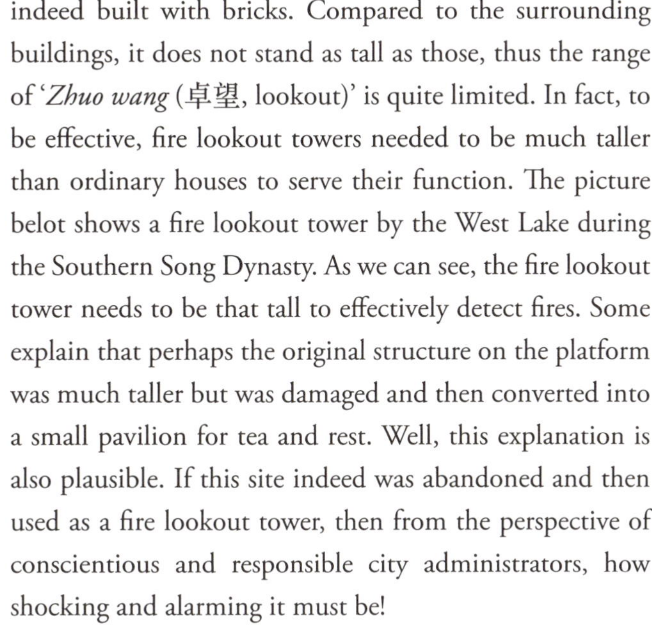

indeed built with bricks. Compared to the surrounding buildings, it does not stand as tall as those, thus the range of '*Zhuo wang* (卓望, lookout)' is quite limited. In fact, to be effective, fire lookout towers needed to be much taller than ordinary houses to serve their function. The picture belot shows a fire lookout tower by the West Lake during the Southern Song Dynasty. As we can see, the fire lookout tower needs to be that tall to effectively detect fires. Some explain that perhaps the original structure on the platform was much taller but was damaged and then converted into a small pavilion for tea and rest. Well, this explanation is also plausible. If this site indeed was abandoned and then used as a fire lookout tower, then from the perspective of conscientious and responsible city administrators, how shocking and alarming it must be!

All right, we've walked from the small bridge to the dock, and now we're about to explore water transportation. What can we find on the waterways? Of course, there are more boats and...

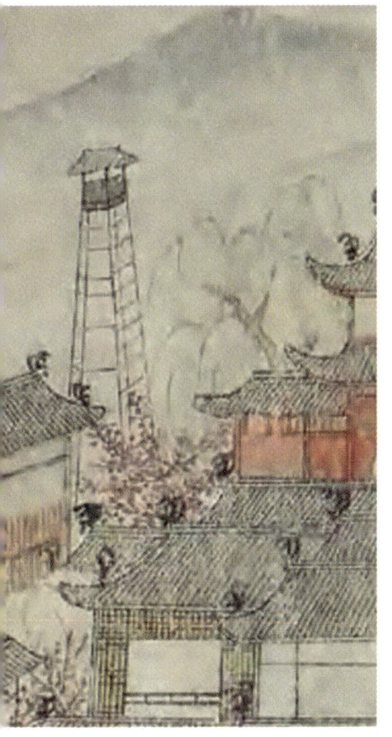

LEFT: A fire lookout tower by the West Lake during the Southern Song Dynasty (Attributed to), *Scenic Attractions of West Lake* (《西湖清趣图》) in the collection of Freer Gallery of Art Collection

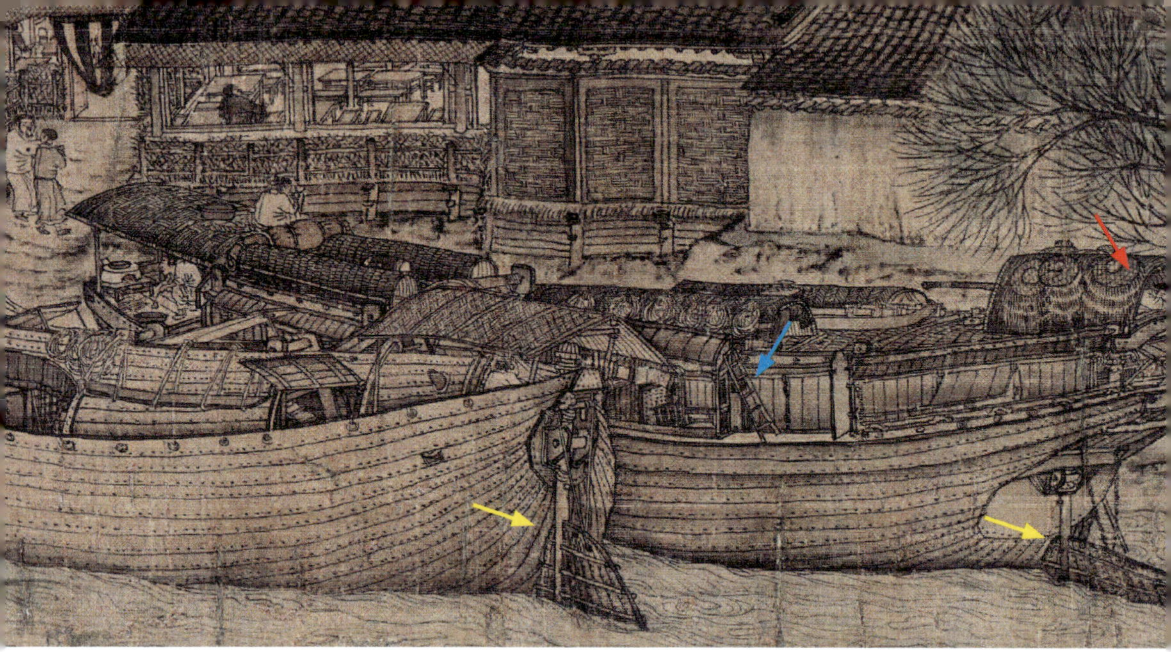

8. Look at the large boats on the river!

Passing the dock, we'll see even more large boats!

Looking at the picture above, this boat appears to be considerably larger than the grain transport boats we saw earlier. We can estimate its length by comparing it to the houses on the shore. Additionally, we can infer its height using the ladder (indicated by the blue arrow, with an enlarged view on the right) – the ladder has five or six rungs. However, this is not the largest boat in *Along the River During the Qingming Festival.*

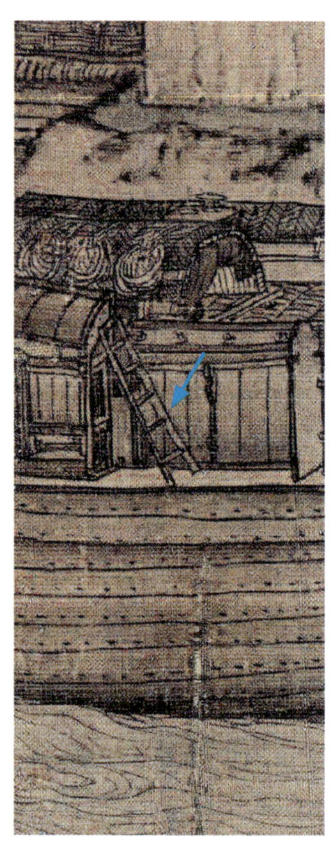

The red arrow in the picture above points to a helmsman responsible for operating the boat's rudder. The rudder is just below him (indicated by the yellow arrow). This type of rudder is called a 'balanced rudder', which can be freely raised and lowered. The helmsman manipulates the rudder using a *Gun* (辊), which is a roller device, under the canopy. Upon closer inspection of the rudder blade's structure, it is made by vertically joined planks and reinforced with horizontal timbers. 'Balanced rudders' are

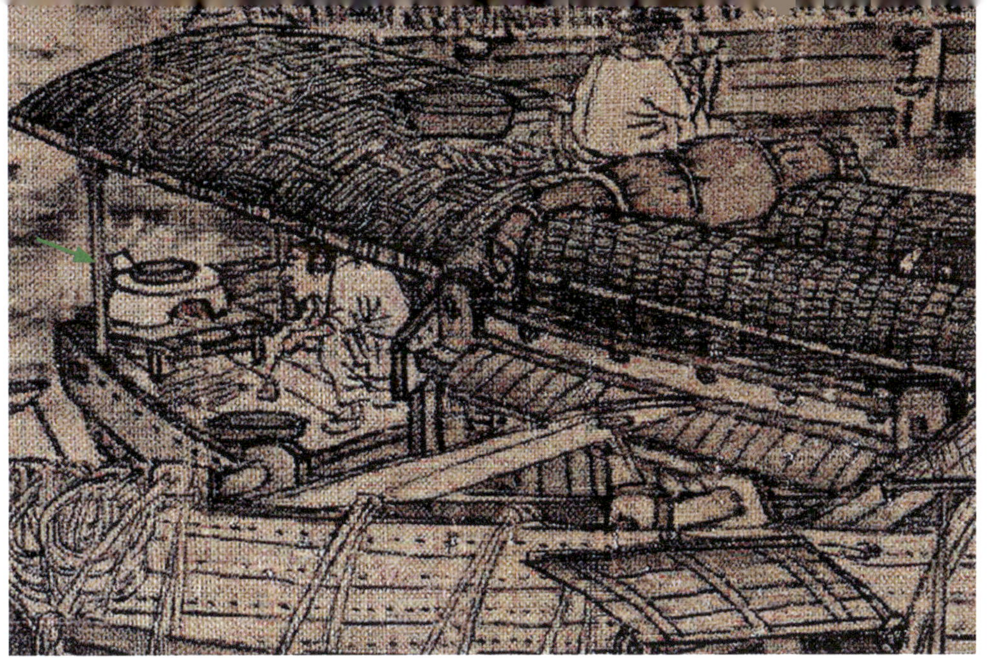

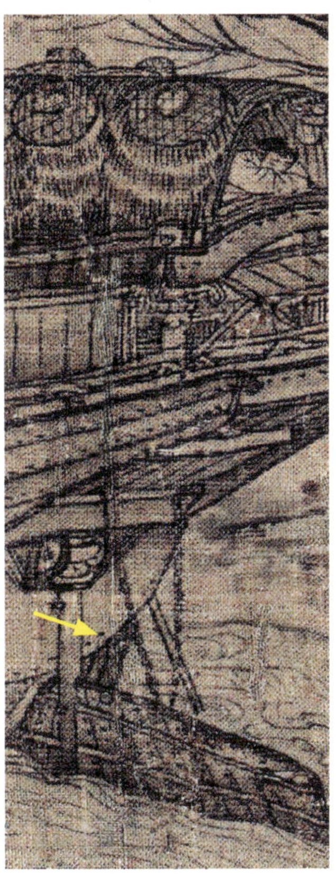

lighter to operate and offer a stronger control over steering, making boats more stable during navigation, which was a world-leading technology at the time. In the painting, the helmsman is resting inside the canopy at the stern of the boat. He has his hands tucked in and half of his face buried, appearing to be asleep. The artist, Zhang Zeduan, is particularly adept at embedding subtle details like this to set the stage for more significant events unfolding later in the scene.

The green arrow in the picture above points to a small stove. The boat crew is cooking their own meals, while the boat owner has likely gone ashore to drink at a tavern. Along the shore, the windows of the restaurants are wide open allowing patrons to enjoy the scenery while drinking. Free from responsibilities and with nothing to do for the moment, people idle away the time for a while. Just the thought of it is quite pleasant. Unfortunately, this short moment of tranquillity will soon be disrupted!

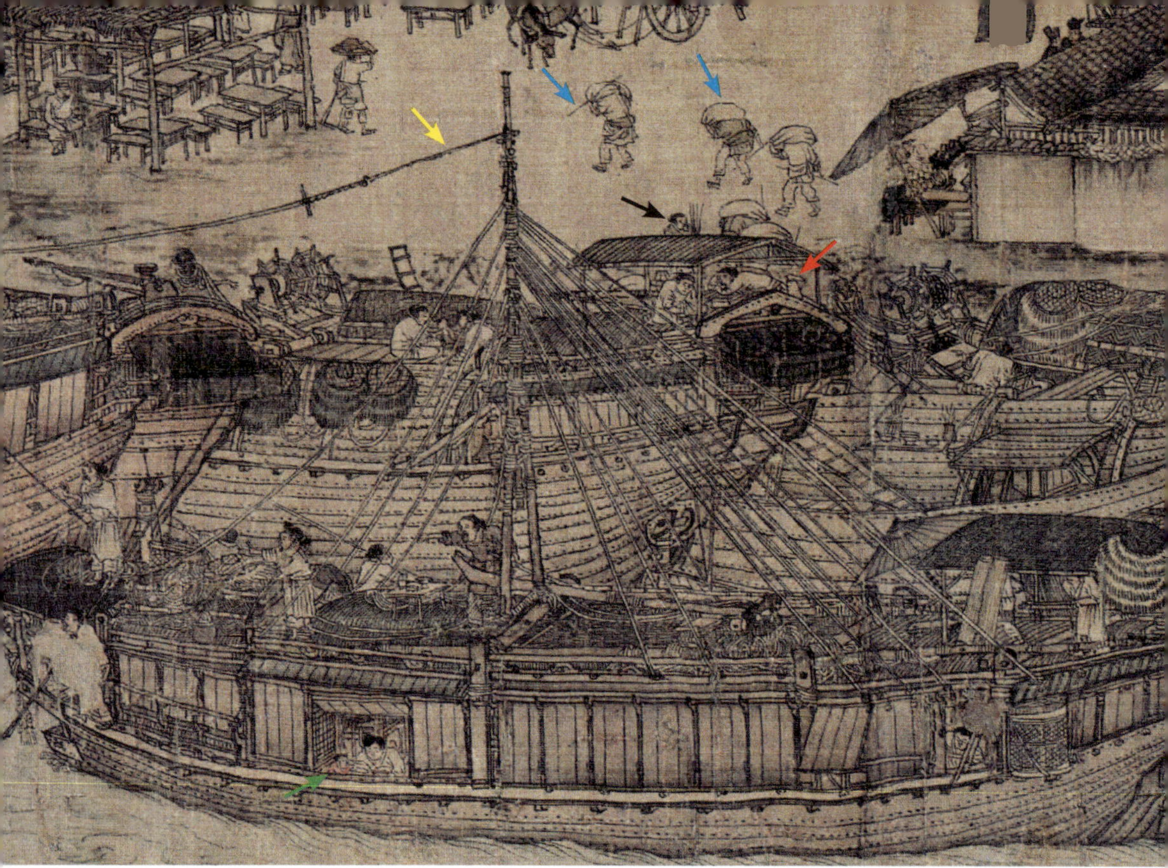

9. What are the large boats gathering for?

In this scene, we see even more boats. These boats are densely packed in the river, making it difficult to distinguish one from another. According to the regulations at that time, on the first sailing day during the Qingming Festival, the official grain transport fleet was required to assemble and set sail from the Rainbow Bridge Dock. This dock was the grain distribution centre in the southeast of Bianjing.

Now let's look at the details. The blue arrow in the picture above points to the porters, each clutching a thin stick, known as a *Chou* (筹), which means a tally used for counting. Look further, and we'll see the foreman, highlighted by the black arrow, holding a handful of these counters. Each porter who carries a sack of goods receives a *Chou*, and his wage is calculated based on the total number he collects. This counting system has a long history; I've even seen it used in documentaries from the first half of the 20th century. The red arrow points to an older man with a thick beard, who is likely quite old. He is lying down, watching his companions with his lower limbs casually bent back, appearing

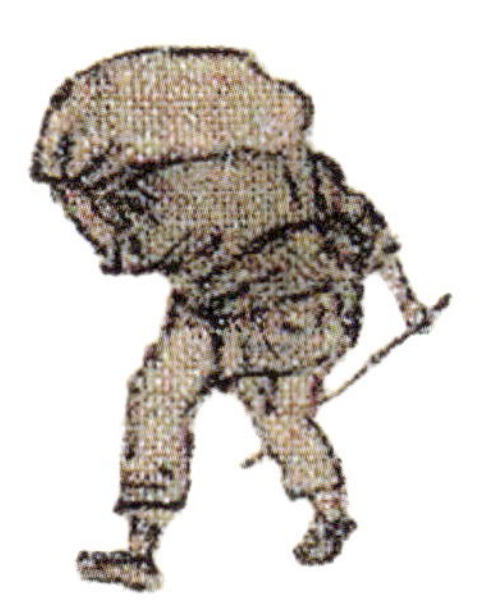

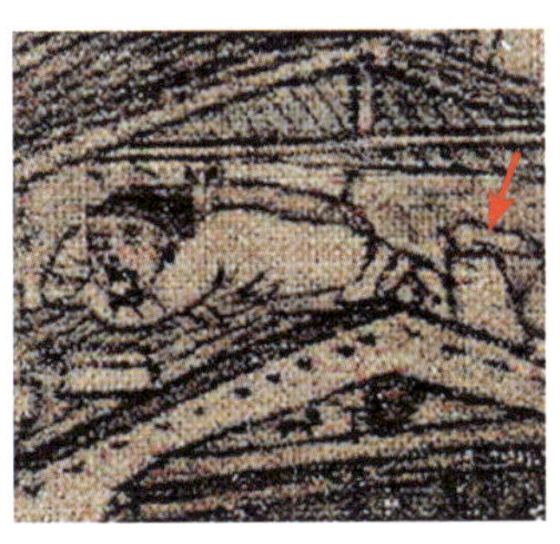

relaxed and playful – how cute! Meanwhile, a window in the front cabin is open (indicated by the green arrow). A child in red is looking at his mother, who is lost in thought, gazing at the flowing river, seemingly oblivious to the nearby boatmen's shouts. Where is she taking her child? What might she be pondering at that moment?

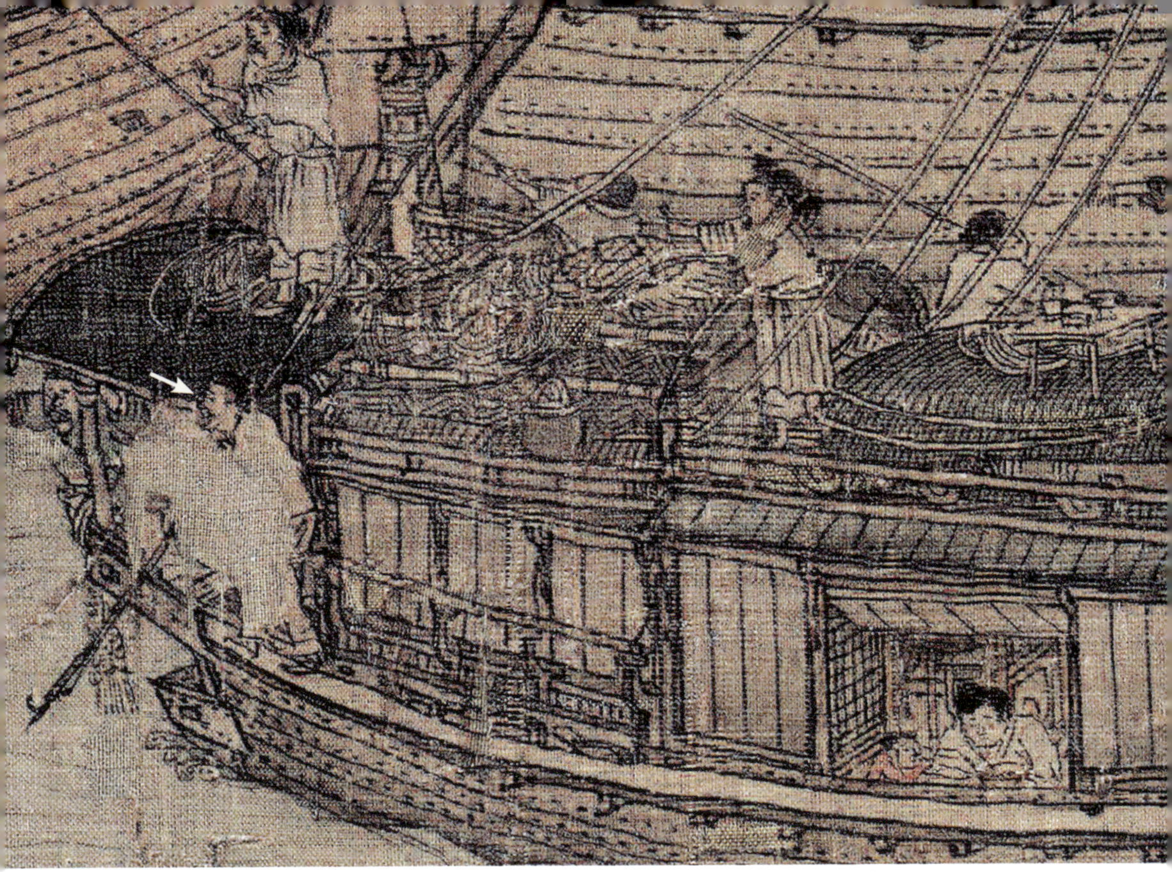

The yellow arrow on the left page points to a tow rope that extends far out, where five trackers (see in the panoramic view on the next page) are pulling this large boat upstream. Judging from the cabin's windows, this is a dual-purpose passenger/freighter boat. Due to its large capacity and the crowded condition on the river, the crew is visibly on high alert, busy managing the navigation. The picture above on this page is an enlarged view of the boat.

Five trackers

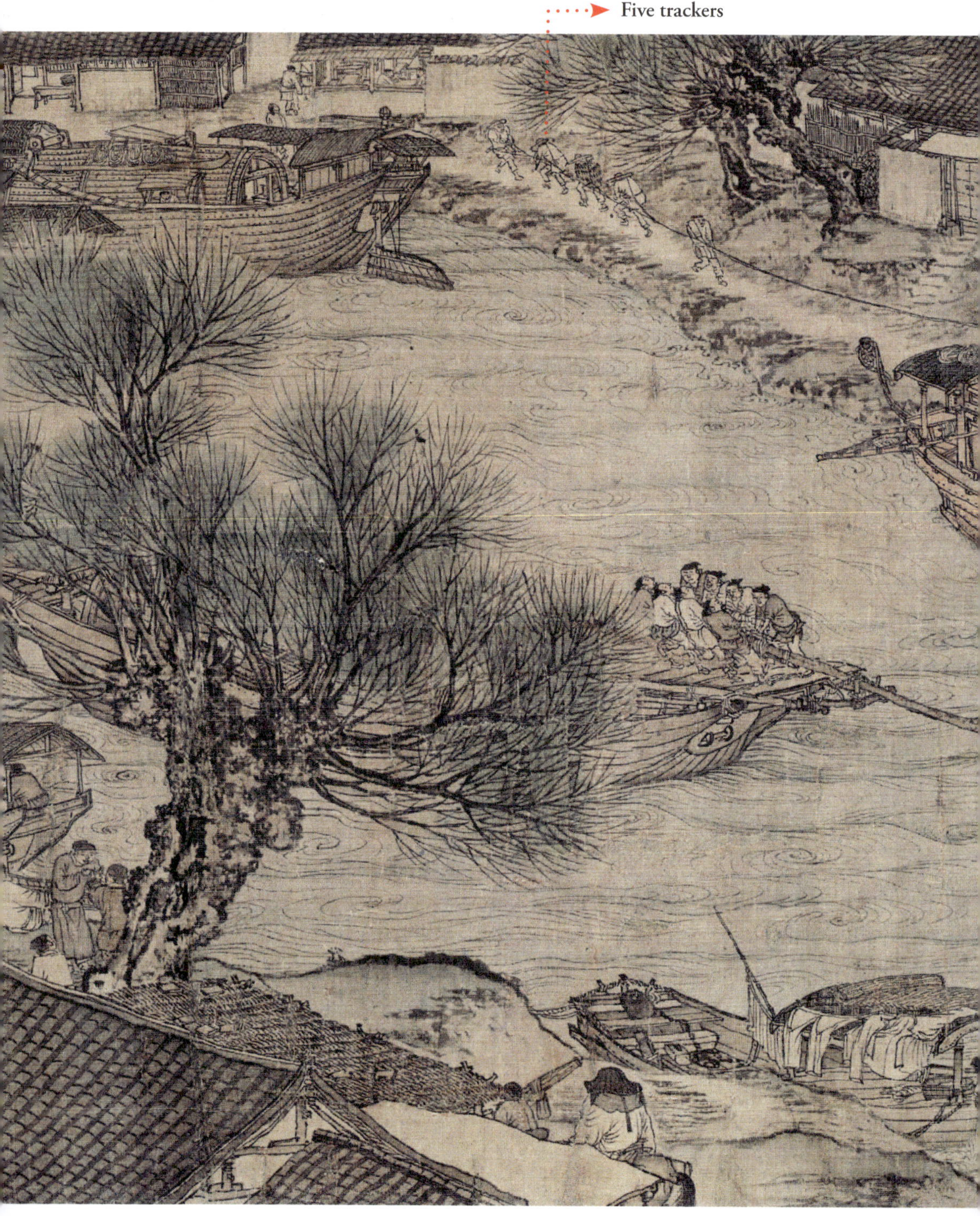

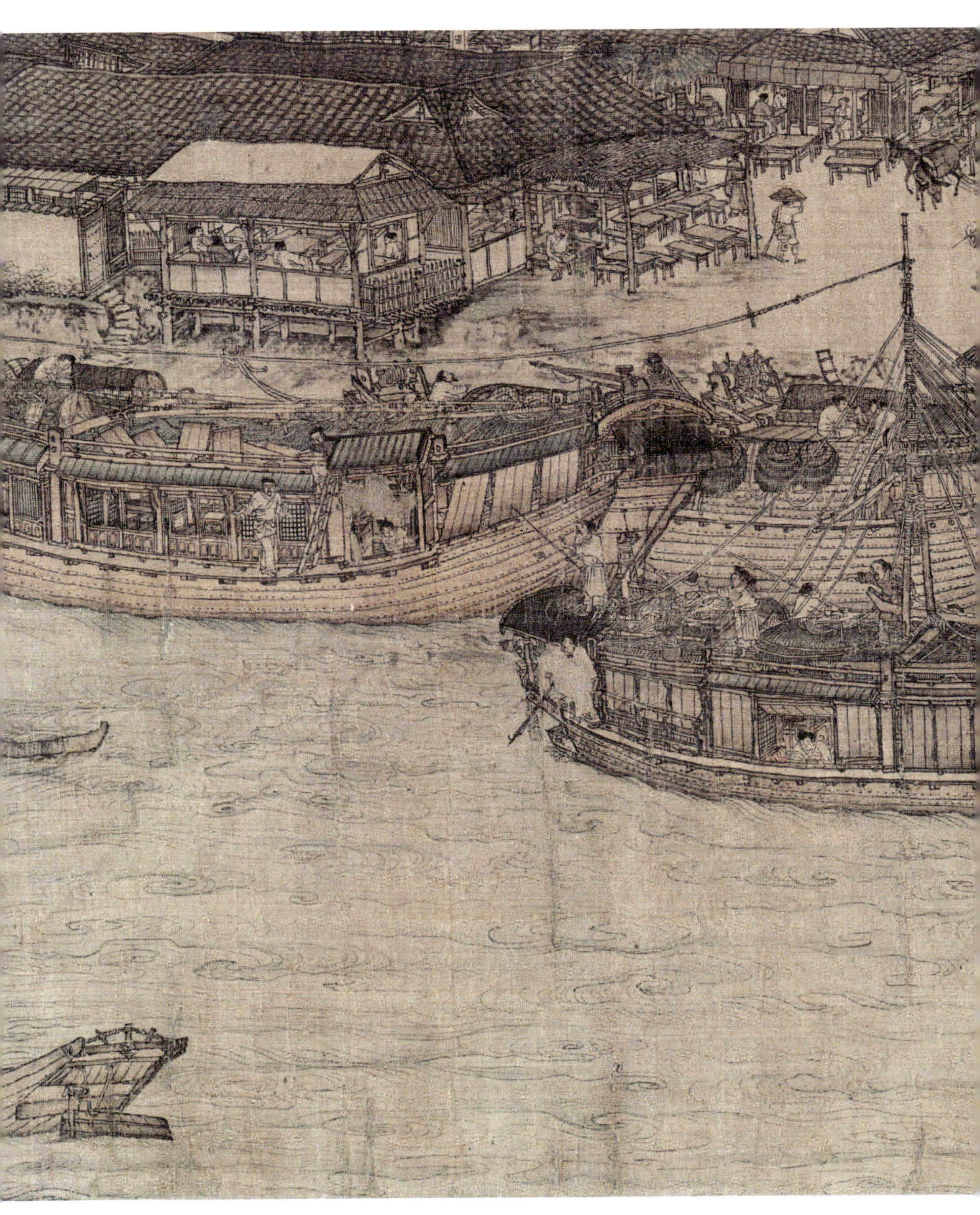

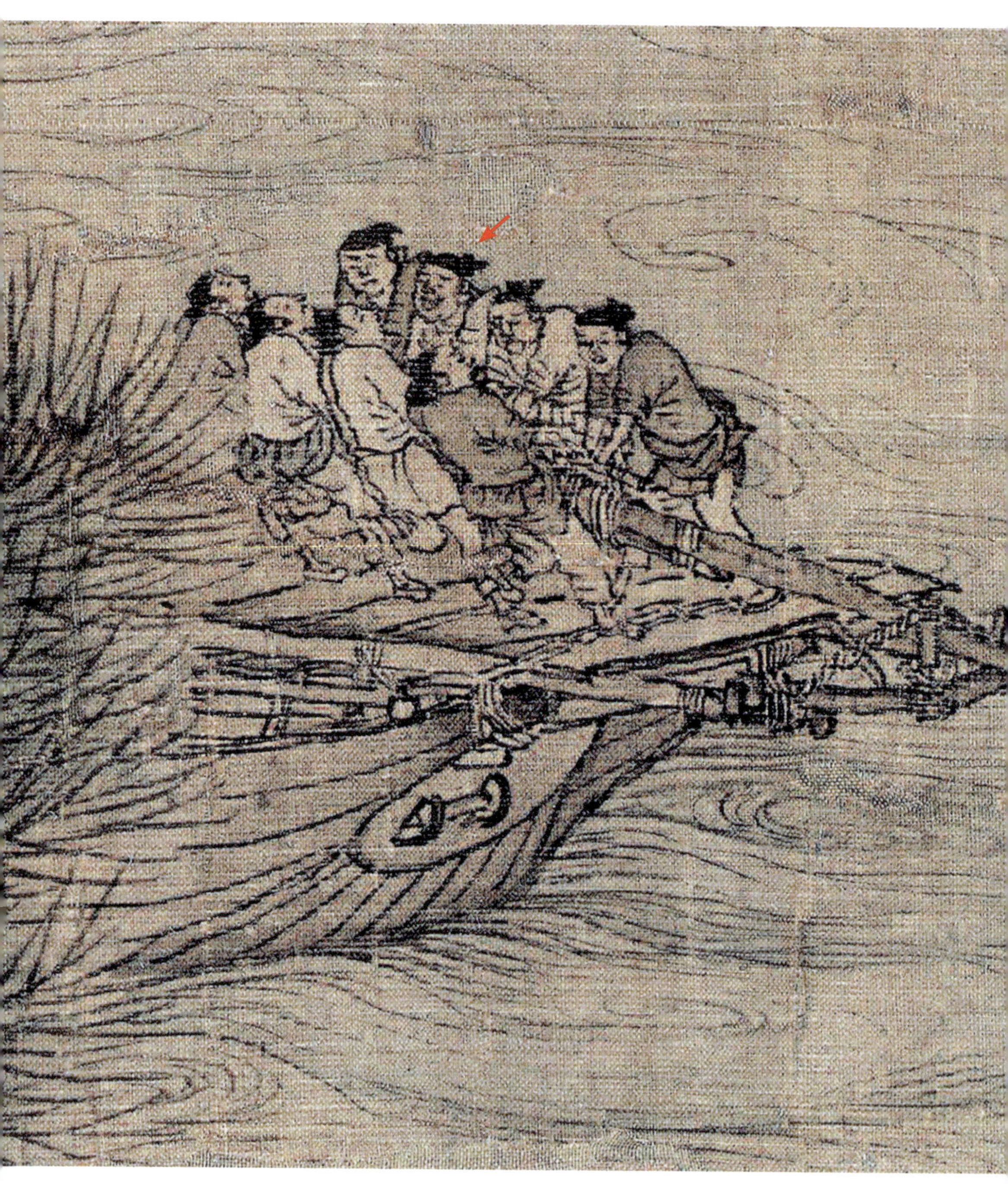

The owner, crew and even a woman, are all reaching out and signalling to alert other boats to avoid collisions. Two crew members standing on the canopy and larboard are holding long poles, ready to steer the direction at any moment. The one on the larboard (indicated by the white arrow in the picture above) appears to be quite skilled in the water. For me, I wouldn't dare stand there myself.

10. On the dual-purpose passenger/freighter boat equipped with huge oars, what are the people really worried about?

In the previous panoramic view, we figure out the 'power' behind the dual-purpose passenger/freighter boat: on the small path along the distant shore, five trackers are pulling the large boat upstream. The boat that had previously caused great anxiety among the people on the dual-purpose passenger/freighter boat also appeared. It is a heavily laden boat, navigating through the river channel. At the bow and stern are two huge oars, each manned by eight crew members working together. The picture on the left page shows the eight crew members at the stern. There are also eight at the bow, but they are hidden by foliage.

What's the difference between an oar and a paddle? The ancients said that a large and long one is called an oar, while a short and small one is called a paddle. Of course, the difference between oars and paddles is not just in size and length. Both are tools for propelling boats, but paddles work intermittently – with each stroke, the paddle is dipped into the water, pulled back, then lifted and returned for another stroke, pushing the boat forward gradually. Oars, by contrast, mimic the motion of a fish's tail, offering continuous propulsion. Typically installed at the bow and stern of a boat, oars are swung from side to side, propelling the boat in a manner akin to a fish flicking its tail. As the saying goes, 'the efficiency of one oar equals that of three paddles', underscoring the superior efficiency of oars over paddles. This efficiency stems from the leverage principle, which makes oar operation comparatively easier. However, the oars in this picture are so huge that it takes many people working together to row with them.

Now, let's take a closer look at the boatmen rowing the oars. Eight of them are aligned on both sides, four on each side, vigorously rowing the large oars. The men on the left are leaning backwards, clearly pulling the oar back. Can you see their left legs?

Their lower left limbs are raised and pulled back, indicating the extensive range of their rowing motion. Meanwhile, the four men opposite are pushing down the oar, working together to control the angle of the oar blade and its direction of motion. Notably, the boatman indicated by the red arrow, unlike his companions who exert their strength with grunts and shouts, is caught with a wide-open mouth in a foolish grin, looking carefree. However, absorbed in their vigorous rowing, the boatmen are unaware of the looming danger. As we continue to look further, we'll discover that the people on the dual-purpose passenger/freighter boat are shouting not out of concern for themselves but for another boat. These clueless boatmen on that heavily laden boat, focused solely on rowing, are completely unaware of the serious crisis ahead!

11. Clothes drying on the boat's canopy

Before we explore what danger the heavily laden ship is about to cause, let's first take a look at a small boat nearby.

On the bank of the Bian River, close to our side, a boat is moored. Unlike the large, luxurious cargo boats and passenger boats, this is a fisherman's boat. It is so small in size that the whirlpools stirred up by the large oars of that heavily laden boat can rock it unsteadily. A woman has just been washing clothes on the boat, and now, the clothes are drying on the boat's

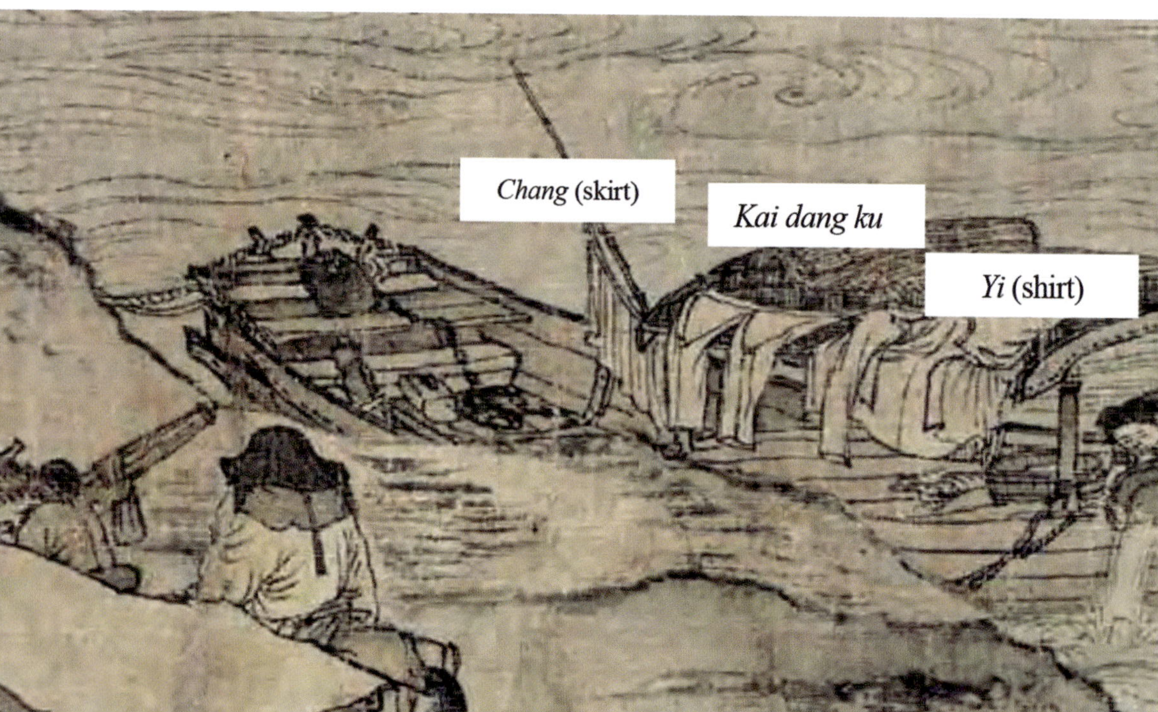

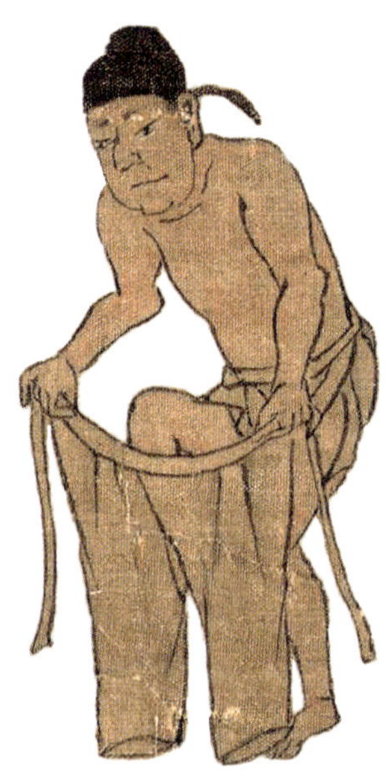

The person putting on his *Kai dang ku, from Hundred Horses*, the Tang Dynasty, in the collection of the Palace Museum in Beijing

canopy. Shirts and skirts are on both sides, with pants in the middle. Please take another look at those pants – what's special about them? Those are *Kai dang ku,* as we mentioned earlier. More precisely, we call those *Ban kai dang ku* (半开裆裤), because only the back is exposed. In ancient paintings, such *Ban kai dang ku* are not uncommon. They can be found in the *Early Snow on the River* (《江行初雪图》) and *Watergate Gristmill* (《闸口盘车图》) during the Five Dynasties (picture on the next page). Besides, there is a person just putting on his *Kai dang ku* depicted in *Hundred Horses* (《百马图》) in the Tang Dynasty (picture on the right). This might be the only scene of someone putting on *Kai dang ku* in ancient Chinese paintings, making it extremely valuable!

Now, from this scene of clothes drying in *Along the River During the Qingming Festival*, we can also learn that *Kai dang ku* were worn by both men and women.

Some might say, 'Exposing your buttocks, how embarrassing!' Of course, adults generally wouldn't only

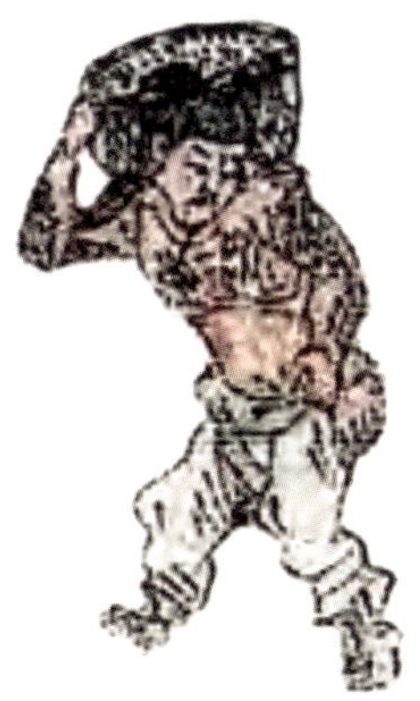

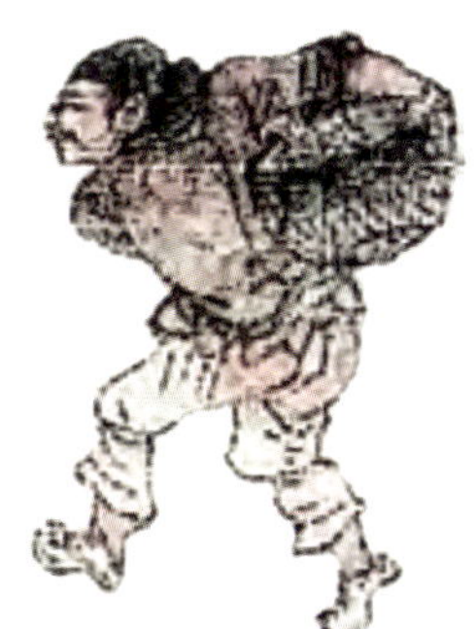

A bare-buttock labourer in *Kai dang ku* from *Watergate Gristmill*, the Five Dynasties,in the collection of the Shanghai Museum

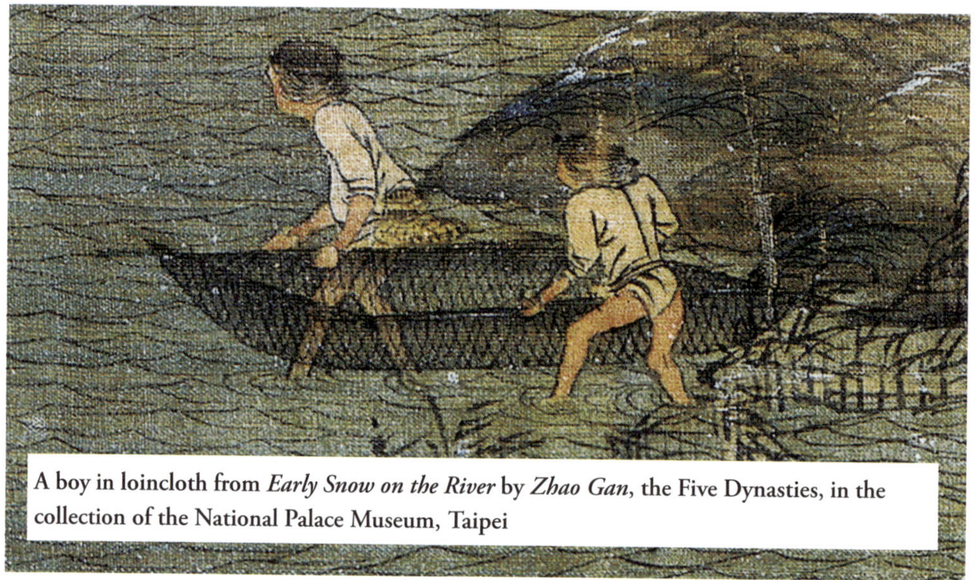

A boy in loincloth from *Early Snow on the River* by *Zhao Gan*, the Five Dynasties, in the collection of the National Palace Museum, Taipei

wear *Kai dang ku*. After putting on *Kai dang ku*, they usually wore a shirt or skirt over them to avoid accidental exposure. Why did I say 'generally'? This is to be precise in my expression, because in situations without women present, male labourers might directly wear *Kai dang ku* without minding about their exposed buttocks (such as the labourer in the *Watergate Gristmil* on the left side). So, some naughty kids (or a mischievous adult like myself) might ask, 'if an ancient person was walking down the street and bent over, or if a gust of wind suddenly blew, could his buttocks be exposed?' The answer is, yes, such situations could occur. For instance, at the end of *Along the River During the Qingming Festival*, there is a man bending over to draw water from a street-side well, wearing short *Kai dang ku*. No wind is needed at all – his buttocks are unabashedly bare, right on the bustling streets of Bianjing city.

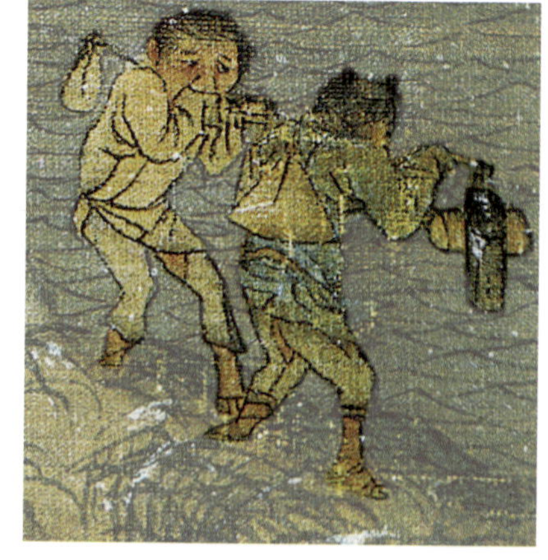

A boy in *Kai dang ku* from *Early Snow on the River* by *Zhao Gan*, the Five Dynasties,in the collection of the National Palace Museum, Taipei

12. The mysterious traveller

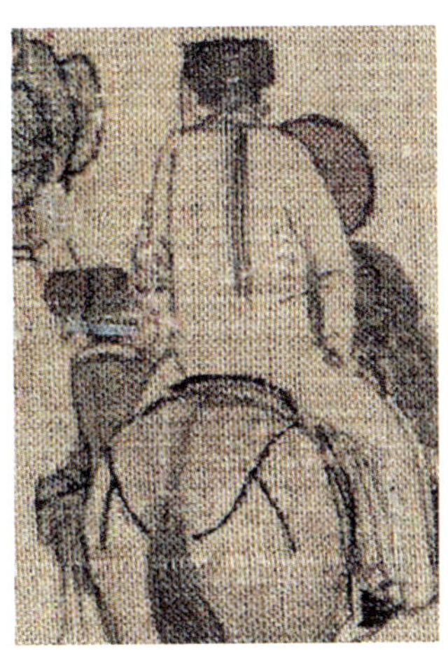

Across from that clothes-drying boat, a traveller is riding a horse towards the city (see the picture below). He is dressed unlike anyone else we've seen in the scroll – wrapped up particularly heavily from head to toe. His head is covered with an angular hood to protect against the cold and sand, from which dangles a rope-like object resembling a 'braid'. Some speculate that this person might be Jurchen, or even possibly a spy sent by Jin. This speculation is intriguing; however, we cannot be certain that the rope-like object is indeed a 'braid', as in *Along the River During the Qingming Festival*, there are two other figures who are clearly dressed in Song attire who also have similar 'braids' hanging down (see two pictures on the bottom of this page).

However, there should be no doubt that this man comes from afar.

Is he from the north? Where is he headed? What secrets are hidden beneath his distinctively thick, almost bulky clothing and his tightly covered hood? In *Along the River During the Qingming Festival*, this is the silhouette that most piques my curiosity: he pays no attention to the woman pouring water nearby, and turns a deaf ear to the shouts of the boatmen on the river. It seems that nothing can stir any interest; he just walks without any words, as if driven by a profound purpose. Looking at him, one cannot help but feel a sense of melancholy.

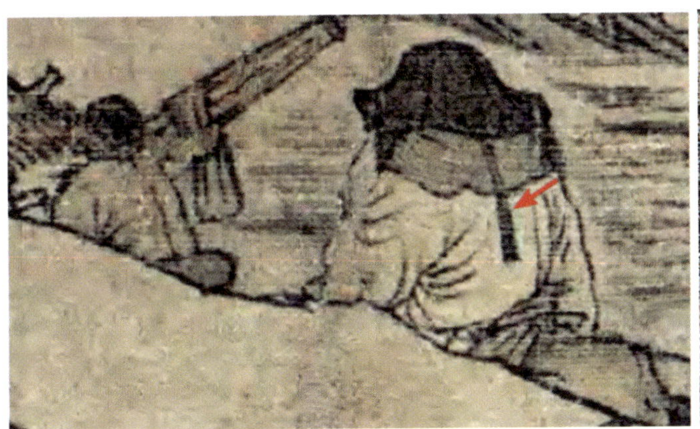

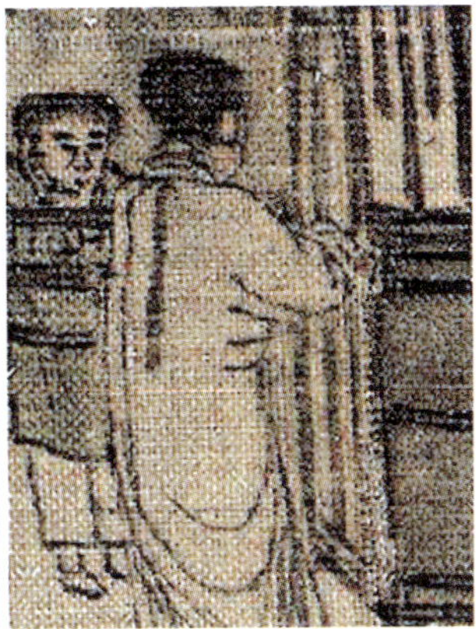

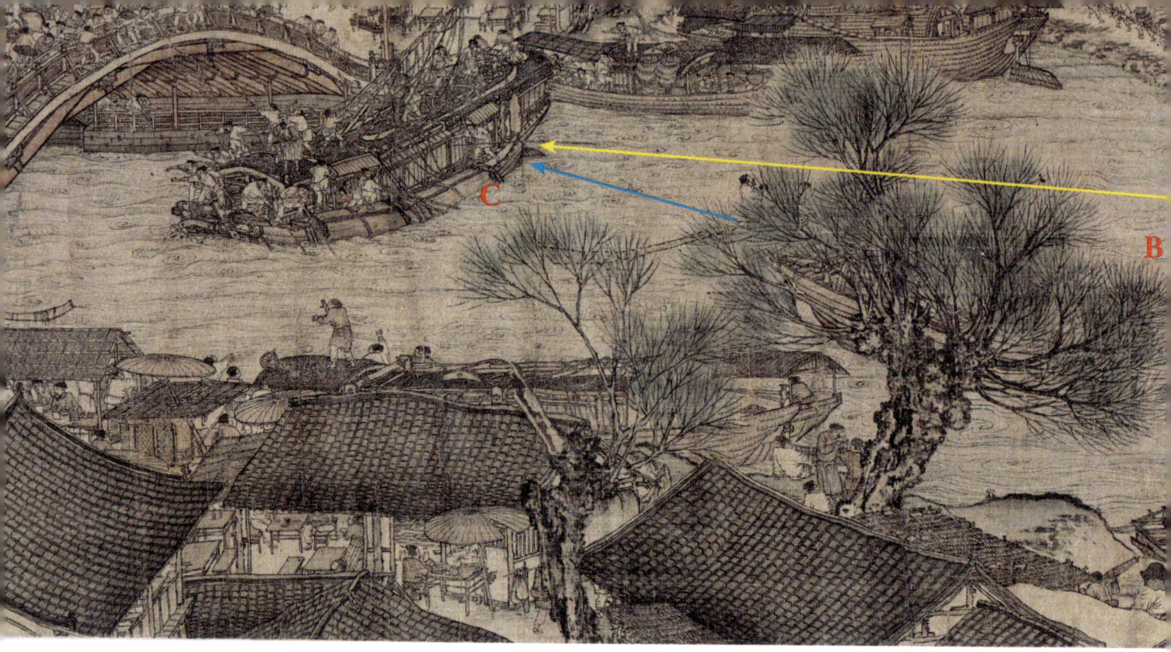

13. The chain of crisis for large boats – explained!

In the previous two sections, we 'interpolated' the stories of the laundry woman and the traveller. Now it's time to discuss the peril the laden boat is about to face. Please unfold your book flat, and the long picture spanning the top of two pages shows the complete relationship among the three boats. Let's call the three boats A, B and C, respectively (see the picture above).

As we've mentioned, the traditional way of viewing a handscroll is to unroll it section by section shoulder-width, rather than viewing the entire scroll at once as one might in a modern museum nowadays. Thus, when the scroll unfolds to reveal boat B, we might initially assume that boat A's warnings are for its own safety. However, as the scroll continues to reveal boat C, our understanding changes. Do you find that the lookout aboard boat A can see not only boat B but also boat C in the distance? It's even possible that the people on boat A first notice the danger to boat C, and then realise that the rowers on boat

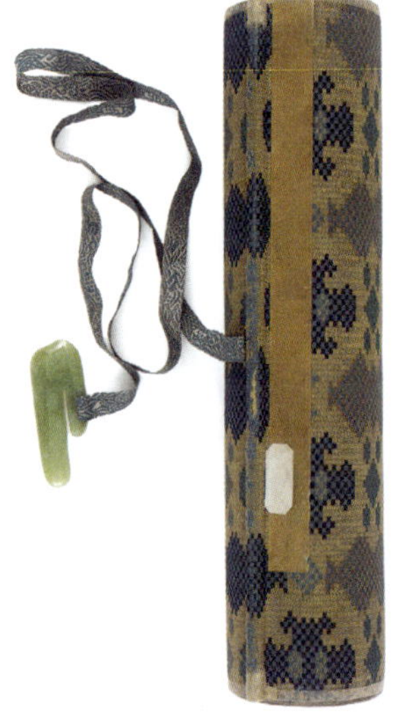

Photo of a rolled-up handscroll. The following discussion will mention how ancient readers would unroll the scroll from right to left, pausing to admire and study it, shoulder-width section by section.

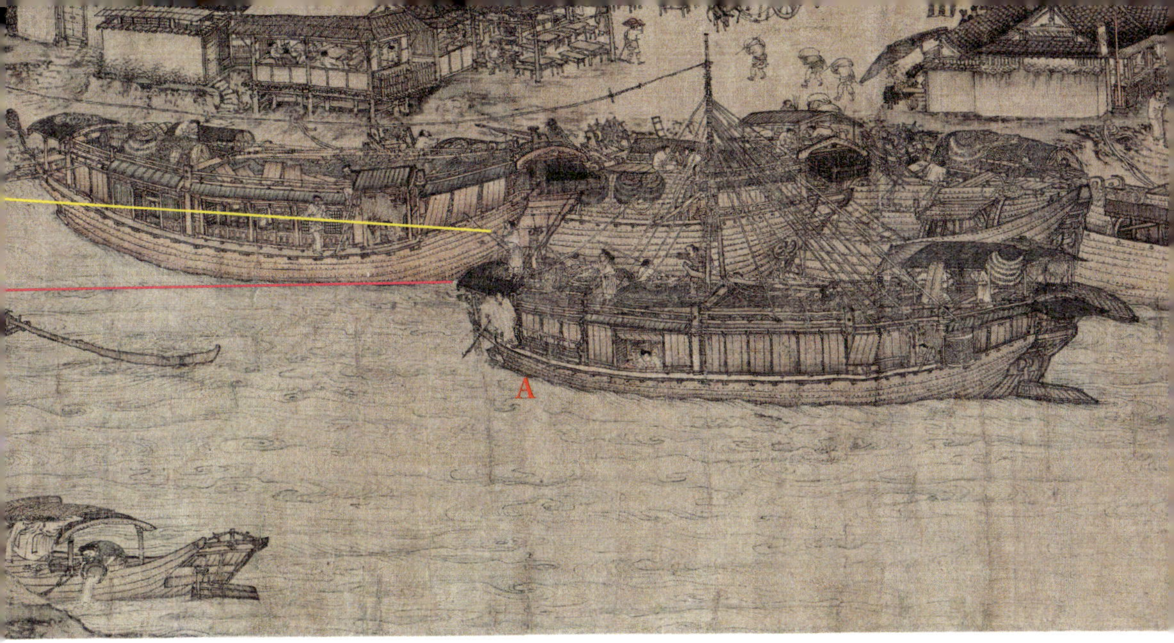

B, far from slowing down, are vigorously rowing straight towards boat C. At that time, boat C is in a perilous situation (details later), and is barely able to fend for itself, making it nearly impossible to evade a collision with boat B. This, it turns out, is the reason for the people on boat A shouting so loudly.

Then, some might ask, since there appears to be some distance between boat A and C, why do we say that boat A first spots boat C? It is because boat A and C are in 'one family', or in other words, they belong to the same fleet, so boat A has been keeping an

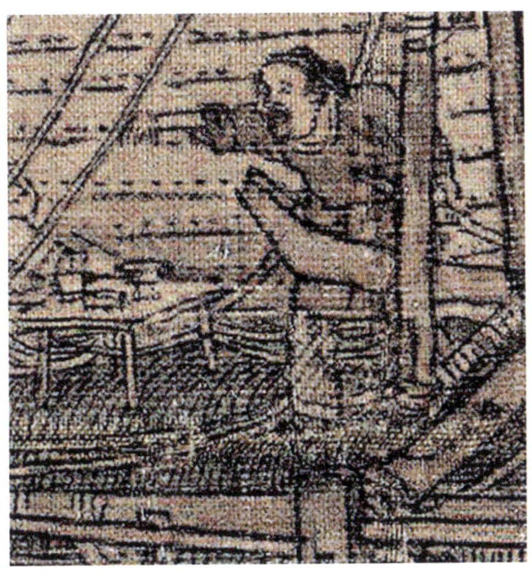

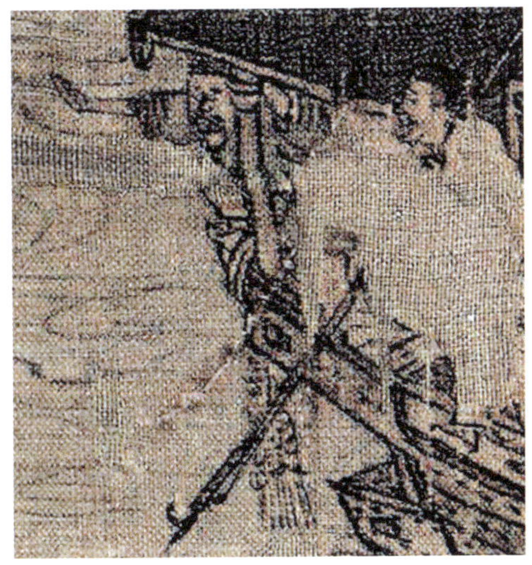

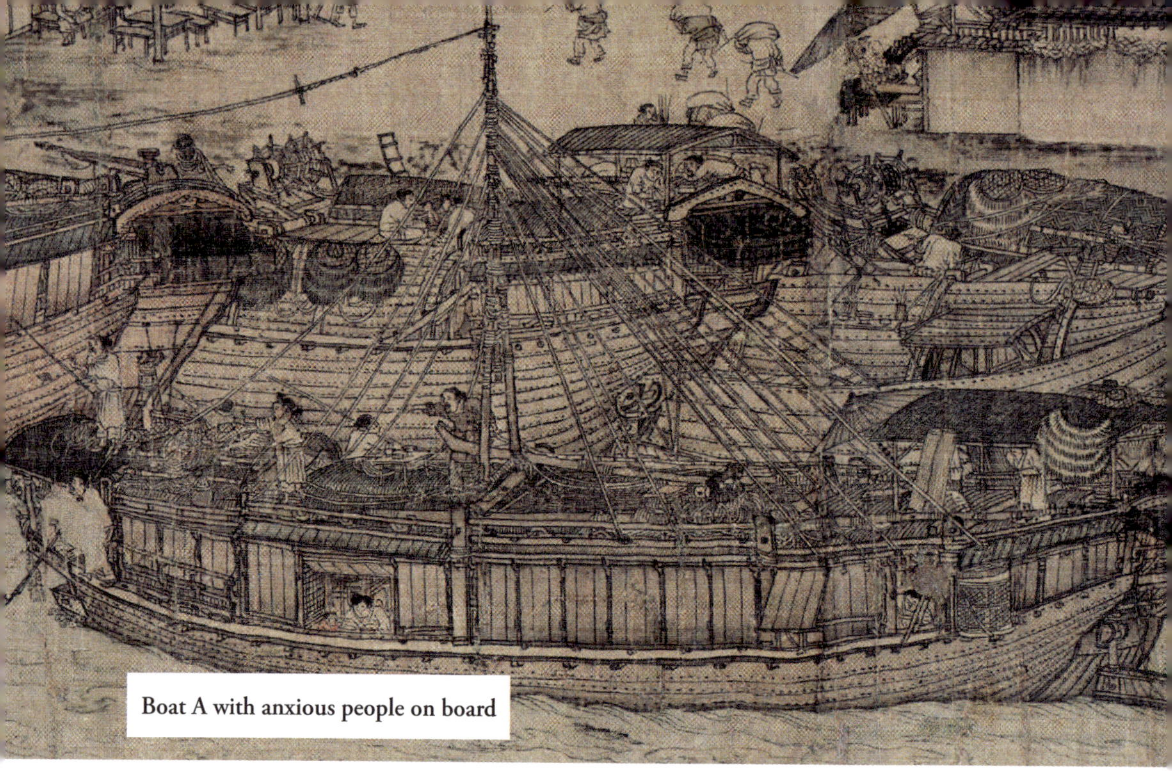

Boat A with anxious people on board

eye on boat C. How can we tell? Boat A and C have many similarities. First, they are both dual-purpose passenger/freighter boats of the same type. The windows on the fore and aft cabins of boat C also open inwards and there are passengers inside, while the windows of the middle cabin are also closed, likely filled with goods on both the lower and upper cabins, similar to boat A. Second, both boats are being towed by trackers. Moreover, even the passengers on both boats are similar, with elderly women, young women and children on each. Furthermore, 'common sense' is also strong evidence: the people on boat A are particularly anxious, indicating a close relationship with boat C.

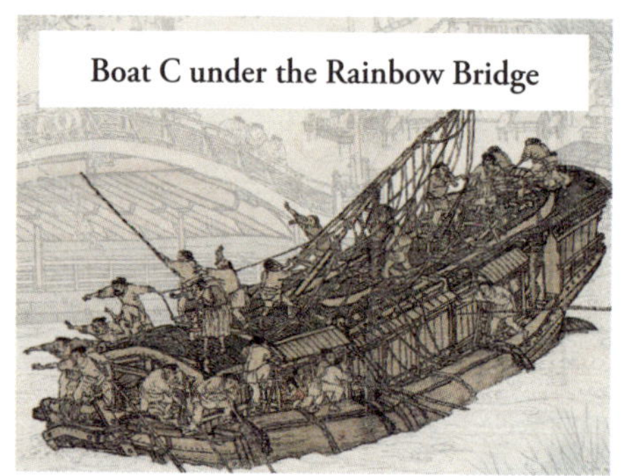
Boat C under the Rainbow Bridge

At this point, reflecting on the rowers of boat B, it takes on a different meaning. These rowers are undeniably putting in a great effort, but without a skilled helmsman, the large boat could find itself in peril and even become both a maker and a victim of a crisis. So, what exactly is the danger that boat C, which boat B is rushing towards, facing?

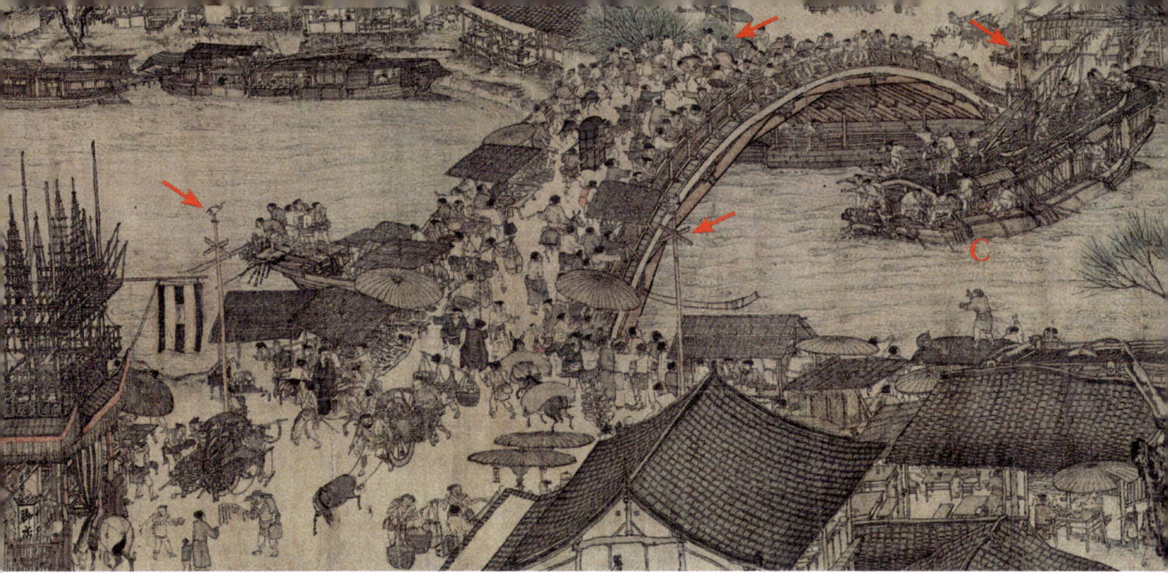

14. The Rainbow Bridge! Rainbow Bridge!

To better understand the dangers faced by boat C, we must start with the Rainbow Bridge. The Rainbow Bridge! Yes, the Rainbow Bridge! Seeing the Bian River is exciting, but seeing the Rainbow Bridge is even more thrilling! This bridge is the centrepiece of the entire scroll, and it is also the most famous. Let's find out what's happening on and under the bridge.

This is a wooden bridge, featuring a deck that is impressively wide; some scholars estimate it to be at least 8 metres in width. Such a large wooden bridge spans the banks without the support of any piers or pillars in the middle, earning it the designation of a *Fei qiao* (飞桥, bridge without piers). Furthermore, the bridge is coated with red lacquer (髹 *xiu*, brushing lacquer onto objects), so it resembles a rainbow from afar. Hence it is known as the Rainbow Bridge.

How was the Rainbow Bridge built? It appears to be made from rows of massive timbers curved into an arch, but the specific construction method has long been lost. Let alone the construction method, without Zhang Zeduan's painting, we wouldn't even know that such a *Fei qiao* was ever built by our ancestors. Then, who is the designer? Recorded in the *Mian Shui Yan Tan Lu* (《渑水燕谈录》) in the Song Dynasty, the identity of the original designer is an 'exiled disabled soldier', which means a disabled soldier exiled to the military for committing a crime. As for his name, it is lost because he was a small potato.

At both ends of the Rainbow Bridge, there stand tall poles (indicated by the red arrows at the top of the page) at each corner. Atop these poles is a cross, and perched on top is not a living crane but an effigy of one. What is the purpose of these tall poles? Some say they are weathervanes used to indicate the wind direction for sailors. Indeed, weathervanes existed in ancient times, initially made of chicken feathers in the shape of birds. The bird would rotate with wind, allowing people to discern the wind direction based on its heading. However, I believe it is unlikely that these poles are weathervanes. It's easy to judge: please look at the picture on the left that shows the two poles on this side of the bridge with cranes facing in opposite directions – one crane's head points right, while the other left. If they are used to indicate direction, well, wouldn't that just confuse sailors?

Another explanation is that they are *Biao mu* (表木) or marker poles, which serve to mark directions and the 'red line' of roads. They are not only found around this Rainbow Bridge but also along many streets in the capital. Why are such *Biao mu* set up? Because during the Northern Song Dynasty, the problem of private encroachment on public streets and even waterways is very serious. Failing to stop, *Biao mu* are installed to warn people not to cross the line.

The problem of street encroachment in Bianjing indeed has historical roots. In the third year of the Xiande era (956) under Chai Rong, the emperor of the Later Zhou Dynasty, an imperial edict was issued stating: 'In the capital city, where the streets are fifty steps wide (about 78m), residents on both sides are allowed to take advantage of five steps (about 7.8m) on each side to plant trees, dig wells, or set up stalls. For streets from thirty to twenty-five steps wide (about 47m), each side is given three steps (about 4.7m), and so forth with variations.'

In other words, one-fifth of the streets in the capital city was allocated for legal occupation by the residents on both sides of the street, where they could plant trees, dig wells and even set up stalls for trades. Can you believe it? There is such a good thing! However, after the Northern Song Dynasty established its capital in Kaifeng, the situation evolved, leading to an increasingly severe problem of street encroachment. Residents excessively occupied the streets, to the extent that carriages could not pass through smoothly on many originally wide streets. Consequently, the Song government was compelled to establish the 'Street Office', an institution specifically responsible for managing the streets to prevent street encroachment. Despite these issues, the Song Dynasty's approach to urban street management remained relatively open, which contributed to Bianjing (and

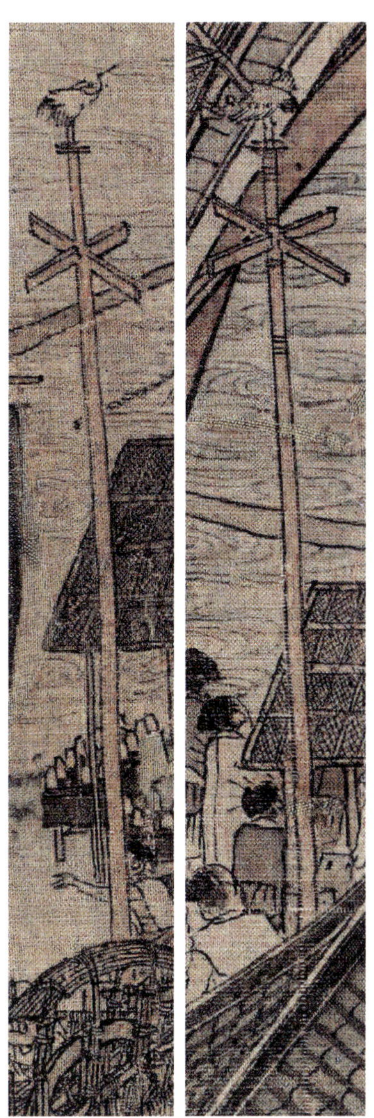

Biao mu (or *Hua biao*,华表) at both ends of the Rainbow Bridge

later Lin'an) becoming one of the most bustling metropolises in the world at that time. If you asked me to take you on a historical journey to any city, I would definitely choose Bianjing of the Northern Song Dynasty. Although slightly chaotic, the city was fascinating. It was a true city of human life with endless streets to explore, countless snacks to taste and a variety of lively scenes to witness.

Let's talk a bit more about *Biao mu*, also known as *Hua biao*. Legend has it that *Hua biao* was initially used by wise and virtuous emperors to accept public advice. How did this work? They would erect a wooden pillar at the intersection of main roads, with a horizontal beam crossing the top of the pillar. People from all walks of life could easily come to write criticism of government policies. These people would write their suggestions on placards, tie them with a rope and hang them on the horizontal beam, waiting for the king's emissaries to collect them. *Biao* signifies the practice of the emperor's acceptance of advice, thus giving the pillar its name. Over time, however, the original purpose of accepting advice faded and eventually disappeared completely, and the significance of *Biao mu* as a landmark for main roads becomes more prominent. Bridges, often situated on crucial thoroughfares, typically have these pillars built. Using *Biao mu* as boundary markers becomes a derived function. As for the crane-shaped tops of the *Hua biao* in the picture, it is to symbolise auspiciousness and good fortune, as the crane is one of the symbols of a peaceful and prosperous era.

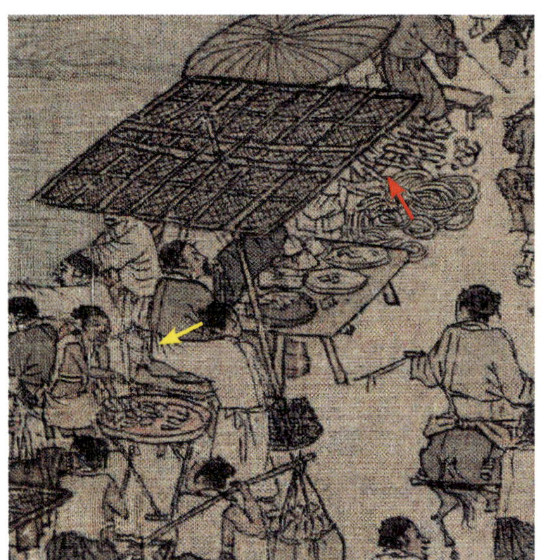

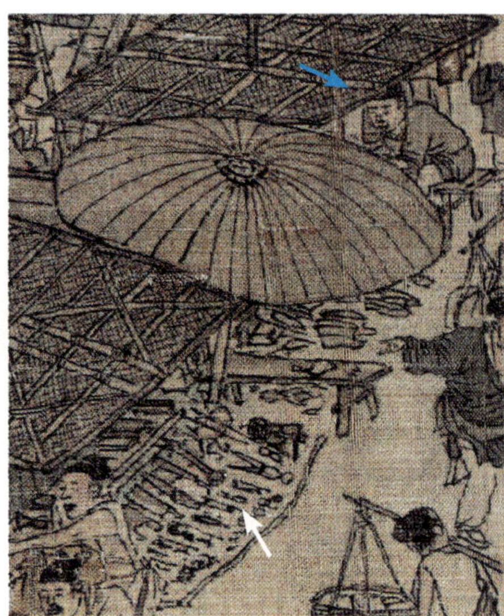

15. Stalls and hazards on the bridge

As mentioned earlier, the deck of this Rainbow Bridge is at least 8 metres wide. Precisely because of its width, vendors have set up stalls along both sides. And, because of these stalls, the bridge is particularly crowded with people and horses shuttling back and forth.

Let's take a closer look at what these stalls are selling. Some are selling ropes (indicated by the red arrow on the left), some appear to be selling snacks, some are selling shoes (the blue arrow likely points to a customer trying on shoes), and some are selling items like kitchen knives and scissors (indicated by the white arrow).

In the upper picture on the left, underneath a circular tray (indicated by the yellow arrow) is a portable folding rack. While walking, the stand can be folded up and either carried or tucked under the arm. Upon reaching a suitable location, the stand can be opened, and the tray placed on top of it. Once the goods are arranged on the tray, the vendor is ready to start selling.

At the end of the bridge, there is a woman. Some say she is selling steamed buns, while others say she is selling *Huang pang* (黄胖), which is a clay figurine used for rituals during the Qingming Festival. Some people may ask, 'Isn't it said that women in ancient times were not allowed to leave their homes freely? How come there is a woman selling steamed buns in the market?' But it all depends. Indeed, in ancient

Well, well, Sima Guang, the pot-smashing man, you are great in every way, but you're just not down-to-earth. Female sumo wrestling? Even the common people enjoy it, so why can't I? It's precisely because I share in my people's joys that happiness abounds among them!

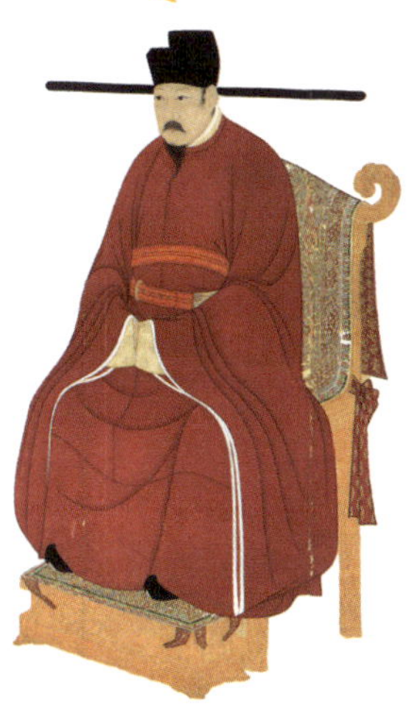

Seated Portrait of Emperor Renzong of Song, Anonymous, Northern Song Dynasty, in the collection of the National Palace Museum, Taipei

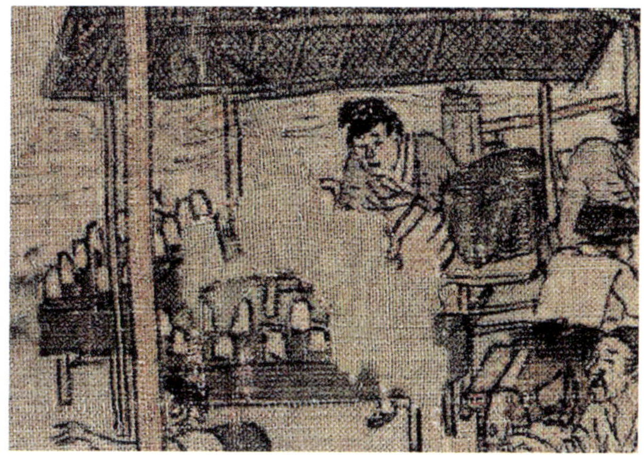

times, women from upper and middle-class families rarely appeared in public places, but it was different for women from poorer families. They, like men, also needed to sell goods in the market or earn a living through their skills and crafts. Speaking of which, it reminds me that during the Song Dynasty, there were even female sumo wrestling performances which could be considered living by their skills. They not only performed in the streets but also performed for Emperor Renzong of Song, and received rewards just like other performers. When the minister, Sima Guang, heard about this, he wrote a memorial to protest against the emperor watching women's naked performances which went against etiquette, and suggested that Emperor Renzong abolish the female sumo wrestling event. Therefore, at that time, women could even engage in sumo wrestling and it was not a big deal for them to do some small business. It is recorded in ancient books: 'Women are not hidden away, and they even go to the market to do embroidery for others, which is not considered strange.'

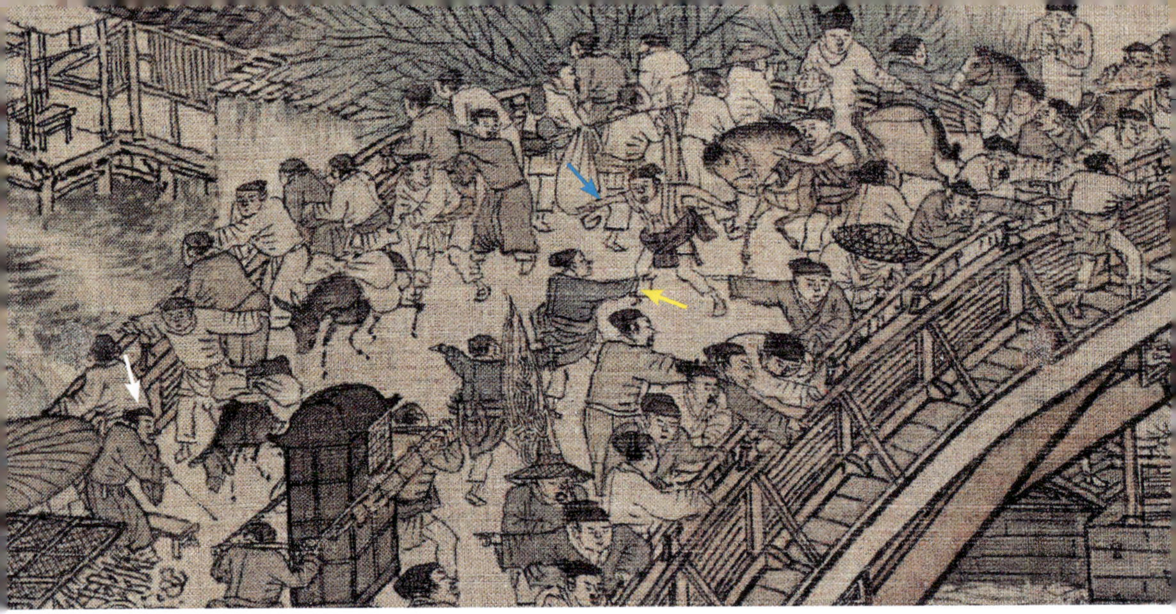

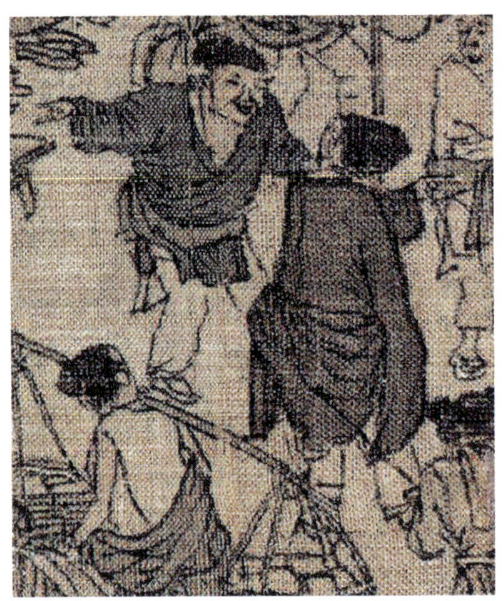

In the middle of the bridge stand two figures (in the picture on the opposite page). One of them, with a notably long right sleeve, is a *Ya ren* (牙人) or *Ya lang* (牙郎), a broker in trading. The reason for his long-sleeved garment is to allow the sellers and buyers for discreet finger-touching inside the sleeve during negotiations. This method of bargaining is to leave room for compromise, ensuring that the transaction proceeds amicably.

At the bottom page 76, the scene about 'horses and sedan chairs jostling for the way', is another classic on the Rainbow Bridge. The originally spacious bridge becomes congested due to the crowd on both sides, leading to a conflict between the horses and the sedan chairs. Some say that the horse-faction and the sedan-faction started fighting, but it's not that serious. Look at the horseman frantically pulling the reins back, causing the horse to uncomfortably twist its neck. At the front of each group, one figure with a raised right hand (indicated by the blue arrow) seems to be saying, 'Let's go to the right!' Another, also with a raised right hand (indicated by the yellow arrow), appears to be saying, 'We'll take the right side!' They are not about to fight; indeed, depicting a brawl would be vulgar, something that Zhang Zeduan would absolutely not do. However, he did not shy away from portraying arrogance and commanding gestures. Look, the official on horseback is holding a whip in his left hand, pointing towards someone on the bridge, likely uttering something unpleasant, causing a commoner to turn his head and look at him. 'It's all because of you onlookers that the bridge is so jammed with horses!' I guess that's what he's saying.

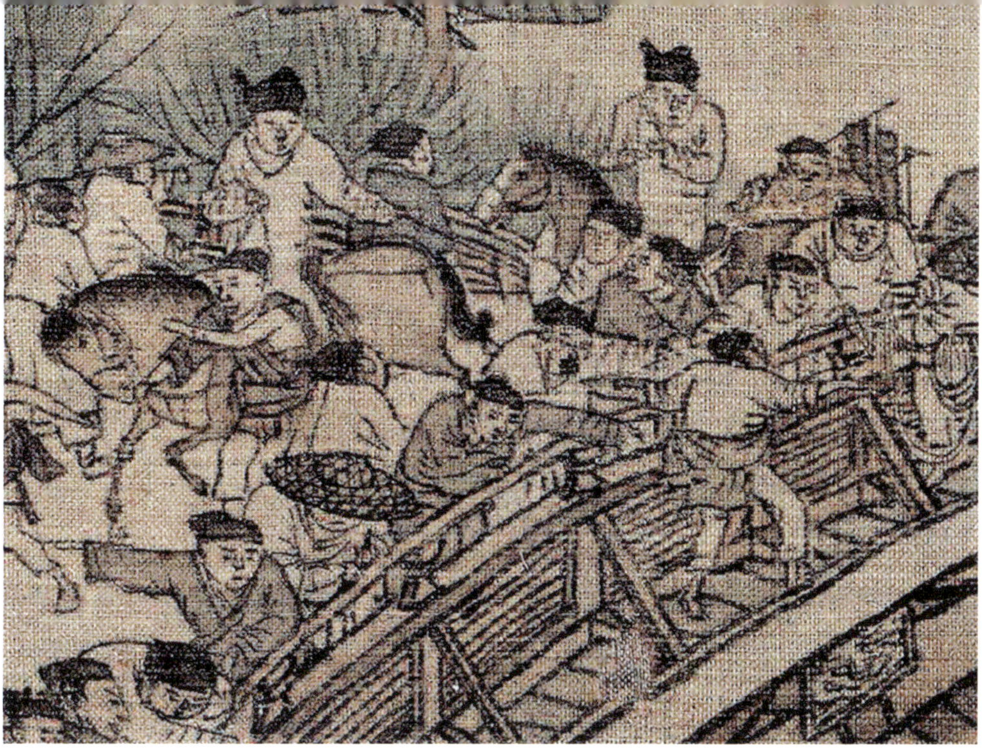

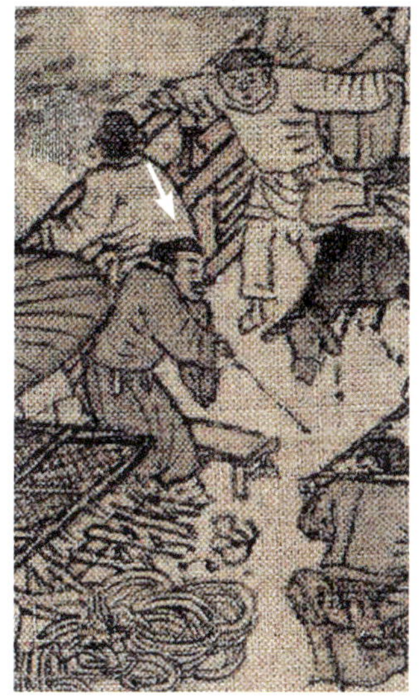

While such a scene captures the viewer's attention, a less noticed but imminent danger is happening nearby. A blind man (indicated by the white arrow in the picture above) using his cane to navigate the path, is unaware that two donkeys laden with goods are rushing down the bridge. One of the donkeys is already right in front of the blind man, and what's even more worrying is that there is little room for the donkeys to dodge him due to the nearby sedan chairs.

Back to those onlookers gathered on the bridge, what exactly are they watching?

Alas! A large boat under the bridge is facing a perilous situation!

That boat! It is boat C!

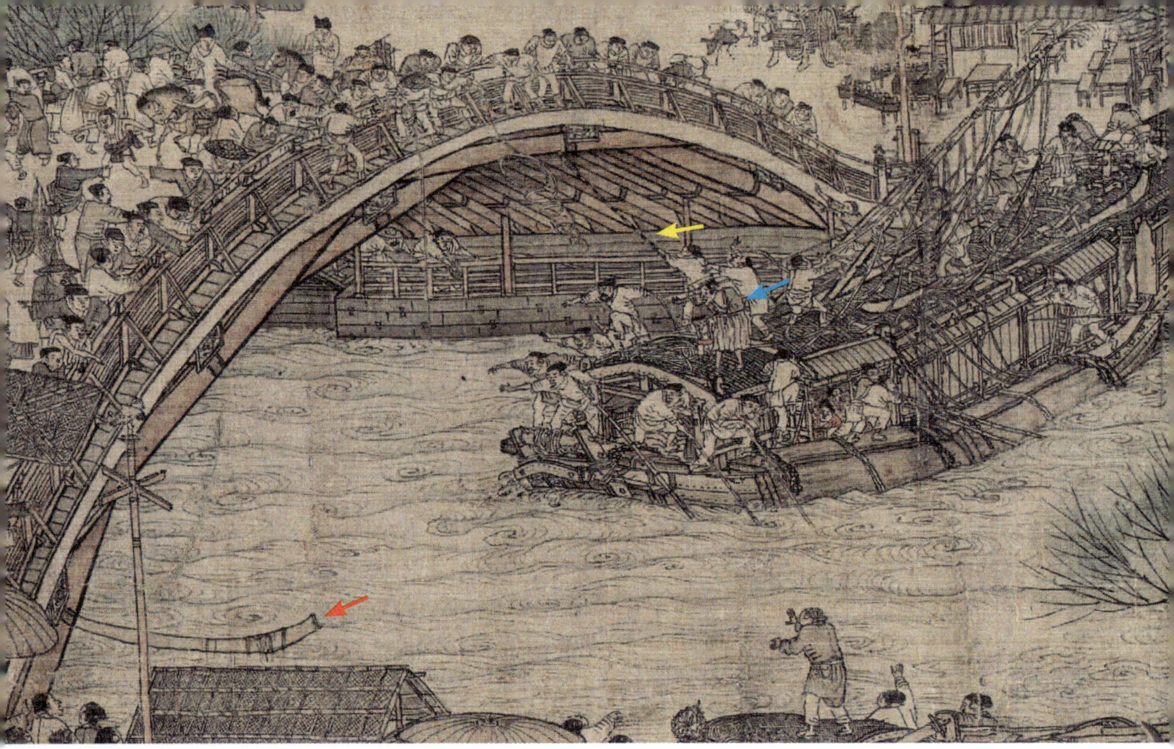

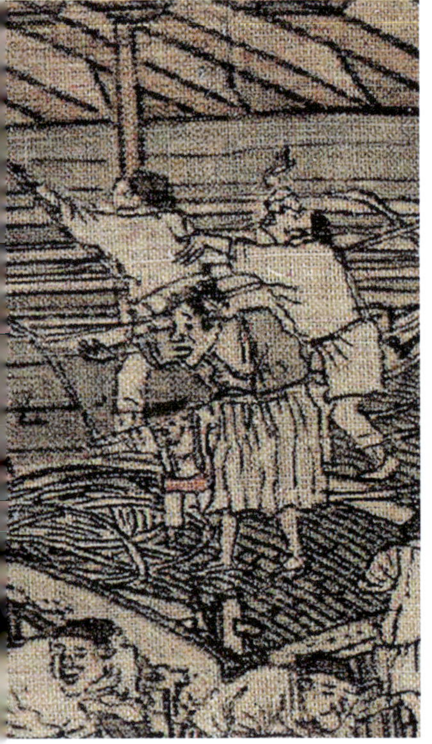

16. The truth behind the large boat crisis

Let's recall the chain of events in the large boat crisis: Boat A warns boat B, boat B charges towards boat C, and boat C is in a state of chaos. But what exactly is causing the chaos on boat C?

Passing under the Rainbow Bridge, the mast on a large boat must be lowered. However, as boat C reaches the bridge, its mast has not been fully lowered. To make matters worse, possibly due to the swift currents, the boat is also drifting sideways, dangerously close to colliding with the bridge. At this critical moment, all the crew members spring into action. Some are loosening the ropes and lowering the mast, others are shouting warnings to nearby boats, some are using poles at the bow to adjust the direction, and a few are leveraging a black and white striped long pole (possibly a water level measuring pole, indicated by the yellow arrow above) against the bridge's beams for support. It's still worth noting that there is also a child and an elderly woman standing on the canopy at the bow (indicated by the blue arrow above), sparing no effort to shout loudly. Despite their age, the little one tries his best to help in such a dangerous situation.

The child and several adults are all pointing in the same direction. It turns out that there is another danger under the bridge – a large oar is just under the Rainbow Bridge (indicated by the red arrow in the picture on the previous page), clearly showing that there is another boat there! (For a full view of this boat, please see the cross-page picture on page 80.) Boat C is trying to avoid colliding with the bridge, but it may end up crashing into the large boat under the bridge instead. And at this very moment, a group of boatmen on boat B are rowing vigorously towards boat C!

It must be noted that not all the people on the bridge are mere lookie-loos. In fact, as many as five people have climbed over the railing to lend a helping hand to the large boat below. Imagine the scene: Standing at the edge of the bridge is quite dangerous, don't you think? Two of them are throwing ropes down. Where did they get the ropes? There happens to be a vendor selling ropes on the bridge, so they must have borrowed them from there. You see, a great painting withstands close scrutiny like this, revealing layers of action and interaction that enrich the narrative.

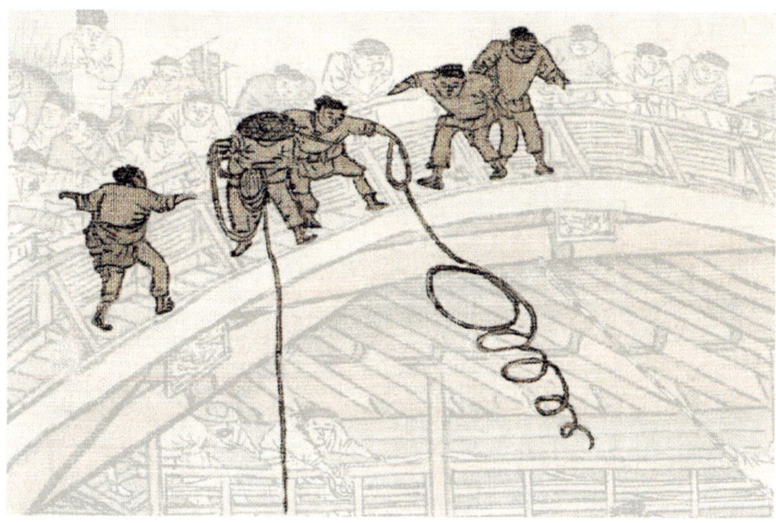

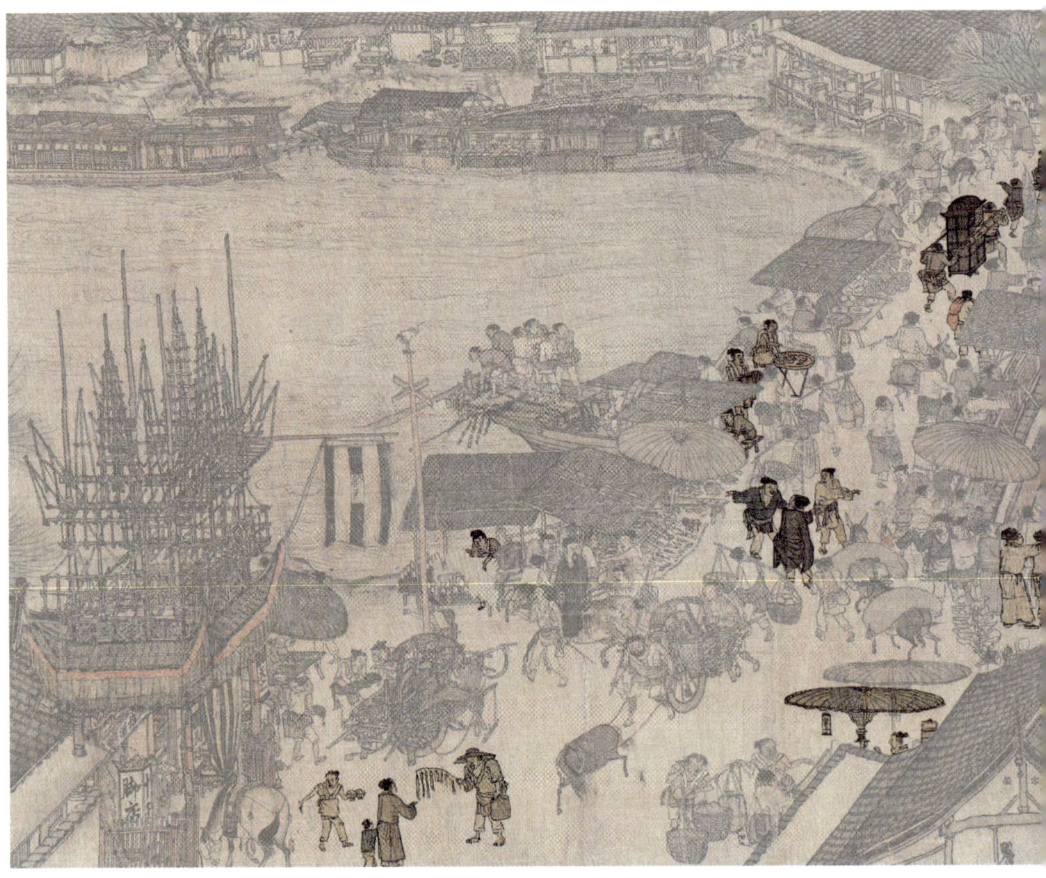

Finally, let's review the full story of the 'large boat crisis'. Firstly, Zhang Zeduan is a painter particularly skilled at narrative painting. The events he depicts always have direct and indirect connections. For example, the crisis facing boat C is not isolated but linked in multiple dimensions. The narrative always transcends the isolated events, generating a broader significance. Second, regarding its narrative significance, some perceive the cooperative effort of the labourers, while others see the perilous situation of the large boat as symbolic of the nation's difficult circumstances (facing formidable enemies to the north in addition to internal chaos). The large boat will eventually pass through the crisis, providing viewers with relief from the tension. However, the lingering danger around the boat – even after overcoming the crisis – serves not only as a comfort but also a warning.

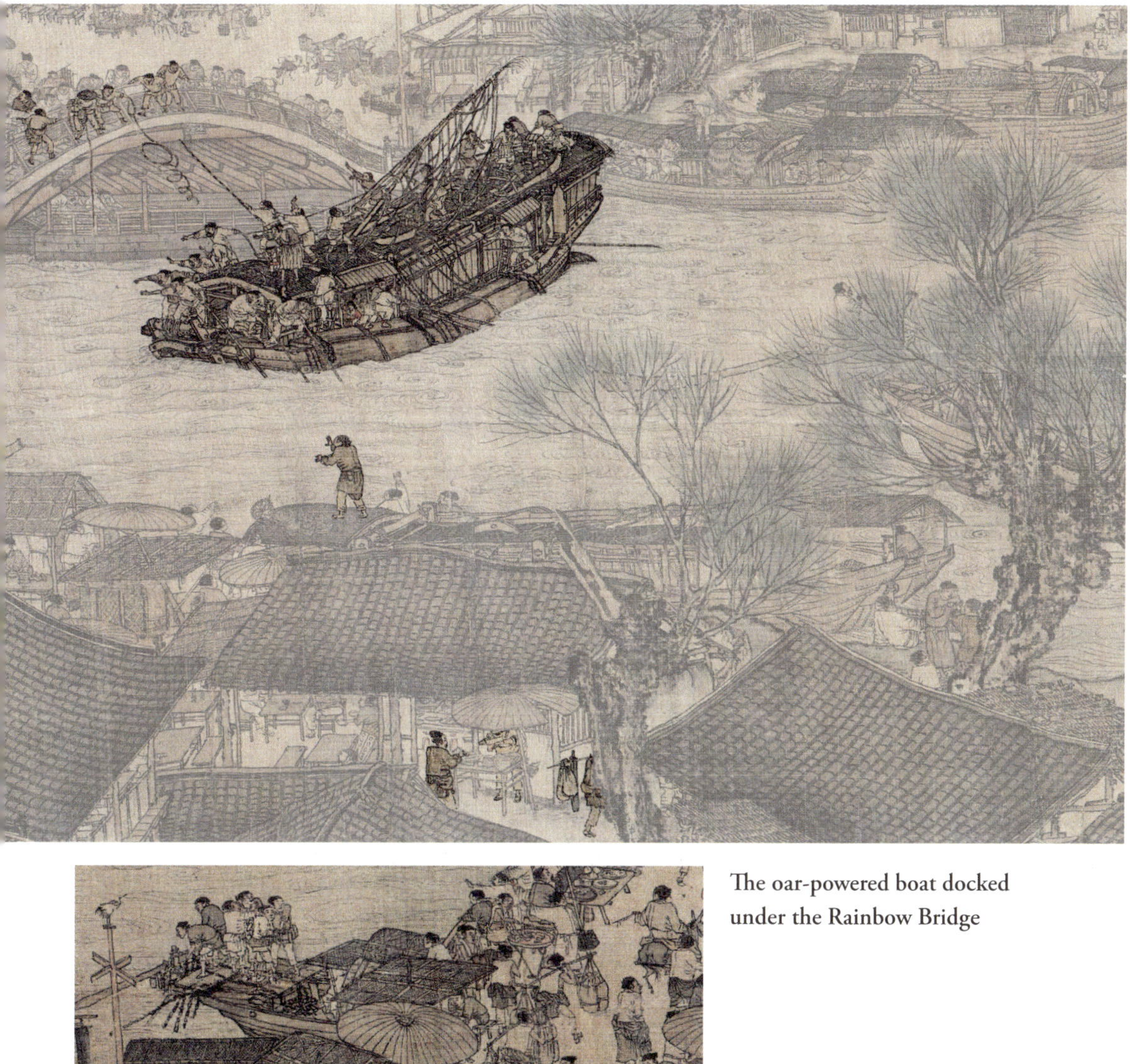

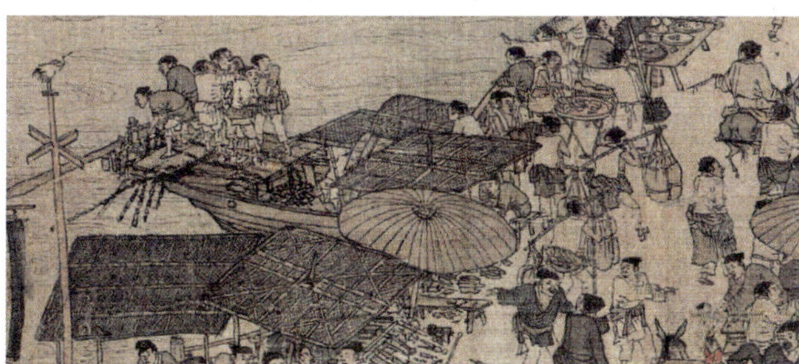

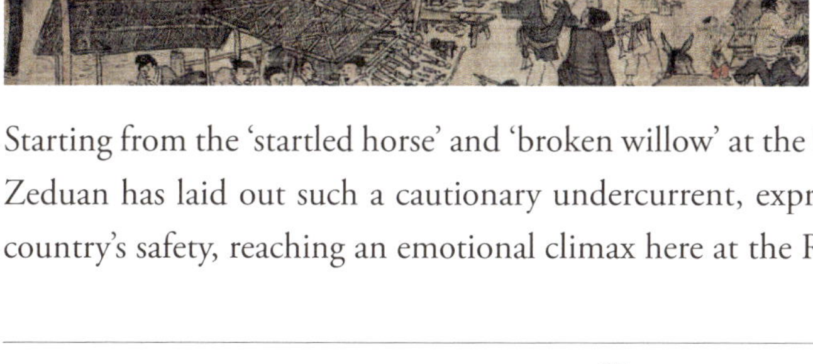

The oar-powered boat docked under the Rainbow Bridge

Starting from the 'startled horse' and 'broken willow' at the beginning of the scroll, Zhang Zeduan has laid out such a cautionary undercurrent, expressing his concerns about the country's safety, reaching an emotional climax here at the Rainbow Bridge.

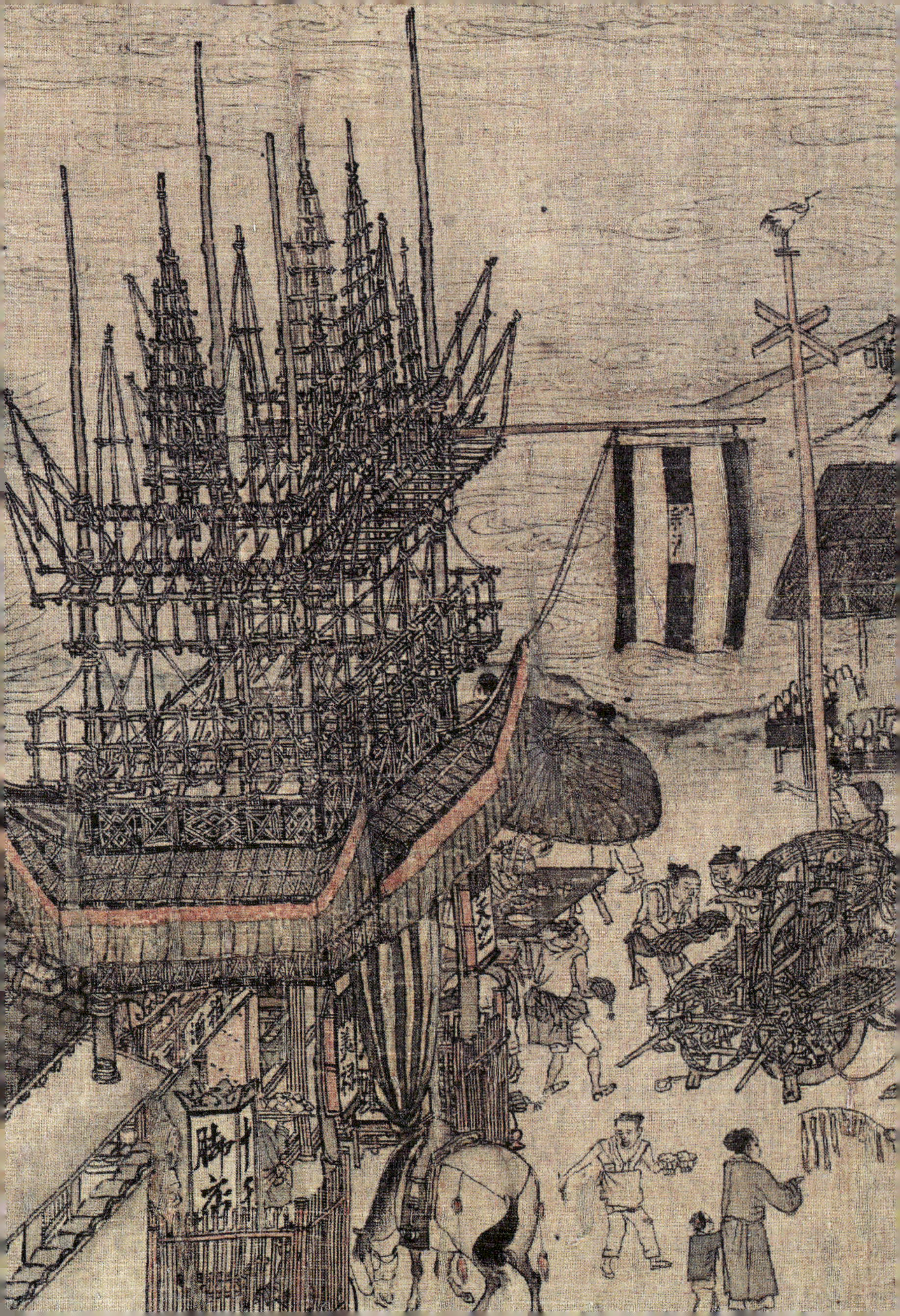
十千
腳店
美祿

17. *Jiao dian* (脚店): What kind of shop is it?

Having experienced the perilous situation with the large boat, let's now take a moment to relax with a visit to the tavern at the end of the bridge. Inside the red wooden fence at the entrance of the tavern, there is a lantern box (indicated by the blue arrow on the left page; please note that there is also a person squatting, hardly noticeable, near the lantern box inside the fence). On one side of the lantern box, it reads *Jiao dian,* and on the other side, *Shi qian* (十千), which is a moniker for fine wine ①. *Shi qian Jiao dian* is likely the name of this shop. At night, candles can be lit inside the lantern box to attract more patrons. So, what exactly is a *Jiao dian*? In the *Dongjing Meng Hua Lu* (《东京梦华录》, *The Eastern Capital: A Dream of Splendor*), it is stated: 'There are seventy-two licensed taverns in the capital… the rest are called *Jiao dian*.' A licenced tavern, or *Zheng dian*, is a luxurious and large tavern authorised to brew and sell its own alcohol. These taverns not only operate their own wine houses but also sell wholesale wines to *Jiao dian* and other liquor vendors. Taverns that do not have the right to brew alcohol are generally referred to as *Jiao dian.* On the wooden pillars at the entrance of this *Jiao dian*, there are also two signboards hanging, which read *Tian zhi* (天之) and *Mei lu* (美禄) respectively – *Tian zhi Mei lu* is another moniker for fine wine ②, and here it is likely used as an advertising slogan.

In front of the shop, the tall, upright wooden structure is called a *Cai lou huan men* (彩楼欢门), which means a decorated tower gate. On important occasions, the wooden frame is adorned with lanterns and decorations, creating a lively and impressive atmosphere to attract patrons. Extending horizontally from the *Cai lou huan men* is a long pole from which a wine curtain hangs. According to the historical notes in *Rong zhai xu bi* (《容斋续笔》) in the Song Dynasty, taverns of the time would hang a large curtain outside their entrance, typically made of several pieces of blue and white cloth. This curtain could be left blank and people would still recognise it as a symbol of a tavern; alternatively, it could feature a concise advertising slogan. For instance, in *Water Margin*, the advertising slogan on the wine curtain of the tavern at Jingyang Ridge reads, 'Three bowls down, even the strongest man gets drunk'. The characters on the wine curtain here are partially damaged, but they likely read *Xin jiu* (新酒), which means new wine.

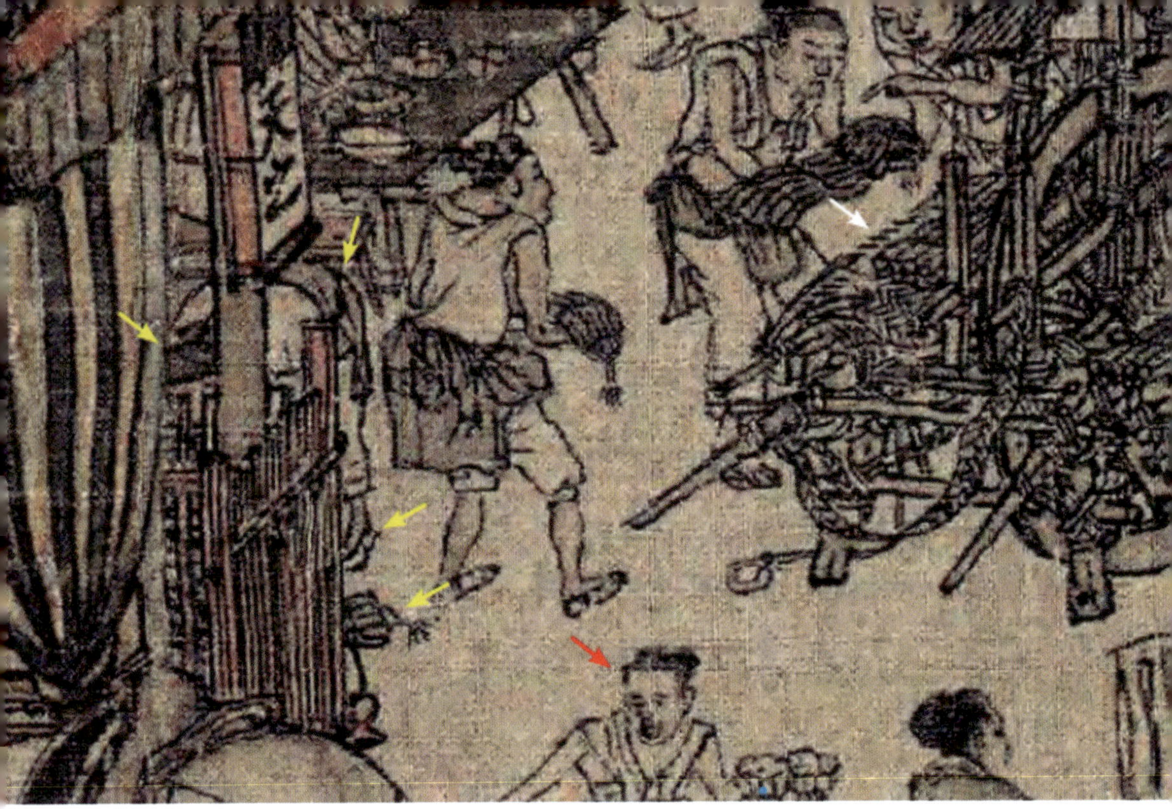

① In *Fu on Ming du* by Cao Zhi from the state of Cao Wei in the Three Kingdoms period of China, there is a line that reads: 'I return to feast in joy, drinking fine wine which is worth thousands of *Qian* (currency) a *Dou*.'

② In the *Book of Han*, Volume 24, Part 2, *Treatise on Food and Money* (*Shi huo zhi*, 《食货志》), Ban Gu of the Eastern Han Dynasty wrote: 'Wine is the blessing bestowed upon mankind. It is a means by which emperors and kings nourish their people, offer sacrifices and pray for blessings, support the weak and heal the sick. In all ceremonial gathering, nothing proceeds without wine.'

The waiter in the *Jiao dian* (indicated by the red arrow) is holding two bowls in his left hand and chopsticks in his right. Today we call him a 'delivery guy'. Yes, the concept of food delivery was already popular during the Song Dynasty. Carrying two bowls

The 'delivery guy'

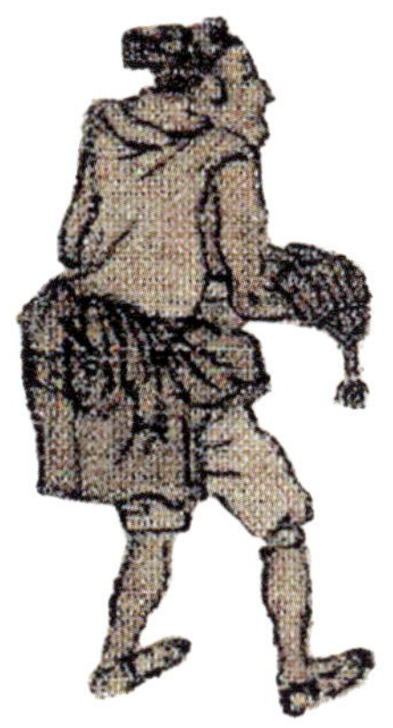

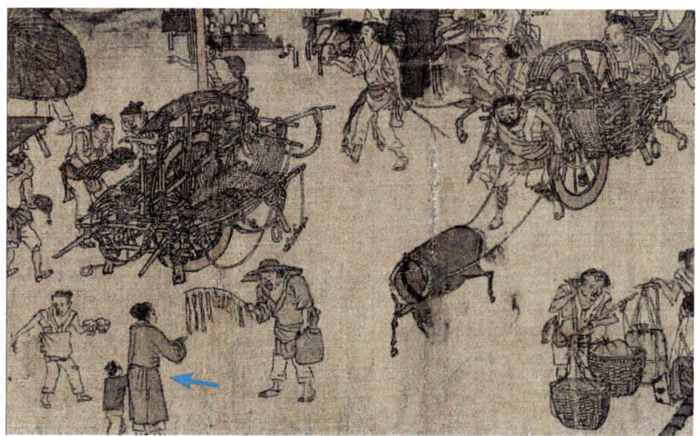

in one hand might seem impressive, but it's actually nothing compared to what is described in the *Dongjing Meng Hua Lu* (《东京梦华录》, *The Eastern Capital: A Dream of Splendor*): 'The waiter carries three bowls in his left hand and stacks about twenty bowls from his right hand to his shoulder. Amazingly, he managed to deliver these as ordered without any mistakes.' (It's hard to imagine how they managed to do that!)

The white arrow points to a money transport cart. In ancient times, people threaded copper coins together with ropes. A string of one thousand coins was called a *Guan* (贯). In the picture, five or six *Guan* are bundled together, and we see a person delivering a bundle to the transport cart for counting. Of course, the amount of money that needs to be transported is not limited to just this single bundle. Another person carrying money follows behind, and there is still one bending over to carry money behind the red fence. On the left page, where the yellow arrow points, we can discern his head, raised buttocks and feet, along with the coins on the ground. It seems that this *Jiao dian* is doing quite well!

18. Series of crises on the Rainbow Bridge

Near the *Jiao dian*, two more dangerous situations occur (the conflict between a horse and a sedan chair, and another between a donkey and a person), making a total of four perilous situations on the bridge. Considering the numbers of these incidents on such a crowded bridge, it's undeniable that the bridge is fraught with danger. When a phenomenon is frequently depicted, we cannot help but think that it is related to the

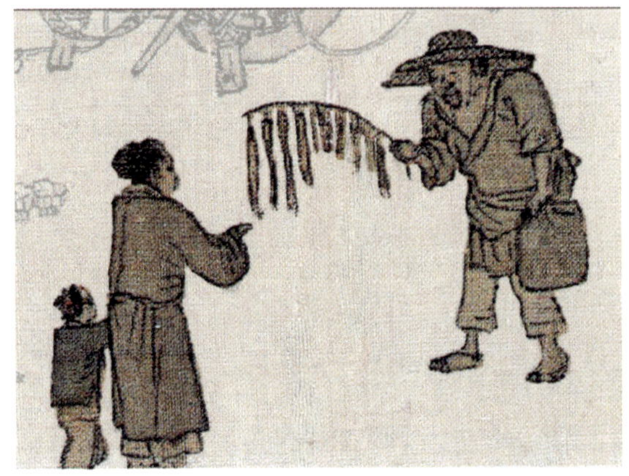

theme. It might even be said that the primary focus of the Rainbow Bridge scene is a concentrated expression of dangerous situations. Given that the Rainbow Bridge is at the centre of the entire scroll, a sense of 'crisis' becomes an unavoidable theme in *Along the River During the Qingming Festival*. Now, let's delve into what exactly happened.

An adult (indicated by the blue arrow on the opposite page), standing next to a delivery guy, holds a little girl's hand. He is buying something from a vendor across the way. The vendor grips a slender stick in his right hand. The stick is adorned with strip-like items – likely toys favoured by children. He also clutches a bag in his left hand – presumably to replenish his stock as items are sold. As they are engrossed in their transaction, a donkey abruptly barges into the scene from behind. This donkey is pulling a single-wheeled cart, manoeuvred by a person pulling at the front and another pushing from behind. Such a configuration – a donkey, a single-wheeled cart, and two people – is known as a 'single-wheeled tandem cart'. The cart, not yet laden with goods (the loaded cart outside the city gate at the top of the next page will be discussed later), dashes briskly down from a bridge. The donkey, being the first to notice the vendor absorbed in his sales, makes a sudden swerve to avoid a collision, turning its head to one side. We can imagine the potential mishap had the donkey not turned away – it might have nearly bumped right into the vendor's back! Tandem carts require precise coordination between the front and rear; might the donkey's sudden movement cause an overturn of the cart? It seems highly likely!

Now, let us turn our attention to another scene. Just behind the single-wheeled tandem cart, two donkeys are ascending the bridge (indicated by the yellow arrow on the opposite page). Both donkeys are laden with large sacks of goods, which appear to be quite heavy. As they round the bend to cross the bridge, they unexpectedly encounter a child (indicated by the red arrow on the right page) at the turning point. The young man driving the donkeys is on the left side; being quite short, his view is obstructed and fails

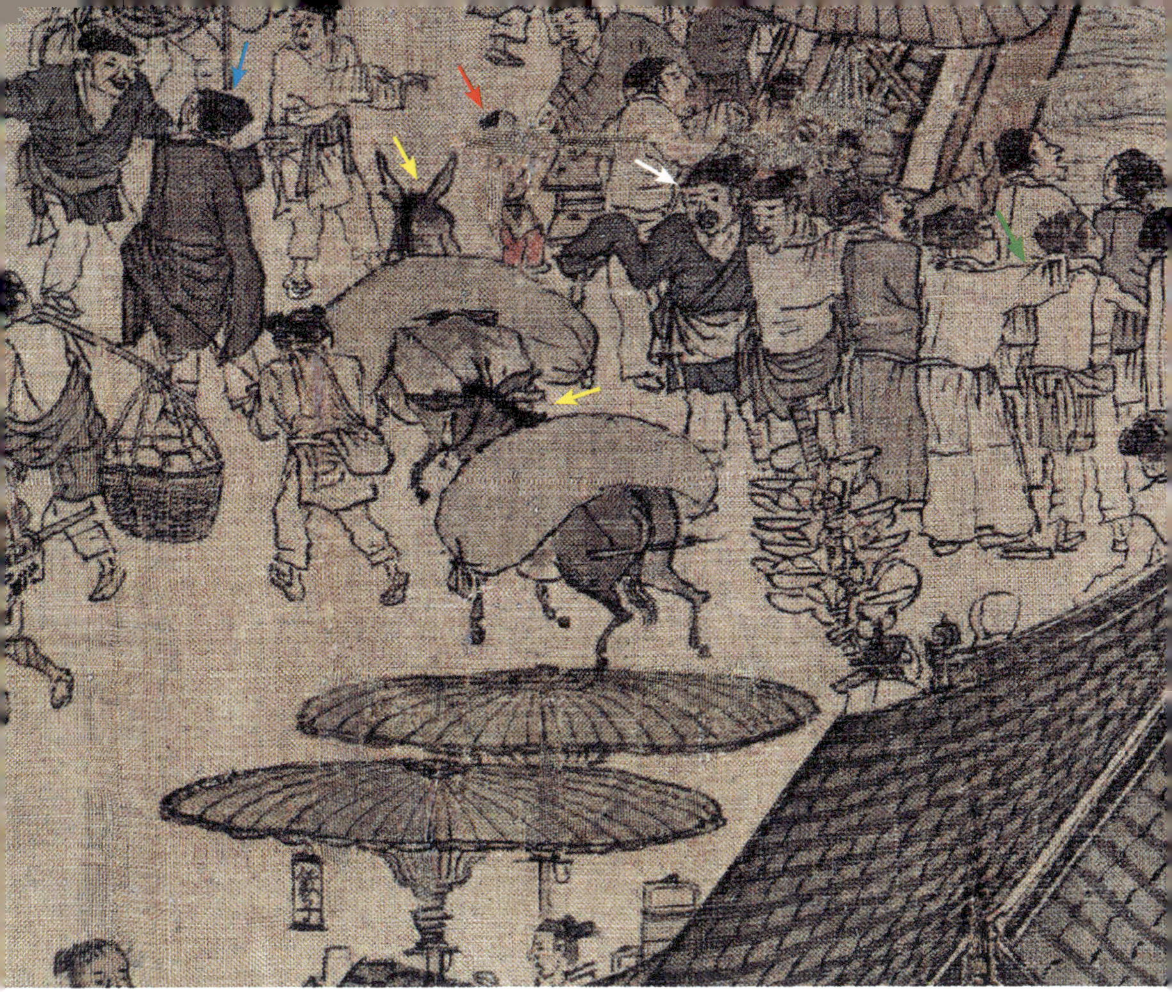

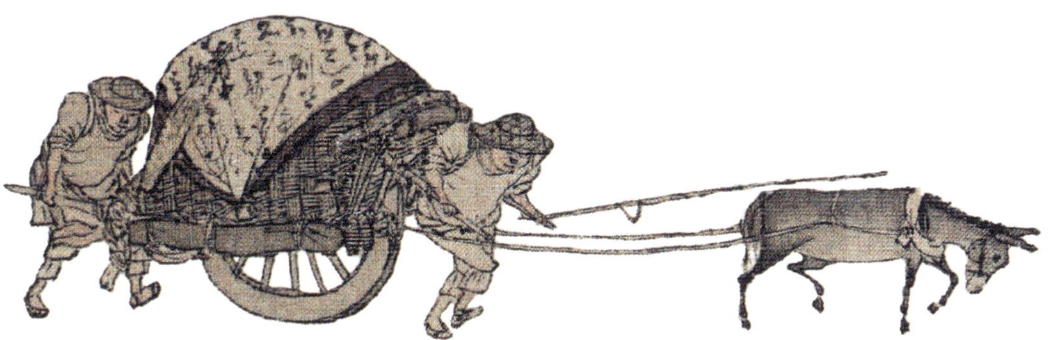

The loaded single-wheeled tandem cart

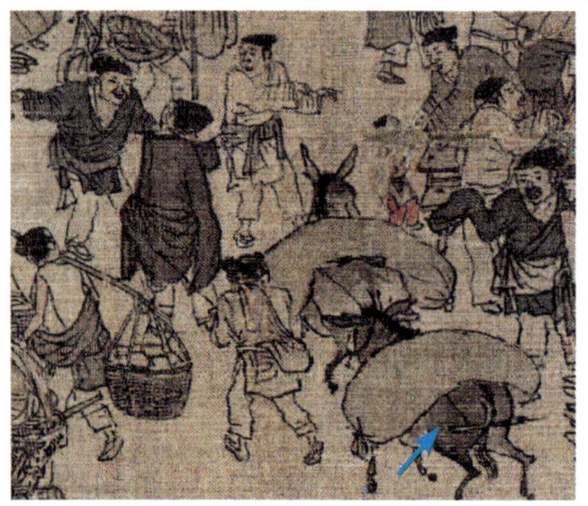

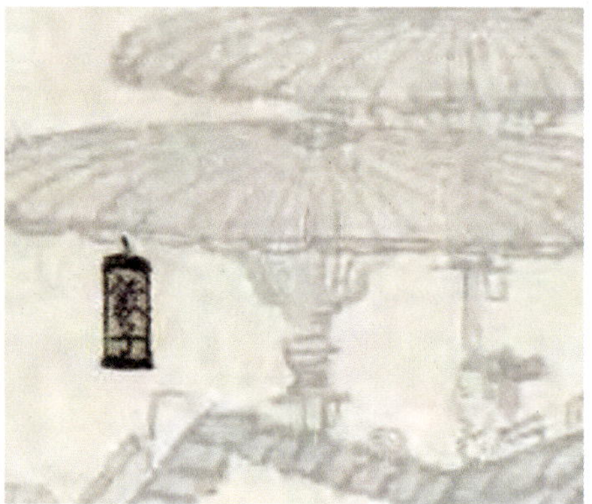

to notice the child in time. The child, dressed red trousers, appears to be only four or five years old based on his height and hairstyle, although his facial features are obscured due to damage to the painting. From his perspective, the suddenly appearing donkeys must seem like enormous beasts. Startled, he quickly calls out to an adult nearby. His parents, just like others, are likely distracted by the large boat crisis in the river. Hearing the child's shout, they hurriedly turn around to pull the child to safety.

The narrow escape from danger can be partly attributed to the efforts of a *Ya ren* (indicated by the white arrow in the on page 87). By waving his long sleeves, he shooed the donkeys away from him, indirectly saving the child. Otherwise, the donkeys, already irritated from heavy loads and the sharp turn, might have inadvertently charged headlong into the child, potentially causing serious harm.

Did the crisis end there? Not at all! As we look closer, near the donkey's head, another *Ya ren* (indicated by the blue arrow in the picture on page 87) is talking with two others. I imagine their conversation goes something like this: One of them, with a face full of smiles, says, 'Come with me; I need your services.' The other retorts, 'Hey, that's not fair! He's supposed to come with me; I was here first!' The *Ya ren*, feeling flattered by the unexpected demand for his services, points to the man in white and tells the first, 'All right, all right. I'll go with him first, and then I'll come and take care of your business later.' As the trio heatedly discuss at the end of the bridge, they unwittingly block the donkey's path. The donkeys, already spooked by being shooed, are stumbling towards them...

Up to the Rainbow Bridge, more than half of the scroll has been unveiled. Zhang

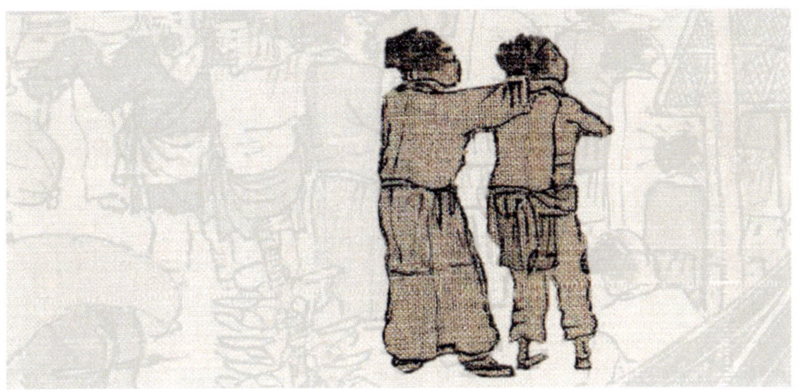

Zeduan has depicted several crises, yet none are rendered into actual accidents. Indeed, throughout the scroll, the artist has not portrayed any accidents that have already occurred, but rather the moments just before they might happen. No one can deny that Zhang Zeduan truly masters the art of narrative. In fact, it is this portrayal of imminent but impending action that maximises narrative tension. It's like a balloon inflated to the brink – not burst yet, but on the verge of popping at any moment; or like a row of dominoes, where the fall of a single one could trigger the rest falling down. In such a state of tension, emotions, meanings and all else are at their most intense and profound.

Now, let's take a moment to discuss other details in this scene.

A man (indicated by a green arrow in the picture on page 87) rests his hand on another man's shoulder. This gesture of shoulder-holding is a sign of intimacy, which may be seen as taboo even in modern times, to the extent that the phrase 'putting an arm around someone's shoulder' carries a negative connotation. However, in *Along the River During the Qingming Festival*, this gesture is depicted multiple times, not just between men on the streets but also between women and men (which we will see later in the city). Judging from their relaxed demeanour and the nonchalance of those around them, it is evident that shoulder-holding was perfectly natural among the people of the Song Dynasty. This leads me to two reflections: firstly, shoulder-holding is an external expression of warmth and affection, and such intimacy is a characteristic of traditional Chinese emotional expression nurtured by the Confucian culture; secondly, intimate behaviour in public reflects the concept of 'being as close as family'. Indeed, the act of shoulder-holding and the phenomenon of street encroachment actually share a common ideology. Residents and vendors constructed arbours, creating transitional spaces between private dwellings and streets. This blurring of the boundary between public and private makes the bustling yet chaotic atmosphere of street life in Bianjing, both a boon and a bane to the city's vibrancy.

Look at the donkey (indicated by the blue arrow in the picture on page 88). There is a horizontal stick at the rear of the donkey, known as a *Hou qiu gun* (后鞧棍, rear stabilising stick). According to those with experience, a donkey's body is wider at the back and narrower at the front. So, when using donkeys to carry people or goods, *Hou qiu gun* is necessary to prevent the load from slipping forward. Now, please take a look picture page 88. There are two large parasols in front of the street-facing houses at the end of the Rainbow Bridge. Hanging from the edge of one of the parasols is a rectangular sign that reads *Yin zi* (饮子), a popular beverage at the time ①. It is somewhat similar to the herbal tea brewed with traditional Chinese medicine today.

① Some scholars argue that it is inappropriate to use the term *Yin liao* (饮料, beverage) to refer to the ancient *Yin zi*, as its medicinal purposes in ancient times may have outweighed its use as a drink. However, I believe that *Yin zi* was a broad concept in ancient times and its meaning evolved over time. The *Yu Tang Xian Hua* (《玉堂闲话》) by *Fan Zi* of the Five Dynasties records that during the Tang Dynasty, *Yin zi* was sold in the Western Market of Chang'an. It was made from common herbs, no more than a few ingredients. Without feeling the pulse, and regardless of the illness, a dose costing a hundred *Wen* (文, currency) purportedly treated thousands of ailments. They often placed large pots in spacious houses, *Cuo* (剉, chopping) (zhuó) and *Zhuo* (斫, brewing) day and night, barely able to meet the demand. Isn't that interesting? It was cheap and claimed to cure everything! In the Tang Dynasty, *Yin zi* was not taken for thirst but for medicinal purposes. By the Song Dynasty, *Yin zi* had become more 'specialised'. It no longer claimed to cure all diseases but was used to treat corresponding ailments with specific types, such as Rehmannia *Yin zi*, Rose *Yin zi*, Antelope Horn *Yin zi*, Fructus Aurantii *Yin zi*, and Kudzu Root *Yin zi*. On the other hand, beverage-type *Yin zi* was also developed, for disease prevention in healthy individuals as well as for curing the sick.

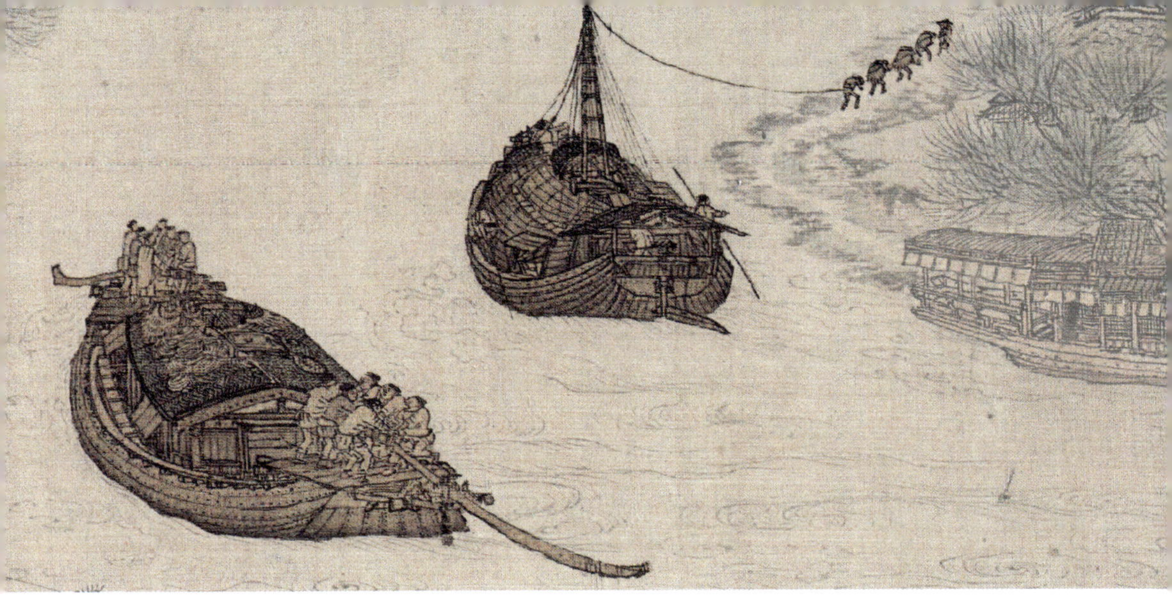

19. The Bian River running eastward

Running across the Rainbow Bridge, the Bian River turns and flows into the distance. From a narrative perspective, the story of the Bian River concludes here. We are about to unfold the scroll further and once again set foot on land, heading towards the city. But, let's not hurry along just yet. There are still some 'highlights' that we haven't explored here. We'll start by looking at the distant and then focus on the nearby surroundings.

In the distance, four or five boats are moored on the left bank. Between the side of the boats and the riverbank, long planks are laid out, serving as gangways for people to board and disembark. A person carrying a shoulder pole is already on the gangplank, while an elderly person and a child on the shore are preparing to board the boat (indicated by the red arrow in the picture below). Looking further towards the centre of the river, there is another heavily laden boat propelled by oars. However, this boat is manned by a group of six instead of the usual eight (as shown in the picture above). Near the oar-powered boat, there is a tracker-powered boat. The boatmen on the oar-powered boat are still calling out their rhythmic chants, although their voices are barely audible from this distance. The tracker-powered boat, in contrast, is quiet and free from the hustle and bustle of the

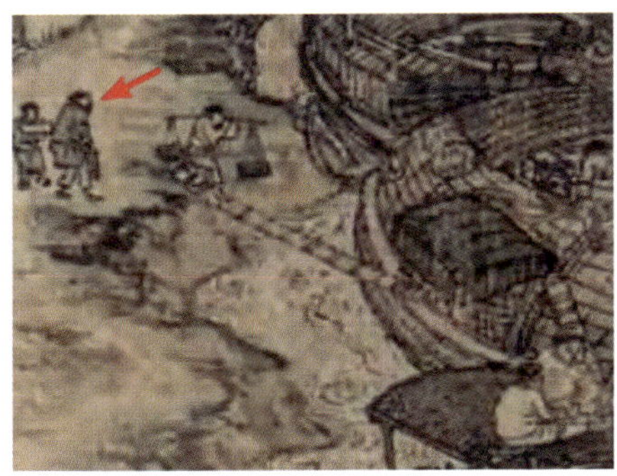

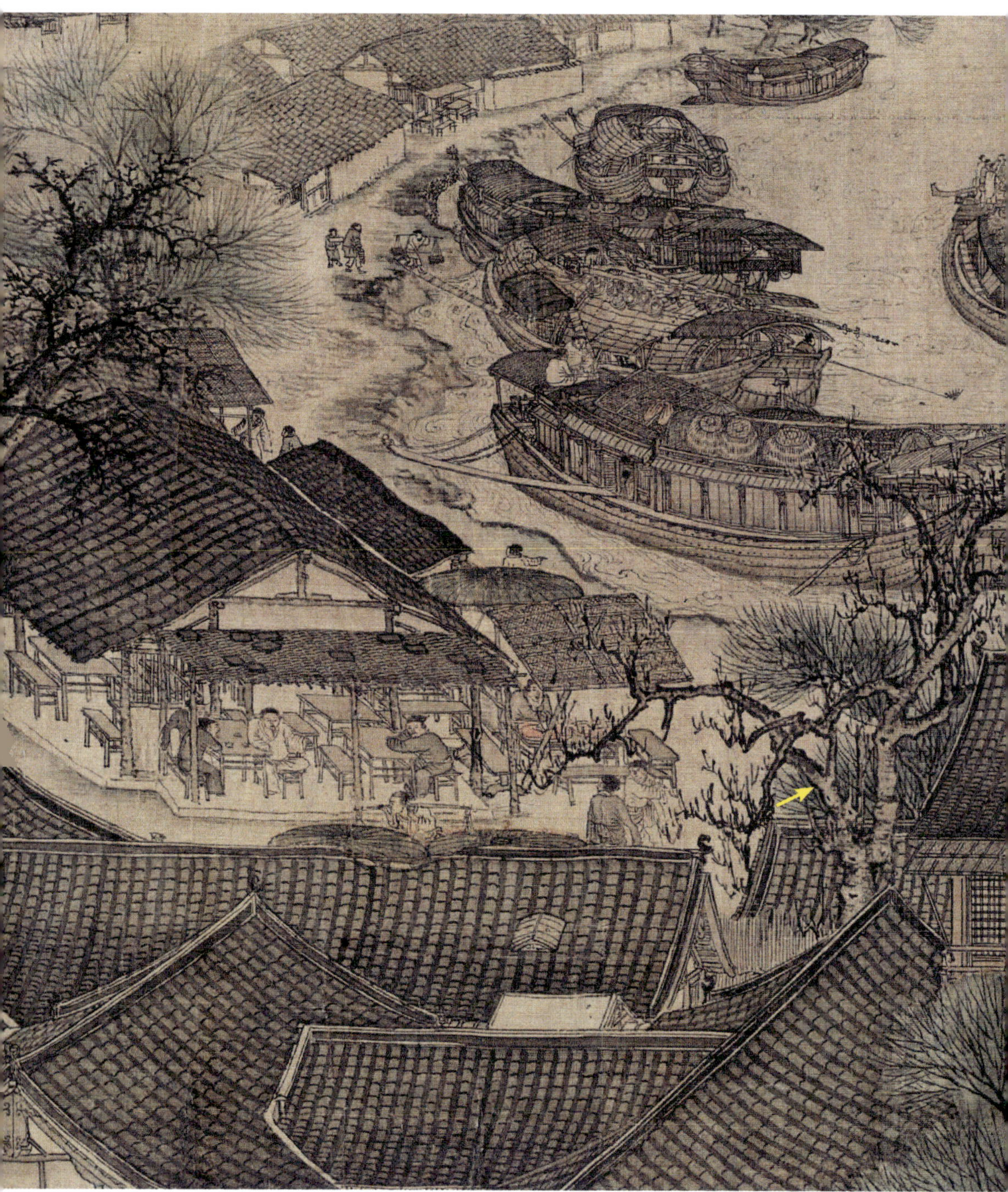

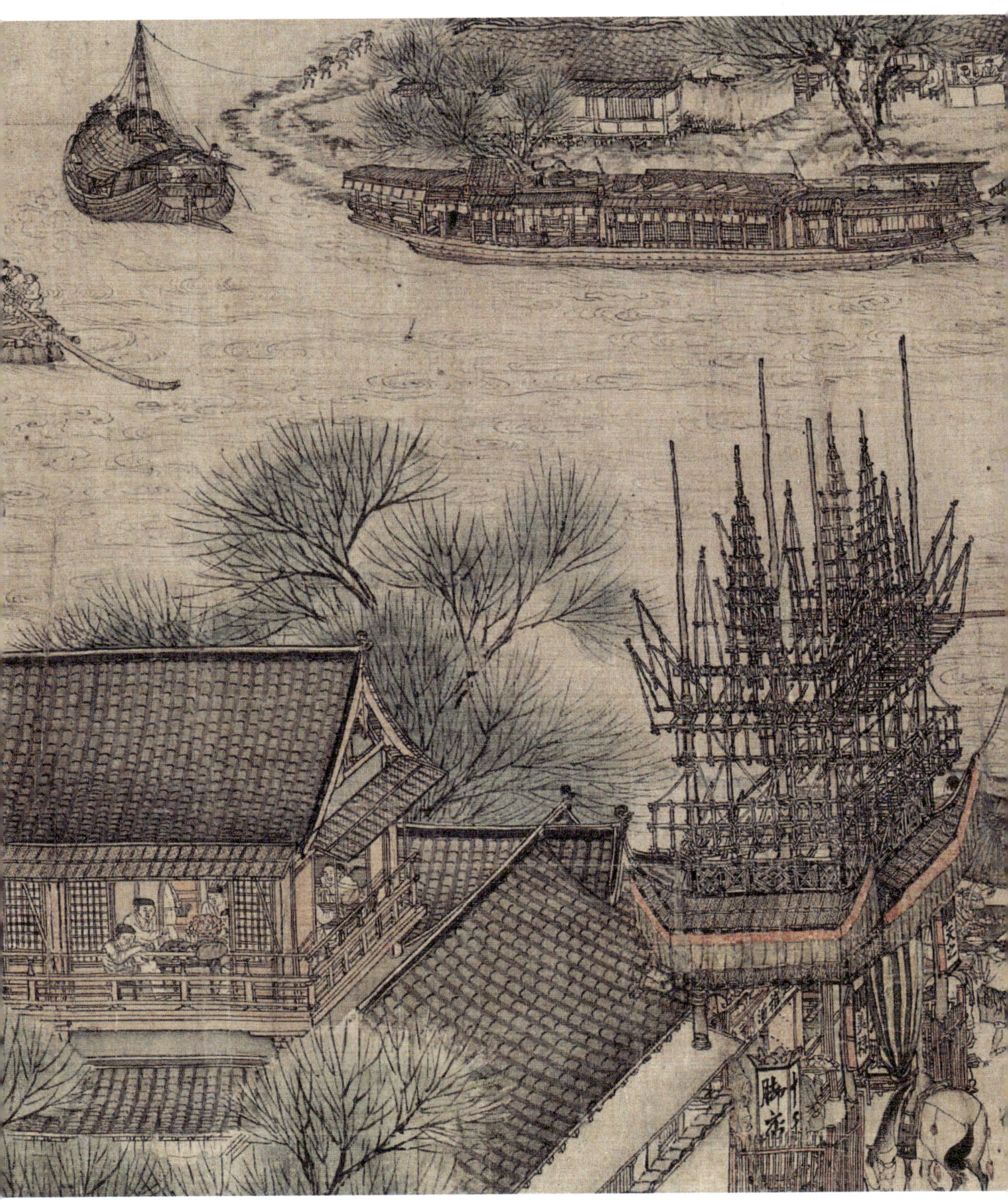

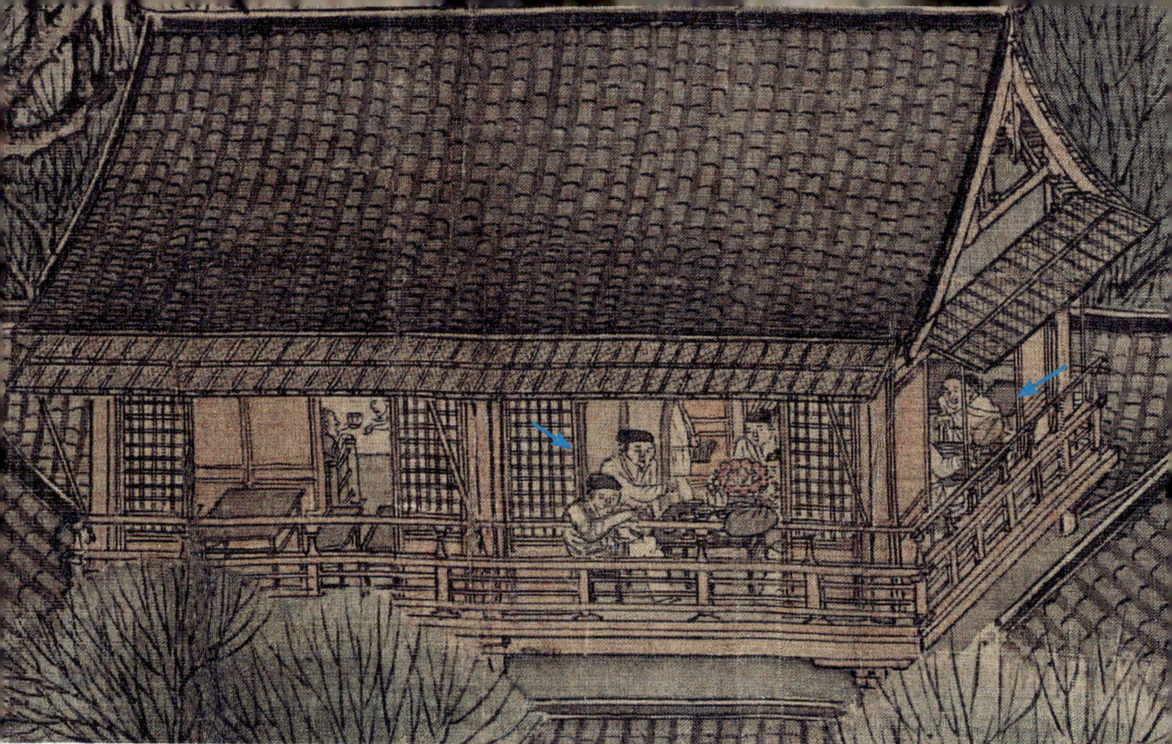

Rainbow Bridge. Here, where the river is wide, the two types of boats no longer need to worry about colliding. By repeatedly depicting these two types of boats here, the artist may be hinting that the crisis faced by the large boat under the Rainbow Bridge will eventually be over, so as to ease our tension.

On the second floor, we can see two groups of diners: one group is directly in front of us, while the other is on the side (indicated by the blue arrows in the picture above). They are not seated in the spacious hall but rather in private rooms, which is called *Ge zi* (阁子) in the Song Dynasty. These *Ge zi* are separated by wooden partitions, offering limited privacy. However, the soundproofing is relatively poor, so if people in one *Ge zi* speak loudly, their voices can be heard in the adjacent *Ge zi*. In the classic Chinese novel *Water Margin*, the heroes often drink in such *Ge zi* at taverns. When we read the passages about the heroes drinking in these *Ge zi*, the scene here will help us vividly imagine their activities.

Now, let's look at the group of people directly in front of us. One of them is leaning against the railing, looking downwards. Can you notice that his right leg is raised, resting on his left thigh? Let's try this posture to experience a sense of leisure. In the poetry of the Song Dynasty, *Ping lan* (凭栏, leaning against the railing) is a classic imagery, as seen in the lines

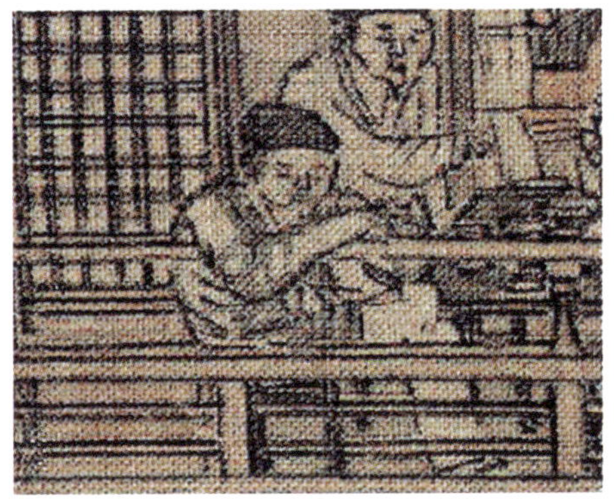

The person on the second floor of the *Jiao dian*, leaning against the railing with one leg crossed

'凭栏久，墙外杏花香' (Leaning against the railing for a long time, the fragrance of apricot blossoms wafts from beyond the wall) by *Cao Zu* from the Northern Song Dynasty, or '凭栏处，潇潇雨歇' (Leaning against the railing, the drizzling rain ceases) by Yue Fei from the Southern Song Dynasty). The scene here helps us understand how ancient people used to lean against railings. Of course, not everyone leaning against the railing is as languid as the person in the painting. Yue Fei, with his 'vigorous and passionate aspirations', would naturally have a different demeanour when leaning against the railing.

Now, let's look at the periphery of the second floor. Have you noticed anything unusual? It seems to have only doors and no walls, right? In fact, its 'walls' are composed entirely of doors. These doors are known as *Ge zi men* (格子门, lattice doors), also called *Ge shan* (隔扇) or *Ge zi* (格子). Their general structure is as follows: the upper part consists of

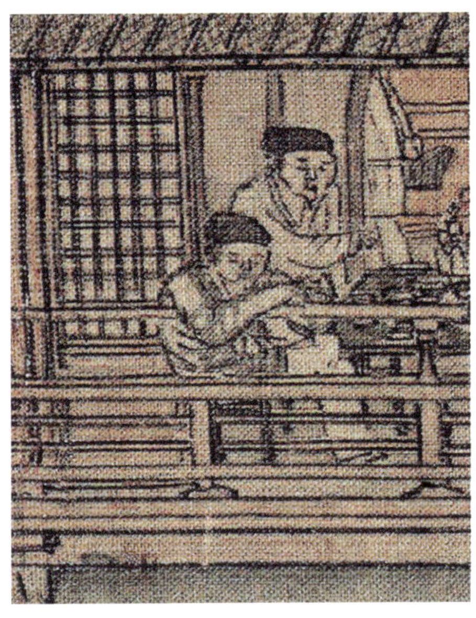

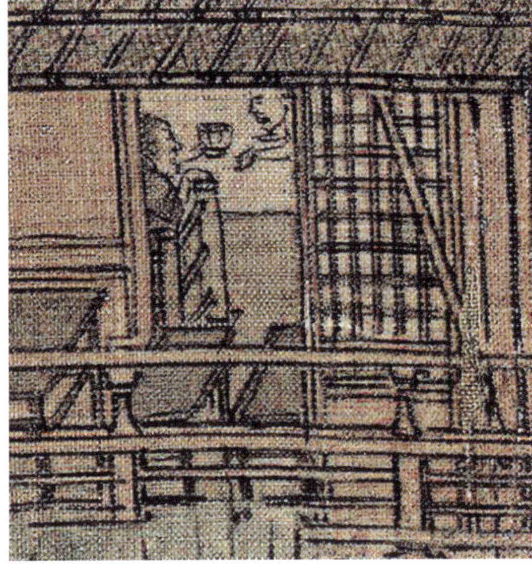

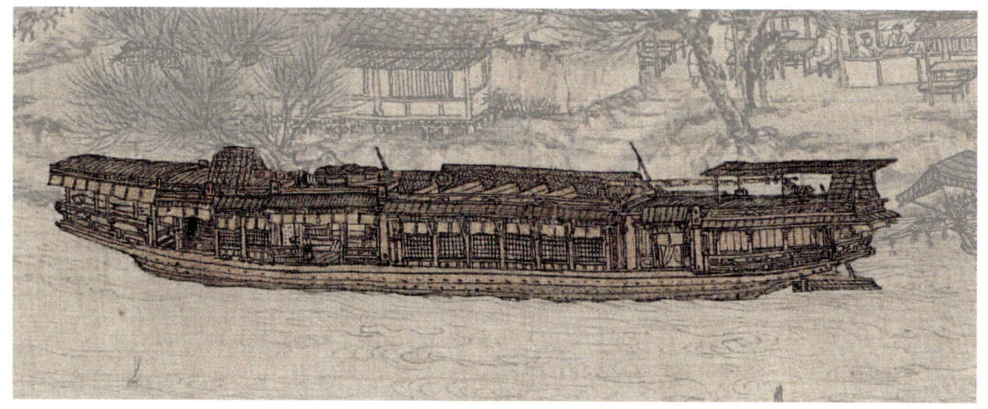

A large passenger boat at the bend of the Bian River

square, grid-like patterns, occupying about two-thirds of the door's height; the lower part is a water-resistant blockboard, occupying about one-third of the door's height. *Ge zi men* can be freely opened, closed or removed: with them in place, they create a closed, private space; with them open, the room becomes well-ventilated and bright. Speaking of this, I recall a hot debate from a few years ago about what exactly is the 'bed' in Li Bai's line '床前明月光' (Before my bed lies a pool of moon bright). The controversy arose because some people felt that rooms in ancient times had small windows, making it impossible for moonlight to shine in front of the bed. As a result, some interpreted the 'bed' as a *Hu chuang* (胡床) or *Ma zha* (马扎), which is a low stool, while others interpreted it as a *Jing lan* (井栏), which is a well curb. In any case, they insisted that Li Bai's bed should be outdoors. However, the poem is quite clear that the moonlight shines 'before the bed', and since moonlight naturally illuminates everything outdoors, why emphasise '前 (before)' if it were truly outside? The reluctance to acknowledge the word '前 (before)' in the phrase is still due to the disbelief that ancient rooms could be very well-ventilated and bright. In addition to this example, there is another scene in the *Landscape of Four Seasons* (《四景山水图》) in the Southern Song Dynasty, which depicts the autumn scene in Jiangnan (see the picture opposite). The room in this picture is even larger, making it feasible for moonlight to shine directly before a bed. Of course, our examples are paintings from Song Dynasty, and may not exactly represent the Tang Dynasty. However, they can at least make the scene of 'Before my bed lies a pool of moon bright' less easily questioned.

Let's continue talking about the *Ge zi men*. These large, operable doors on the upper floors must be paired with a 'partner' – the railing. The reason is simple: without a railing for protection, it would be too dangerous. Additionally, the railing and the door are almost adjacent to each other, with no corridor in between for people to stroll along. This is precisely why that person can sit at the table while leaning against the railing.

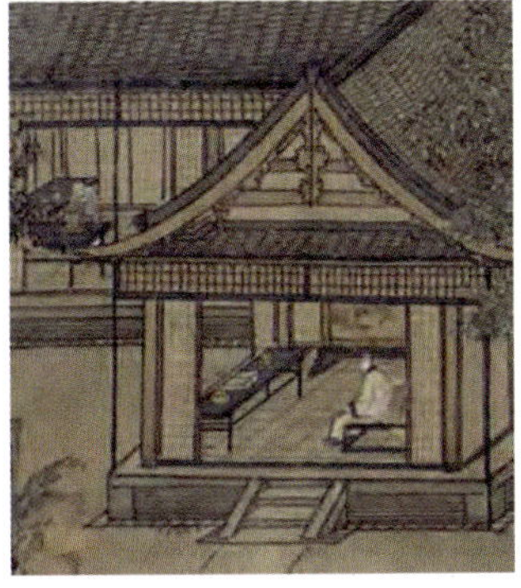

Part of *Landscape of Four Seasons* by Liu Songnian, from the Southern Song Dynasty, in the collection of the Palace Museum, Beijing

There's another interesting detail happening on the second floor: a waiter downstairs is passing a bowl to another waiter upstairs (as seen in the picture on the right on page 95). Although we can't directly see the stairs inside the building, the interaction between the two waiters informs us that the stairs are just there. Looking more closely, the waiter passing the dish is holding the bowl out with his left hand while his right hand is resting on the baluster of the staircase railing. It's really impressive and touching to see how attentive and diligent the artist is, even in such subtle details!

Finally, let's talk about that tree in the courtyard of the *Jiao dian* (we can refer back to the previous panoramic view, pointed out by the yellow arrow). That tree stands out as unique in the entire scroll of *Along the River During the Qingming Festival.* Some researchers believe it is a magnolia tree for the following three reasons: First, the bark of a magnolia tree is silvery-grey or greyish-whiter, with thin twigs. Its solitary flower grows at the tip of a main stem or branch, pointing sharply upwards. Second, magnolia trees were originally planted in Henan regions in ancient China. Finally, in ancient times, magnolia trees were often planted in front of pavilions, terraces and towers. They are important flowering trees in the northern regions during the early spring. The Qingming Festival falls right around the time when magnolia buds are about to bloom.

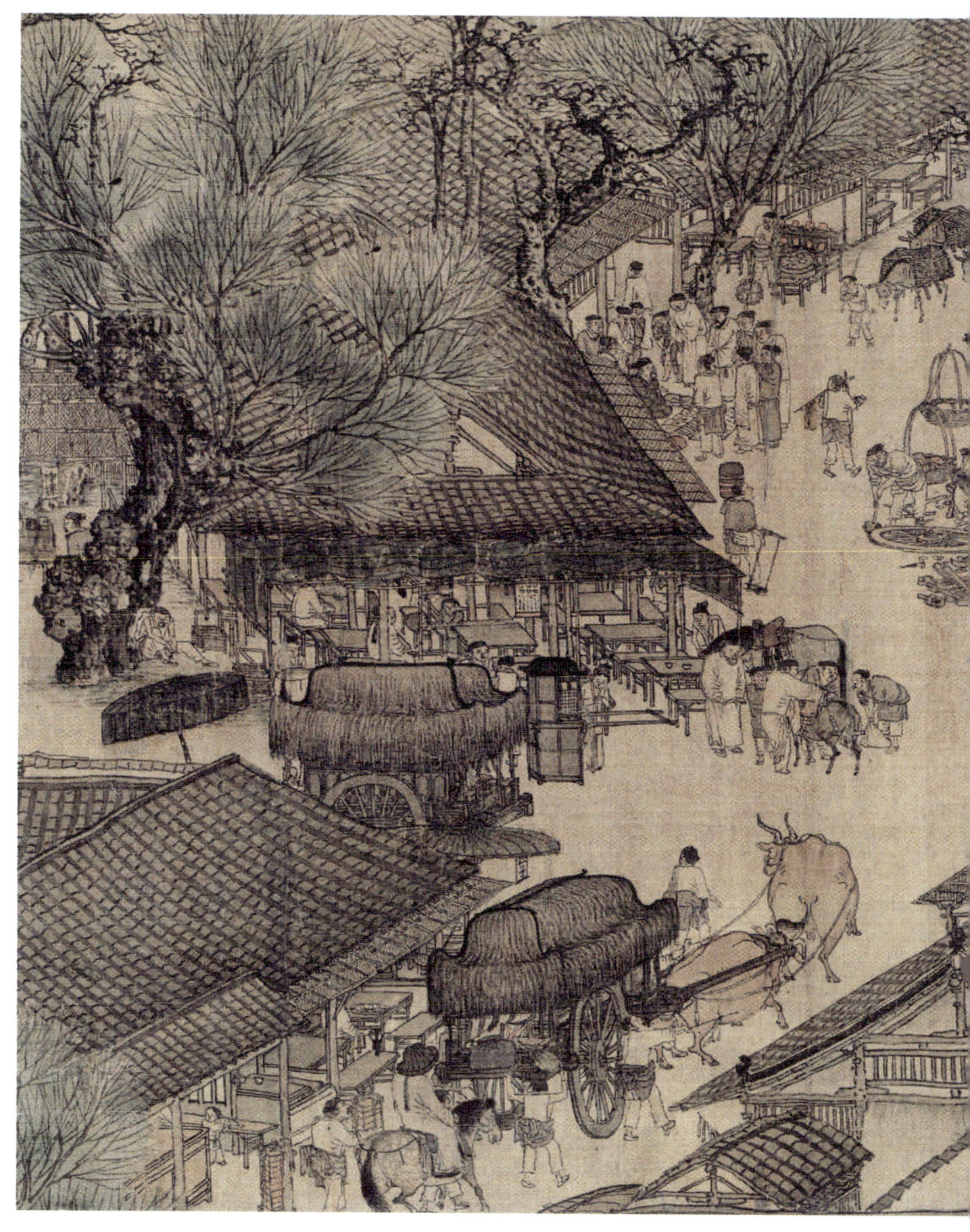

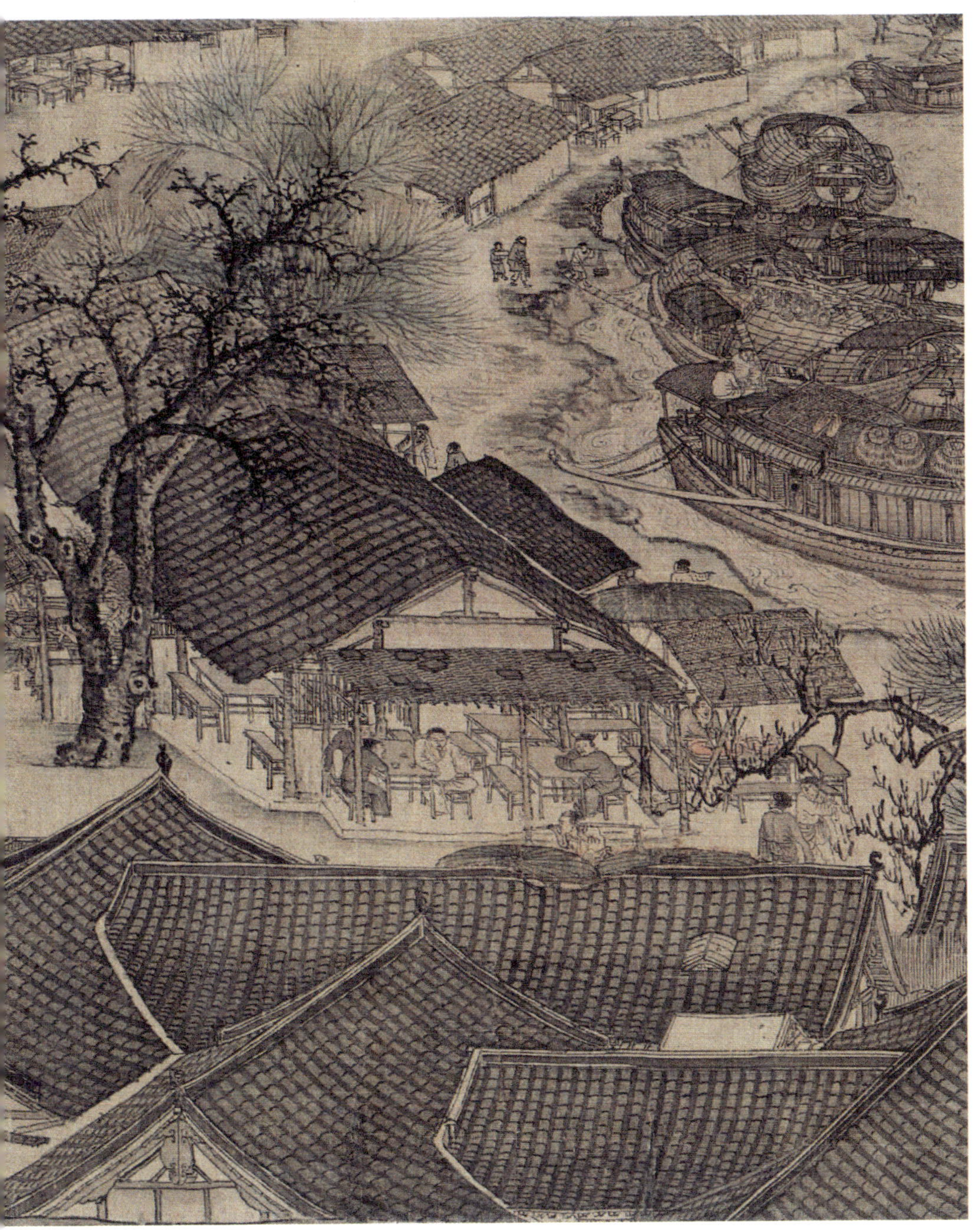

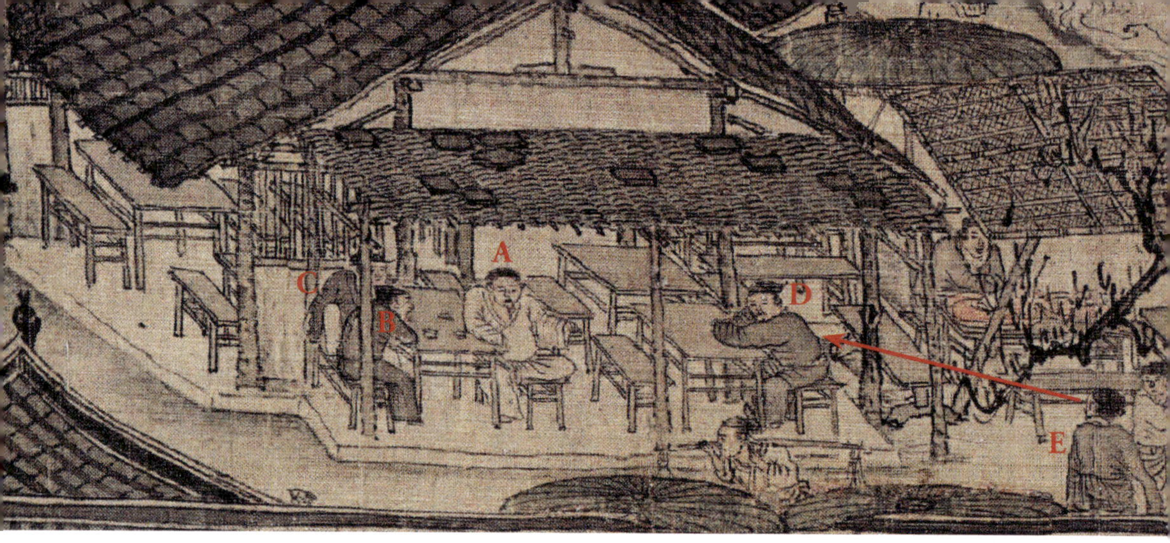

20. Stories happening at the crossroads outside the city

As the Bian River bends, the story along the waterway comes to a close. So, we continue strolling along the street towards the city gate.

Leaving the dock, we immediately arrive at a crossroads (a panoramic view on the previous page). Since it's close to the dock, there are quite a few 'stories' happening here. Let me take you around to see for yourself.

First, let's take a look at the four corners of the crossroads.

At the top of this pace is the street-facing storefront on the northeast corner, where the floor inside this store is about one or two bricks higher than the street level. There are four people sitting idly (labelled A, B, C, D and E for clarity). Once we take a closer look, we can find them in an intriguing manner. The three people on the left, clearly are acquainted. The person in white (A) having a higher status than B and C. We might notice that when B and C talk to him, A doesn't face them directly, but looks towards the street and raises his left hand as if pointing at a passing porter, possibly saying to B and C, 'Hey, you've been living well under my wing; if it weren't for me, wouldn't you end up toiling like that porter?' B, who is slightly older than C, nods and bows eagerly, saying, 'Yes, yes, yes!' On the other hand, C, who is still younger, does not say a word but simply looks in the direction A is pointing. Do you notice how C is sitting? His right leg is bent with his foot resting on the stool, giving off a bit of a hooligan vibe. Now look at A's sitting: it is far from elegant, with his right arm resting on the table and his left leg casually crossed over on the stool, giving an impression of casualness and self-satisfaction.

Now, let's look at D, who is sitting alone at the next table. Do you see what he's

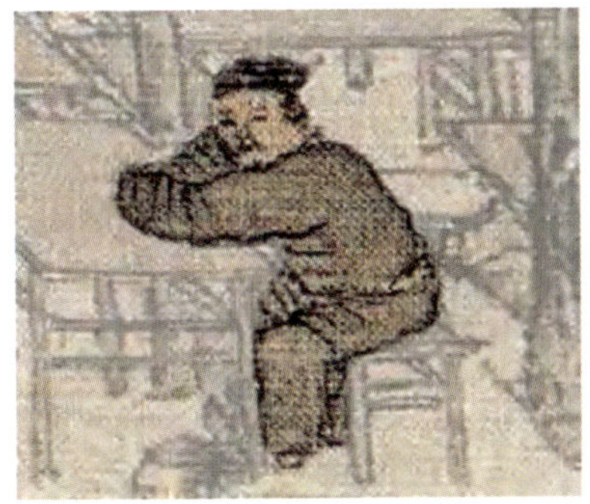

doing? At that moment, he might be overhearing A commenting on the porter and unconsciously looked in the porter's direction as well. However, his gaze seems distant and unfocused, more like he is lost in thought than truly observing. Now, look at his hand – he's actually resting his chin on his hand, a gesture also referred to as *Zhi yi* (支颐, supporting the chin)①. This solitary figure, sitting alone without even a teacup on the table, is a character that invites curiosity.

① *Zhi yi* (支颐) is a very evocative image in Tang and Song poetry. Bai Juyi, a poet from the Tang Dynasty, wrote in his poem *New Year's Eve:* 'In the evening, I sit with my chin resting on my hand; at midnight, I fall asleep on my arm.' Qin Guan, a lyricist from the Northern Song Dynasty, wrote in his poem *Yu lou chun: Awakening from a nap at noon by the window, the scent of incense fades*: 'Resting my chin on my hand, I'm lost in melancholic thoughts, my brows furrowed with sorrow; Biting my delicate fingernails. Few people know my heart is broken; I idly watch the pair of butterflies flirting by the flowery curtain.'

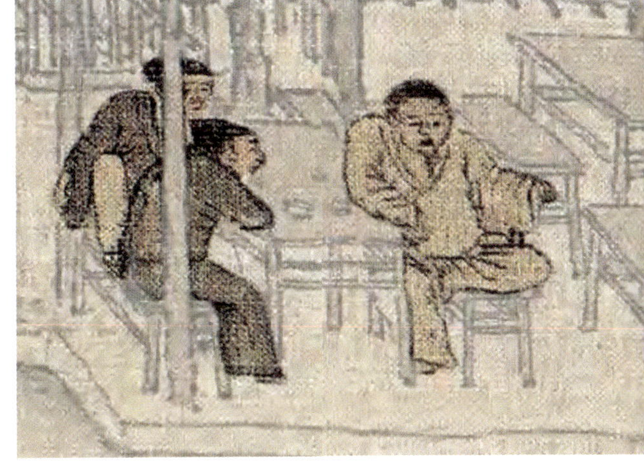

Zhang Zeduan was a master at using the gaze of his characters to establish relationships between them, thereby telling a silent story. For instance, D is looking at others, while E is also looking back at him. Urged by his companions, E seems to be saying, 'Wait, I think I might know him.'

Of course, the above interpersonal relationships and dialogues are merely my own speculation and should not

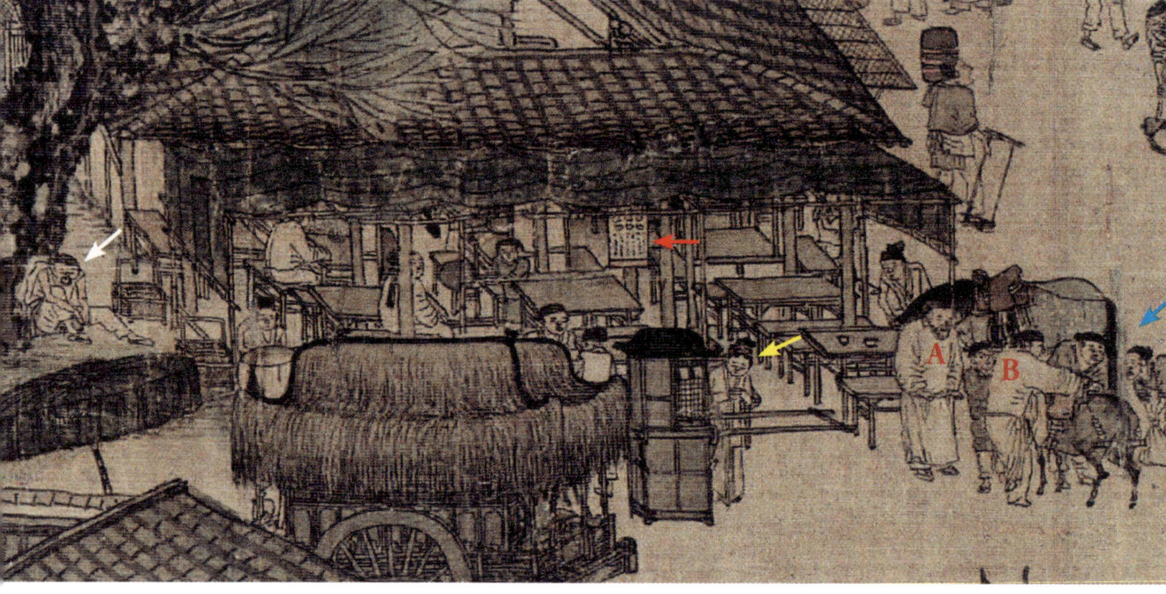

Details of the street-facing storefront on the southeast corner of the crossroads

limit your imagination. I believe that if this scene were used for a writing exercise, it would undoubtedly spark a wealth of creativity and inspiration.

The image above depicts the street-facing storefront on the southeast corner of the crossroads. If the theme of the northeast corner is 'idleness', then the theme here is 'farewell'. Zhang Zeduan employed a technique of contrast to portray this scene of parting.

In the scene indicated by the blue arrow, we observe the moment of farewell. A and B are most likely friends. They just enjoyed a farewell drink at a nearby restaurant, and a young waiter is busy clearing the cups and dishes. A stands aside, watching his friend B mount a donkey. Some might mistakenly think B is mounting a horse, but that is not the case. Behind A stands a big horse, markedly contrasting with the small donkey B is about to ride. Zhang Zeduan's deliberate painting of both a big horse and a small donkey in this scene is likely meant to reflect B's humble condition. I speculate that B might have once been an official eligible to ride horses but, having been demoted, he can now only dejectedly ride a small donkey as he leaves the capital city behind.

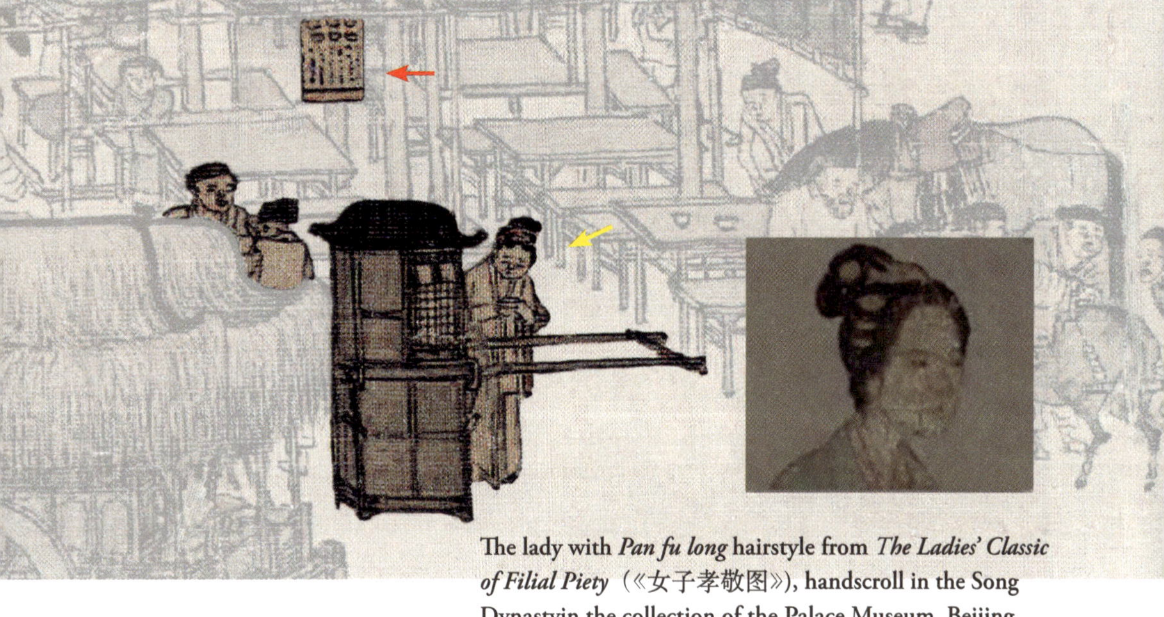

The lady with *Pan fu long* hairstyle from *The Ladies' Classic of Filial Piety* (《女子孝敬图》), handscroll in the Song Dynastyin the collection of the Palace Museum, Beijing

The yellow arrow points to a sedan chair, beside which stands a woman ①. It seems that she is holding something in her hands while talking to the person inside the sedan chair; alternatively, she could be the passenger herself, merely waiting to board. Two men stationed beside the sedan chair are likely the sedan chair bearers. Could there be a connection between the sedan chair and the small donkey? There are arguments for both possibilities. On one hand, the closeness of the sedan chair to the donkey might imply that the person inside or beside the sedan chair is related to the man mounting the donkey, possibly his female kin. On the other hand, they appear unrelated because B is already mounting the donkey, ready to depart, while the sedan chair shows no signs of following, with the two chair bearers still chatting on the side. In any case, there seems to be a relationship between the two that is both connected and detached, sparking curiosity about their relationship. What is certain, however, is the striking contrast between the modest sedan chair and the luxurious carriage approaching from the opposite direction, much like the contrast between the small donkey and the big horse. In comparison to the luxurious carriage, the small sedan chair appears rather poor and humble.

① I kindly ask my dear readers to look at the hairstyle and attire of this woman. Some believe she is styled with a hairdo known as *Pan fu long* (盘福龙), a popular hairstyle during the Chongning and Daguan periods (1102–1110). However, this depiction alone is not definitive enough to confirm the hairstyle (for a more definitive example, see the *The Ladies' Classic of Filial Piety* 《女子孝敬图》 from the Song Dynasty on page 103). What can be confirmed, though, is her attire: she is wearing a loose, short jacket called *Bei zi* (褙子). This type of garment, an overcoat with a straight collar and slits on the sides and back, emerged during the same period as the *Pan fu long* hairstyle, which helps us date the creation of *Along the River During the Qingming Festival*. Before the popularity of the short *Bei zi*, women in the Song Dynasty commonly wore long *Bei zi* that reached down to their feet. Starting from the Xuanhe period of Emperor Huizong's reign (1119–1125), the style shifted from loose to form-fitting. The picture on page 107 depicts a woman from the Southern Song Dynasty in a red, form-fitting long *Bei zi*.

Finally, let's take a look at two subtle details: Inside the shop, a small banner hangs from a wooden pillar (indicated by the red arrow on page 102), likely advertising the best dishes

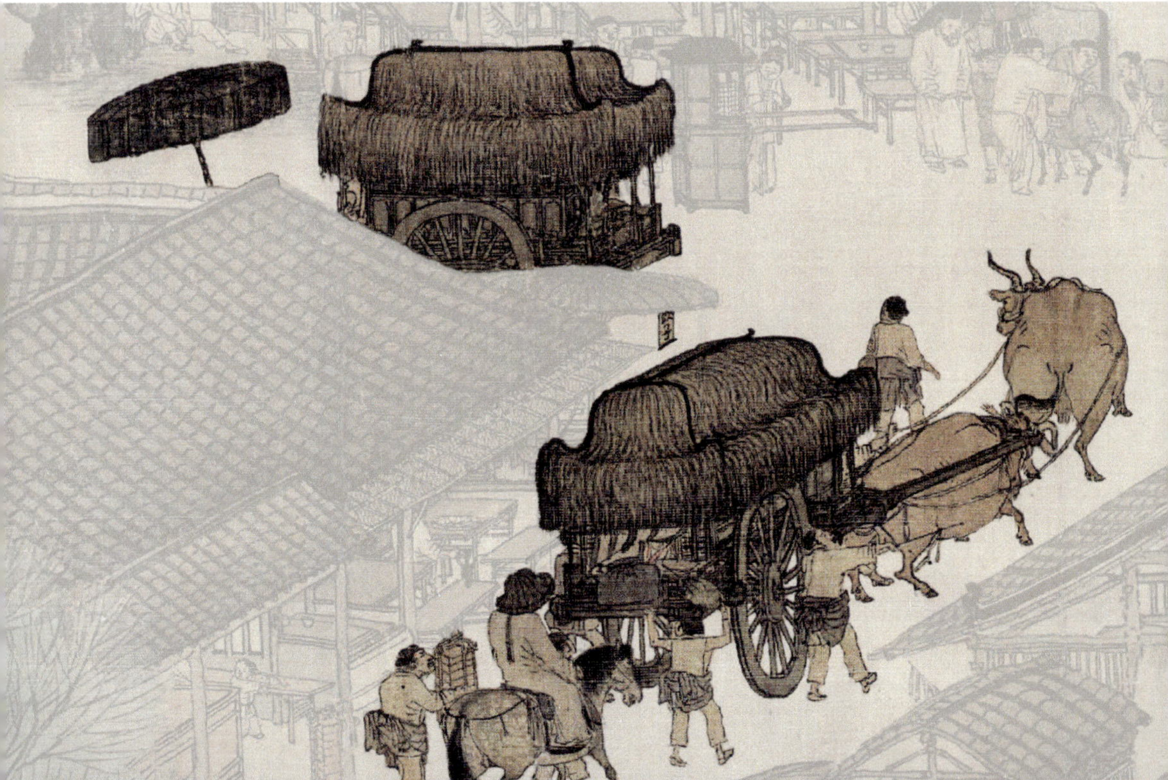

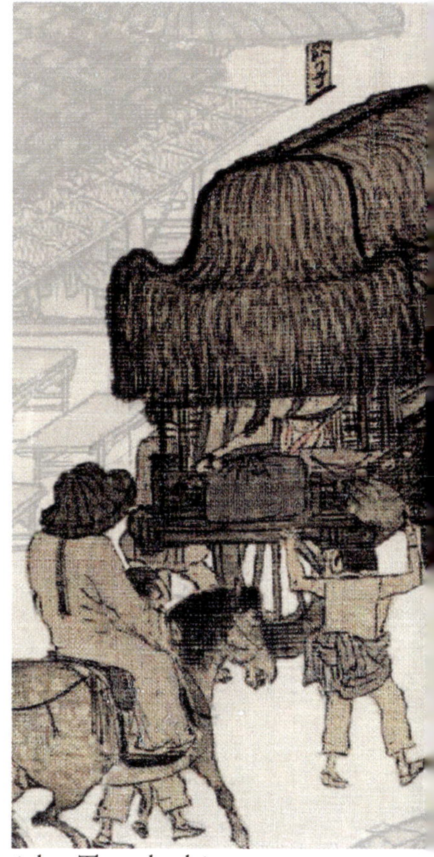

here. Outside, under an old willow tree, a shirtless, middle-aged porter sits on the ground, taking a nap (indicated by the white arrow on the left page). This figure is one of the most sympathetic characters I find in *Along the River During the Qingming Festival*.

Now let's take a look at the opulent carriages that make the sedan chair and donkey appear so humble in comparison.

Behold, the picture on the opposite page that shows those two opulent carriages.

The carriage in front has already turned the corner, heading towards the city gate. A flat-topped cyan umbrella canopy is visible at the front of the carriage, indicating the extraordinary status of this convoy. ①

Following behind, this carriage is flanked by attendants and guards on both sides. On the right, an attendant brandishing a bullwhip looks up and shouts as if commanding, 'Make way, everyone make way!' Interestingly, there is actually no one nearby at all. Just looking at him, we can see what it means to be imperious and overbearing! This figure serves another purpose as well: by comparing him to the carriage, we can gauge its height. The wheel is over a person's height, and the entire carriage stands about twice the height of a person, so we can imagine what it would feel like to stand next to such a massive carriage. Moreover, there are two robust oxen in front pulling the carriage (the front ox is harnessed, while the rear ox is yoked), enhancing the sense of grandeur.

① In ancient China, the use of umbrellas was strictly regulated, reflecting one's social status. During the reign of Emperor Huizong of the Song Dynasty, when someone travelled under a cyan umbrella, all officials were expected to yield the way. As recorded in *The History of Song*, Volume 150, Chapter (*zhi*, 志) 103: *military dress II*: 'In the third year of the Zhenghe era during Emperor Huizong's reign, when the princes of

Yan and Yue were travelling, officials did not yield the way. As a result, they were granted a three-tiered cyan umbrella... This practice then became an established rule.' (Here, 'established rule' refers to systems, rules and conventions.)

The carriage's canopy looks quite unique, doesn't it? It's made from palm fibre, which is very high-grade and opulent. There are doors at the front and back of the carriage, with curtains hanging over them. As these curtains sway, we could see a woman sitting inside the carriage. According to *Dongjing Meng Hua Lu* (《东京梦华录》, *The Eastern Capital: A Dream of Splendor*), this type of carriage was specifically used for 'the ladies of the household to ride in'.

Finally, let's take a look at the man on horseback following the carriage. Think about the traveller passing by the clothes-drying boat – doesn't he seem familiar? Like the traveller, he also wears an angular hood, with a 'braid' hanging down. And he is also a mysterious figure seen from behind! It really looks like he has been through a lot... Given that the main purpose of this book is to guide our readers to appreciate the painting, rather than to engage in fanciful storytelling, I won't share too many stories I've come up with. However, my dear readers, with your imagination, it will certainly enrich your appreciation of the painting.

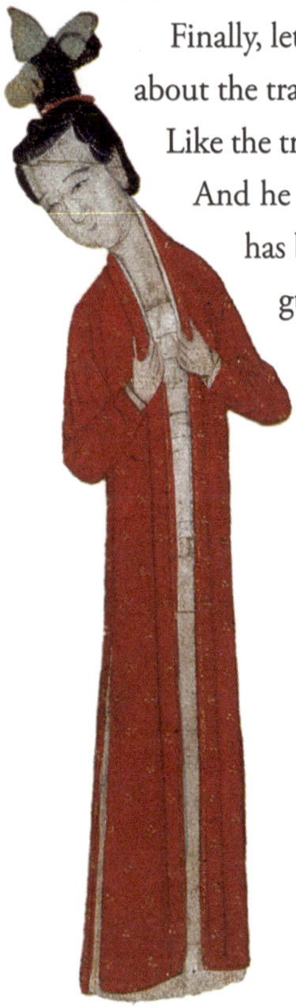

The female court musician in a red, form-fitting long *Bei zi* in the Southern Song Dynasty from *Ladies Playing Music* (《歌乐图》), handscroll, in the Southern Song Dynasty in the collection of the Shanghai Museum

21. The tools in the carriage repair shop

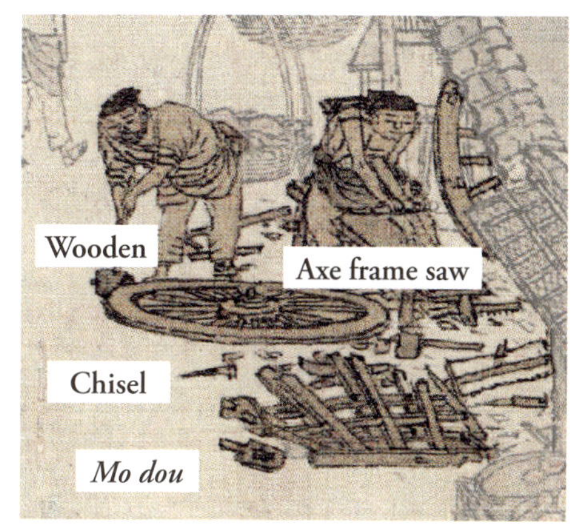

Not far from the crossroads, there is a carriage repair shop. Two craftsmen are working there. Among the tools they are using and those scattered on the ground, we can see a wooden mallet, frame saw, chisel, axe and *Mo dou* (墨斗, an ancient measuring tool in traditional Chinese woodwork). Typically used for cutting wood, the frame saw, consists of a rectangular wooden frame, a saw blade and hemp ropes. The frame saw in *Along the River During the Qingming Festival* confirms that the frame saw was already in use during the Northern Song Dynasty. *Mo dou* is another essential tool for carpenters, used to mark straight lines. It operates by pulling an ink-soaked string out, placing it taut across the wood, and then snapping it to leave a straight, dark line.

The older craftsman is using a wooden mallet to adjust the wheel, while the younger one is sitting astride a stool, busily smoothing a long piece of wood with a tool. Some people believe that he is using a plane, but no archaeological evidence supports the existence of planes used in the Song Dynasty so far (the earliest known example of a plane in China comes from a Yuan Dynasty shipwreck in Heze, Shandong). Therefore, it is highly unlikely he is using a plane. What he is using looks more like a scraper. Before the invention of frame saws and planes, when people needed to split large pieces of wood, they would drive a row of wedges into the wood to crack it. To flatten wood, they would first use an adze to roughly level the board, then use a scraper to scrape it, and finally polish it with a whetstone.

The carriage repair shop provides essential services for carriage maintenance, but it also causes inconvenience to traffic. Do you note that the craftsman holding the mallet is almost in the middle of the street?

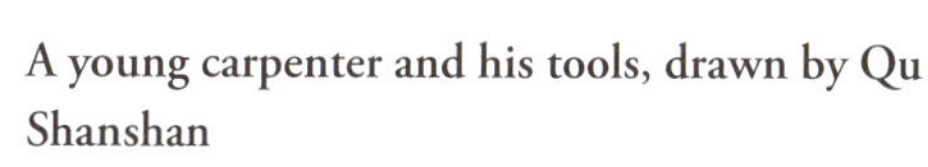

A young carpenter and his tools, drawn by Qu Shanshan

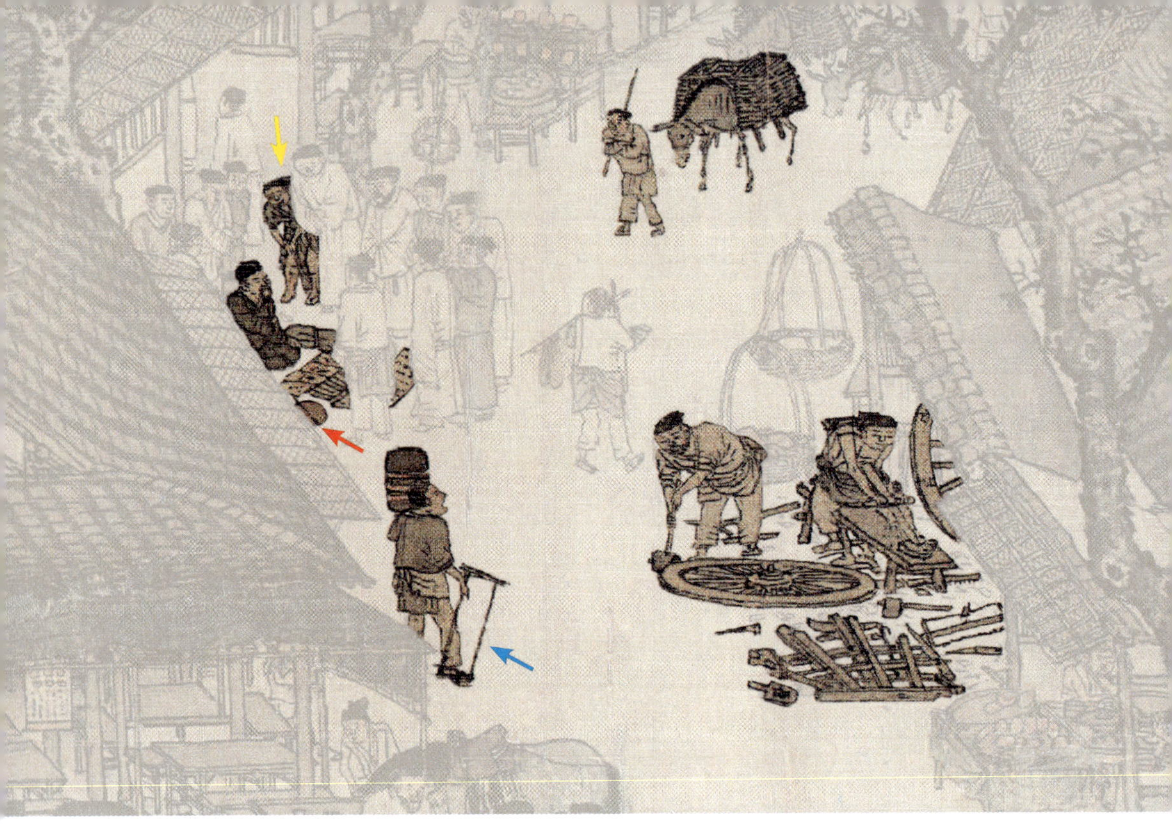

22. The vendor with his portable rack, the itinerant doctor and the charcoal-selling donkey caravan

A man is walking towards the carriage repair shop, carrying goods on his shoulder and holding a long wooden rack in his right hand – it's a folding, crossed-leg goods rack (indicated by the blue arrow in the picture on the page 107). This rack is similar in principle to a folding stool, with two legs crossing each other. When unfolded, it can be used to display goods. It greatly facilitated the vendor's business. We have seen this type of portable goods rack unfolded and laden with goods on the Rainbow Bridge. Now, this scene makes us see that it is indeed convenient to carry. The vendor, mouth wide open, was likely calling out to passersby, hawking his wares. As noted in the *Dongjing Meng Hua Lu* (《东京梦华录》, *The Eastern Capital: A Dream of Splendor*), various vendors in Bianjing city 'chant and call out in a hundred ways', allowing people to know what they are selling just by hearing their unique calls. These hawkings, engaging but never annoying, were melodiously called as '*Chang Mai* (唱卖, singing sales)' or '*Ge jiao* (歌叫, melodious calls),'① resonating like music through the streets.

① *Dongjing Meng Hua Lu* (《东京梦华录》, *The Eastern Capital: A Dream of Splendor*), volume VIII: During this most beautiful month of spring, with myriad flowers in dazzling bloom – peonies, kerrias and Rosa banksiae, etc. Flower vendors put their flowers in bamboo baskets, enticing customers with their melodious calls.

Across from the repair shop, a group of people are gathered around an elderly man seated on the ground, rows of goods arrayed before him. He is likely an itinerant doctor, setting up a stall here to sell medicines②. How can we tell? Look at the man pointed out by the yellow arrow: he is lifting his clothing to reveal a swollen thigh, evidently waiting for the doctor's examination. The red arrow points to a fan. This is neither the first nor the last fan in the painting; later, we will explore more about the unique functions of fans in the Song Dynasty. For now, let's look at the donkey carrying charcoal. The baskets flanking its back are empty, yet it does not seem relieved of its burden but rather looks somewhat dispirited. So is the young man in front of it, with his arms crossed over his chest, listless and weary. This scene calls to mind Bai Juyi's poem *The Old Charcoal Seller* (《卖炭翁》): 'The ox is tired out and the old man hungry. They rest in the slush outside the south gate of the market.'

② Though someone suggests that this man is selling calligraphy and paintings, not in this book. Whether or not itinerant doctors can cure illness, there is an interesting record: Ouyang Xiu once suffered from diarrhoea and the court physicians failed to cure. However, he was healed after taking medicine sold by a vendor on the street. Not only was the medicine effective, but it was also affordable, costing just three *Wen* (文, currency) per prescription. This is documented in Zhang Gao's *Yi shuo* (《医说》 The Medical Theory), Volume VI, *Zang Fu Xie Li* (脏腑泄痢, Treatment of Diarrhoea) in the Southern Song Dynasty: Ouyang Xiu once suffered from severe diarrhoea, which court physicians could not cure. His wife said, 'There is a medicine sold in the market, three *Wen* per prescription, which is very effective.' He replied, 'I'm different from those common folk; how can I take it!' Then his wife mixed it with the court physician's prescription and he was cured.

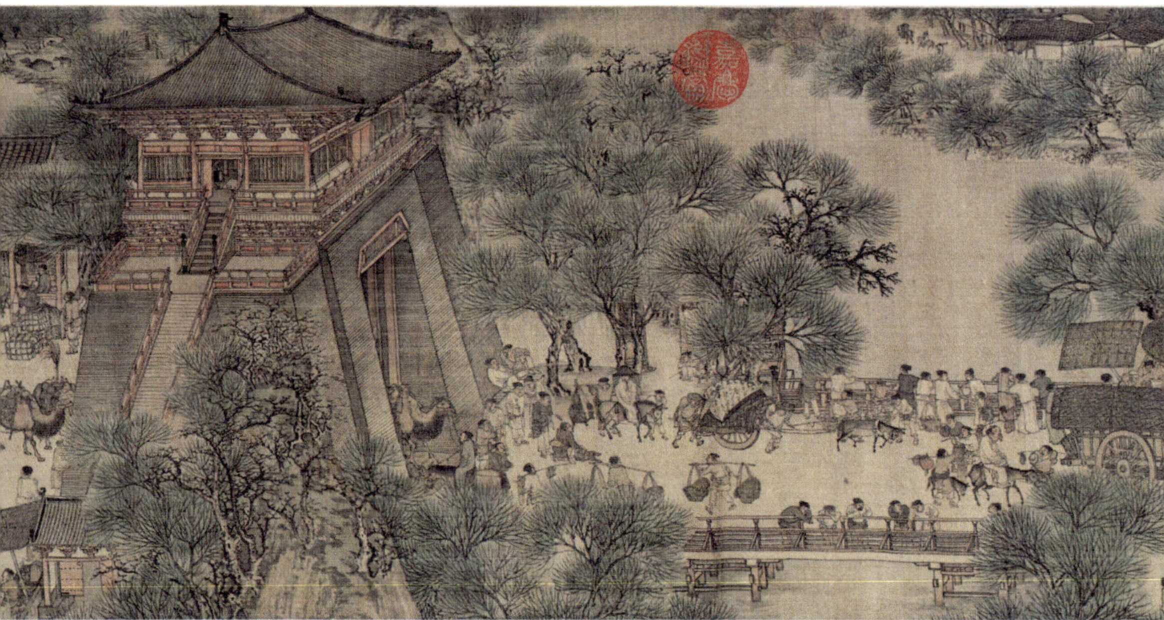

23. A mysterious mansion

Passing the crossroads, behold, the city gate was in sight!

Please lay the book flat, and before us unfolds a panoramic view from the crossroads to the city gate of Bianjing. The scene can be divided into two sections: the right page as the first section, from the opulent ox cart to the end of the Rainbow Bridge; the left page as the second section, from the head of the bridge to the city gate.

Let's look at the first part. Have you noticed how the scene suddenly shifts, becoming more open and quiet? This is because there is an extraordinary 'mansion' on one side of the street. Let's take a closer look at what makes it so unique.

First, there is a small river and a small bridge in front of the mansion. Does this remind you of anything? It's a bit like a miniature moat, isn't it? Especially considering that the real moat and the city gate are nearby, there seems to be a kind of structural similarity. Thus, the painter has imbued this mansion with a symbolic meaning. Second, there are some 'strange' people at the gate and along the fence. But what makes these figures stand out? Let's look at their surroundings: in addition to the river and bridge, the wall is topped

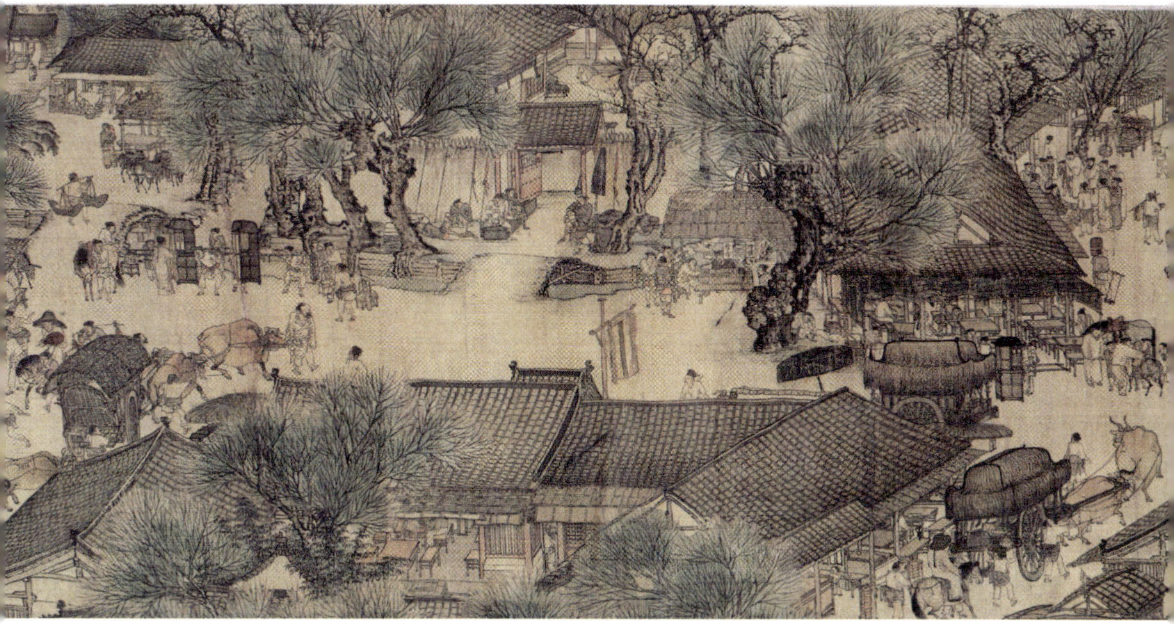

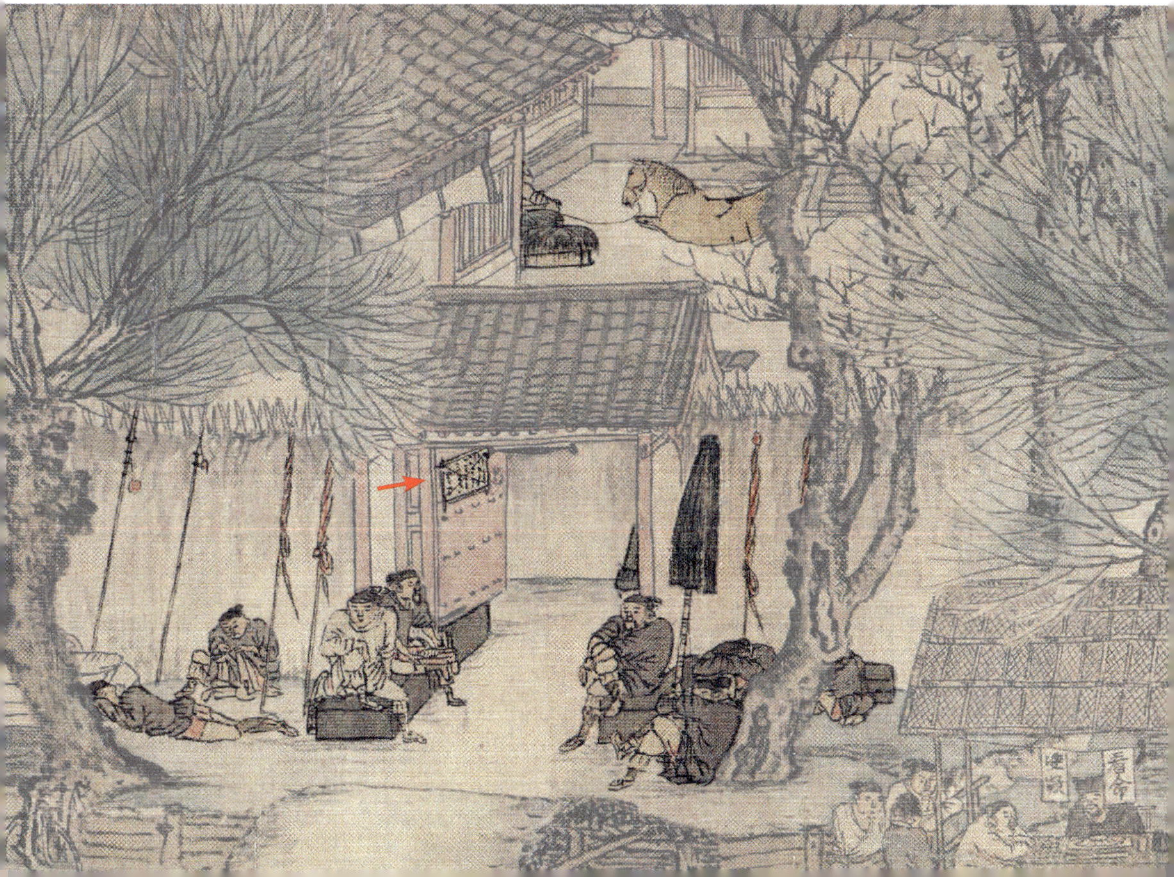

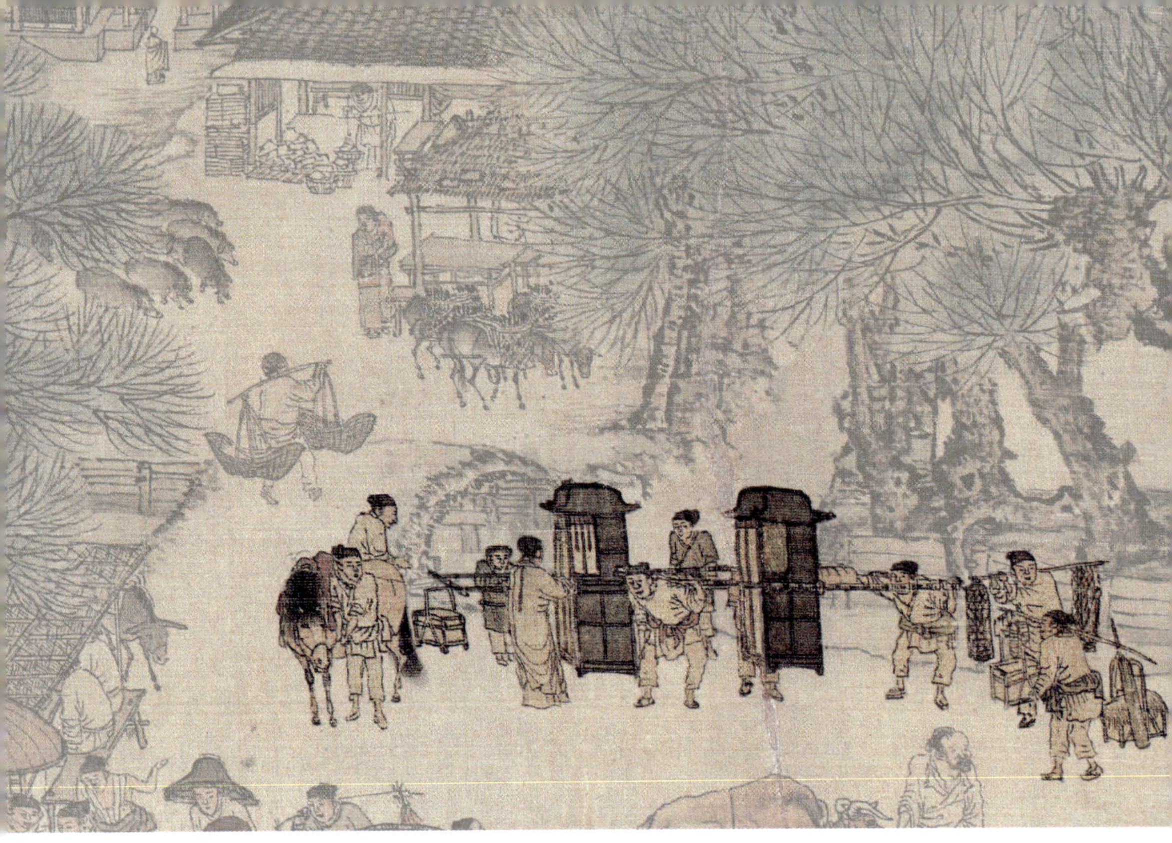

with anti-climbing spikes, three rows of studs are on the red door and a notice is posted on the door (indicated by the red arrow on the previous page). Inside the courtyard, there is a horse tended to by a dedicated caretaker. Therefore, this is likely a government office. Looking back at the wall behind, not only are there a cyan umbrella and a flag (rolled up in the picture), but there are also long spears! Generally speaking, the Song Dynasty implemented strict weapons control policies, prohibiting private ownership and manufacture of weapons, especially during the reign of Emperor Huizong. Long spears were regulated weapons①. Their presence here, particularly given the strict weapons control policies, leaves little doubt that these people are government soldiers.

① Notably, short spears, intended for self-defence, were permitted for private ownership. As recorded in the *Song Jian Long Zhong Xiang Ding Xing Tong* (《宋建隆重详定刑统》, *The Detailed General Penal Code of Jianlong Period of Song Dynasty*): 'Bows, arrows, knives, shields, and short spears – these five weapons are allowed in private households.' However, armour, crossbows, long spears, *Shuo* (矟,

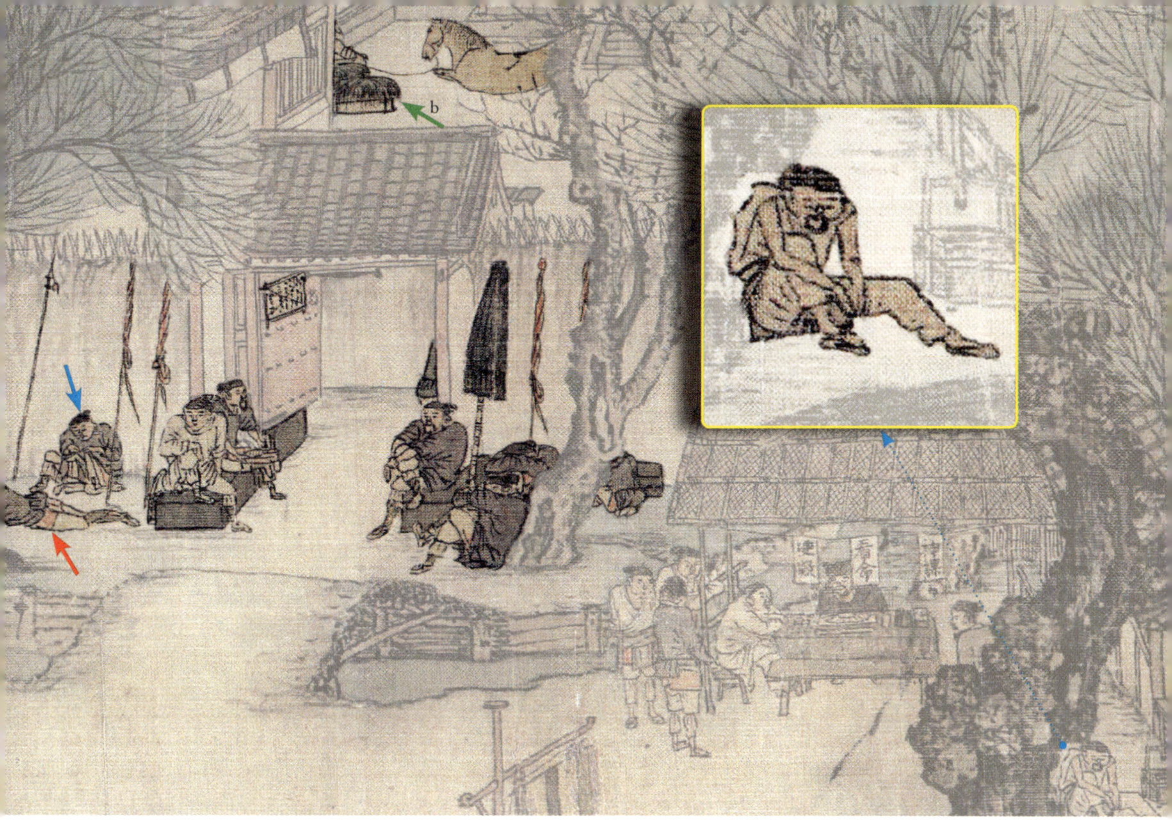

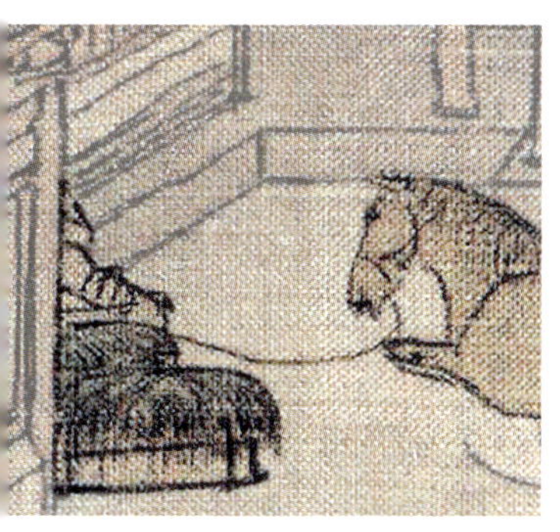

also written as 槊, a heavy weapon similar to a spear but with a much longer blade), and horse armour are not permitted in private households. Those individuals who possess long spears or *Shuo* shall each be sentenced to a year and a half of hard labour.

Their status as government soldiers makes their behaviour more intriguing. Do their actions align with our expectations? Some are lounging about while others are sprawling on the ground. Take, for example, one (indicated by the red arrow) is lying on the ground asleep. His posture is incredibly 'wanton', exposing his thighs and red underpants. In such a public place, under the gaze of others, isn't he embarrassed and ashamed? Then look at another (indicated by the blue arrow) – he isn't much better. He sits at the base of the wall, actually mending his clothes! The others either cross their legs, bend their knees, rest their feet on a box-like object under their buttocks or bury their heads in sleep.

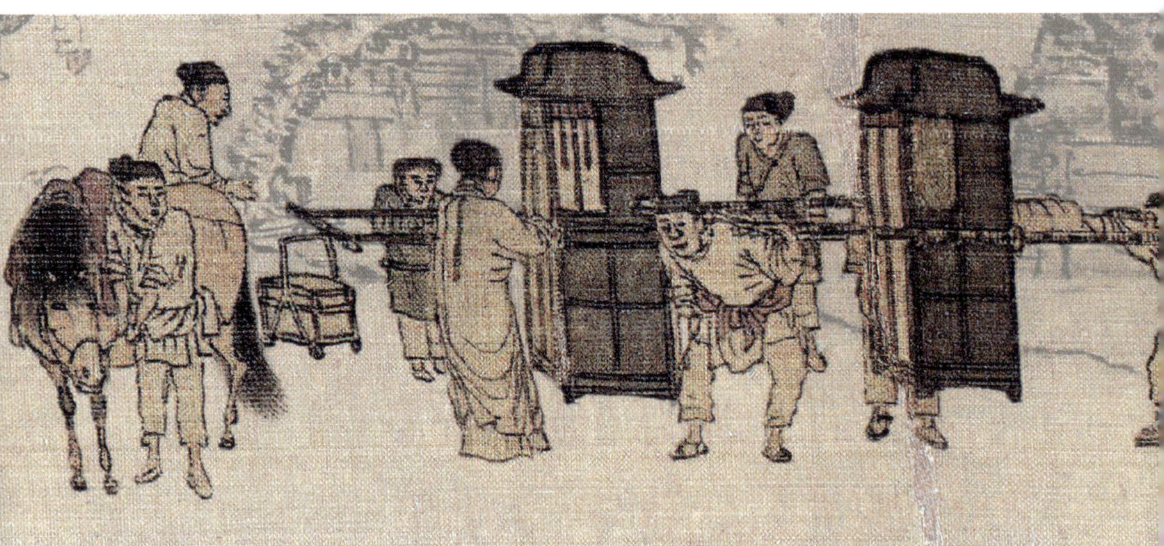

Some argue that they 'all appear extremely fatigued, as if they had just arrived after a long, arduous journey'. However, I find this interpretation not entirely accurate. If we talk about genuine 'fatigue', the middle-aged man under the big willow tree truly embodies exhaustion. These soldiers, on the other hand, seem merely indolent. There is a subtle distinction between the postures of fatigue and indolence. Take another closer look and consider this distinction – do you see it as well?

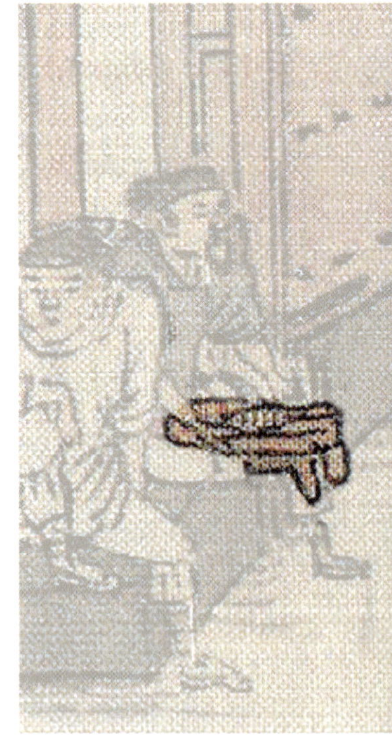

② In the courtyard of the government office, there is a detail worth noting: a horse lies on the ground while the groom sits against the wall, holding the reins. Beside him appear to be two troughs filled with what looks like grass (indicated by the green arrow). Please notice how the grass 'overflows' from the troughs, cascading around the edges. Its vibrant green, a stark contrast to withered yellow, reveals that

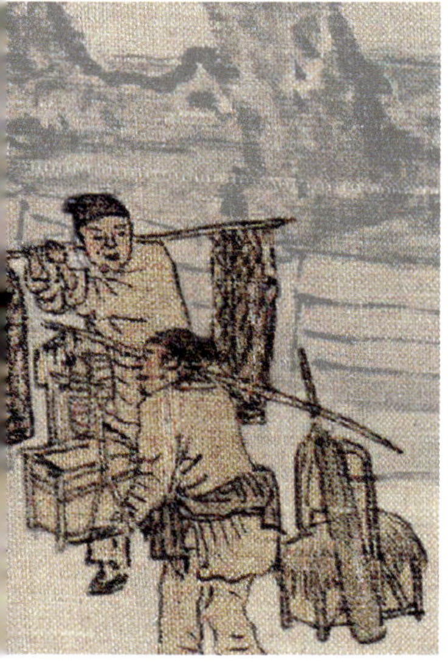

the stored fodder is not dry hay but rather freshly cut grass – a testament to the season of lush, verdant growth.

A curious question emerges: why are soldiers at the front of a government office so indolent and bored? Shouldn't they be alert and attentive? Some believe that this office is a courier station, an institution for the transmission of official documents and that the people at the door are courier soldiers, with the horse in the courtyard being a courier horse. Their laxity, then, could be interpreted as a sign of government inefficiency. This sounds reasonable. If this is indeed a courier station, then high-ranking officials, perhaps even the emperor himself, would be outraged to witness his soldiers slacking off to such an extent, just as a boss would be furious to find his employees attending to personal matters during work hours or a teacher catching their students napping in class. My dear readers, let me ask you a question: the bearded soldier, sitting by the door, holds a plate with a fish on it. What could this signify? Some suggest he might be waiting to give it to a courier station official, though this seems unlikely. My initial thought was that perhaps the fish is intended for Qingming Festival rites. However, this theory conflicts with the interpretation of a courier station. Could a courier station also be responsible for delivering Qingming Festival offerings? After much contemplation, I confess, I'm stumped.

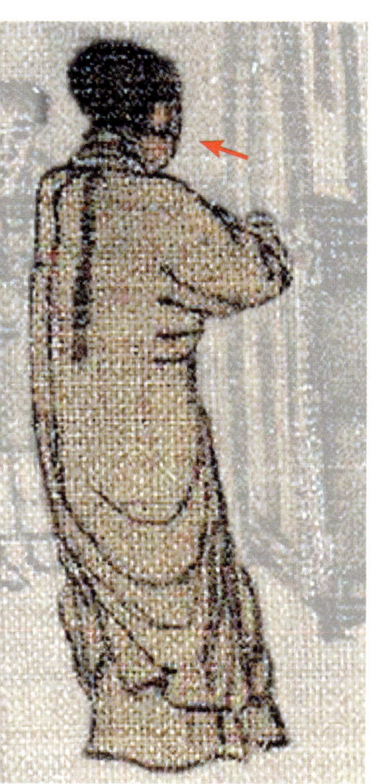

Where historical evidence is lacking, imagination rushes in to fill the void. Some let their imaginations run wild and connect the group by the river with the mansion. Look at the person ahead of the sedan chair, dressed as a scholar but with an awkward demeanour, possibly disguised as a woman or even a eunuch from the palace, masquerading as a scholar accompanying his master. (As an aside, there is also a 'braid-like' object hanging behind this person – similar braids appear in two other places, yet the attire is clearly that of the Song Dynasty, thus the assumption that the horse riders behind the laundry boat and the opulent carriage are both Jurchens is unfounded.) A woman in disguise, or a camouflaged eunuch... what an intriguing idea! I couldn't help but join in the speculation and noticed a peculiar detail. Look at the red arrow on the left: it points to a black line beneath the person's face and ear, seeming to wrap around from the back of his head. Could it be a mask? How fascinating! Some even speculate that this is Emperor Huizong of the Song Dynasty sneaking out for a clandestine date with Li Shishi (a famous courtesan in the late Northern Song Dynasty). The fish, they imagine, is for their meal after the rendezvous. All right, all right, I'm quite fond of 'gossip' myself, but too much of my personal imagination would seriously undermine this book. Hmm, let's leave it at that.

24. The fortune teller's three advertising boards

Near the courier station, a simple booth made of bamboo mats sits beside the small river, under the shade of the willow trees. It is a fortune-telling booth (see the picture opposite). The fortune teller sits under it, reading someone's fortune. Do you remember the street fortune teller we encountered at the dock? This one seems a bit more 'upscale', with a stronger sense of marketing. Look, he has strung up a rope and hung three advertising boards that read: '*Shen ke* (神课, divination)', '*Kan ming* (看命, fortune-telling)', and '*Jue yi* (决疑, casuistry)'. The character '课(*ke*)' in *Shen ke* (神课, divination) does not signify a 'lesson' or 'class' but rather represents a method of divination. It often involves tossing copper coins to observe their faces or pinching fingers to calculate the heavenly stems and earthly branches to predict good or ill fortune. The word *Shen ke* essentially boasts of his remarkably accurate divination. The artist's decision to draw the fortune-telling booth adjacent to the courier station inevitably evokes a certain association: with the government's indolence, people must turn to divination to inquire about their destinies.

In *Along the River During the Qingming Festival*, there are three fortune-telling scenes: the first is at the docks, reading the fate of labourers; the second, presented here, caters to the wealthy; and the third, in the city, for an examinee. It is said that Bianjing housed up to ten thousand fortune-telling shops and stalls at that time and these three scenes are emblematic of the practice.

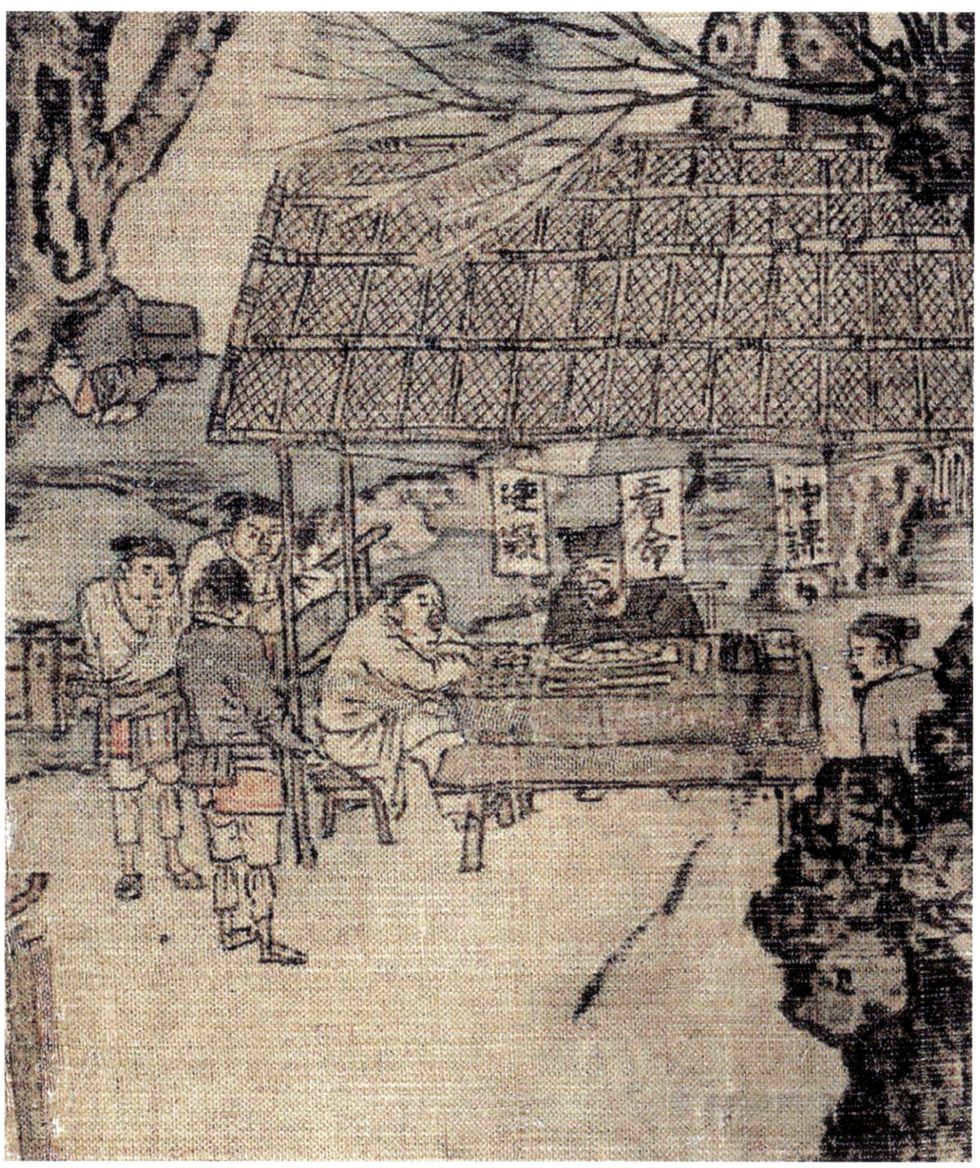

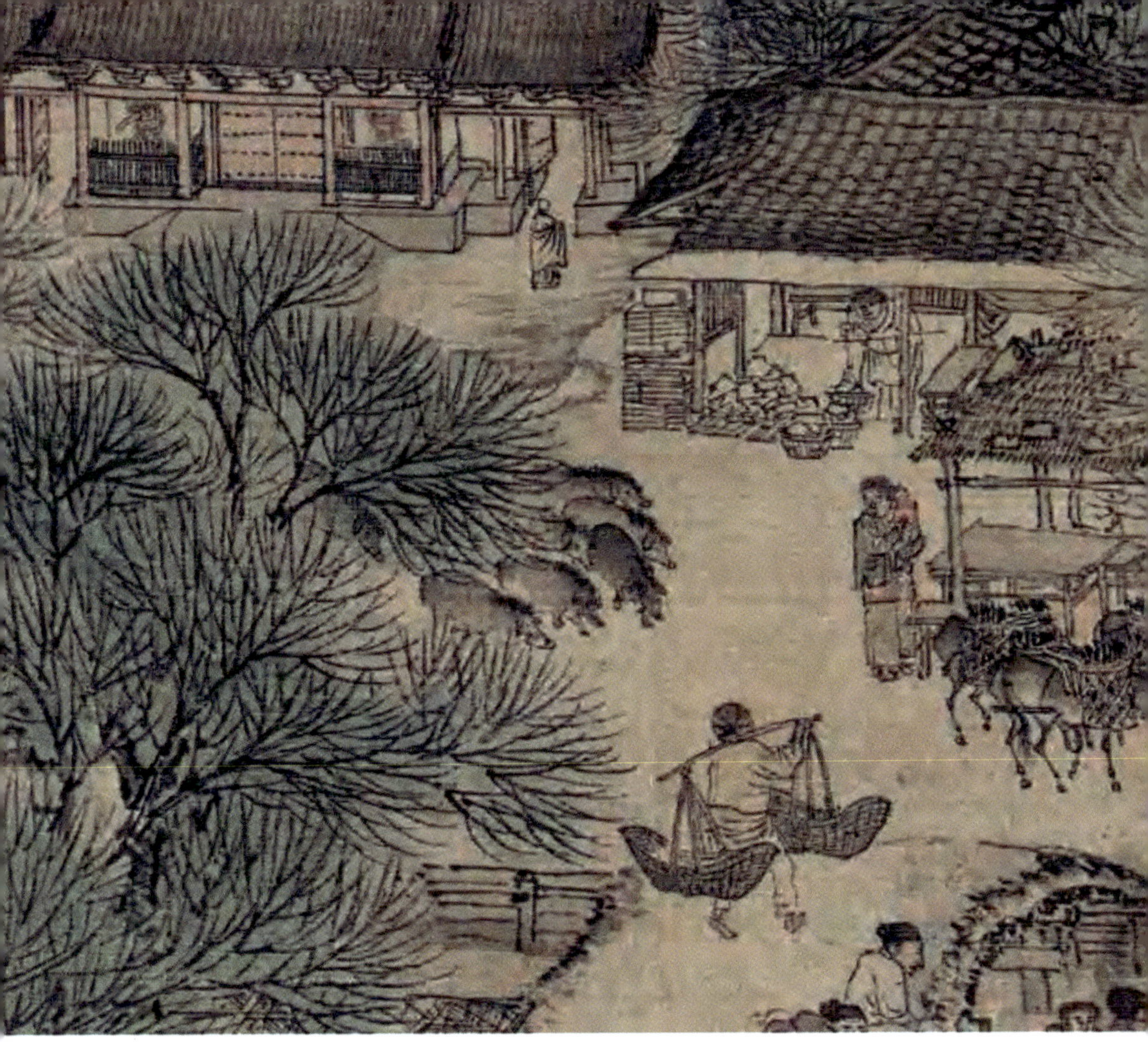

25. A temple in the distance and a sounder of wandering pigs

Leaving the main road and crossing a small bridge towards the back streets, a temple comes into view.

The temple seems quite desolate. Standing at the end of the bridge, we can find the main gate of the temple is tightly shut, with only the side doors on either side open. A monk is seen returning to the temple. Although the temple here appears quiet, in reality, the temples in Bianjing were not merely secluded places for spiritual cultivation as people might imagine. As recorded in *Dongjing Meng Hua Lu* (《东京梦华录》, *The Eastern Capital: A Dream of Splendor)*, 'during the Double Ninth Festival, two temples (Kaibao Temple and Renwang Temple) held lion dance performances'. All the monks sat atop the lions, performing rituals and preaching, attracting throngs of spectators. Ha! Preaching from atop a lion – how could that not draw attention? Another temple, Xiangguo Temple, opens to the public five times a month as a market. If we fancy kittens or puppies, we could head to Xiangguo Temple. Daily necessities, such as toiletries, are also sold at the temples, along with bows, arrows, books and paintings. Not only could commoners engage in trade, but, perhaps surprisingly, nuns from various temples would also come to sell embroidery, flowers, jewellery, hats and silk threads. Furthermore, dismissed officials sell their local specialties and aromatic medicines as well. ①

① *Dongjing Meng Hua Lu* (《东京梦华录》, *The Eastern Capital: A Dream of Splendor*), Volume III: 'Xiangguo Temple opens five times a month for people from all walks of life to trade. At the main gate, birds, cats, dogs, rare fowls, and exotic animals are sold. The second and third gates are filled with various daily necessities. In the courtyard, colorful tents, open-air stalls, and booths are set up, selling rush mats, bamboo mats, screens, toiletries, saddle mats, bows and swords, seasonal fruits, and dried meats. Near the Buddha Hall, one can find *Mi jian* (traditional Chinese medicine), brushes, and ink. The two corridors are occupied by nuns from various temples selling embroidery, collars, flowers, pearls and jades, headdresses, colored gold-threaded hats, special hair buns, triaras, and silk threads. In front of the Zisheng Gate behind the hall, there are books, antiques, paintings, as well as local specialties and aromatic medicines from dismissed officials. The rear corridor is filled with fortune-tellers, vendors, and portrait painters.'

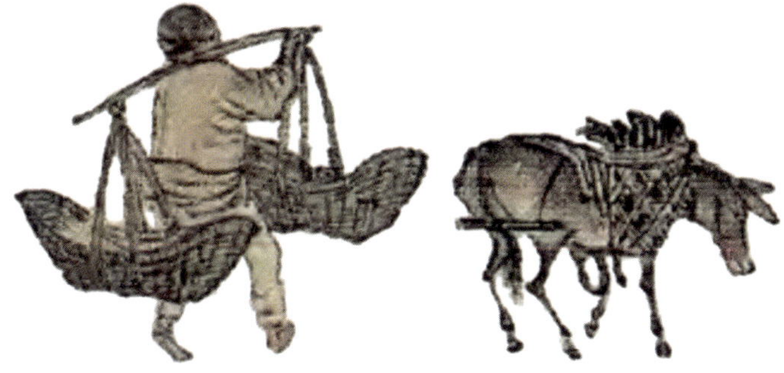

Zhang Zeduan paints lively daily life, yet imbues temples with a sense of desolation. This possibly reflects his Confucian ideology and mundane sentiments: 'if we are the people heading towards the temple with the shoulder pole, we would realistically be hindered by a sounder of pigs.' It remains uncertain whether the artist intentionally or coincidentally drew a sounder of pigs 'strolling' on this path.

Some might wonder how pigs could roam freely outside the city gates. However, these few pigs are nothing compared to what is recorded in the *Dongjing Meng Hua Lu* (《东京梦华录》, *The Eastern Capital: A Dream of Splendor*). It states that pigs are brought to the capital through the Nanxun Gate to be slaughtered, 'driven by merely a dozen people, tens of thousands of pigs would arrive every evening, yet none stray from the path'. Can you imagine the sight of tens of thousands of pigs obediently marching into the capital?

Once again, we see donkeys carrying charcoal, resting under the shade of trees. Their owner is nowhere in sight, and their charcoal has yet to be sold. Nearby, there's a shop where the shopkeeper is weighing something by a steelyard balance, with no customers present, so he is likely pre-packaging goods for sale. What kind of shop is this? Some speculate it might be a salt shop, though this is uncertain. What can be confirmed is that during the Song Dynasty, the government implemented a 'salt monopoly' policy, meaning that the government had a monopoly on the trade and distribution of salt, allowing it to be sold only under specific, limited conditions (here, trade mainly refers to merchants transporting and distributing salt on behalf of the government). The word *Que* (榷) originally meaning a single-log bridge, extends to the exclusive selling rights. As the ancients said, '*Que* is to monopolize its benefits to make them enter the government.'

We will discuss more about the salt trade in the Song Dynasty later on. For now, let's take a look at the mother and her son in this scene.

This mother is holding her baby, with one hand supporting its bottom and the other gently on its back, just like how mothers today cradle their infants. The child, nestled comfortably against his mother's shoulder with his little head pressed close, is also no different from babies today. The mother's right foot is in front, her left foot behind, as she turns her head to look at something. Following her gaze across the moat, we see the city gate of Bianjing (the capital of the Song Dynasty).

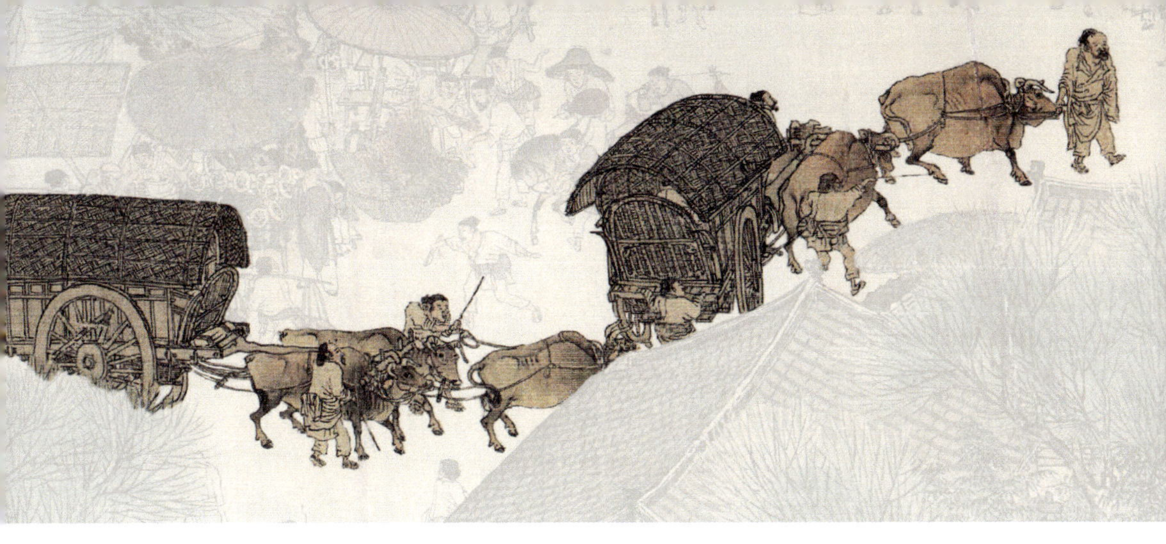

26. Three scenes at the end of the bridge: traffic, trade and digression

We now arrive at the end of the bridge, ready to enter the city.

Like the Rainbow Bridge, the bridge over the moat is also bustling and crowded. We will explore this scene in three categories: traffic, trade and digression. We'll start with the traffic situation.

Look, two ox-carts are about to leave the city. Compared to the opulent ox-carts at the crossroads, these two are much more modest, without cyan umbrellas or palm canopies. We can only imagine the awkward encounter that awaits, as these modest carts reach the small square in front of the government office, only to be dwarfed by their opulent counterparts. This will be even more embarrassing than the contrast between the lavish ox-carts and the sedan chair and donkeys, as both are using similar forms. It's a bit like wearing the same outfit, with one being a named brand and the other a knockoff. However, even the opulent ox-carts are not the most impressive. The *Dongjing Meng Hua Lu* (《东京梦华录》, *The Eastern Capital: A Dream of Splendor*) records several types of vehicles in Bianjing. One type is the *Tai ping* (太平) cart, which is 'pulled by more than twenty mules or donkeys in two lines, front and back, or by five to seven oxen'. We can imagine how large a cart pulled by over twenty donkeys or mules, or up to seven oxen, must be. Once it appears, the opulent ox-carts might only be considered 'toys' in terms of size. These super *Tai ping* carts, while capable of transporting numerous passengers, also face risks on steep downhill roads due to their heavy loads and potential difficulty in braking. For this reason, two donkeys or mules are tied behind to 'sit backward' as a form of 'braking system' when going downhill. There is also a smaller carriage similar to the *Taip ing* cart, called the '*Ping tou* (平头) cart', commonly used by inns to transport barrels of wine (which we will see later in the city). The carts used by women resemble *Ping tou* carts, but are modified with a cabin top for the comfort and privacy of the female passengers.

Having just discussed a few types of carts in Bianjing, let's now go back to the traffic situation at the end of the bridge. Alongside the ox carts, a small group of people and horses are returning to the city, at a fairly brisk pace. But a man carrying a shoulder pole blocks the way, so the groom is forcefully reining in his horse to slow it down. This horse behaves almost identically to that of the horse on the Rainbow Bridge. Let's compare the two horses – aren't they very similar? Of course, we can also play a game of 'spot the difference' with our family and friends to see if there are any dissimilarities between the two.

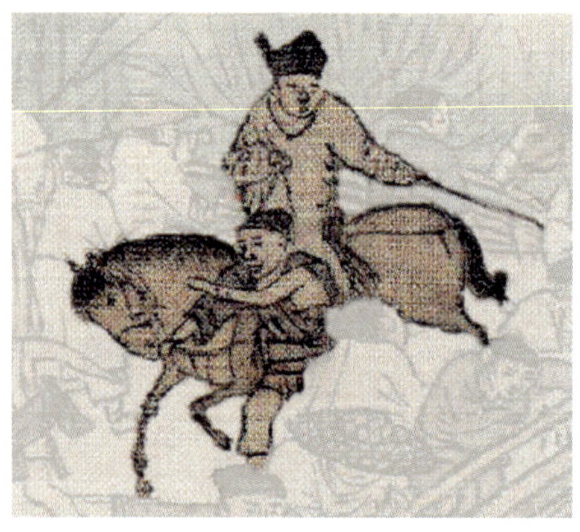

The horse on the Rainbow Bridge

Now, let's look at the man on horseback. He is wearing an angular hood (maybe with a 'braid' hanging down the back of his head), identical to the hood worn by the two men near the clothes-drying boat and behind the opulent carriage. Initially, the appearance of the first two individuals sparked curiosity about whether they might be the Jurchens, as some had speculated. This assumption, however, seems less probable now, as we glimpse the face beneath the hood, and he is quite handsome. This at least proves that the angular hood and the so-called 'braid' are not reliable indicators of Jurchen identity. The man also holds a fan in his hand. This is not the first time a fan appears in *Along the River During the Qingming Festival*, nor will it be the last. This time, we can clearly see that the fan appears to be wrapped in silk. Some speculate that perhaps the weather is still cold during the Qingming Festival and fans are not yet needed. However, carrying a fan is a custom in the Song Dynasty, for example, to 'shield themselves from dust'. Additionally, some have suggested a startling idea that what these individuals are holding are not fans at all, but fan-shaped objects – perhaps woven from branches and wrapped in cloth – used for ritual purposes. I question this view, especially considering the itinerant doctor who seems unlikely to be heading to the countryside for a ritual, yet also has a fan at his stall. How can you explain this? In any case, I still tend to believe that what they are holding are fans, as a part of their lifestyle, just as women nowadays carry bags when they go out. Moreover, their fans serve more than one purpose beyond 'shielding from dust'. What else you might ask? We will discuss that once we enter the city.

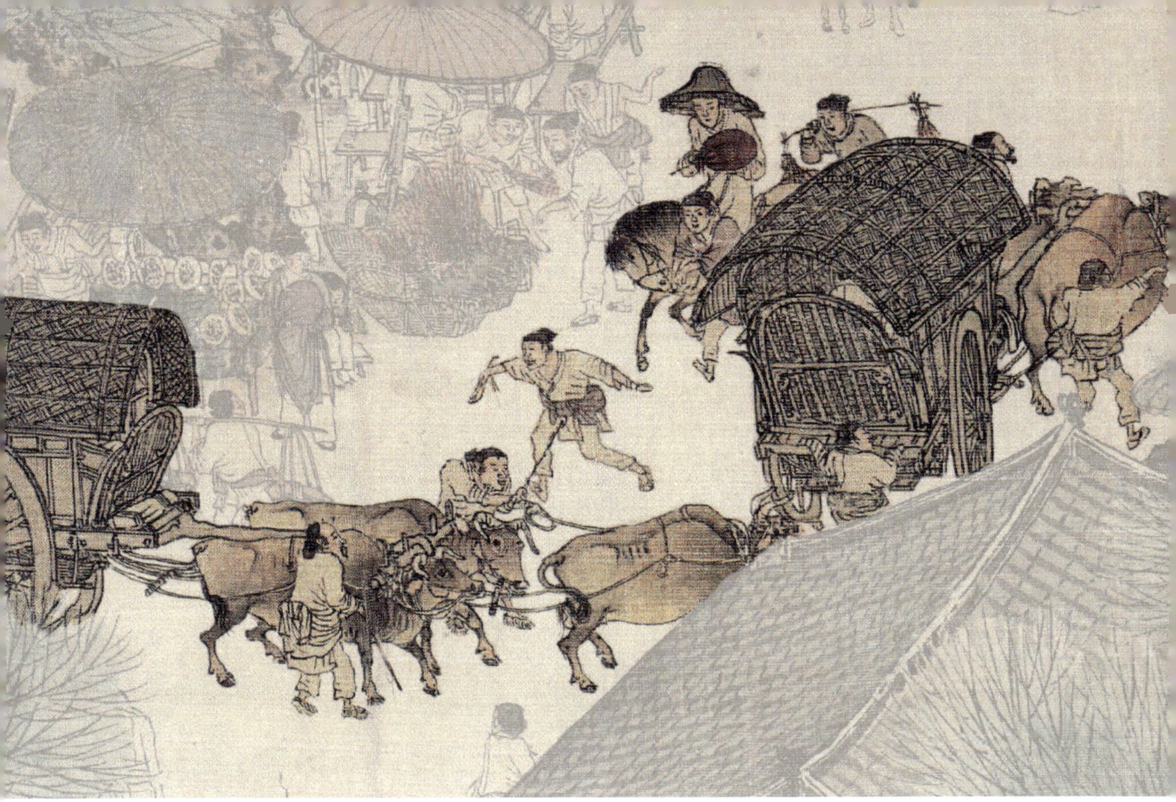

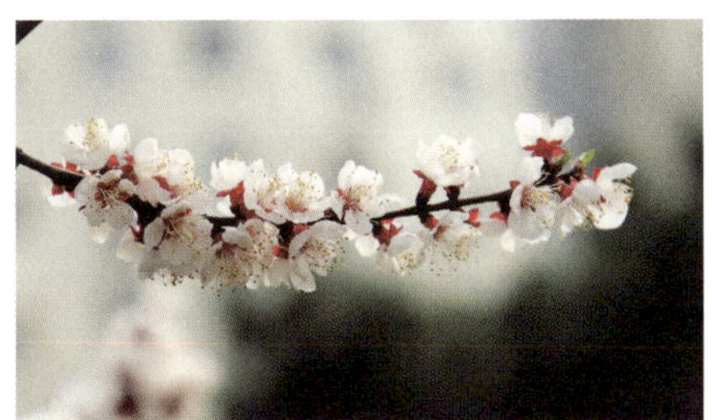

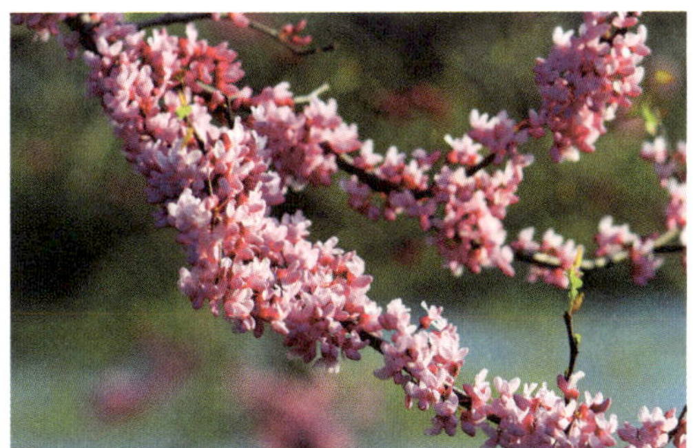

ABOVE: Apricot blossoms
RIGHT: Chinese redbud flowers

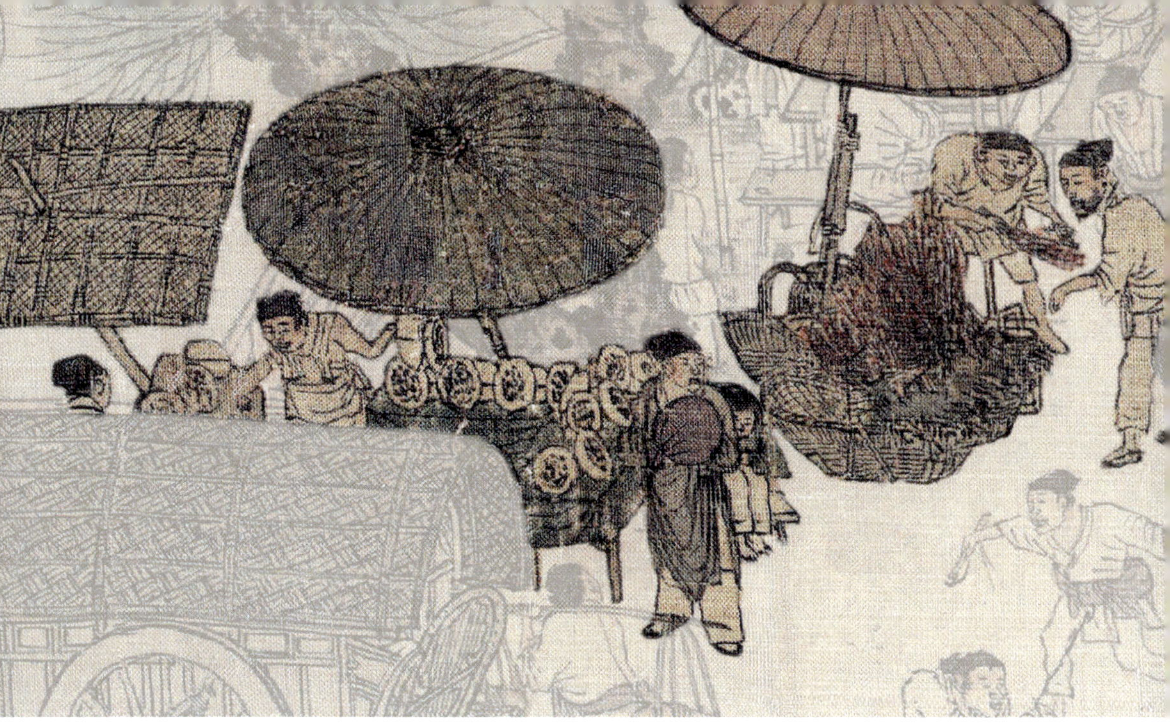

Let's see what intriguing businesses are happening at the bridge's end. At the top of this page, there are two stalls. One is selling flowers, and the vendor is recommending a bouquet to his customer. What kind of flowers are those? Some say they are apricot blossoms. Apricot blossoms are deeply intertwined with the Qingming Festival, as in the poems: 'All night I listen to the spring rain in the room, tomorrow morning deep in the alley they'll sell apricot flowers in bloom' (*Just Clearing up after a Spring Rain in Lin'an* by Lu You, in the Song Dynasty) or 'When I ask a shepherd boy where I can find a tavern, he points at a distant hamlet nestling amidst apricot blossoms' (*Qing Ming*, Du Mu in the Tang Dynasty). Others say they are Chinese redbud flowers or Cercis chinensis, which are 'deep purple and small... densely clustered, covering the branches in full... in full bloom by the end of March' (*Xiaoshan hua pu*, Qing Dynasty). Now, look at the customer – a bearded man! In fact, there was nothing unusual about men buying flowers in the Song Dynasty. The people in the Song Dynasty harboured an ardent love for flowers, a passion shared by people from all walks of life – men, women, the old, the young, the emperor and the common people alike. They didn't just place flowers in vases – they also wore them in their hair. In the fifth year of a Xining reign by Emperor Shenzong of the Song Dynasty (1072), in March, Su Shi wrote a particularly amusing poem: 'When an unabashed old man wears a flower hairpin, shame is not on him, but the

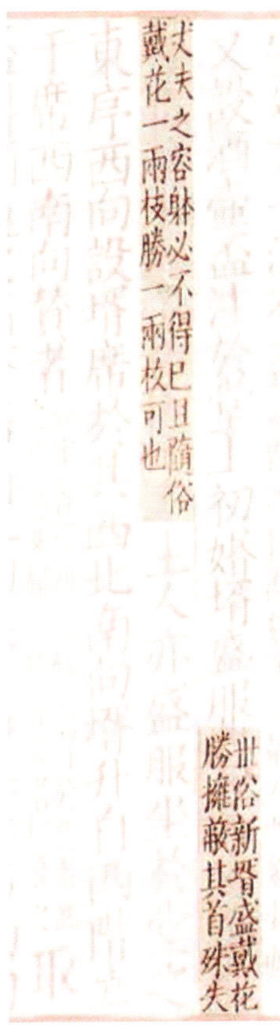
丈夫之容躰必不得已且隨俗
戴花一兩枝勝一兩枝可也
世俗新壻盛戴花
勝擁蔽其首殊失

Simashi Shuyi, by Sima Guang from the Nothern Song Dynasty (reprinted in red _Fang song_ font by _Jiangsu Shuju_ in the 7th year of the Tongzhi reign, 1868, during the Qing Dynasty)

flower-humiliatingly blushing. The passersby all laugh at me – staggering and drunken, miles along the street, behind windows half open' (*Admiring Peonies at Jixiang Temple*). That day he was quite drunk and people kept rolling up their pearl curtains to look at him, not just because of his drunken state but also because he was wearing flowers in his hair. He mocked himself, saying that he, an old man, was not ashamed to wear flowers, but the fresh flowers must be embarrassed to adorn his aged head. Interestingly, Su Shi was not even forty years old at that time. Yet, unlike today, where people often keep their age a secret, people in the Song Dynasty frequently referred to themselves as old. Regarding the custom of wearing flowers, not everyone was fond of it, with Sima Guang being a typical representative. As previously mentioned, he opposed women's sumo wrestling and he also disliked the practice of wearing flowers. However, wearing flowers was, after all, a widespread custom, so he couldn't completely reject it. In his book about family etiquette, *Simashi Shuyi* (《司马氏书仪》), he said, 'It is customary for grooms to wear an abundance of flowers and jewellery, covering their heads, completely altering the dignified appearance of a man. If it is unavoidable, then following the custom of wearing one or two flowers or ornaments is acceptable.' Isn't that interesting? Looking around, above the neck, all we could see were flowers and ornaments, hardly a face visible. Where is the manly appearance in this? Sima Guang was quite helpless, thus advising his family not to wear too many. His use of 'if it is absolutely necessary' and 'following the custom' just indicates how widespread and dominant the custom of wearing flowers was.

While it is fairly clear that the neighbouring stall is selling flowers, we just cannot be certain about what kind of flowers are being sold. However, it is not easy to say

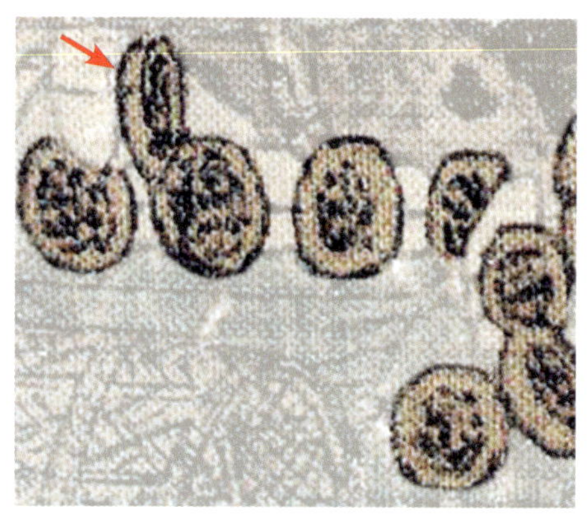

what the adjacent booth is selling either. Some say they are selling watermelons... of course, not whole ones, but cut into pieces, with watermelon seeds on the top. Such a view is truly ridiculous. In fact, although watermelons were already being cultivated in the Yan region of China during the Northern Song Dynasty, they had not yet spread to the Central Plains until after the Jin conquered both the Liao and Song. A large number of *Mengan Mouke* households ① migrated to the Central Plains, bringing watermelons with them. However, to determine whether they are selling watermelons or not, one need only observe the details – no argument is necessary.

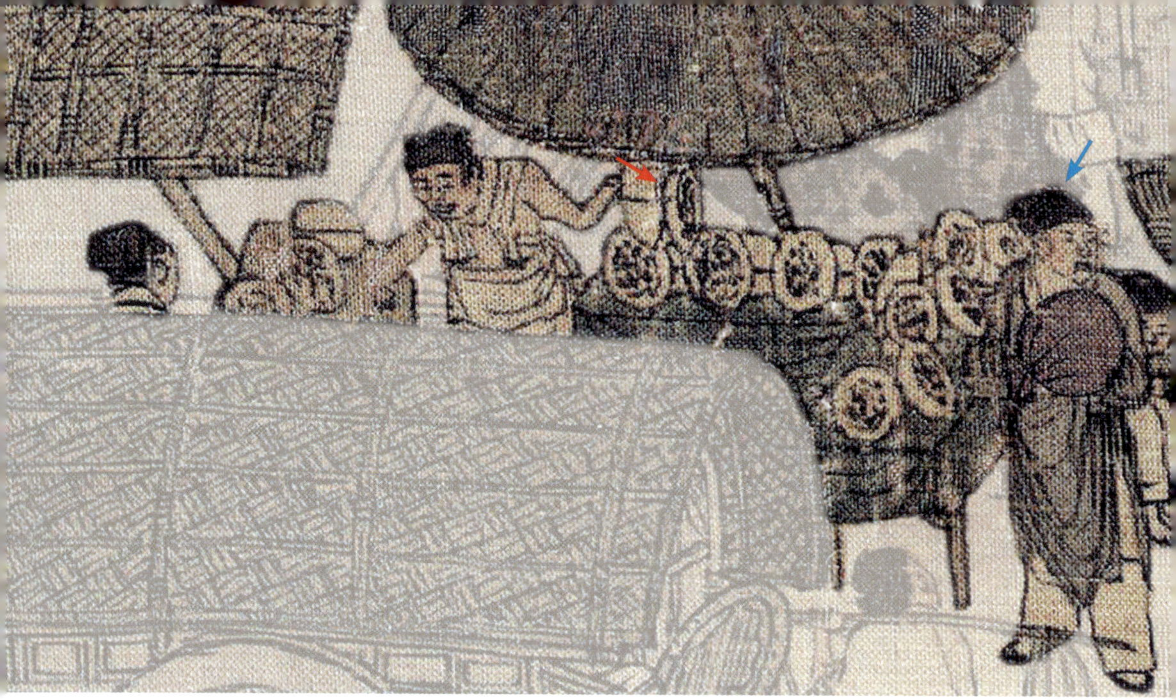

My dear readers, please look at the side view of the object (indicated by the red arrow). Who sells watermelons sliced like that? Take a closer look – they are round, slightly thick and the black spots on the surface look like scorch marks... Doesn't it look like some kind of cake? In *Dongjing Meng Hua Lu* (《东京梦华录》, *The Eastern Capital: A Dream of Splendor*): 'As for flatbreads, there are deep fried bread shops and *Hu* (胡) bread shops.'

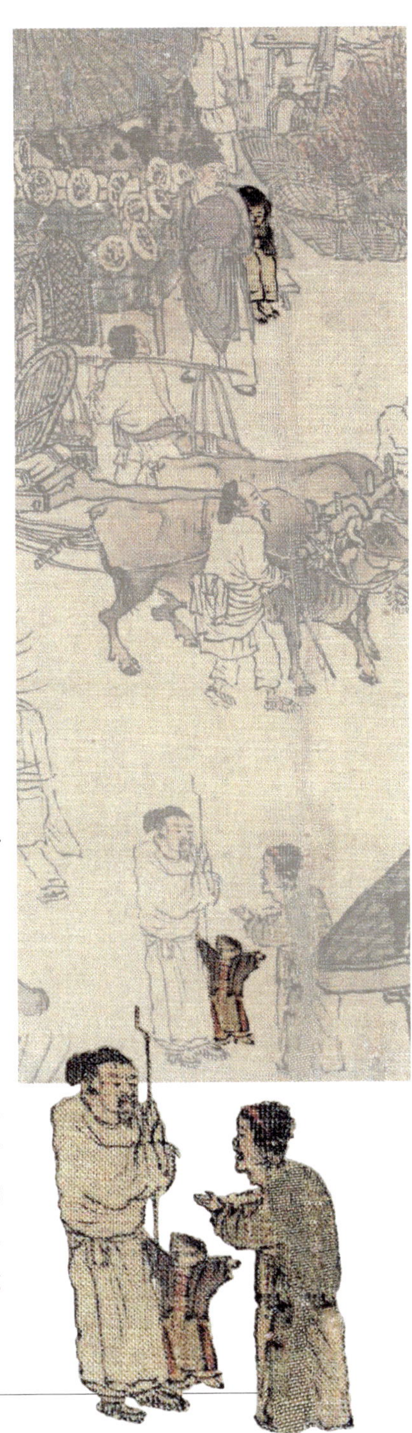

What is being sold here should be flat breads, similar to the *Nang* (馕) that can be eaten in Xinjiang today. *Nang*'s long shelf life makes it ideal for travellers. The vendor may have set up his stall outside the city gate with such consideration – people travelling far from the city would conveniently buy some *Nang*. Now, look at the vendor. Compared to the person indicated by the blue arrow, his outfit is much cooler. There also appears to be a fan to his right, presumably because he is baking cakes in the baking pit. But some people say these 'round cakes' are *Zao hu* (枣餬), made from dough and dates, but we will only mention it here briefly without going into detail.

① The Jurchen people of the Jin fell under the influence of *Mengan Mouke*, living separately from the civilian households, and were referred to as *Mengan Mouke* households.

In a quiet corner of the *Hu* bread stall, a young boy sits with his arms folded, his feet bare. He looks quite distressed as if he has been wronged. Could the vendor be his father? The boy might have been scolded for some reason and, in a fit of pique, has chosen to sit defiantly, refusing to help, while his father is busy attending to customers and has no time to address his son's sulking.

Whether intentional or not, Zhang Zeduan painted another, even younger, child seeking attention on the other side of the bridge, almost in a straight line with the first young boy. At that moment, an elderly man and an old woman were chatting, oblivious to the little child stretching out his arms, yearning to be embraced by his grandfather.

This subtle detail, as depicted by Zhang Zeduan, might hint at something deeper. Could this be a reflection of his own childhood – a stubborn child longing for affection? This reminds me of an anecdote from the childhood of Emperor Huizong of Song. On his way north after being captured, he was once very thirsty and asked someone to pick mulberries from the roadside. While eating, he told the minister Cao Xun, 'When I was a child, I saw my wet nurse eating these, so I took a few to eat. Just when I was enjoying them, she snatched them away. Today, as I eat mulberries again, misfortune strikes once more. Isn't it as if the mulberries have stayed with me through thick and thin?'① His words carried a mix of self-mockery, bitterness and a poignant sigh. The Song people's recollections of childhood events carry psychological details that resonate strongly with modern people, as well as the warmth of human nature expressed with genuine emotion. Such seemingly insignificant details in *Along the River During the Qingming Festival* are indeed worth savouring.

① In *Beishou jianwen lu* (《北狩见闻录》) by Cao Xun in the Song Dynasty.

27. Leisure on the bridge and beggars

As we step onto the bridge, the vibrant chaos of the Rainbow Bridge fades, replaced by an atmosphere of leisurely tranquillity. Look, an old man is riding a donkey out of the city and his attendant walks beside him, chatting away, but he appears self-content without saying any word in response. A small donkey, likely the foal, trails behind, its head lowered in apparent boredom as it blindly follows – a scene reminiscent of our own childhood, when we often trailed behind adults, compelled to match their pace. This simple scene carries no profound meanings nor offers grand insights. Life itself is often this way – a wordless tapestry of experience that we see, feel and intuitively understand.

Quite a few people stand by the railings on both sides of the bridge, gazing at the scenery and watching the fish swimming in the river. Can you see the fish in the river? The fish depicted by Zhang Zeduan in this painting are probably the most simplistic yet lively and interesting fish in the history of Chinese painting. Let us imagine what these five onlookers might be saying or thinking. A exclaimed, 'Look, there are fish!' B responded indifferently, 'Hmm...' showing little interest. He looked at the water but not

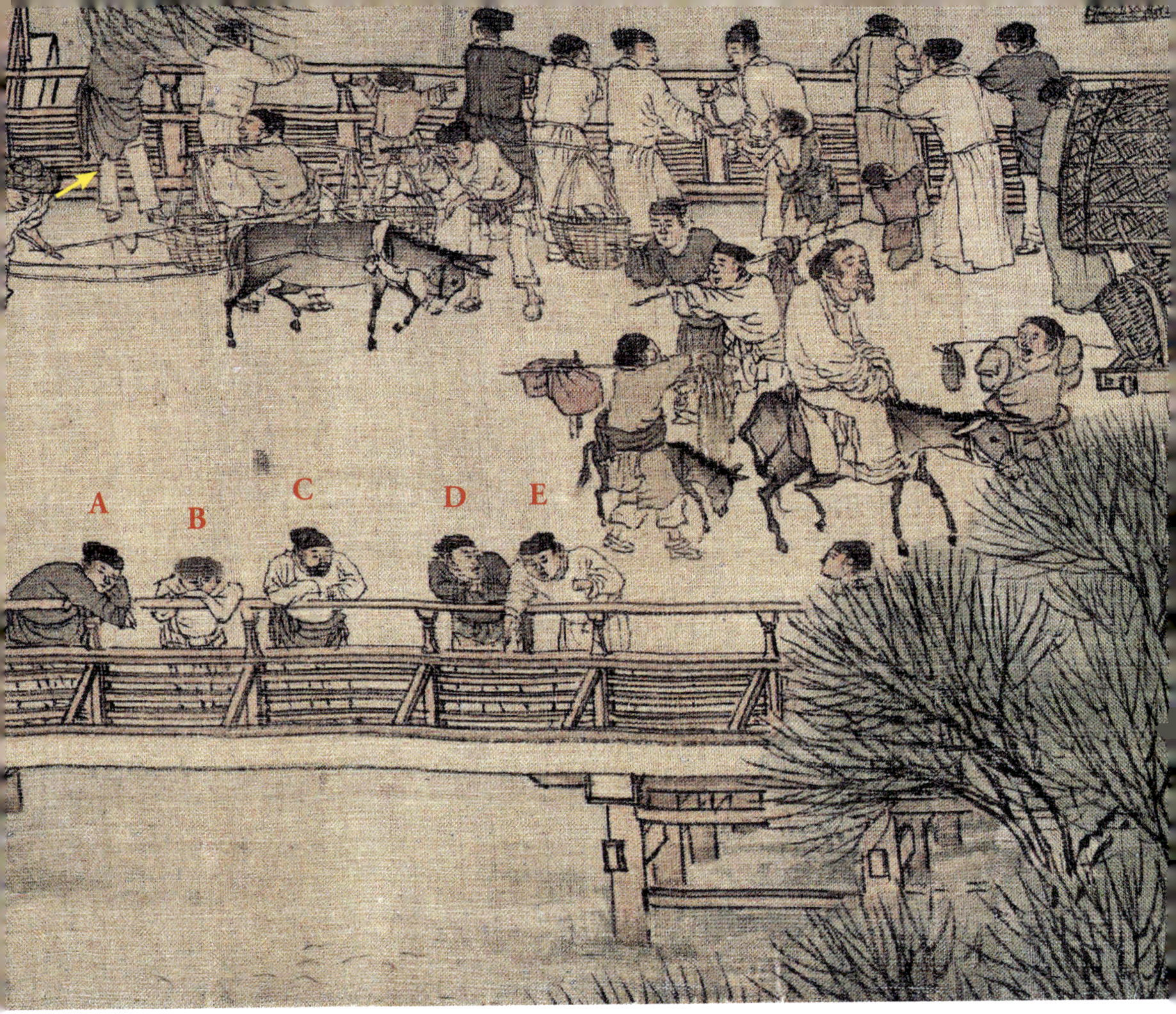

A
B
C
D
E

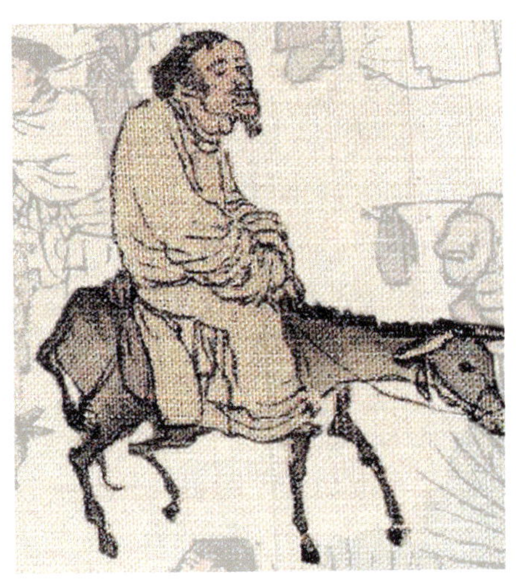

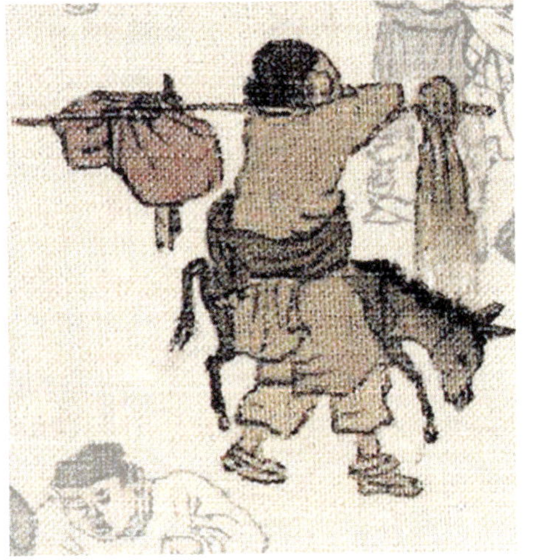

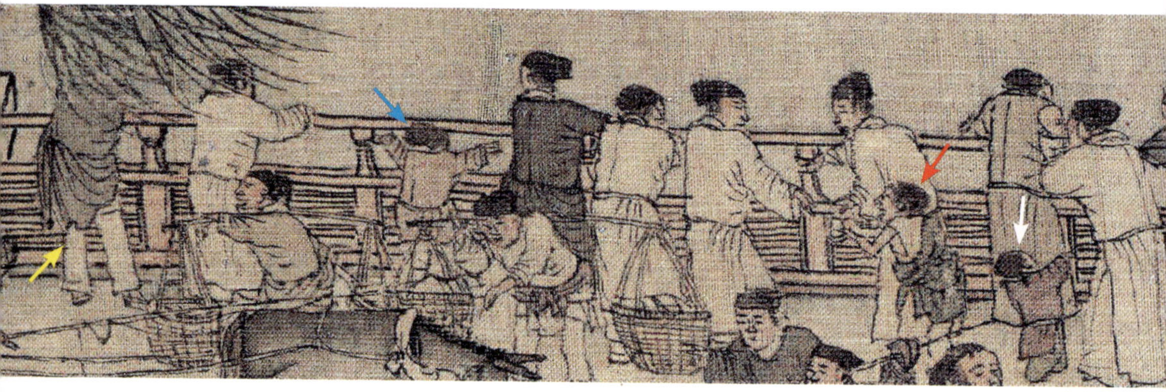

really at the fish, his grunt was barely a response to A. C doesn't look at anyone, neither at the water nor the fish, but thinking, 'Ah, the young men, always so youthful.' C is likely a middle-aged, chubby fellow from someone's family who has come to the bridge for a short break. E, with the loudest voice, pointed at the fish in the water and declared, 'Hey, look! There are six fish!' D teasingly countered, 'Seven, it's definitely seven.' E sputtered, his face turning red with indignation.

On the other side of the bridge, obscured by willow branches (indicated by the yellow arrow), stands a figure whose long garment, perhaps intentionally or accidentally, has hitched up and is tucked around his waist. Among the numerous characters in *Along the River During the Qingming Festival*, he is not eye-catching at all. And yet, once spotted, he draws our eyes with an inexplicable allure. Could it be admiration for his long legs? Perhaps the modern look of his trousers? Or maybe the artistic flair exuded by his casually lifted garment?

The figure indicated by the red arrow is generally believed to be a young beggar, hand outstretched in a plea for alms. Some argue that the one indicated by the white arrow might also be a beggar. Indeed, this is possible, as the 'child's' proportions appear unusual, resembling that of a dwarf. However, it's also conceivable that this is the child of the person in white. Given the child's height, he can't see the spring scenery that the adults are admiring, thus needing to be lifted up for a better view. Now, please take a look at the figure indicated by the blue arrow. Unlike the younger ones, he can appreciate the landscape all by himself.

When discussing the attitudes of the Song Dynasty towards beggars, *Dongjing Meng Hua Lu* (《东京梦华录》, *The Eastern Capital: A Dream of Splendor*) mentions that in the capital Bianjing, it was customary to treat beggars with respect and not to slight them, as disdain for them was frowned upon by society. ① This respect extended beyond common courtesy; the Song government enacted laws and established welfare institutions specifically to provide for the poor and destitute. ② For instance, during the winter of the second year of Xining era (1069) under the reign of Emperor Shenzong, a severe snowstorm struck Bianjing. Emperor Shenzong issued a decree instructing the official welfare institution, *Fu tian yuan*, to shelter the homeless beggars until the warmer spring. Later, under Emperor Huizong at the beginning of the Chongning era, institutions like *Ju yang yuan* (居养院) and *An ji fang* (安济房) were established, adopting even more favourable policies towards the destitute. Some prefectures and counties went overboard in their implementation, even hiring wet nurses and maids for the poor, leading to a situation where 'the poor were content while the rich were disturbed'. *Along the River During the Qingming Festival* depicts the street life of Bianjing during the Qingming festival, a time when the weather turns warmer. At this time, the government had ended its shelter and relief efforts, causing the beggars to reappear on the streets.

① *Dongjing Meng Hua Lu* (《东京梦华录》, *The Eastern Capital: A Dream of Splendor*), Volume V: 'As for treating beggars, there is also a code of conduct. Any slight negligence or disrespect towards them is not tolerated by the public.'

② *The History of Song*, Volume 178. *Treatise on Food and Money* (*Shi huo zhi,* 《食货志》): In the capital of the Song Dynasty, there were originally East and West *Fu tian yuan* (Welfare Institutes) that distributed public grain (*lin*, 廪) to the elderly, the sick, orphans and beggars. Initially, only twenty-four people received additional financial aid. Emperor Yingzong later decreed the establishment of additional South and North *Fu tian yuan*, along with the expansion in the East and West, to support daily distributions for three hundred people. Annually, five million units of internal treasury funds were allocated for these expenses, which was later increased to eight million through the profits generated in *Sizhou* (泗州). Furthermore, another edict stated that in cases of heavy rain or snow, local magistrates were to waive the rental fees for lodgings for up to three days, not to exceed nine days in a year. In the second year of the Xining era, during a particularly harsh winter, an edict was issued stating, 'Those who were old, young, ill or impoverished without support were to receive additional financial aid and shelter in the four *Fu tian yuan* until the warmer spring.' By the ninth year, Han Jiang, the administrator of Taiyuan, said, 'By law, the elderly and sick should be given rice and beans by the prefecture from the first day of November to the end of March of the following year. In Hedong, where the weather is colder, this support starts a month earlier and, depending on the surplus, possibly extends through March.' This proposal was accepted. Those widows, orphans, childless, the disabled elderly, the sick and disabled and the poor were housed either in their own homes, if available, or in government residences. Their living expenses were covered without a time limit. They were given rice and beans abided by the law for beggars; if it was insufficient, they were supplemented by standard welfare funds. In the early years of the Chongning era, under the administration of Cai Jing, *Ju yang yuan* and *An ji fang* were established, significantly increasing the rice allocation beyond the usual amount. Officials and soldiers were assigned as attendants, and kitchens were set up to provide food and drink. However, some local administrations went beyond what was necessary, even providing canopies and hiring wet nurses and maids, leading to unrestrained expenditure. Consequently, the poor were content while the rich were disturbed.

28. Two big mysteries at the city gate

All right, we've finally arrived at the city gate!

Although we've reached the city gate, let's not hurry inside. Beneath the gate, there are two intriguing details (indicated by the black and green arrows in the picture at the top of the opposite page). One of these has a relatively satisfactory explanation, while the other, to this day, I have yet to find a convincing interpretation.

Let's first look at the mystery that has been relatively well explained. We have encountered this earlier in the text – it is a single-wheeled cart (indicated by the black arrow) pulled by a donkey and a person in the front, and pushed by another person at the

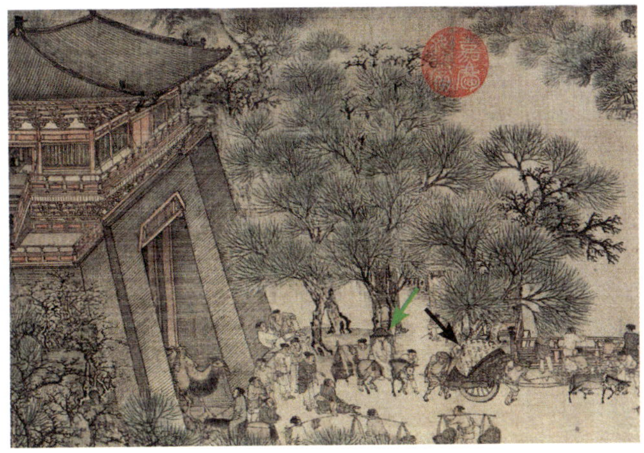

back. It is known as a 'single-wheeled tandem cart'. The goods on the cart appear to be very heavy, with the little donkey striving to move forward. Here comes the crucial part: the cart is covered with a tarp (*shan*, 苫布), upon which there are calligraphic inscriptions. This is quite unusual, isn't it? What could this be all about?

Generally speaking, ancient Chinese people were respectful and cherished written paper. However, there were exceptions. For example, during the reign of Emperor Shenzong of the Song Dynasty, there was a painter named Guo Xi. His painting style was imbued with a rustic charm and a concern for daily life, reflecting a humanitarian spirit. Emperor Shenzong highly praised Guo Xi. However, during the reign of Emperor Huizong, preferences had shifted, and Huizong did not favour his style. Consequently, painters in the imperial academy even used Guo Xi's silk landscape paintings as rags. Now, back to the tarp with inscriptions, could this also be related to the fluctuating fortunes of officials

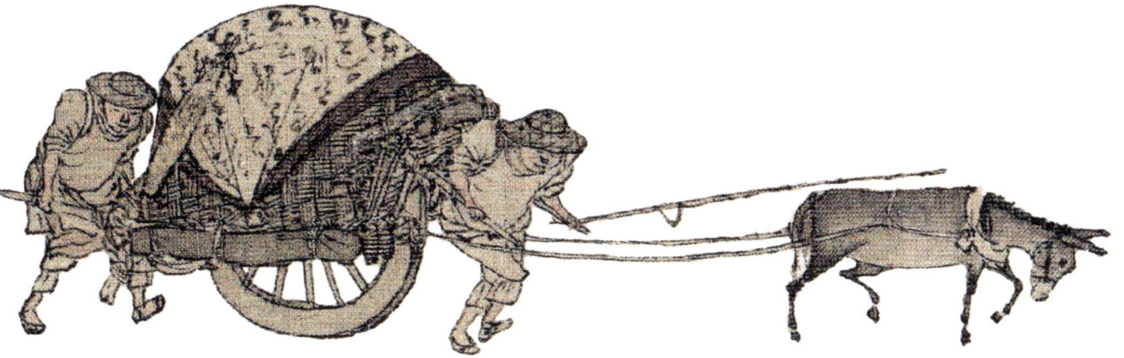

in the imperial court? It is generally believed so. The Northern Song was troubled by the 'New and Old Faction Strife' for many years, where one faction of officials advocated for reform and changes, while another favoured stability and conservatism. With the shifting power between these factions, those who fell from grace saw their works and belongings discarded. Thus, the inscribed tarp on the single-wheel tandem cart might subtly suggest that it covers books and other items belonging to an ousted official. Where are they taking these items? They might be hauling them to the outskirts to be burned. At this point, the seemingly inexplicable crises scattered throughout the scroll suddenly have a main thread, don't they? For example, the startled horse and broken willows at the beginning, the large boat under the Rainbow Bridge in the middle section, the lazy 'courier' we just saw, and various traffic problems, all express Zhang Zeduan's sense of crisis. Considering the geopolitical tensions – first with the Liao and later the destruction at the hands of the Jin – the international environment was fraught with danger, yet the imperial court was constantly engaged in internal strife and administrative neglect. The city management was also a mess. While people basked in the illusion of a 'peaceful and prosperous age', vigilant intellectuals like Zhang Zeduan could not help but feel deeply anxious.

Now, let's discuss the other mystery, for which I have yet to come across a satisfactory explanation. Let's begin by determining the gender of a character. Please look at the

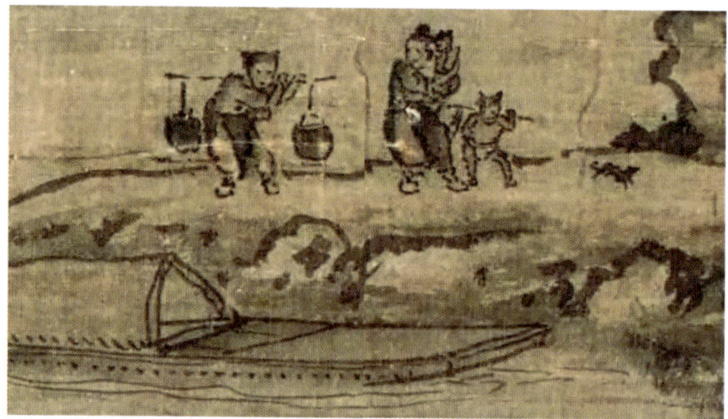

Part of *Early Spring* (《早春图》), by Guo Xi from the Northern Song Dynasty, in the collection of the National Palace Museum, Taipei

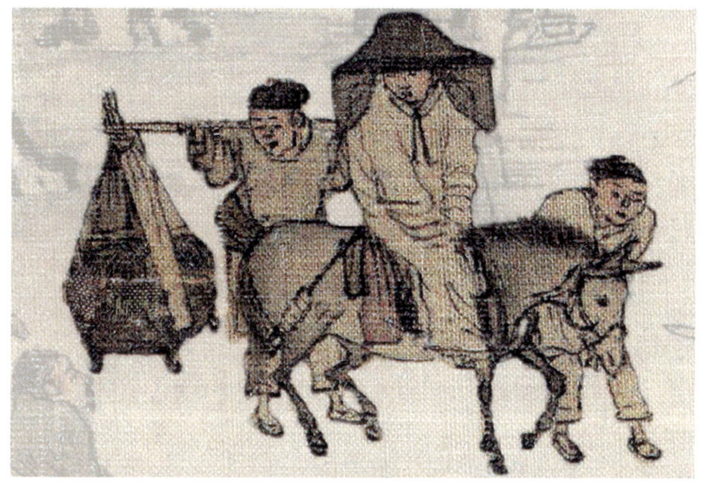

picture on this page, the person mounted on the animal – do you think it's a man or a woman? Some scholars refer to this figure as 'gentleman on horseback'. And many believe this person to be a male, but in fact, it is a woman. She is wearing a *Wei mao* (帷帽, veil hat), a broad-brimmed hat around which a curtain of fabric drapes down (either in the front and back or on both sides), typically to the shoulders. During the Song Dynasty, women would also ride donkeys or mules outdoors, but they generally wore a veil or a *Wei mao* to cover their faces. After all, riding donkeys or mules was not considered very dignified, so most noble women would travel by sedan chair. Now, let's take another closer look and examine what exactly this woman wearing a *Wei mao* is riding. Some say it's a donkey. That's incorrect. She is neither on a horse nor a donkey, but on a mule. If we compare the mule she is riding with the donkey ridden by the old man at the bridge – the differences are quite obvious, aren't they? So, how do you usually distinguish between donkeys, horses and mules? It's not too difficult. We can focus on their ears, mane, body and tails. A short-eared, long-maned animal is a horse, otherwise it's a donkey. A mule has a larger body than a donkey, and its mane stands upright, unlike a horse's mane, which hangs down. Some might ask, is it necessary to distinguish so clearly what they are riding? It is indeed crucial. In ancient times, what one rode represented different social statuses – for instance, scholars and hermits rode donkeys, while officials rode horses. It also carried cultural significance, such as Zhang Guolao, one of the Eight Immortals, rode a donkey,

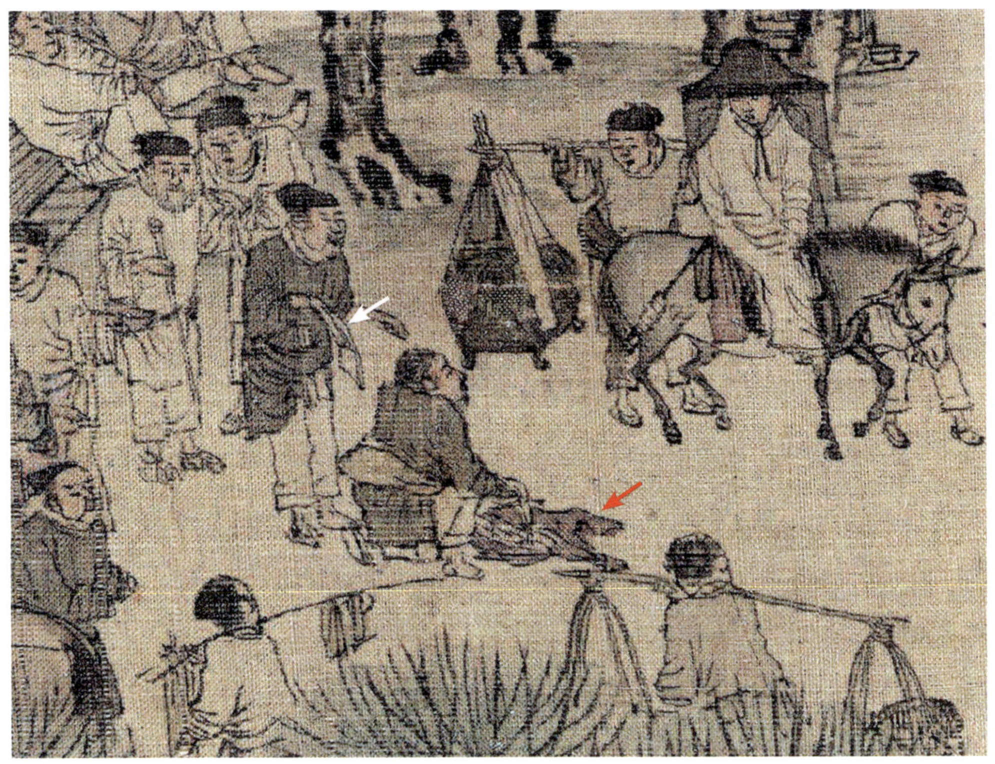

or Laozi, the first philosopher of Chinese Daoism, rode an ox. As for this woman, she might have no choice but to ride on a mule, though perhaps I am overthinking it.

At that moment, the woman was looking sideways at something on the ground. Please look at the red arrow in the picture at the top of the page. What do you think that is? Some say it is a slaughtered yellow sheep. They believe that the person kneeling on one knee before the sheep and the one beside him holding a prayer scroll (indicated by the white arrow), are worshipping the road god for the woman wearing *Wei mao*, praying for their friend's safe journey. I agree that it is a sheep, but the woman riding the mule appears to be just passing by; the relationship doesn't seem to be that of friends. It looks more like they are forcibly soliciting the woman on the mule, doesn't it? Of course, we cannot be certain of what exactly is happening. Another interpretation suggests that the person on

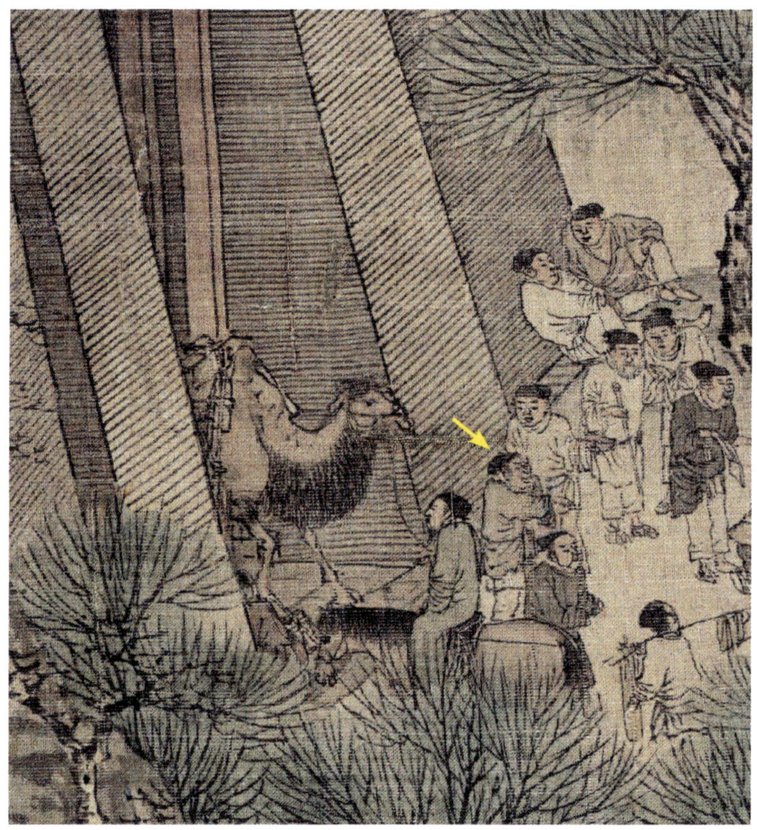

the ground is an old man, who is 'prostrating' and begging from passersby. The 'gentleman on horseback' passes by, merely glancing back without any intention of giving alms. This interpretation, however, is clearly flawed. For instance, it misidentifies a woman as a man, a mule as a horse, and describes 'kneeling on one knee' as 'prostrating'. They haven't carefully observed the image at all, so how can their viewpoint hold water?

All right, now we are about to enter the city.

Please look at the city entrance, where a camel is partially visible, half-emerging. The person leading the camel (indicated by the yellow arrow on the left) is pointing forwards with his right hand, seemingly shouting for people to make way. At the same time, a scholar on horseback is entering the city – he sits upright and elegantly, forming a stark contrast with the rugged appearance of the camel rider.

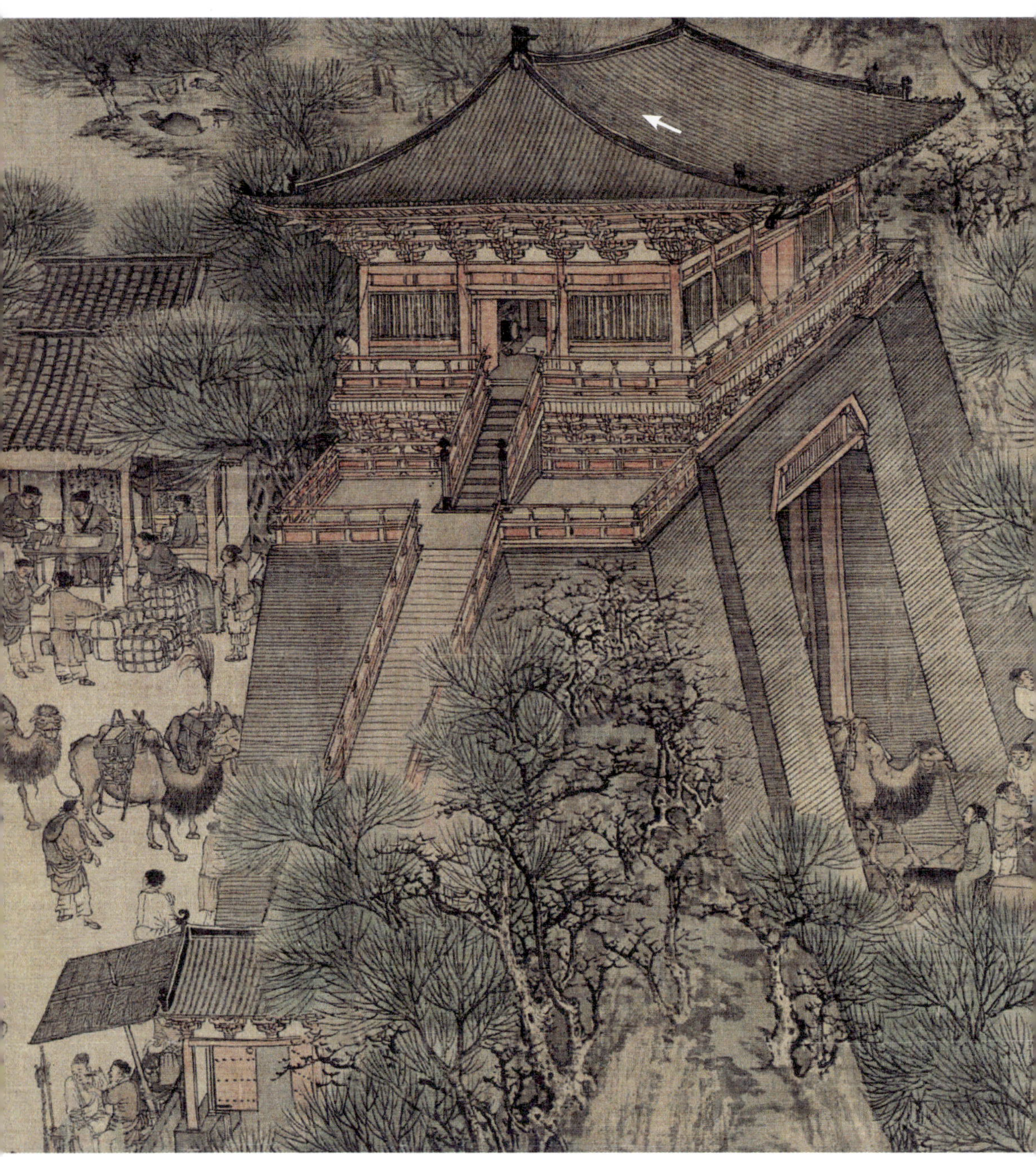

29. The great gate of the capital

Now, let's take a good look at the city gate.

Please look at the full view of the city gate (on the left page). What are your impressions? It's quite tall and grand, isn't it? Its wooden structure is also painted with red lacquer, making it look even more magnificent. For someone like me, if I were to stand in front of the city gate and look up at the gate tower, I would definitely feel a bit excited. The roof style of the gate tower is known as a 'single-eave *Wu dian* roof (庑殿顶, Chinese Hipped Roof)'. This term may be unfamiliar to most people, but it's not difficult to understand. A *Wu dian* roof is one of the traditional roof styles in ancient Chinese architecture, featuring a main ridge and four sloping ridges that create a four-sided slope, which is why it is also known as a five-ridge hall. The *Wu dian* roof can be either single- or double-eaved. A double-eave roof has an additional short eave added to each of the four corners under the upper roof layer, forming a second tier of eaves. With two layers of eaves stacked, it is known as a double-eave. The double-eave *Wu dian* roof represents the highest grade of ancient roof styles, with the single-eave following it. The components under the eaves (indicated by the white arrow on the left page) are called *Dougong* (斗拱). *Dougong* is a unique structural element in Chinese architecture: it is characterised by layers of interlocking bracket sets, formed by placing a large wooden block (*dou*) on a column to provide a base for the bow-shaped brackets (*gong*) which in turn support either the horizontal structural beam or another bracket above. What is the function of *Dougong*? It can transfer the weight of the eaves to the columns, allowing the eaves to extend outwards.

The artist has depicted the access stairway of the tower, guiding us on how to ascend to the gate tower. The 'stairway' is divided into two sections. The shorter section at the top, with one step per level, is called *Ta duo* (踏跺), or *Ta dao* (踏道) in the Song Dynasty. The longer section below is quite different: the steps are ridged like a washboard. So it is known as *Jiang Cha* (礓碴). Unlike the *Ta dao*, which is designed specifically for people to walk on, such an anti-slip ramp can facilitate the transportation of goods by wheeled carts and horses, hence it is also called a 'horse path'.

After examining the exterior of the city gate, some people might say, 'It looks quite normal. What other stories could there be?'

Is it necessary to inspect everyone entering or leaving the city? There is no need at all. Camel caravans are leaving the city and a person on horseback is entering the city. Everyone is free to come and go without being questioned. Some researchers have pointed out that the person leading the camel at the city gate is a *Hu* (胡人). Could the *Hu* come and go freely? One explanation is as follows: with generations of *Hu* merchants coming to do business, the images of camels and the *Hu* have become familiar to the Han Chinese in the Central Plains. Moreover, the *Hu* families who have lived in Bianjing since the Five Dynasties period have long assimilated into Central Plains culture. Not only do they consider themselves Han Chinese, but the surrounding Han people also recognise them as such. In this context, foreign merchants and envoys are no longer surprises to anyone anymore; it has become the norm. As we can see, the camel handler who must shout to remind people of his camel caravan, suggests that no one is even looking at them. However, the issue here is not about who is being inspected, but rather that there is no one assigned to check or guard the gate at all. The city gate, a critical defence point, especially during the tumultuous final years of the Northern Song Dynasty, when the dynasty was on the brink of collapse, is unguarded! How odd it is that there isn't even a gatekeeper! Of course, it's not accurate to say there is no one at all. Look up at the city tower where a man overlooks the bustling streets. He might be a night watchman, responsible for the big drum inside the tower (indicated by the white arrow in the picture on the right). Here, I want to draw your attention to another detail. Do you see the rectangular shape on the ground next to the big drum? That's a sleeping mat. To confirm our

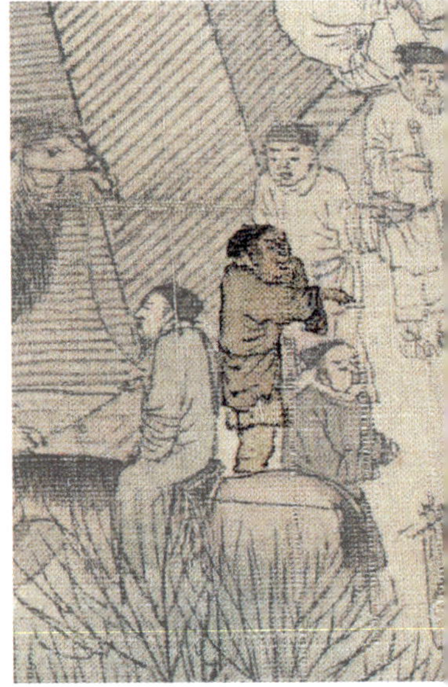

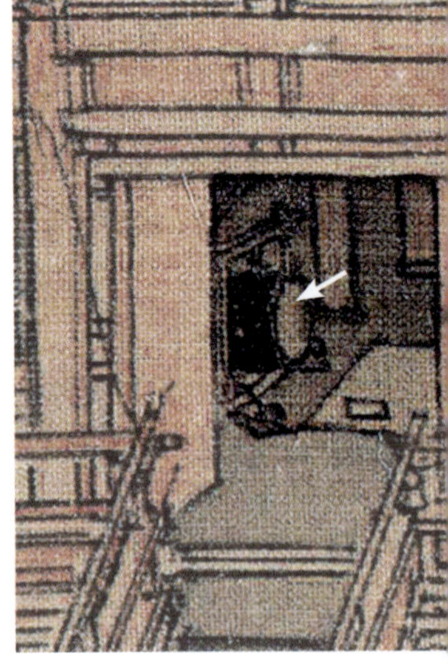

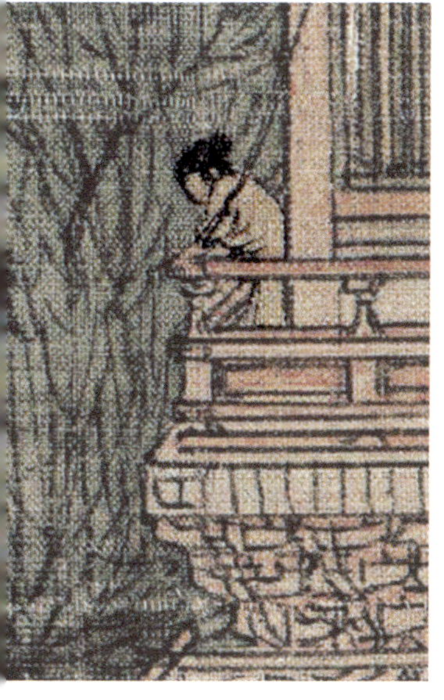

understanding, the artist has even drawn a small rectangle, which is a pillow. Since there is no one else in the gate tower, this watchman can lie down whenever he wants to rest and look around whenever he feels like it (what a pleasant job). The fact that he has his own sleeping mat spread out on the ground by the gate also indicates that few people come by. Staying alone and bored is, after all, a lonely experience. So, unable to bear the solitude any longer, he has leaned over the railing to watch the lively scene below.

Where there is a city gate, there must exist a city wall. So where is the city wall in this picture? If you noticed the city wall in the full view of the city gate on the previous page, you are excellent, as even some researchers overlook it. In fact, the city wall (indicated by the yellow arrow) is a rammed earth wall, overgrown with miscellaneous trees (which, judging by their age, the city wall has been in disrepair for quite some time). Besides, the wall is quite 'thin', so it's no wonder many people fail to recognise it (or rather, they didn't expect it to look this way). We might wonder why the capital's city wall wasn't built of brick, a material already in use since the Western Zhou Dynasty. By the Song Dynasty, brick walls were common, as seen in cities like Yangzhou, Guangzhou and Chengdu. However, the segment of the Bianjing city wall in *Along the River During the Qingming Festival* is still a rammed earth wall. Could such a seemingly fragile earthen wall withstand an enemy invasion? Clearly not. Thus, some scholars interpret this as a sign of weak city defences. Yet, others argue that this doesn't necessarily indicate a weakening of defences, because the wall depicted is

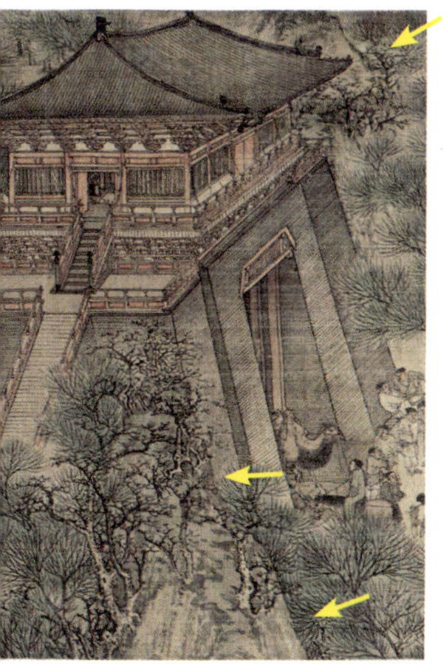

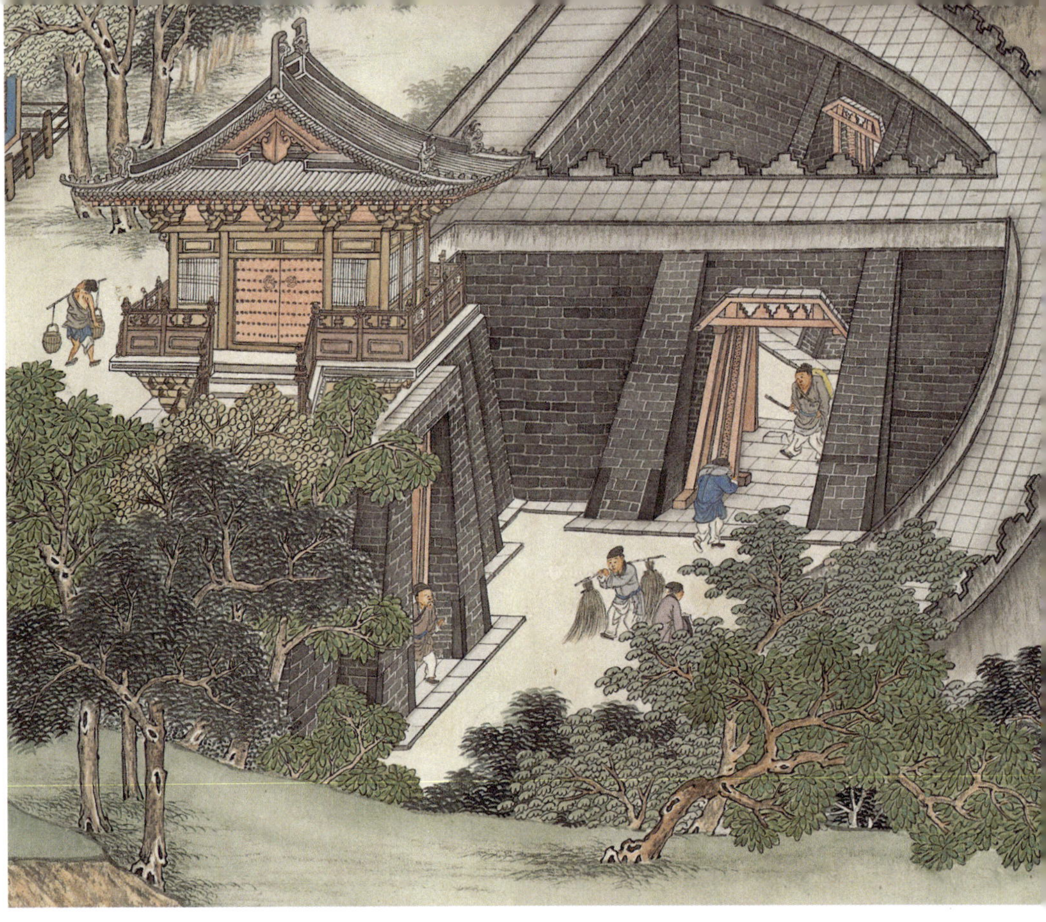

actually the inner-city wall, which no longer plays a significant role in military defence. This might explain why it is 'allowed to remain low and overgrown with miscellaneous trees'. Records in the *Dongjing Meng Hua Lu* (《东京梦华录》, *The Eastern Capital: A Dream of Splendor*) describe a much more formidable outer city wall. It was more than 40 *li* (里, 20km) in circumference, and the moat was over 10 *zhang* (丈, 33m) wide, with willows planted on both sides of the river banks, and pedestrians were prohibited from walking along the banks. Moreover, the construction and maintenance of the outer city wall were highly focused on defence and actual combat. For example, on the outer city wall, *Ma mian* (马面, Chinese bastion) were set up every hundred steps. It's hard for us to imagine – a protruding platform built along the city wall, on which a bastion could be quickly built. It is named for its narrow façade and long shape similar to a horse's head. Should the enemy attack, they would not only face direct assault but also crossfire from both sides. *Ma mian* was set up every hundred steps,

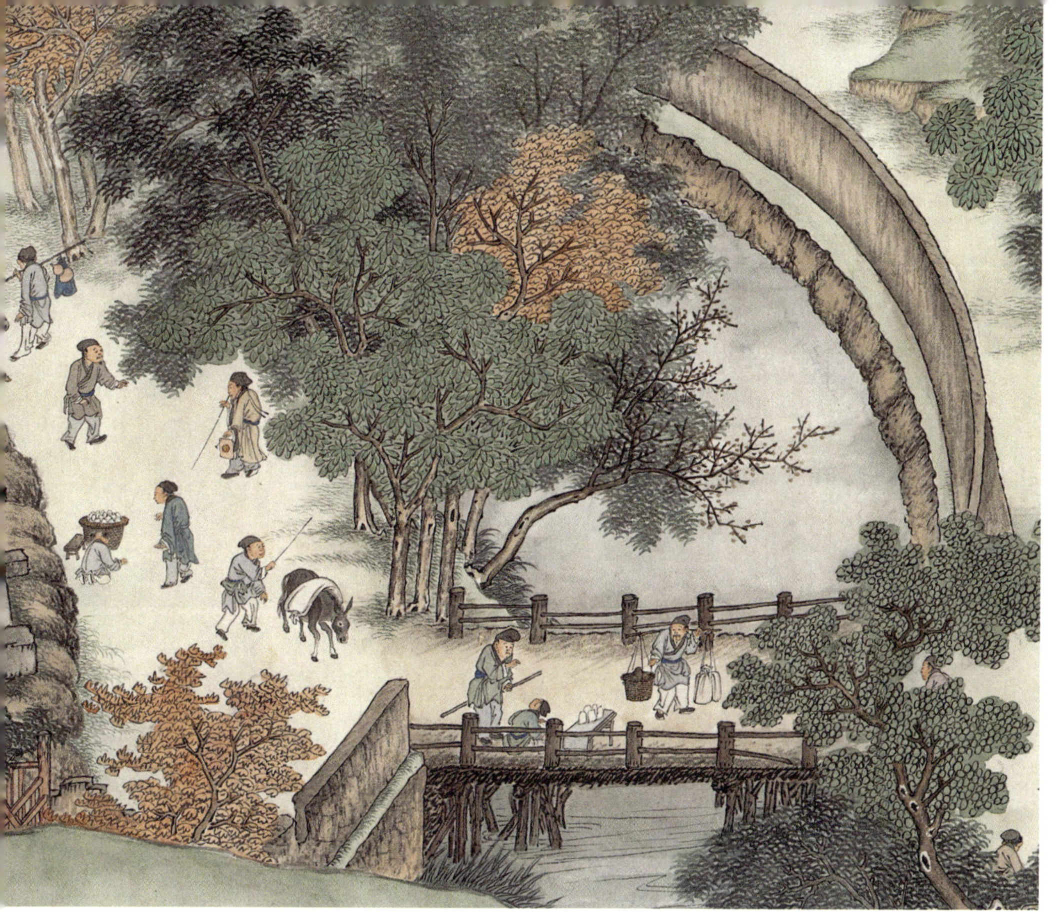

ABOVE: Part of *An Era in Jinling* by Xie Sui from the Qing Dynasty, in the collection of the National Palace Museum, Taipei

and armories were set up every two hundred steps. In addition, ten thousand combat engineers were responsible for the daily maintenance of the city wall ①. Such city wall and its maintenance measures are obviously different from those depicted in *Along the River During the Qingming Festival*. As for the gates, the records in the *Dongjing Meng Hua Lu* (《东京梦华录》, *The Eastern Capital: A Dream of Splendor*) are also very different: While the four main gates, such as the Nanxun Gate, were 'straight gates' with a double-layered design, all other city gates featured outer barbicans and a triple-layered construction for enhanced security ②. What does a barbican look like? To illustrate this, I've included a picture of a Song Dynasty barbican from Nanjing (formerly known as Jinling) for your reference ③.

① The original text reads: 'Every hundred steps along the new city wall, a *Ma mian* was built. The protruding parts on the city wall, from which the enemy can be attacked from both sides. This fortification made attacking a daunting illusion. Additionally, the wall was densely fitted with crenellations (merlons). Maintained and repaired day and evening, it presented an imposing sight. In the city, elm and willow trees were planted along the *Ya dao* (牙道, an official road). Every two hundred steps, a defensive arsenal was placed to store weapons. Ten thousand combat engineers from the *Guang gu* (广固, a type of combat engineer troop) were responsible for daily maintenance and mud plastering of the city walls, with a special commander from the capital overseeing their work.' In the Song Dynasty, the military system was organised from large to small into *Xiang* (厢), *Jun* (军), *Zhi hui* (指挥) and *Du* (都). Each *Du* consisted of a hundred men, and five *Du* formed one *Zhi hui*. A *Zhi hui* was led by a commander and one or two deputy commanders. So, twenty *Zhi hui* mentioned here would thus comprise ten thousand soldiers.

② The original text reads: 'All city gates were constructed as triple-layered barbicans with staggered openings, where the gates on both sides of the outer city gate were not aligned directly. Only the Nanxun Gate, Xinzheng Gate, Xinsong Gate and Fengqiu Gate were designed as straight, double-layered gates. These were the four main gates, all reserved for imperial passageways.'

③ This picture was originally from the Song Dynasty court painting '*An Era in Jinling* (《金陵图》)', which was later recreated by Xie Sui in the fifty-second year of the Qianlong era (1787) during the Qing Dynasty. A barbican is an important defence facility in ancient times. The barbican in the picture is semi-circular, with a straight wall vertically dividing it in the middle. To enter the city, one would first pass through the gate on one side of the outer circle, then a gate in the middle straight wall to the other side, and finally enter the city through the front city gate. This is the 'staggered opening' described in the *Dongjing Meng Hua Lu* (《东京梦华录》, *The Eastern Capital: A Dream of Splendor*).

Then, is it still possible that the city gate and city wall in *Along the River During the Qingming Festival* actually indicate weak city defences? Or are they reasonable given the circumstances? I prefer the former illustration. Why? Because the realism in *Along the River During the Qingming Festival* is literary in nature, which means that the details he paints are factual, what is chosen is selective. Just as he ostensibly painted a journey from the outskirts to the city, but the sequence and details were meticulously crafted. As a result, the key images take on symbolic meaning, for example, the plaque on the city gate. Zhang Zeduan makes us see the character '門 (*Men*, gate)', but intentionally omits its specific name. This is a literary skill: What he painted was not any gate of Bianjing, but rather a gate of the prosperous Song Dynasty, both real and fictional. The contrast between the lofty, splendid gate and the low, dilapidated city walls carries a certain symbolic meaning. As for those who hope to determine exactly which gate this is (with theories such as Dongjiaozi Gate, Shangshan Gate and Xinzheng Gate), it should be viewed separately. While seeking historical knowledge from the painting is important, one should also be cautious not to over-emphasise factual verification at the expense of intuitive understanding and emotional interpretation. Otherwise, it will make vain efforts and miss the essence.

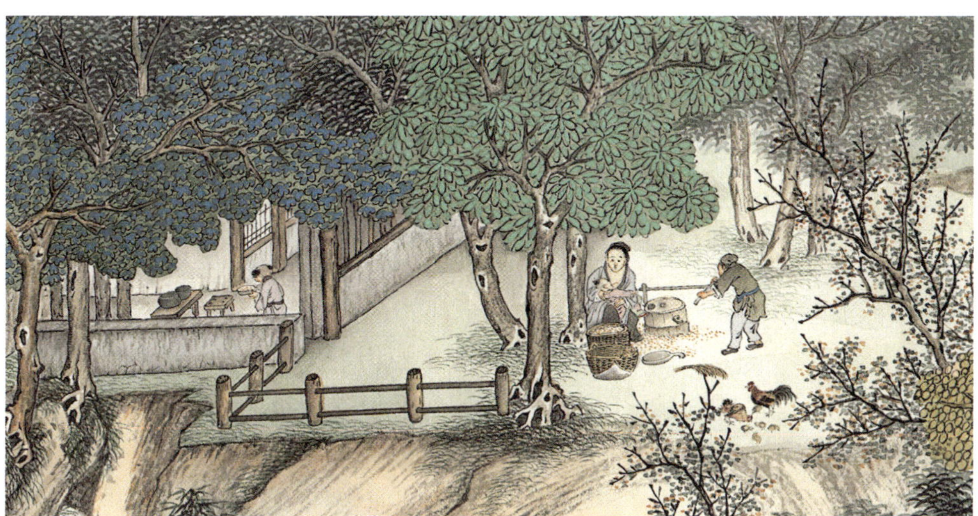

30. The scale, sugarcane and razor

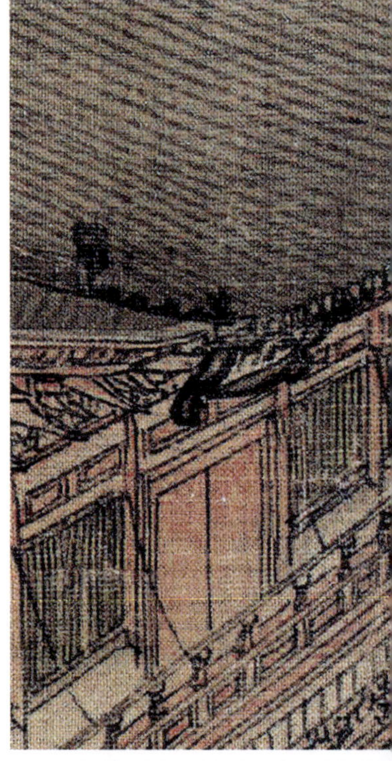

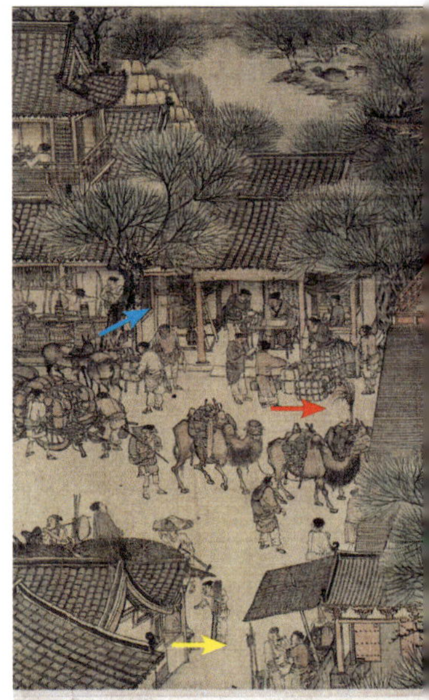

Now, we find ourselves inside the city.

Immediately upon entering the city, three objects are sure to pique our interest. Allow me to weave them together for you.

Please look at the spot pointed out by the yellow arrow in the picture bottom right (detailed opposite). There, we will find a simple stall made of bamboo mat, supported by a thick wooden pole with its sharpened end piercing through the centre of the mat. Two people are sitting under it. One person, in his long robe with his chest exposed, turns his face sideways to be shaved. A makeshift barbershop! The barber, with his left hand gently cradling the customer's chin, wields a razor in his right hand, skilfully shaving his customer. The barber's right pinky finger slightly raised in a somewhat affected pose, isn't that quaintly charming?

In the Song Dynasty, barbers were known as *Dao nie gong* (刀镊工), or simply *Nie gong* (镊工). They earned a modest living by providing haircuts and shaves. Some of them, who were astute, had opportunities to enter wealthy households and interact with rich young masters. As a result, they would often engage in other businesses, such as brokering a trade or selling flowers and paintings. These barbers had a special name at that time, called *She'er* (涉儿), which probably meant cross-disciplinary or engaging in multiple fields.

At the barber's stall, there are two more details. Please look at the spot indicated by the white arrow in the picture opposite. A thin wooden stick supports the corner of a square mat, and something is hanging from the top. Can you guess what it is? Some people say it's a braid. That makes sense, as it would serve as a physical advertisement. As for the other detail, please pay attention to the barber stall's location – it's right at the entrance to the city wall. We can see that half the gate is open, unguarded, suggesting that anyone can go up there. Well, let's not talk about its weak city defences and such. If it were today, someone would definitely charge an entrance fee at the gate!

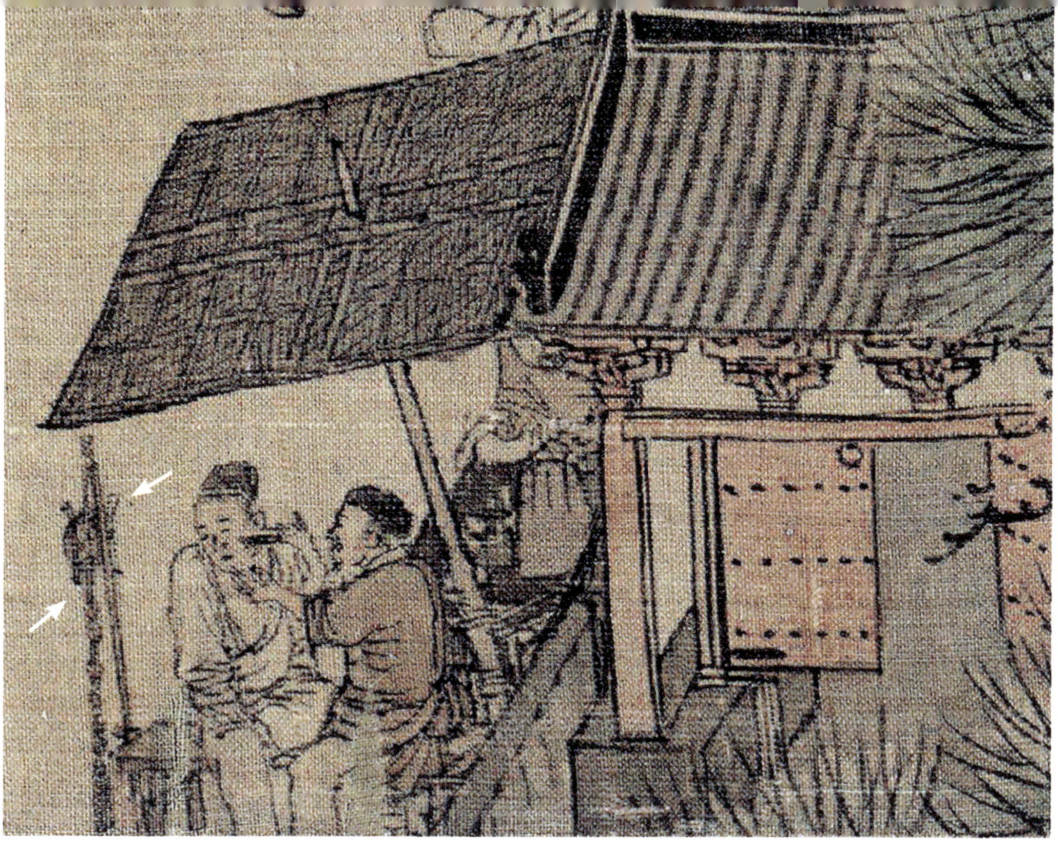

Having discussed the razor, let's move on to another item: sugarcane.

Walking through the city gate, we'll brush past camels. Just outside the gate, we would notice something inserted into the saddle on the side of a camel (indicated by the red arrow in the picture on the right). It is long, its tassels – or perhaps leaves – fluttering conspicuously, making it quite eye-catching. However, it's rarely mentioned what exactly

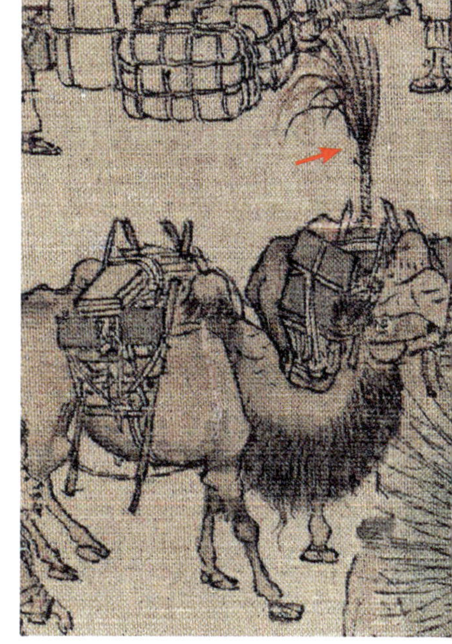

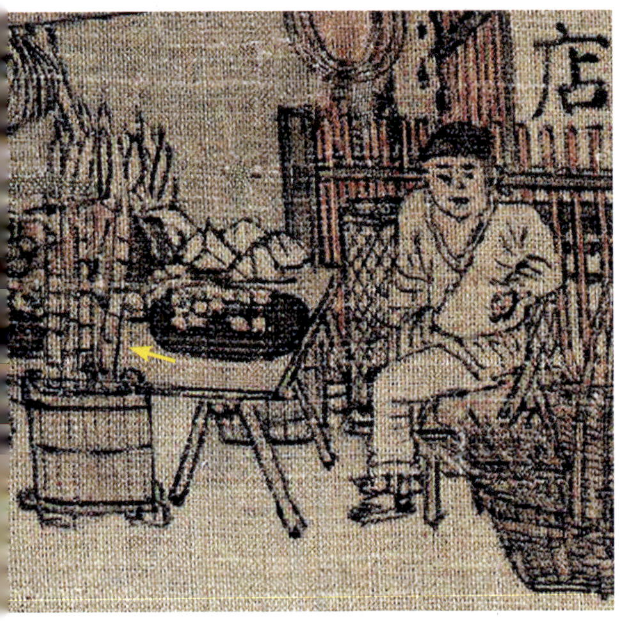

this is, probably because no one knows it. It could be a stalk of sugarcane ①; the conspicuous 'tassels' are actually its leaves. Sugarcane appears twice in *Along the River During the Qingming Festival*. Another one is in front of the *Sun Yang Zheng Dian* (a licenced tavern), which we will see later. Several stalks of sugarcane with their leaves stripped off are neatly placed in a wooden bucket (indicated by the yellow arrow in the picture on the left). The stall owner, originally facing his sugarcane, turns his head at that moment, with his body facing the street, giving the impression of facing the 'camera'.

① Some people believe that it is not sugarcane, but rather a *Jing jie* (旌节). A *Jing jie* is an emblem or banner that envoys carried as a symbol of their authority and mission in ancient times. The camel caravan of the *Hu* envoys is leaving the city to go back to the north.

Then, we ask, was sugarcane available during the Northern Song Dynasty? Yes, it was. Kou Zongshi, a pharmacologist of the Northern Song Dynasty, recorded in his *Bencao Yanyi* (《本草衍义》) that 'Sugarcane is found today in Sichuan, Guangdong, northern Hunan, Zhejiang, Jiangsu and Jiangxi'. This indicates that although sugarcane was not grown north of the *Yangtze* River during the Northern Song period, it could be transported to Bianjing from the south. As previously mentioned, the climate entered a 'Little Ice Age' towards the end of the Northern Song Dynasty, which would prolong the growth cycle of sugarcane. Thus, sugarcane planted in the autumn would be ready for sale just in time for the Qingming Festival.

Now, let's look at the third one. This is the first shop encountered in the city, but it's

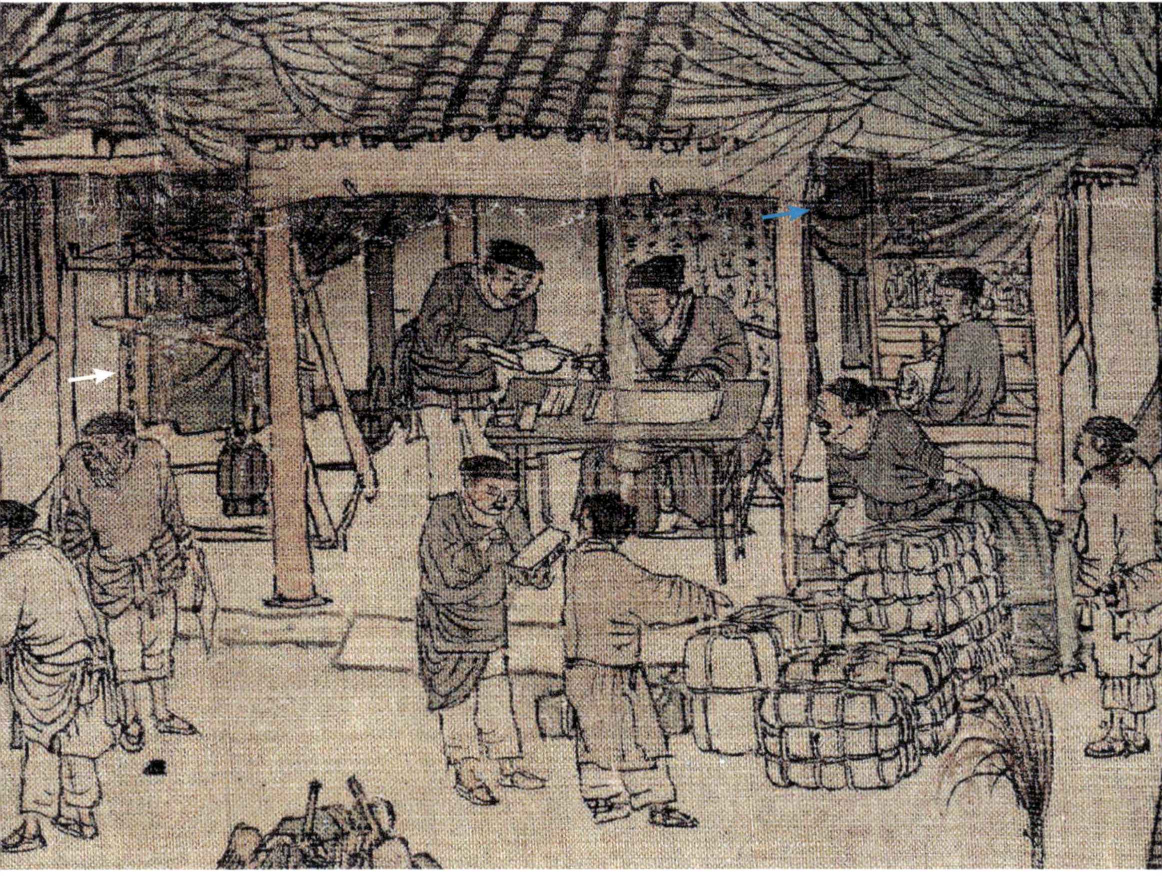

not selling goods. Some scholars believe that this is a government institution – a tax office. That's a bit ironic, isn't it? While the city's defences may be lax, tax collection certainly isn't. The man sitting behind the desk on the chair is likely the tax officer. His subordinates are busy with their tasks – some reporting, others filing documents, registering details, or supervising the loading of goods. The 'large rack' (indicated by the white arrow) is probably a large scale used for weighing goods. The bundles, bound with rope and showing clear indentations, appear to be soft textiles. During the Northern Song Dynasty, textiles were taxed heavily, which also caused the deepest resentment among the people. The man (indicated by the blue arrow) has his mouth wide open, and is likely shocked by the high amount of tax being levied.

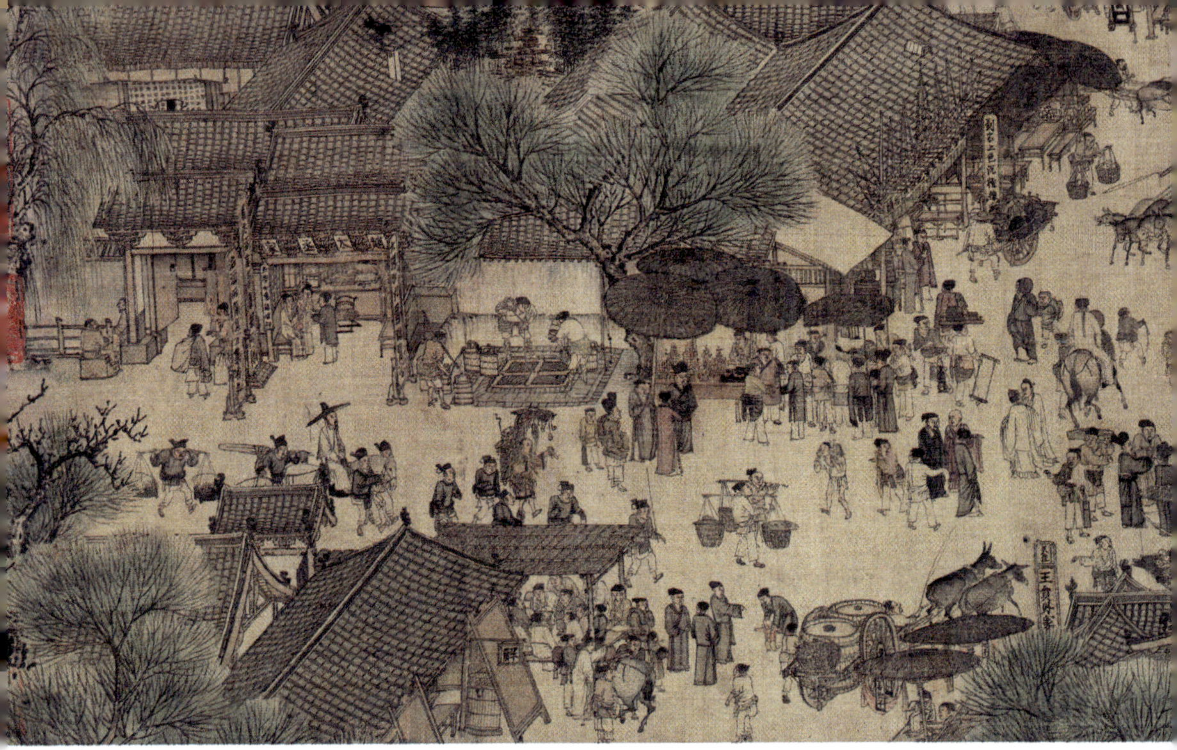

31. The grand *Sun Yang Zheng Dian*

After entering the city, we were busy observing three details. Now, please spread the book open and we will see the full panorama of the city. On the left edge of the picture at the top of this page is the end of the entire scroll, while the main building on the right page is *Sun Yang Zheng Dian,* one of the 'seventy-two authorised shops in the capital'. Do you remember the *Cai lou huan men* in front of the *Jiao dian* near the Rainbow Bridge? There were no decorative lanterns or banners there, just a tall rack. In contrast, the one in front of *Sun Yang Zheng Dian* is already adorned with a lively array of decorations. Upon closer inspection, we can see flowers, branches, embroidered balls, as well as circular and diamond-shaped ornaments. Interestingly, there are also six goose-shaped ornaments (details can be seen in the yellow arrow on the opposite page). On the left wooden column, a flagpole is raised, with a blue and white

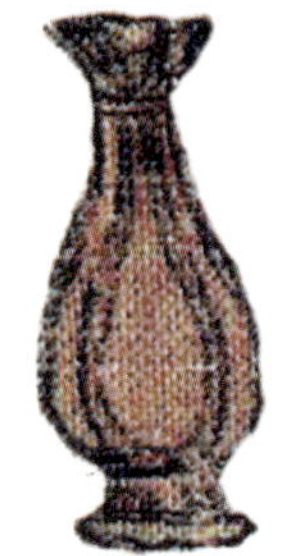

Gardenia lantern

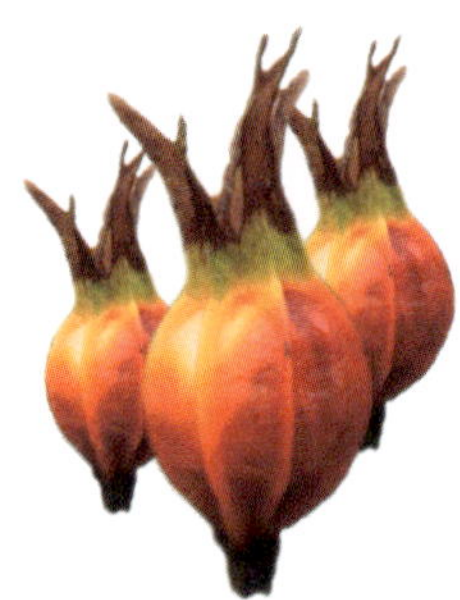

Gardenia fruit

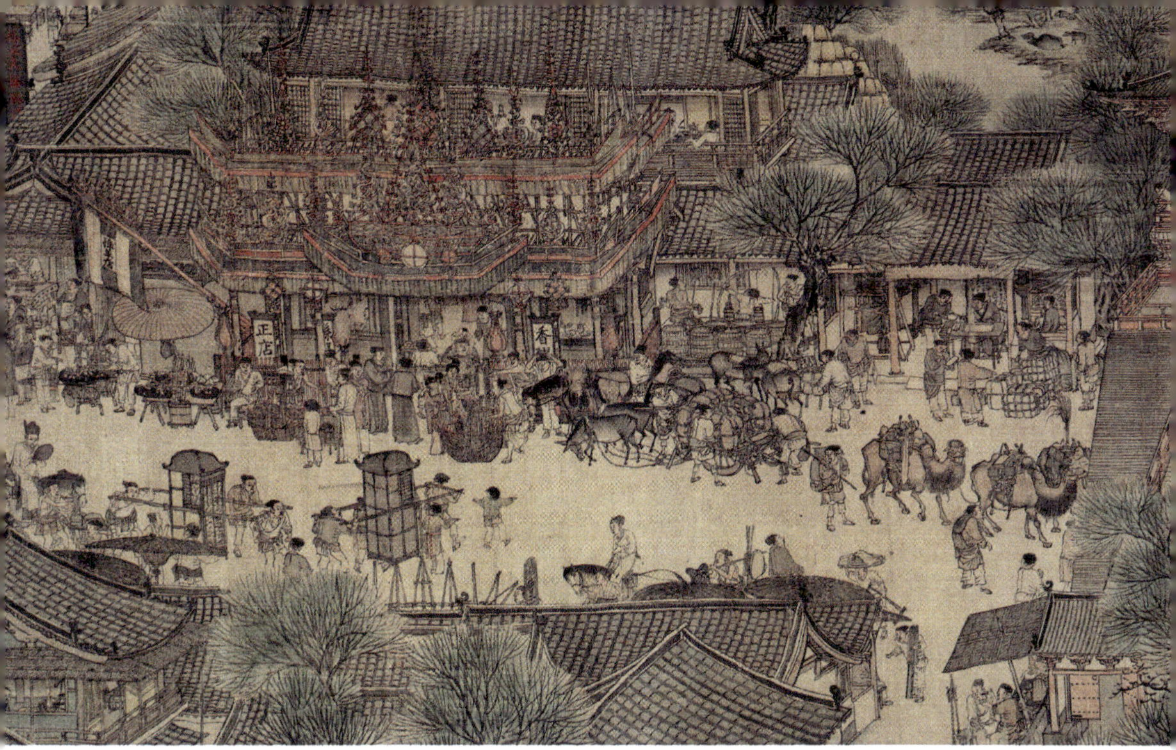

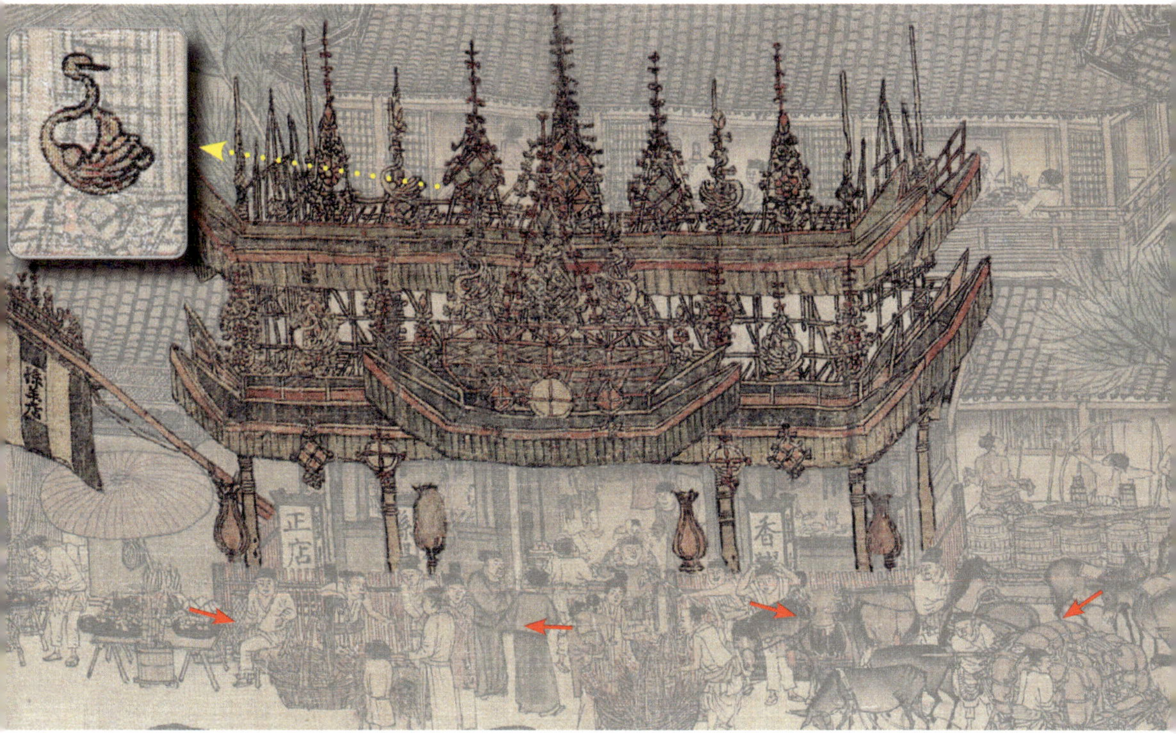

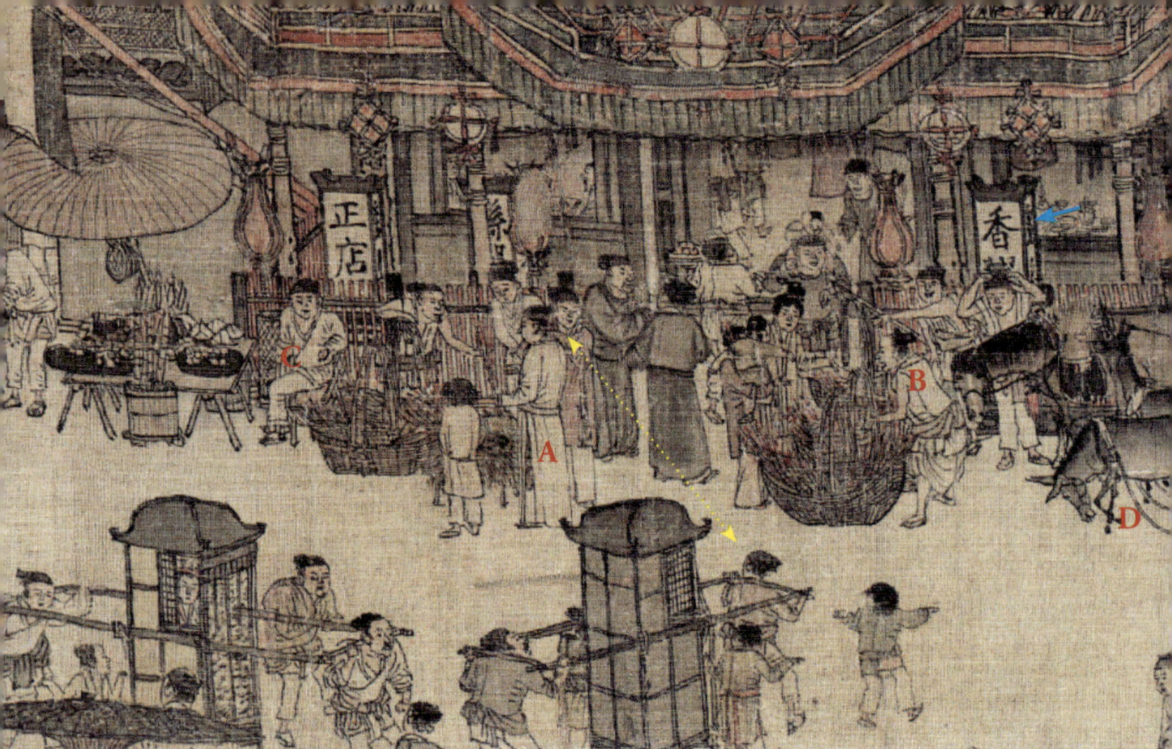

flag bearing the store's name – *Sun Yang Zheng Dian*. Moreover, four lanterns also catch our eyes. These are gardenia lanterns (indicated by the red arrow on page 151)! The design of these lanterns is inspired by the gardenia fruit. Imagine how beautiful it must be when night falls in Bianjing and the gardenia lanterns are lit!

Having just admired the luxurious and lively façade of *Sun Yang Zheng Dian*, let's now explore some details, starting from near to far.

First, let's take a look at the scene in front of its door. While the bustling scene might initially dazzle our eyes, the details are quite straightforward: there is a flower vendor on each side, but the customers buying flowers are markedly different. Let's start with mark A, where there are a man and a woman. To the man's left, a scruffy-looking boy seems to be his attendant; the woman's companion on her right is unknown, but has a pretty face, somewhat girlish. The vendor is pitching flowers, but the man seems disinterested and the woman even more so. She stands very close to the man, her left hand nearly hooking around his neck, yet she turns her head to look down the street. Across the street, two sedan chairs are approaching; the lead sedan chair bearer, distracted by the woman, inadvertently veers off course. The boy and maid on the right side of the sedan chair both raise their right hands, pointing and seemingly shouting, 'Hey, come back, you're going the wrong way!' The woman wears a strange hat and has distinctive features; compared to the person beside her, she might even be considered unattractive and particularly frivolous compared to the lady buying flowers on the right side of the door (as seen in the picture opposite).

C is the sugarcane vendor we saw earlier. He also sells date-filled triangles of steamed bread and round, small pastries. D is the caravan that is reloading goods after inspection and tax payment at the tax office.

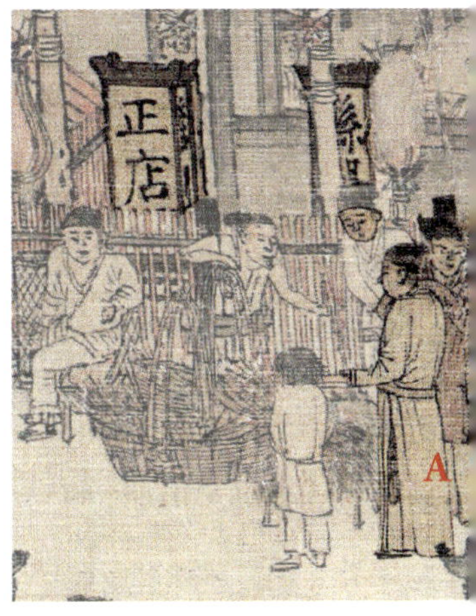

In the picture on the right, we see the illuminated signs on one side of the door. The left sign clearly reads *Zheng dian* (正店) on the front, while the right one is likely *Sun Yang* (孙羊). Additionally, the characters on the front (indicated by the blue arrow in the picture on the opposite page) read *Xiang* (香) on the top and what appears to be *Lao* (醪) below. *Xiang lao* (香醪) is the name of fine wine brew by *Sun Yang Zheng Dian*.

In scene B below, we see a family buying flowers. The father has his baby riding on his neck, much like fathers might do today. His right hand is securing the toddler's leg, while his left hand is pointing at the flowers in the basket, expressing his preference.

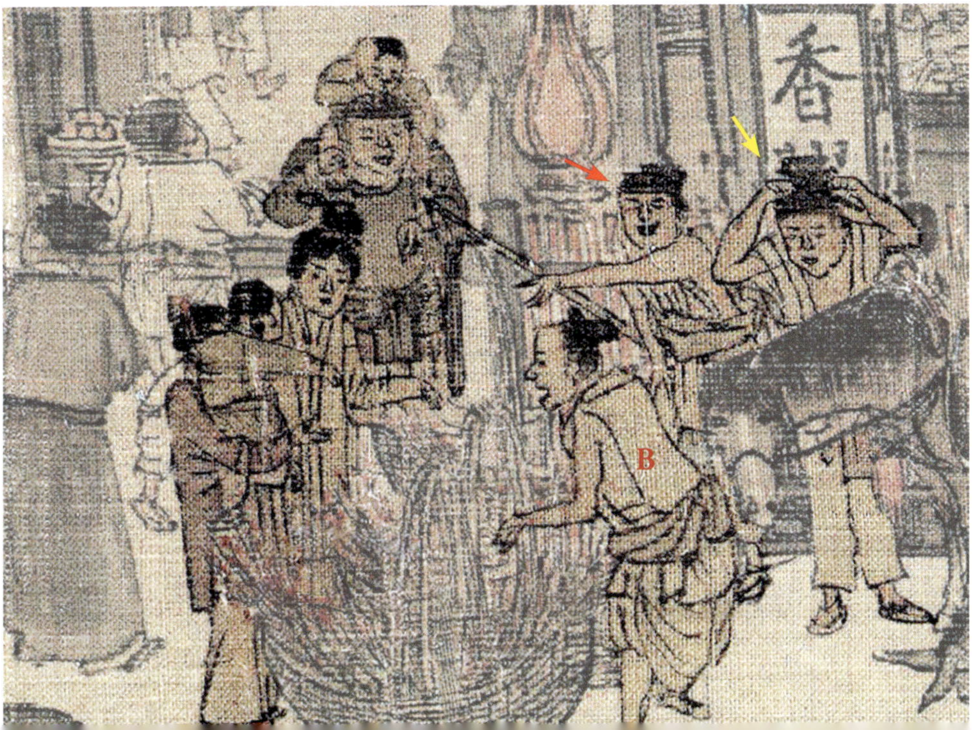

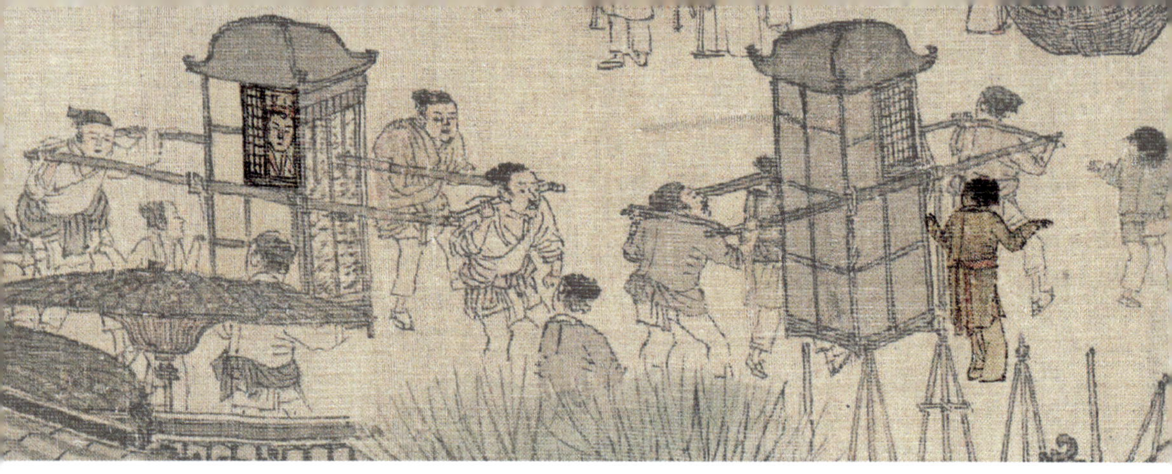

The woman in the middle exudes an air of dignity, her slightly chubby face suggesting a life of comfort and perhaps affluence. By her side stands another woman, perhaps the children's wet nurse, who holds a little girl and accompanies the lady to buy flowers. She wears a loose *Bei zi* and her hair is coiled in *Pan fu long*, which were fashionable during the Chongning and Daguan eras. The expressions and actions of the two secondary characters in this scene are particularly interesting: the one indicated by the red arrow has a comical expression, as if saying, 'Oh my, such lovely flowers, why be picky? Just take it!' The one indicated by the yellow arrow, hearing them bargaining, scratches his head and thinks, 'If I had the money, I'd buy one to wear in my hair...'

Let's delve further into the significance of the sedan chair. The rear sedan chair clearly carries a woman, and although the face of the person in the front sedan chair is obscured, the maid nearby indicates that it is also a woman inside. Do you remember the sedan chair at the crossroads? That too carries a woman. In *Along the River During the Qingming Festival*, it is exclusively women, not men, who are carried in sedan chairs. This is no coincidence. There was a notion in the Song Dynasty that it was disgraceful for men to be carried in sedan chairs. Even Wang Anshi, the prime minister of the Northern Song Dynasty, would only ride a donkey when he went out, not allowing people to carry him in a sedan chair. He once said, 'Since ancient times, even corrupt rulers and nobles have never dared to use people in place of animals.' His view was representative. In *Getting to Know Master Zhu Xi* (《朱子语类》), it is said that 'before the southward migration, scholars and officials seldom use sedan chairs' – officials generally rode horses ①. Even those granted permission by the court to ride in a sedan chair due to old age or illness, they would feel embarrassed to accept it readily and would try their best to decline.

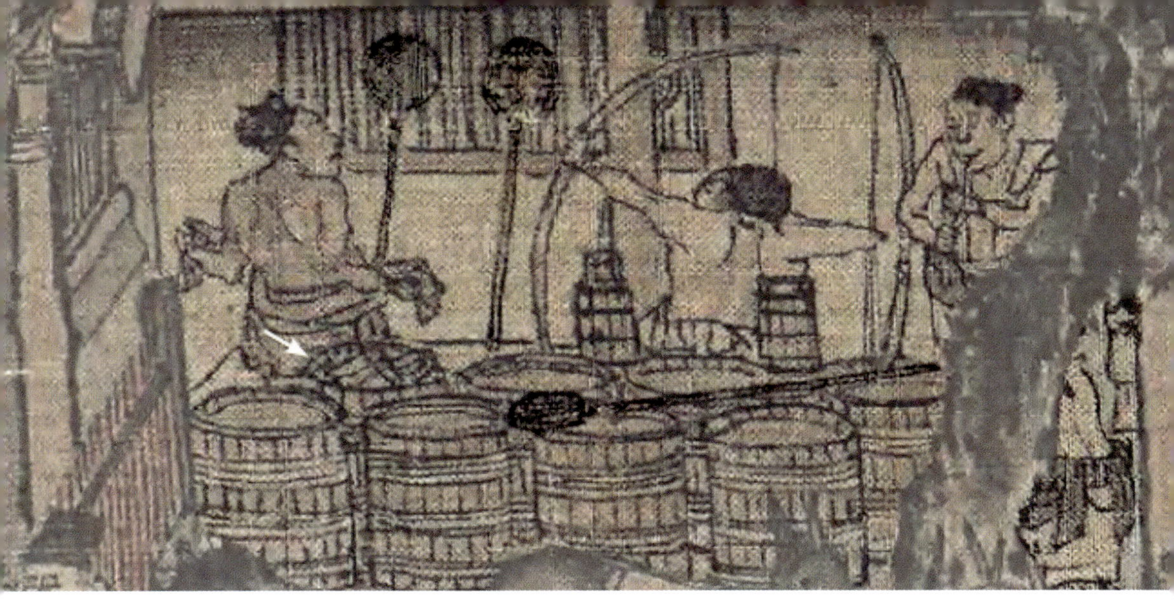

① *Getting to Know Master Zhu Xi*, Volume 128, *Ben chao II: Fa zhi*: 'Before the southward migration, scholars and officials seldom use sedan chairs. For example, as noted by figures such as Wang Anshi and Cheng Yi, who advocated not replacing animals with humans. Court officials generally rode horses. Some, due to old age or illness, when granted the use of a sedan chair by the court, would still strenuously refuse before eventually accepting. However, since the southward migration, there has been no one who does not ride in a sedan chair.' Here, '朝士 (*Chao shi*)' refers to court officials, a general term for government officials.

After observing the scene in front of *Sun Yang Zheng Dian*, let's turn to the street-facing storefronts on its right side. In the picture at the top of this page, we see a small storefront. Outside the storefront are eight large barrels (and two smaller barrels near the wall), and inside are three people (with possibly one or two more behind the trees). The person in the middle is posing as if shooting an arrow; the person on the left is stretching out a long cloth, possibly to tie around his waist; and the person on the right is wrapping his wrist. However, they are not truly practising archery, but mimicking. There are different interpretations of this storefront. Some say it's a bow and arrow shop, which seems too arbitrary and is clearly not the case. Others suggest it's a military wine store, with the large barrels containing wine for the troops. The three men are supposedly soldiers from the

Imperial Guard, ordered to escort the military wine. Excited about the wine, they joyfully show off their strength. However, I do not agree with this interpretation either. I believe this place could be a *Jun xun pu wu* (军巡铺屋) ②, essentially a small fire station, situated next to *Zheng dian* to protect such major taxpayers. The men, then, would be firefighting soldiers. How can we tell? Notice the two long poles leaning against the wall (with another across the barrels), each topped with a circle. These might be the *Ma da* (麻搭), firefighting equipment mentioned in the *Dongjing Meng Hua Lu* (《东京梦华录》, *The Eastern Capital: A Dream of Splendor*) as 'tools for firefighting'. As a firefighting tool, the *Ma da* would have loose hemp tied to the iron hoop at the top, which would be dipped in water to put out fire. But where does the water come from? Normally, it is stored in the barrels. Eight large barrels and two small ones must be what is mentioned in the *Dongjing Meng Hua Lu* (《东京梦华录》, *The Eastern Capital: A Dream of Splendor*). The artist may have intentionally placed one of the *Ma da* across a water barrel to emphasise the relationship between the two. Upon closer inspection, one might also notice that among the eight large barrels, only the one indicated by the white arrow (on the previous page) has a lid, while the other seven are left open, with their lids nowhere to be found. The artist seems to hint at the insufficient water storage in the firefighting barrels. Additionally, the detail of the seven lidless barrels also proves that they are not liquor barrels. Bows without arrows, barrels without water – given Zhang Zeduan's meticulous attention to detail, these elements nearly scream, 'Look, it's all just for show!'

② *Dongjing Meng Hua Lu* (《东京梦华录》, *The Eastern Capital: A Dream of Splendor*), Volume 3: 'In every alley, approximately every three hundred steps, a military patrol station is built. Each station is staffed by five soldiers who patrol at night and handle public affairs. Additionally, there are watchtowers constructed of brick at higher places, where watchmen vigilantly keep an eye out. Below, there are several official buildings housing more than a hundred soldiers, equipped with firefighting equipment such as large and small barrels, sprinklers, *Ma da*, axes, saws, ladders, fire hooks, large ropes and *Tie mao'er* (铁猫儿, grappling hook). Whenever

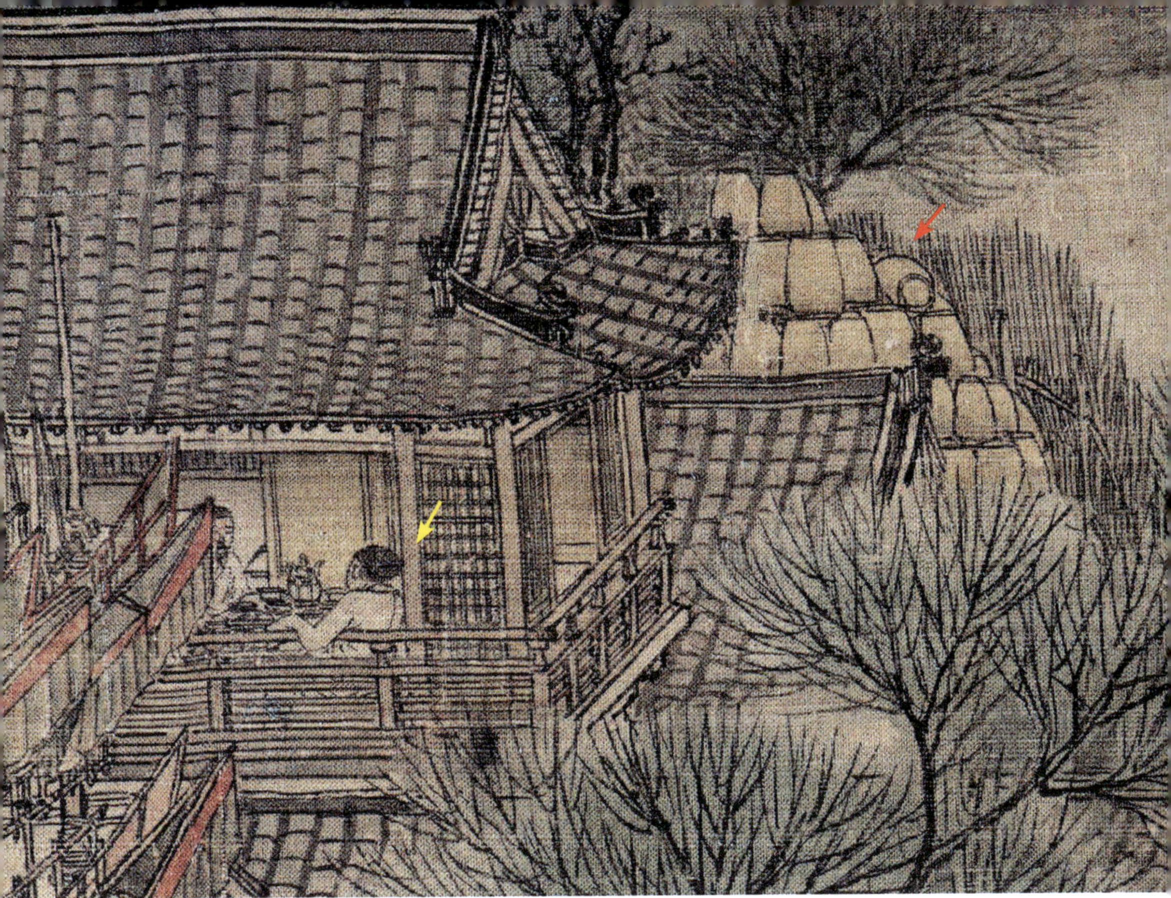

a fire breaks out somewhere, mounted soldiers rush to report it to the commanders and officials. The infantry, palace guards and the judiciary of Kaifeng, take charge of extinguishing the fire, sparing the common people the burden.'

All right, let's discuss the last two details about the *Sun Yang Zheng Dian*.

In the picture above, we can see a corner of the second floor, with a glimpse inside: two men are sitting across from each other at a table. The younger man, leaning comfortably against the railing, is leisurely drinking and chatting with the older man opposite him. Bowls and cups are scattered all over the table; a set of utensils for warming wine (indicated by the yellow arrow), consists of a wine pot and a warming bowl. In use, the wine pot is placed inside the warming bowl, the latter is then filled with hot water to warm the wine in the pot. In *Dongjing Meng Hua Lu* (《东京梦华录》, *The Eastern Capital: A Dream of Splendor*), under the section *Hui xian jiu lou* (《会仙酒楼》, *Hui xian* tavern): 'Generally, the customs of the capital's people are extravagant and more generous. In any tavern, regardless of who the person is, if two people sit down to drink, they must use a set of wine pot and warming bowls, two sets of plates and cups, five plates each of fruits and vegetables, and three to five bowls of snacks, totalling nearly a hundred taels of silver.' Indeed, the illustration perfectly matches the words!

In the backyard of the *Sun Yang Zheng Dian*, there is a large pile of tile jars stacked upon one another. The jar (indicated by the white arrow) is tipped over with its opening facing outwards. Seeing this detail, one can't help but smile. It seems that Zhang Zeduan was concerned that we might not recognise what these were, so he deliberately tipped one jar over to show us what was inside.

These large tile jars are wine jars.

As we mentioned earlier, only the *Zheng dian* had the right to brew wine, while the *Jiao dian* had to purchase their wine inventory from these *Zheng dian*.

Counting them up, the wine jars are stacked up to five layers high! This is only the part we can see, so we can imagine how vast the wine production capacity of this *Zheng Dian* must be. However, *Sun Yang Zheng Dian* is not considered one of the largest among the seventy-two *Zheng dian* in the capital. There is another *Zheng dian,* called *Feng Le Lou* (丰乐楼), which consists of a large complex of five buildings. Later on, one of these buildings was prohibited for climbing because from its top floor, one could look down into the imperial palace. With such scale and prestige, a *Zheng dian* would undoubtedly have a brewing capacity significantly greater than that of *Sun Yang Zheng Dian.*

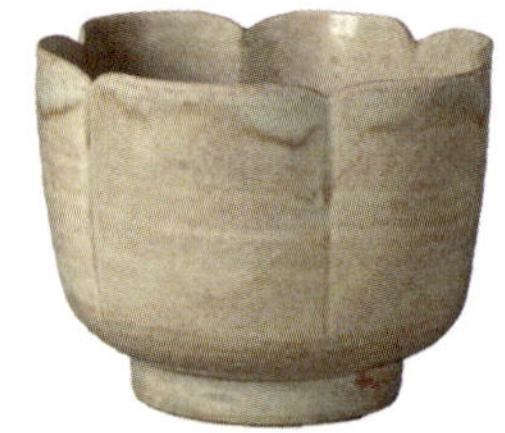

Warming bowl: Height 12.3cm, Opening Diameter 17cm, Base Diameter 9.8cm

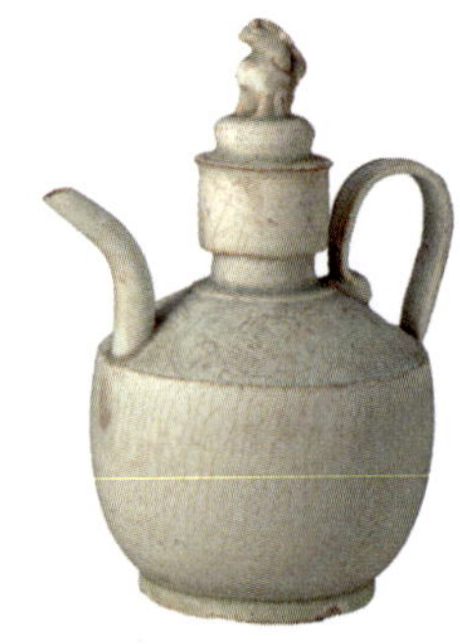

Wine Pot: Height 21.5cm, Opening Diameter 3.5cm, Base Diameter 9cm

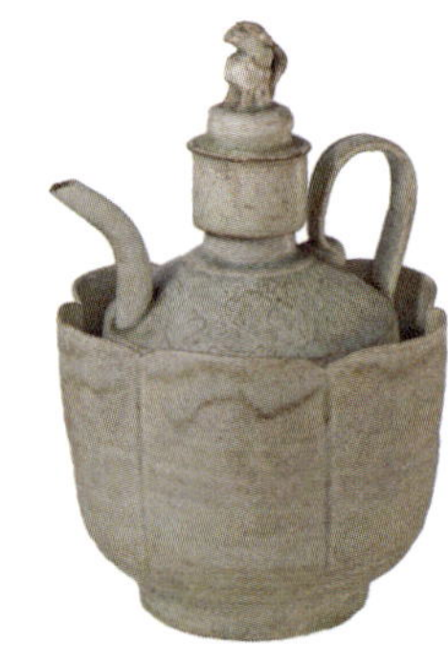

Qingbai glazed warming bowl and wine pot with carved peony designs, Jingdezhen ware, in the collection of the Palace Museum, Beijing

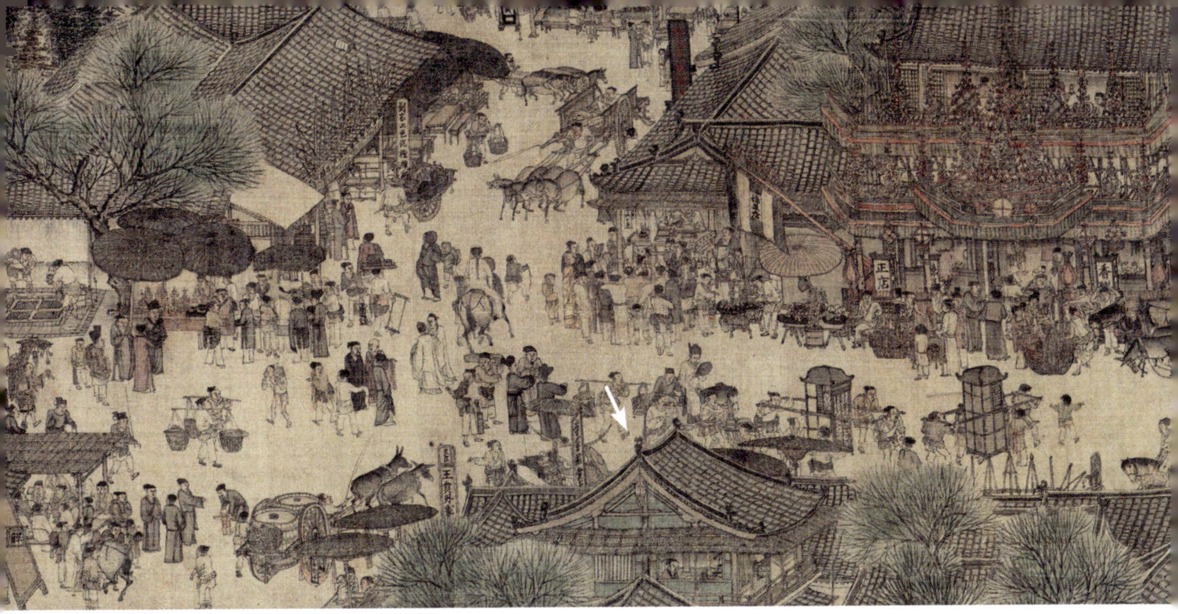

32. The painter's *Hua yan*

Passing the *Sun Yang Zheng Dian*, we arrive at a crossroads in the city.

Now, we gain a special perspective, known as the *Hua yan* (画眼, painter's perspective). It generally has two meanings: firstly, what the characters in the painting are looking at, guiding the audience's gaze to follow them; secondly, certain details in the painting play a crucial role in highlighting the theme. And these key details are also termed the *Hua yan*. The white arrow in the picture above points to the *Hua yan* of this section (and perhaps even the entire scroll): the second floor of the residence, which is a *Jiu zhu* (久住, long-term lodging) named *Wang Yuan Wai* (王员外). *Jiu zhu* is a term used in the hospitality industry during the Song Dynasty, meaning 'suitable for long-term lodging'. For a better understanding, we might liken it to a 'homestay'.

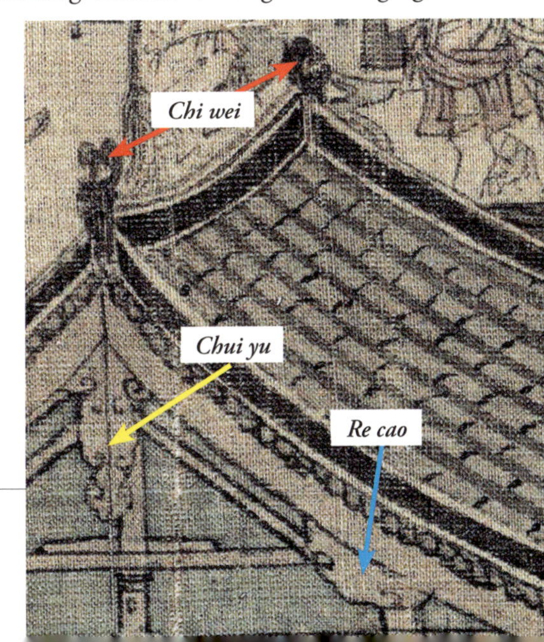

Wang Yuan Wai homestay stands directly opposite *Sun Yang Zheng Dian*, and narratively, it serves as a counterpart. It is much lower in stature – if *Sun Yang Zheng Dian* is likened to a mountain, then the home-stay is a small mound. While *Sun Yang Zheng Dian* is grand and adorned with eye-catching flamboyant decorations, the homestay is predominantly cyan and black, exuding a sense of tranquillity and composure. However, upon closer inspection, we can discern a subtle elegance in its simplicity. How can we tell? For instance, one side of the gable wall is painted with cyan lacquer, a symbol of refined and elegant dwellings. Moreover, *Chi wei* (鸱尾, a kind of ornament) at both ends of the main roof ridge, *Chui yu* (垂鱼, suspended fish) and *Re cao* (惹草, cloud pattern motif) on the gable wall – all display prominently, especially the latter two, which are the only instances presented in the clear front view in *Along the River During the Qingming Festival*. Is this a coincidence or a deliberate design by the painter? The *Chi wei*, also known as *Chi yu* (鸱鱼), resembles mythical creatures capable of spraying water and bringing rain. The *Chi wei*, *Xuan yu* (also called *Chui yu*, suspended fish), and *Re cao*, all aquatic symbols, are auspicious emblems believed to ward off fire and other disasters. They were also once used to indicate social rank and status. Among them is a famous anecdote about the *Xuan yu*: During the Eastern Han Dynasty, when Yang Xu was the prefect of Nanyang, his subordinate presented him with a live fish as a gift. Yang Xu accepted it, but hung the fish in his yard to dry. Later, when the subordinate brought fish again, Yang Xu simply directed him to the dried fish hanging in the yard. Upon seeing this, the subordinate understood. Thereby Yang Xu was known for his integrity and self-discipline, earning him the honourable title of 'The *Xuan Yu* Prefect', and '*Yang Xu Xuan Yu*' a byword for official integrity. Admittedly, as ordinary architectural components, *Xuan yu* and other elements may not hold special significance solely in *Wang Yuan Wai* homestay. However, the artist's choice to showcase them prominently alongside the scholar reading by the window may suggest a deeper symbolic meaning.

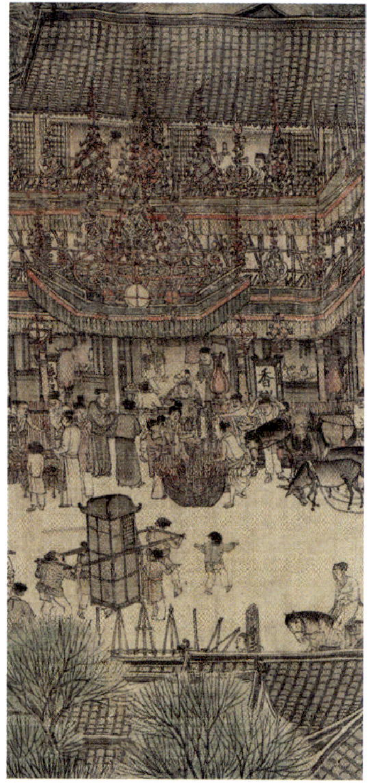

① *Tang Huiyao* (《唐会要》, literally Institutional History of Tang) Volume 44 *Zai za bian* (《灾杂变》): 'In the East Sea, there is a fish with a tail like that of the mythical *chi* (鸱), hence its name.

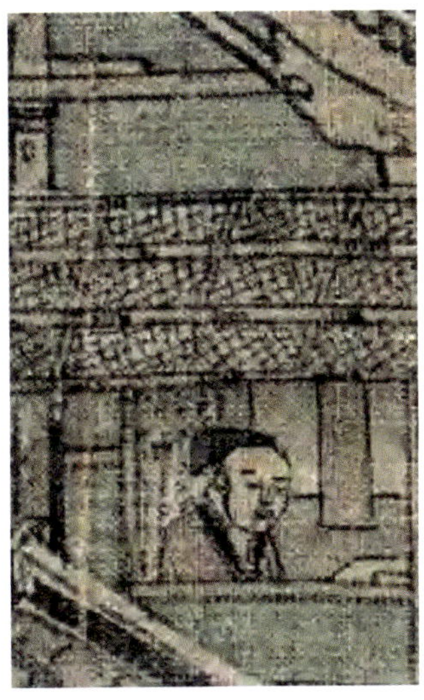

When it sprays water, rain falls. During the Han Dynasty, when the *Bai liang Tai* (柏梁台) suffered a disaster, Wu (巫, shaman) proposed a method to overcome this calamity. Consequently, the Jianzhang Palace was constructed, images of the *Chi yu* were placed on the roof ridges, and auspicious word patterns were painted on the beams to ward off fire disasters.' The *Chi wei* on the roof ridge, representing the tail of the *Chi yu*, was a symbol of the fire prevention. The subsequent evolution of the *Chi wei* is not discussed here.

② *Book of the Later Han: Biography of Yang Xu* (《后汉书·羊续传》): 'At that time, the wealthy and powerful families often indulged in extravagance and luxury, a practice that Yang Xu deeply despised. He always wore shabby clothes, ate simple food and used worn-out carriages and horses. Once, his assistant presented him with live fish, Yang Xu accepted and hung in the courtyard. Later, when his assistant offered fish again, Xu showed him the fish hung in the yard to convey his intention and put an end to such gifts.'

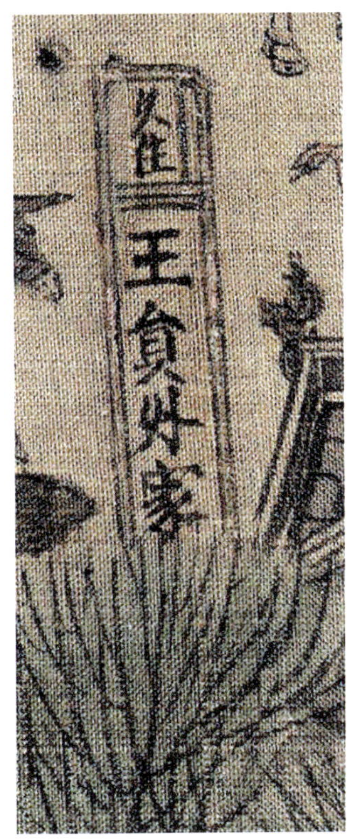

Take a look at the scholar (pictured above on the right). He has a small moustache and appears to be no longer young, likely having experienced the bitterness of failing the imperial examinations. However, his expression is serene, undisturbed by the hustle and bustle of the marketplace, as he remains determined and focused on his studies. There is a particularly harmonious feeling between him and the exterior of the architecture, don't you think? If *Sun Yang Zheng Dian* represents material wealth, then this scholar embodies spiritual nobility. We often find ourselves at a crossroads in life, where the right path leads to indulgence and the left to integrity. How do you choose? I believe Zhang Zeduan already has his answer.

With this, we shall draw a close to our exploration of *Hua yan*.

The close presence of the second floor of *Wang Yuan Wai* homestay makes it impossible to overlook. We are compelled to notice the scholar reading inside the room. It is he who plays the role of bringing the painting to life. Although he doesn't direct our gaze towards the outside world, he endows us with the 'window of the mind' – not in the cunning sense, but a vision of the inner world. Thus, even as we take in the hustle and bustle of the market and the myriad of lives within it, the presence of this scholar will always linger in our minds, allowing us to see beyond the bustling streets.

Zhang Zeduan's design is truly ingenious.

33. The butcher shop and storytelling

Next, let's take a look at the northeast corner of the crossroads in the city. Here lies a bustling butcher shop, surrounded by a crowd and, at first glance, it seems a bit chaotic. Don't worry, we'll categorise and examine in order. At the centre of the butcher shop, there is a relatively large chopping block where an apprentice is busy slicing meat. The chopping block is quite high, so he has his feet on two footrests to make cutting easier. Next to the chopping block sits a plump man with his legs crossed, likely the owner of the shop. A crowd blocks the entrance – a scene that would certainly not be tolerated by shopkeepers today. However, he doesn't seem to mind and is even gleefully watching. Underneath the eaves of the butcher shop, some items are hanging: strips of meat (indicated by the blue arrow opposite), and a small rectangular sign with interesting characters (indicated by the red arrow opposite). The first three characters are '斤六十 (*Jin Liu Shi*)', written clearly without ambiguity. But as for the last character, some people identify it as '邑 (*Yi*)" or "口 (*Kou*)', but its meaning cannot be explained. In fact, it is the character '足 (*Zu*)', making the phrase '斤六十足 (*Jin Liu Shi Zu*)'. What does this mean? Some say it assures customers the full weight and accurate measurement, no short-changing involved. At first, this seems to make sense, but the number '六十 (*Liu Shi*, sixty)' remains unclear, doesn't

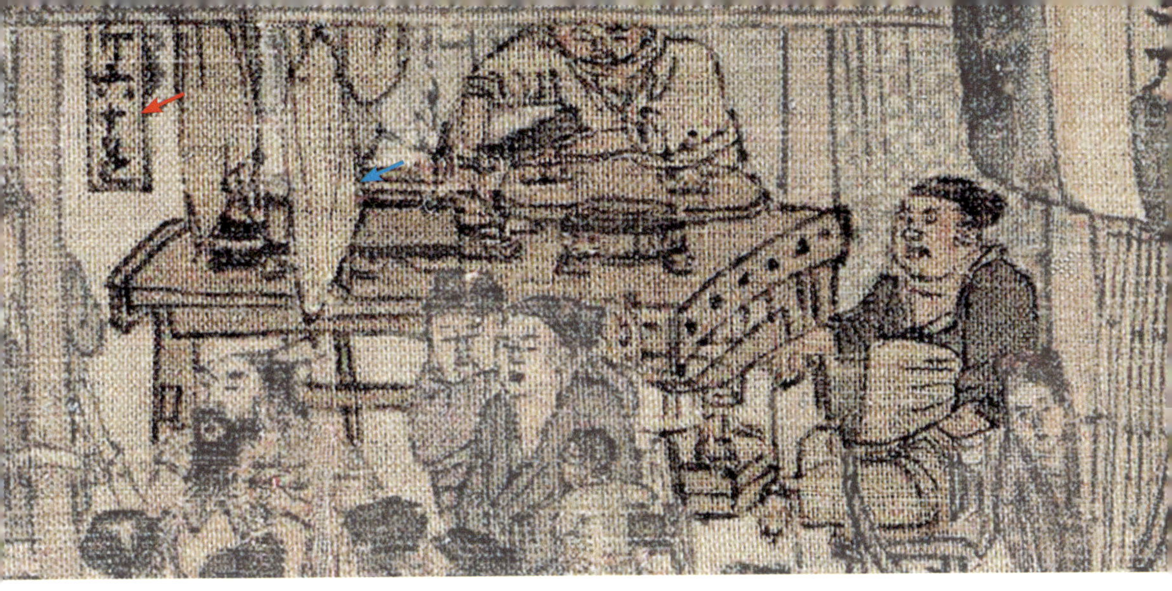

it? To understand the meaning of these four characters, we need to know a bit of historical knowledge. In the Song Dynasty, a currency system called the '省陌制 (*Shengmo* system)' was implemented. Here, '陌 (*mo,* 百)' means hundred, referring to one hundred coins. In this system, 77 coins could be used as 100 coins. Why was there such a regulation? It was due to a shortage of minted coins. As commercial exchanges advanced, the need for currency increased, leading to situations where there were 'not enough coins'. During the reign of Emperor Taizong of the Song Dynasty, the maximum annual production of copper coins could reach more than 1.8 million strings, and iron coins could exceed 500,000 strings, but this was still insufficient. Therefore, the '省陌制 (*Shengmo* system)' was implemented to alleviate the coin shortage. As a result, the Song people often faced a dilemma: is your price calculated based on the *Zu* (足) hundred or the *Shengmo* hundred? For example, a litre of wine could be priced as '149 *Wen* in *Zu* hundred' or '194 *Wen* in *Shengmo* hundred'. The conversion ratio between the two is approximately 100:77, consistent with the 'seventy-seven as a hundred' rule in the *Shengmo*

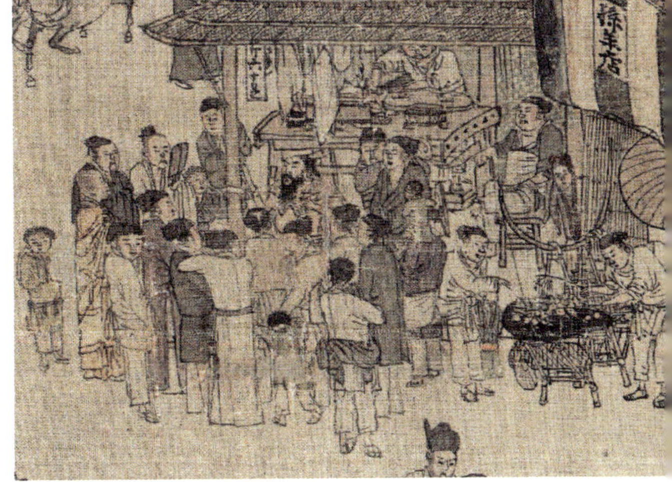

system. With this context, '斤六十足' becomes clearer. It's a shorthand on the butcher's sign, meaning 'the meat price is 60 *Wen* per *Jin* in *Zu* hundred'. This small sign in *Along the River During the Qingming Festival* might be one of the earliest documented price signs in China.

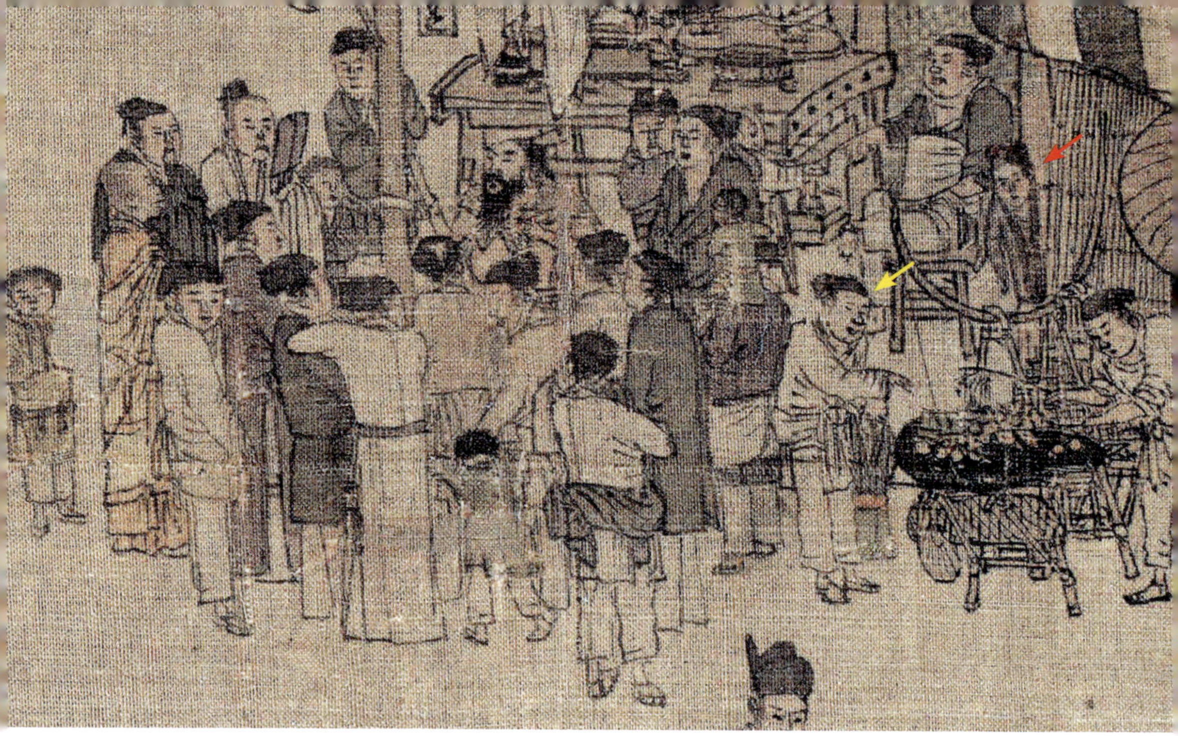

Now let's look at the group of people in front of the butcher shop. The man surrounded in the centre, distinguished by his large beard and distinct demeanour, is a storyteller ①. The crowd around him is interesting; they seem to be casually gathered together, but in fact, their ages and identities are all deliberately designed. Adults, both young and old, are interspersed with several children of varying ages. The youngest child perched atop his father's shoulders, uses his father's head as an armrest. In terms of identity, there are scholars, labourers, as well as monks and Taoists, representing a mix of people from all walks of life, men and women, young and old, are present. Of course,

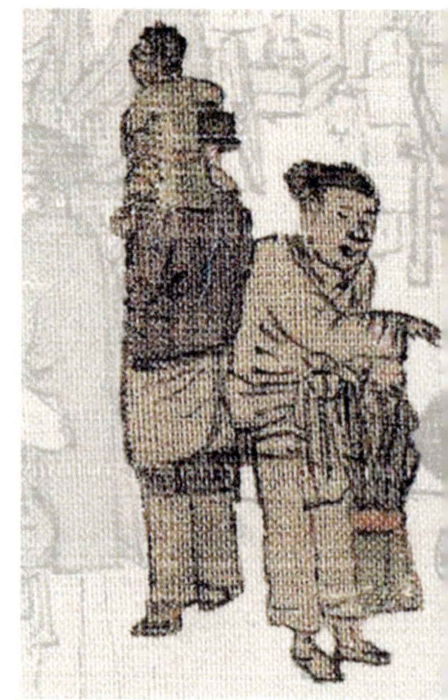

it's not easy for women to squeeze into the crowd. Look, next to the butcher shop owner, a girl peeks out (indicated by the red arrow in the picture above). She seems to be listening attentively, though she may also be watching people buy things. Outside the crowd, a father is holding his child's hand (indicated by the yellow arrow in the picture above) and pointing to the candies scattered on a stall, saying, 'Come on, get me two of these'. The child seems a bit sullen, so his father wants to buy him candies. Zhang Zeduan's depiction of parent-child relationships never fails to evoke our memories of childhood.

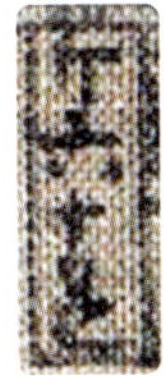

① Some scholars believe that the central figure with the beard is an Iranian merchant, and the people around him are listening to his accounts of exotic experiences from his travels.

34. The *Jie* (解) *Pu* and fortune-telling

Now let's take a look at the southwest corner of the crossroads in the city. This is a *Jie* (解) *Pu*. It is called *Jie Pu* not because we know exactly what it does, but because a pole extends out under the eaves. It carries a banner with only one character – '解 (*Jie*)'.

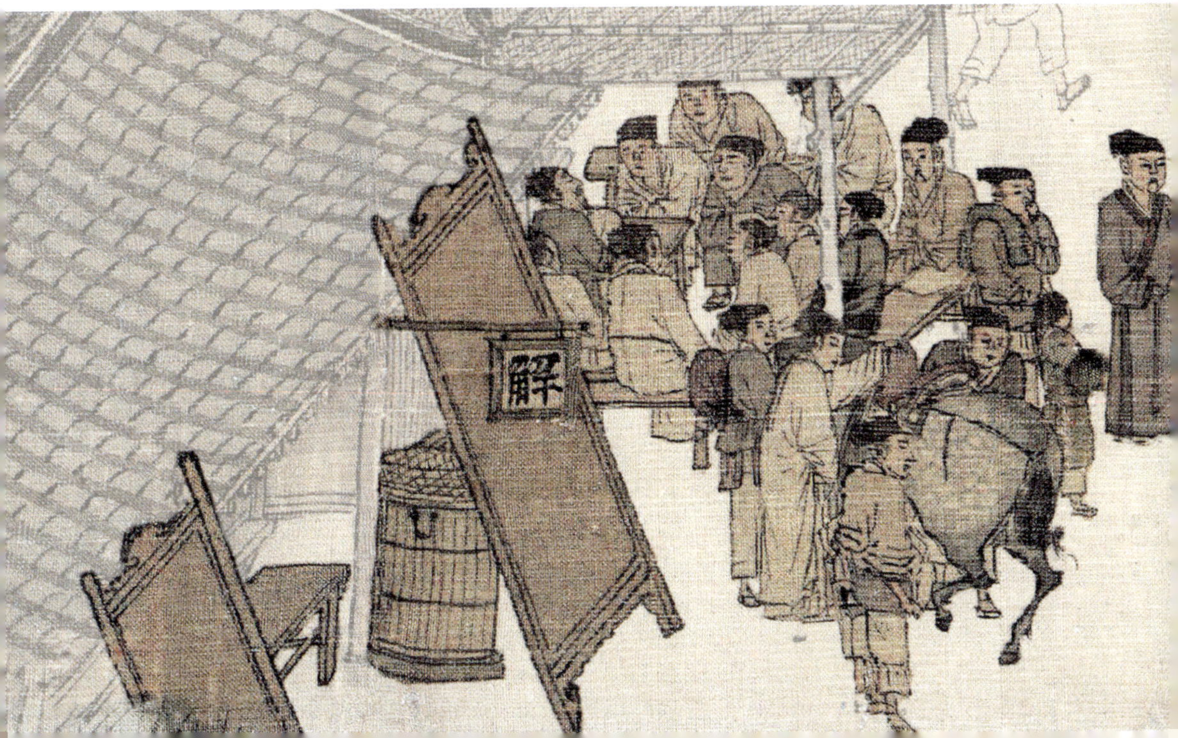

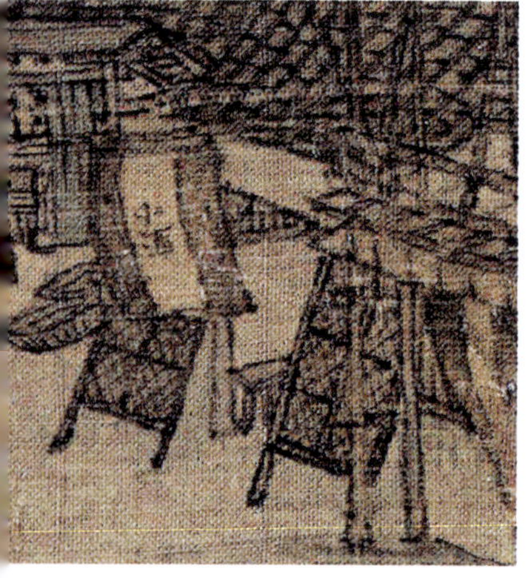

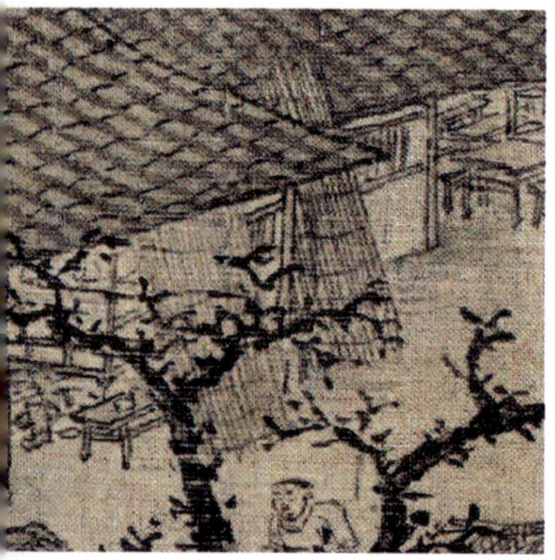

What does the character '解' mean? The most commonly accepted interpretation is that '解 (*Jie*)' refers to '解库 (*Jie ku*)', which is a pawnshop. Additionally, there are many other explanations ①. I will list these interpretations. Feel free to take a look if you're interested.

Rather than the perspectives, it is the details in the painting that truly captivate. Let's take a closer look at a few of these details.

Outside the *Jie Pu*, two movable shutters lean against the eaves. What's their function? Undoubtedly, they can be used as a shield, blocking people's view and protecting their privacy. Or, when it's windy, rainy or sunny, they can be temporarily closed. Similar shields can be found elsewhere in *Along the River During the Qingming Festival*, such as in front of a small tavern on the dock diagonal street (left picture on the top), and in front of a street-facing storefronts outside the city (middle picture on the left). However, although these three shields may have similar functions, their materials and qualities are not the same: one features a wooden frame with matting. One appears to be made of bamboo strips tied with rope, while the one in front of the *Jie Pu* seems to be made of solid wooden boards. It is quite exquisitely crafted, with wooden strips inlaid inside the border and auspicious cloud pattern carvings on the top and bottom. Similar boards also appear in Song Dynasty landscape paintings, like the two smaller pictures on the opposite page. However, there is a difference: the landscape paintings typically show only one side of the board and are associated with rustic households (or shop owners). Zhang Zeduan emphasises daily and practical use, whereas other landscape painters might have artistically transformed that

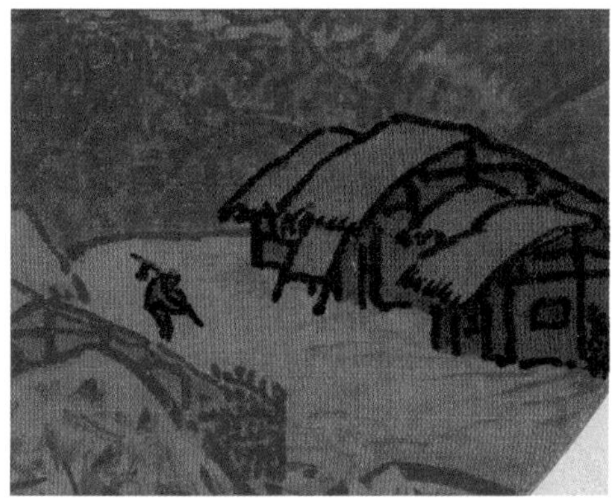

Part of *Picture of Yun Guan Xue Zhan* (《云关雪栈图》), Xu Daoning, Northern Song Dynasty, in the collection of the Palace Museum in Beijing

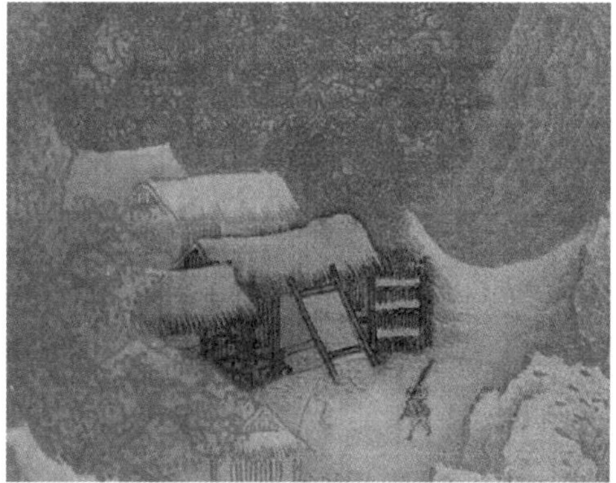

Part of *Picture of Shan Shui,* Ma Yuan, Sourthern Song Dynasty (attributed to), in the collection of the National Palace Museum, Taipei

into a symbol of reclusion, expressing the realm where the 'internal world' and 'external world' are not completely isolated but somewhat detached.

① In addition to a pawnshop, there are other interpretations: First, in ancient times, the character '解 (*Jie*)' was synonymous with '廨 (*Xie*)', indicating a government office where officials work. Second, the character '解 (*Jie*)' has the meaning of transportation of goods, so this could be a freight depot that handles transportation services. Third, '解 (*Jie*)' is the sign for a '解盐店 (salt shop)', as in the Song Dynasty, the salt pools in *Jiezhou* were monopolised by the government. The standardised and formal style of '解 (*Jie*)' suggests that it was uniformly produced by the Imperial Salt Distribution Office. Therefore, it indicates that this shop specialises in selling salt from the *Jiezhou* pools. Fourth, it could be a privately-run '书铺' (book shop) that provides notarisation services for imperial examination candidates. Fifth, it might be an official office that handles affairs related to the imperial examinations. Sixth, this could be a place dedicated to telling fortunes and divining for examination candidates. In short, there are still many different opinions in academia regarding this character '解 (*Jie*)' , and no consensus has been reached.

Beside the door of the *Jie Pu,* there is a barrel-like object, which some people have mistakenly thought to be a 'large birdcage'. This, of course, is not the case. A similar barrel can be seen next to a restaurant at the Bian River dock (top picture on the left), though the one at the *Jie Pu* is more exquisite. Therefore, I suspect that it is a water barrel.

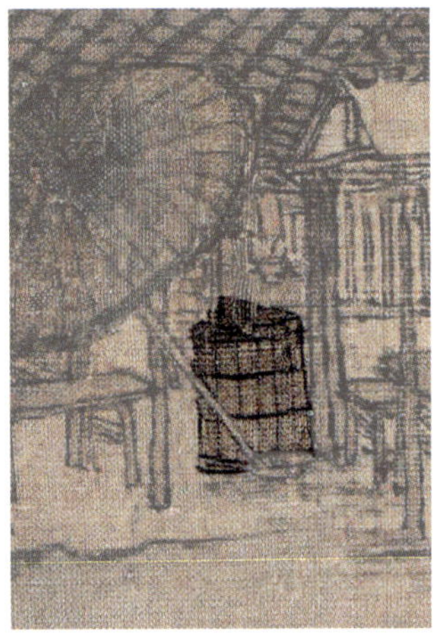

Under the awning beside the *Jie Pu*, a group of neatly dressed young people, likely examination candidates, has gathered. They are listening to a fortune teller (indicated by the red arrow in the picture below left) predict their futures. Upon closer inspection, the fortune teller appears to be blind. Outside the awning, there is a man (see bottom right) who seems to have already had his fortune told and is about to mount his horse to leave. His appearance and demeanour are beyond merely handsome; he could be described as strikingly attractive. The horse he rides is also of an exceptionally high breed, comparable to a luxury car today.

Some people also say that this awning is a storytelling place. Because of the different content and styles of storytelling, the audience it attracts differs from that of the bearded storyteller mentioned earlier.

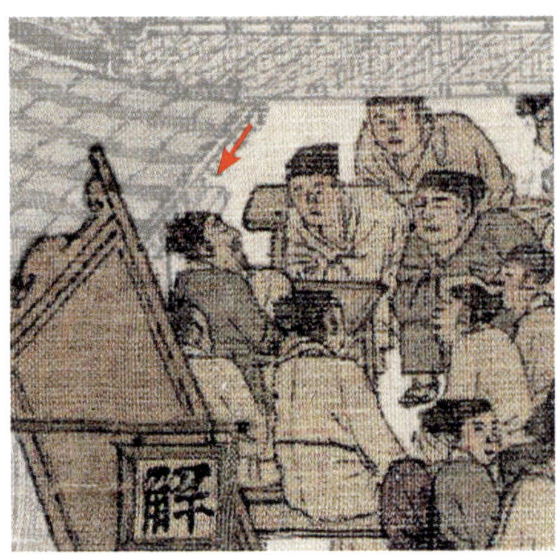

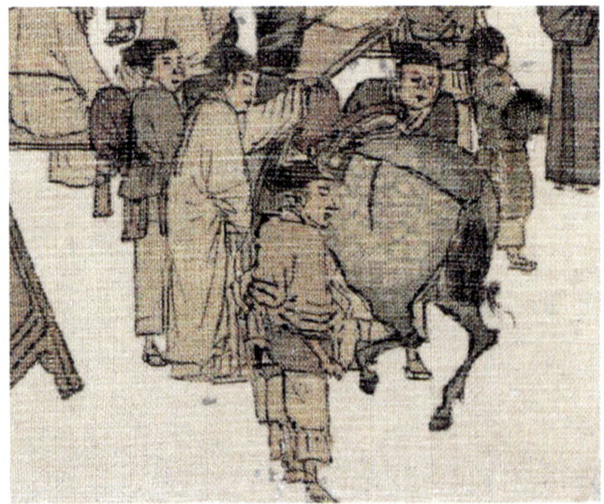

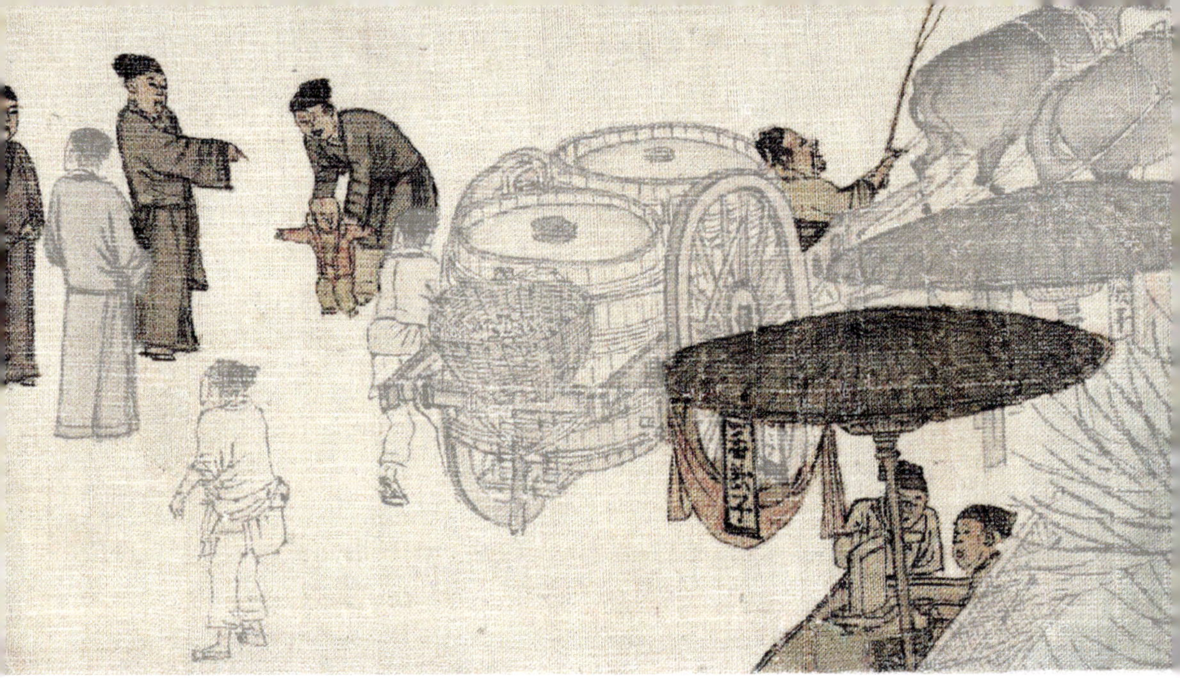

35. Come stroll the city streets with me!

After the butcher shop and the *Jie Pu*, let's casually stroll along the street, looking for interesting details.

The picture at the top of the page shows the scene on the street. A *Ping tou* cart, loaded with two large barrels of wine, recklessly speeds past the street. A child in red is startled, and an adult hurriedly picks him up to safety. An elder scolds the cart driver, seemingly exclaiming, 'Watch where you're going! Can't you see?' The cart driver, unconcerned with the complaints, raises his whip and continues to hurry the donkey along. He tilts his head back, appearing carefree and optimistic, like a drunken man.

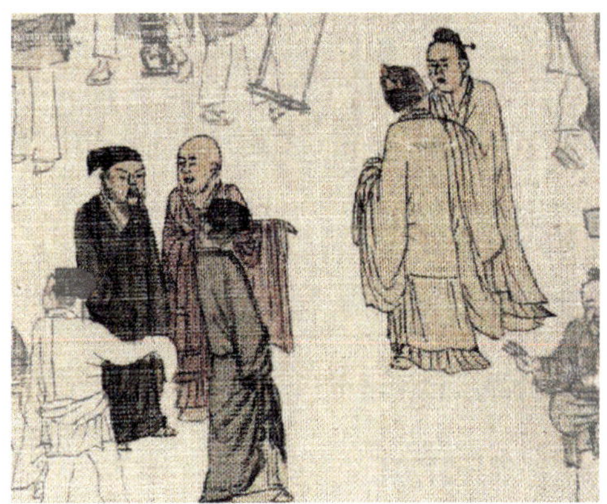

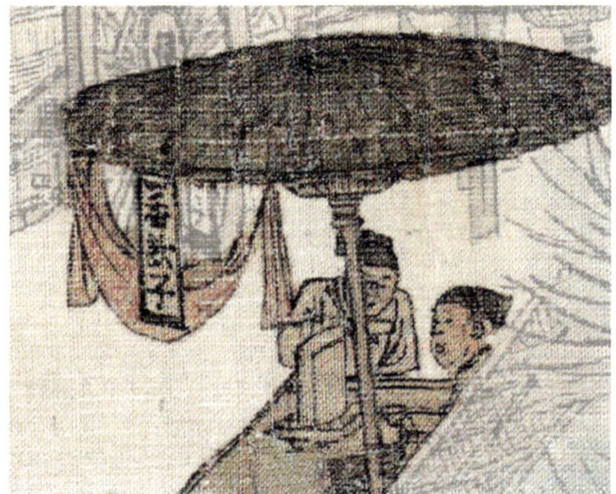

Across from the *Jie Pu*, under the outer wall of *Wang Yuan Wai* homestay, there's a stall selling *Xiang Yin zi* (香饮子, shown in the lower picture on the right on page 167). We've previously discussed *Yin zi* in detail. In the early days, *Yin zi* was mainly consumed as medicine. But by the Song Dynasty, it had become more 'specialised', with the emergence of beverage-type *Yin zi*. The *Xiang Yin zi* here could represent a specialised *Yin zi* – a tasty and healthy beverage. In the picture, the stall owner is seen ladling the beverage with a small spoon, while his customer is savouring his drink.

In the middle of the crossroads stand three people, shown in the lower picture on the left on page 169: a bearded Confucian scholar, a monk in a purple robe speaking eloquently to him, and a third person turning his head to the side in a slightly awkward posture. They might have been engaged in a lively discussion while walking. The Northern Song was an era when Confucianism, Buddhism and Taoism converged, with monks and Confucian scholars often engaging in discussions about Zen and writing poetry together. At that time, there were quite a few temples in Bianjing, with famous ones including *Da Xiang Guo* Temple, *Kai Bao* Temple, and *Tai Ping Xing Guo* Temple. The abbots of these temples were often appointed by the emperor, who would summon distinguished monks from the provinces to the capital to assume the position.

In that same picture, there are two people in white clothes on the right. Some say they are Taoists, while others say they are examination candidates. In the Song Dynasty, people from all walks of life, including scholars, farmers, artisans and merchants, could take the imperial examinations to gain official status. Whenever there were imperial examinations, Bianjing would be filled with candidates from across the country coming to take their exams.

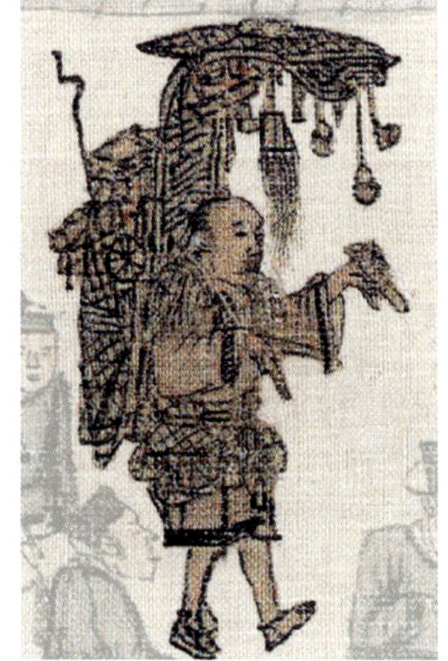

The monk in the purple robe should be of a high status. His robust and healthy appearance, characterised by a plump and rosy complexion, suggests a stable and comfortable life. Not far from him, the walking itinerant monk presents a stark contrast. Let's take a closer look at him. Although he is also bald, his head is not as cleanly shaven as that of the monk in the purple robe – new hair has grown at the back of his head. There are also traces of stubble around his lips, either recent growth or a bad shave. Compared to the round face of the purple-robed monk, his face is much thinner. This is all because he is an itinerant monk, not a monk living locally in Bianjing. Perhaps he has walked through deserts and wastelands, traversed mountains and rivers, and finally arrived in Bianjing. What he holds in his hands and carries on his shoulders are his most important possessions.

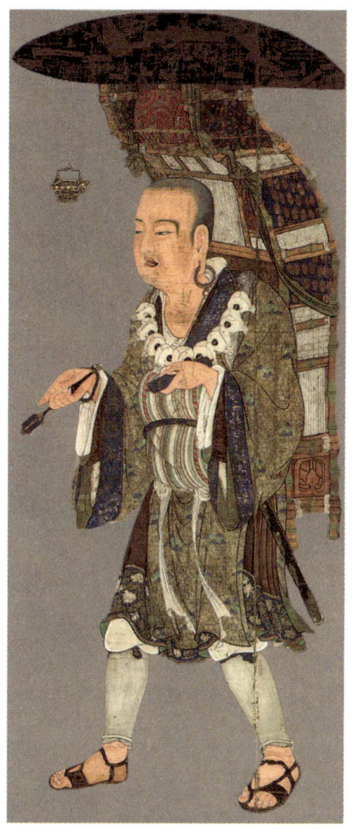

The Monk Xuanzang, Kamakura period, 14th century in the collection of Tokyo National Museum

He is carrying a bamboo frame on his back, which is the '笈 (*Ji*)' in '负笈游学 (*Fu Ji You Xue*, to travel and study with books on one's back)'. A *Ji* (笈) is a book box made of bamboo or rattan. On top of the *Ji*, there is a round hat protecting it from sun and rain. Below it hang objects such as a *Fuchen* (拂尘, a type of fly-whisk), a small lamp, or a tiny incense burner, some scholars call it the *Fuchen* a *Zhuwei* (麈尾). Before the Five Dynasties period, *Zhuwei* and *Fuchen* were two completely different things. The *Zhuwei* originally came in various styles, but they look completely different. Their main uses and periods of popularity were also different. The *Zhu* (麈) is a kind of large deer (some say an elk). Legend has it that deer would

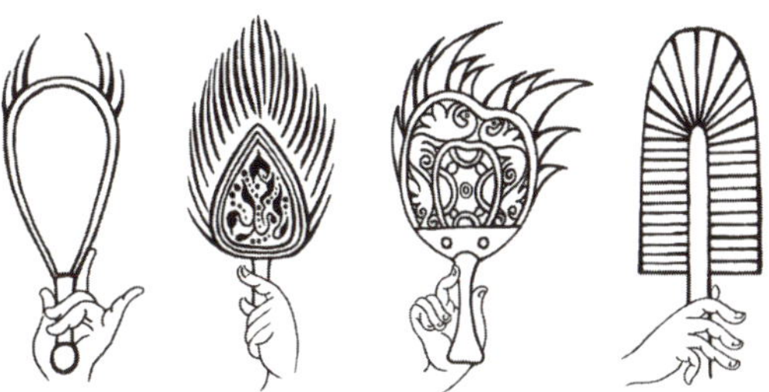

Types of _Zhuwei_ painted by Qu Shanshan

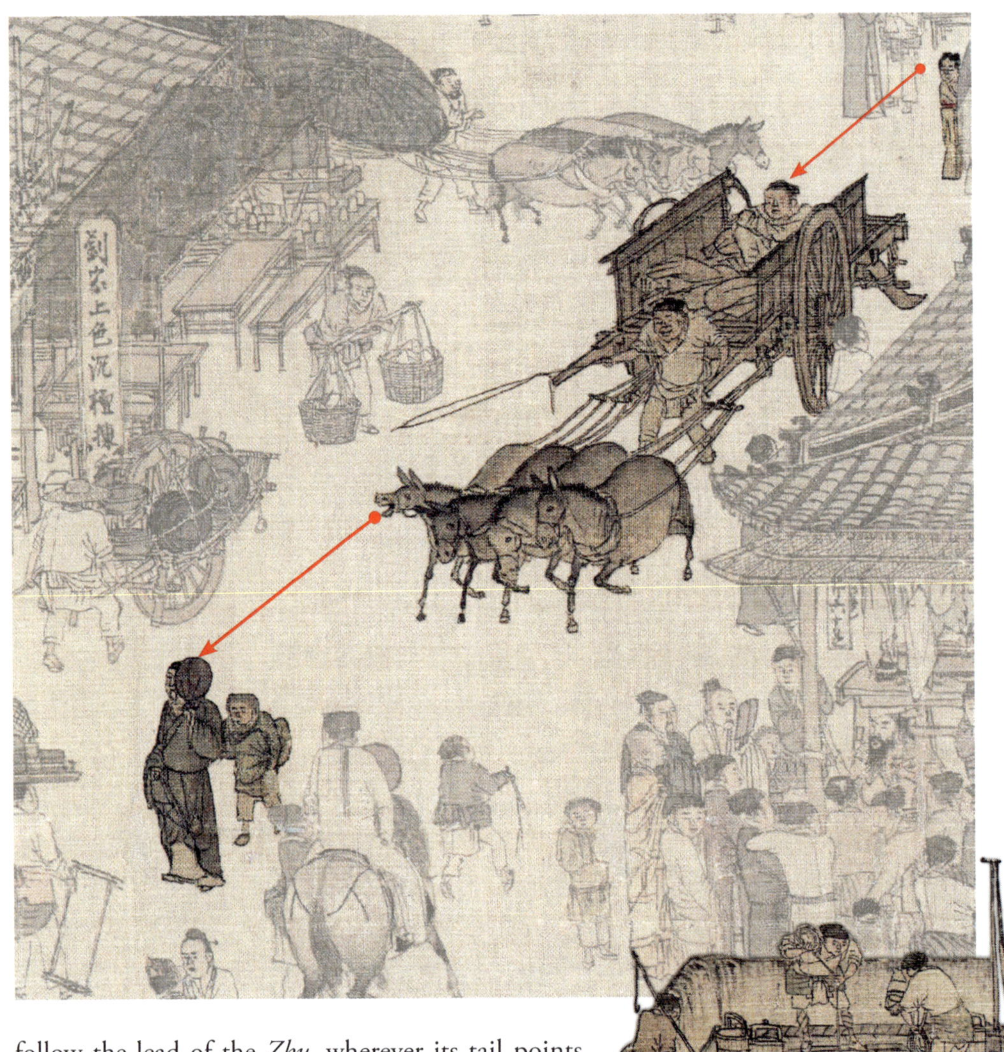

follow the lead of the *Zhu,* wherever its tail points. Thus, during the rise of *Qingtan* Philosophical Movement in Wei and Jin dynasties, scholars enjoyed holding a *Zhuwei* during debates. Eventually, the *Zhuwei* became a sophisticated symbol of the political and intellectual elite, and was often held in hand. After the Five Dynasties, the *Zhuwei* fell out of use, leaving later generations only knowing of its existence without understanding its specific shape. Hence, they created a new *Zhuwei*, which was quite popular in the Ming and Qing dynasties but was actually quite different from its original form, despite sharing the same name. Its shape was similar to a *Fuchen*: a traditional *Fuchen* has a thin, long handle with a relatively small tuft of hair and relatively long hair; the new type of *Zhuwei* has a short, thick handle with a relatively large tuft of hair and relatively short hair. After discussing the *Zhuwei*, let's talk about the small incense burner (indicated by the red arrow in the picture opposite). It has an arched handle in a semi-circular shape, hanging in front of the monk's forehead. Some scholars argue that this is not an incense burner, but rather a small gold container for Buddhist relics. Buddhist relics are 'small crystalline fragments collected from the ashes of eminent monks' and 'are considered to be the embodiment of the Buddha and his teachings'. Monks travelling long distances to spread Buddhism would carry scriptures, Buddhist statues and Buddhist relics, and the relics hanging before their foreheads, as a constant inspiration to persevere in their faith.

Next we will take a closer look at what the itinerant monk is holding in his hands. In his left hand, some say he holds a bamboo clapper, which he strikes while chanting sutras as he walks. Others say it is a scroll of Buddhist scriptures. Around his waist, he has various pouches and bags. On his back, he carries several scrolls of scriptures. Among them, there is a wheel-shaped object, which could be a *Jingzhi* (经帙, a book cover or case for wrapping other scripture scrolls). The stick with a curved top is likely his walking staff.

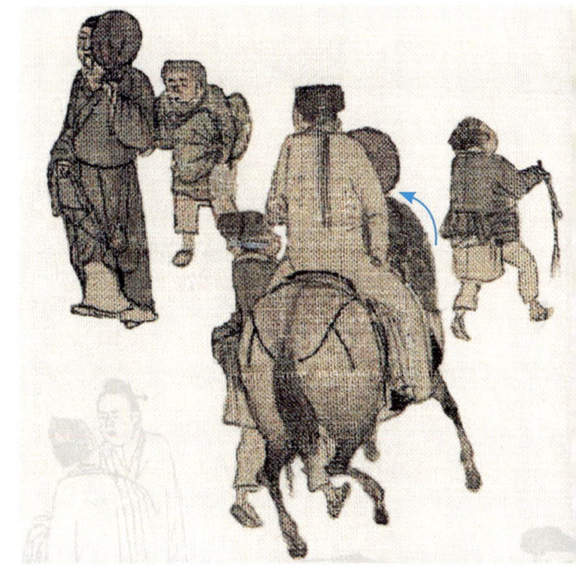

This depiction of the itinerant monk is not unusual. In fact, there is a rather standardised iconography for such figures. Take a look at the picture on page 171, a painting titled *The Monk Xuanzang* (《行脚僧玄奘像》) in the collection of Tokyo National Museum. Overall, it bears quite a resemblance to our monk, don't you think?

In just a few steps away from the purple-robed monk, we encounter one of the most iconic scenes in *Along the River During the Qingming Festival*. Take a look at the picture on page 172, two groups of people are walking towards each other. At this moment, the white-clad man on horseback commands his servant to rein in the horse (as indicated by the horse's turned head, see the blue arrow in the picture on page 173), and he leans to greet an 'acquaintance' approaching from the opposite way. Intriguingly, this 'acquaintance' raises a fan to cover his face, pretending not to see him. Interesting, isn't it? Previously, we noticed quite a few people holding fans, but it turns out that in the Song Dynasty, fans were used not only for fanning, dust protection or blocking the sun but also for a fourth purpose – 'face covering'. When encountering someone they preferred not to meet or it was inconvenient to see, a simple fan could cover their face, sparing both parties any awkwardness. So, why is the relationship between the two so strained?

Some scholars believe it might also be related to the 'factional struggles between the new and old parties'. The dominant faction rides on horseback, while the demoted one can only walk. The different fates of the two sides are also reflected in their attendants. Look, the *Shutong* (书童, a boy serving in a scholar's study) behind this fan-covering man appears quite embarrassed (his little cheeks are flushed red). He dares not look around and follows closely behind his master like a dog with its tail tucked. Interestingly, he is also holding a fan. In contrast, the attendant before the horse rider is in a completely different state. He walks forwards with his head held high and chest puffed out, looking rather haughty and arrogant. Oh, he seems even more pleased with himself than his master!

In Zhang Zeduan's paintings, nothing exists in isolation; everything is interconnected. This scene is no exception. After observing these two groups of people, we must also take a look at the carriage on the other side. If we lay the book flat, we'll see that behind the fan-covering man, two carriages, called '*Taiping* cart', are rushing in! One of them has already turned the corner, with four donkeys or mules running side by side at full speed, while the carriage driver is whipping them on. One of the donkeys brays plaintively. At this very moment, the fan-covering man is still striving to maintain his dignity, but soon he will be knocked over.

In the distance, a girl turns her head to see what has happened. Her gaze, sharp as an arrow, makes our hearts leap into our throats, unable to avoid feeling deeply concerned for the fan-covering man!

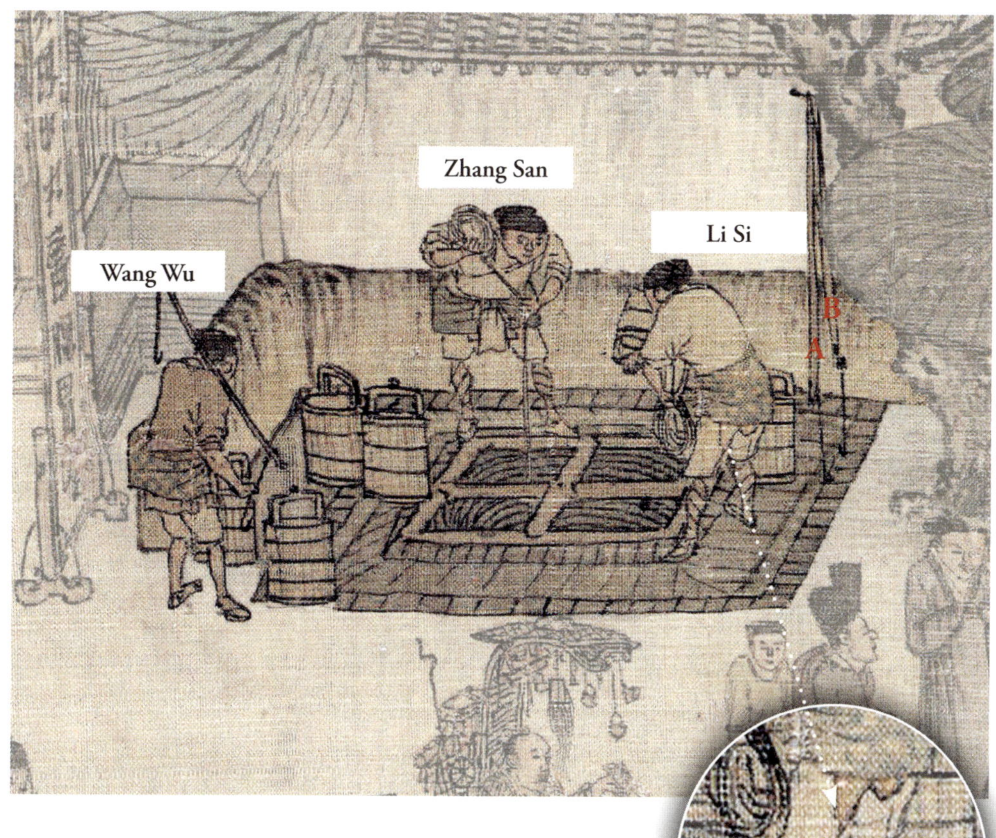

Finally, let's take a look at the water well that the itinerant monk is passing by.

There are a total of two water wells in *Along the River During the Qingming Festival*. One is at the beginning of the scroll, shown in a distant view at the edge of a field. The other is at the end of the scroll, this time in close-up, which is the one we see here. We'll discuss the well first, then the people around it.

This well is under a large willow tree. Although water wells are typically round, the mouth of wells is fitted with a wooden frame in the shape of the character '田 (*Tian*, field)', dividing it into four holes. This can be called a *Si kong jing* (四孔井, a well with four holes) or *Si yan jing* (四眼井). This design enhances safety and facilitating simultaneous drawing of water by multiple people. The well is surrounded by a square platform constructed from cyan bricks or stones, and its inner walls are lined with rectangular bricks. Two rammed earthen walls are built on the well platform, indicating that the well is equipped with protective barriers to prevent contamination from dust and debris.

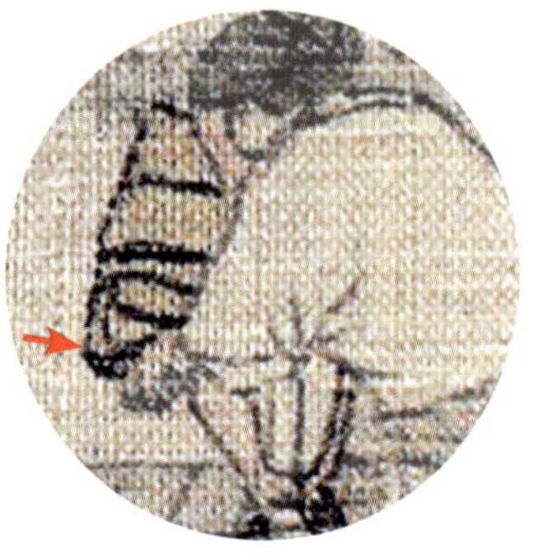

Now, let's take a look at the people. There are three individuals drawing water (for ease of discussion, I've named them, as shown in the illustration on the previous page). First, let's look at Wang Wu in the lower left corner. While some scholars suggest he has just arrived at the well and is about to lower his buckets, a closer look reveals otherwise. Zhang Zeduan's intention is quite clear: the two buckets are sitting steadily on the ground and the man is about to hook the handles with the crook of his carrying pole. He has already drawn the water and is preparing to carry it away. Without any doubt, the details in the artist's depiction invite us to examine carefully, describe accurately and appreciate their exquisiteness.

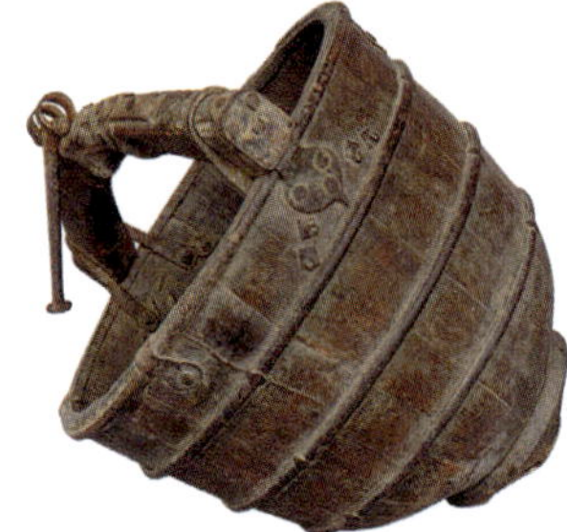

A water bucket with a pointed bottom (Lulu bucket), 54.5cm in height, 42.5cm in diameter, in the collection of Kaifeng Food Culture Museum, Henan province

The other two men are standing by the well. Zhang San is lowering a water bucket into the well. His left hand is pulling the rope and his right hand still has a few coils yet to be released and he is leaning forward to track the bucket's descent. Describing Li Si, however, is more challenging. His left hand holds several coils of rope, but what is his right hand doing? Some say that he is pulling the well rope with both hands and seems to have finished drawing water. However, a closer inspection of the detail on the left reveals that Li Si's right hand is actually about to throw a bucket down the well, indicated by the handle he holds, which matches the arc and thickness typical of a bucket handle. Because, whether throwing or pulling, the rope is unlikely to have such a neat shape. This raises a question: can you count how many buckets are on the ground? We can see a total of five, right? Consider this: one carrying pole carries two buckets, Zhang San is tying one, Li Si is throwing one, and there are five on the ground... Wait, why is there an extra one? A friend reminded me that what Li Si is holding might be a *Lulu* bucket specifically used for drawing water from large wells (locally known in old Kaifeng as *Dao guan*, 倒灌). This makes sense. These buckets are shaped like a spinning top, with a pointed bottom. When drawing water, the bucket tilts automatically to fill with water, then rights itself when full. The lower picture on the left shows a photo of a modern *Lulu* bucket.

The elongated objects marked with letters in the picture on page 175 are two carrying poles, hanging on the branches of a willow tree (more like nailed into the trunk). Three people, three carrying poles – neither more nor less, precisely depicted. Once again, it must be said: great works withstand scrutiny like this.

Lastly, the three men are dressed uniformly (all wearing the same shorts, especially Zhang San and Li Si, who have identical leg bindings), and they operate in a standardised manner (not throwing the carrying poles around). Some suspect they may be professional water carriers. In a large metropolis, fuel and drinking water are significant concerns. Despite the abundance of canals and water sources in Bianjing during the Northern Song Dynasty, there was a severe shortage of drinking water, so severe that many people perished from thirst in years of drought. As a result, the Northern Song government allowed the drilling of more water wells and made great efforts to divert the Jinshui River into channels, allowing wells to be built intermittently for use by palaces, temples and civilian residences. These measures significantly alleviate the problem of drinking water.

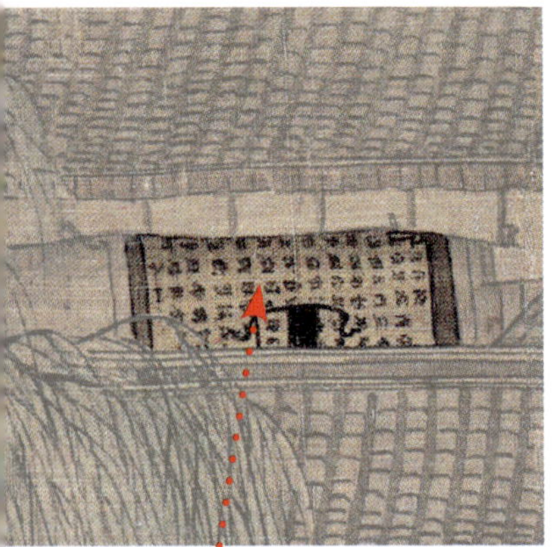

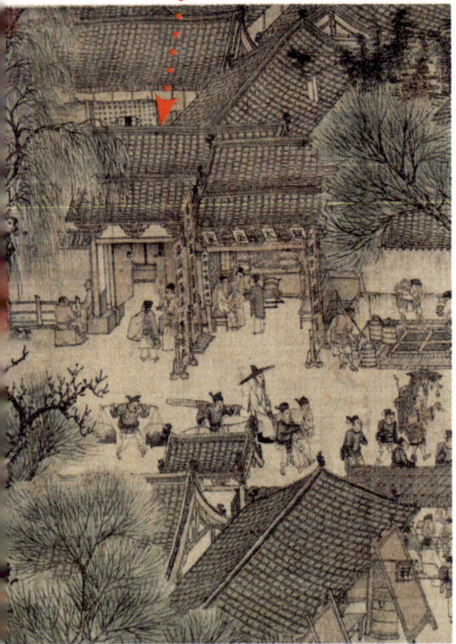

36. Hesitation and determination: two endings of *Along the River During the Qingming Festival*

Here and there, we meander, and before we know it, we find ourselves at the end of the scroll. There is a pharmacy and a tree. Let's first take a look at the pharmacy.

The pharmacy is named *Zhao Taicheng Jia* (赵太丞家). Here, *Taicheng* (太丞) is the title of a medical officer. During the reign of Emperor Huizong of the Song Dynasty, it was prohibited for ordinary people to do business in the market or have official titles on their shop signs, but pharmacies were an exception. Therefore, the large sign reading *Zhao Taicheng Jia* on this pharmacy does not violate any regulations. Although the storefront is not large, it has five *Dougong*, far more than needed for structural support. This can only be interpreted as a display of prestige, implying that this pharmacy enjoys considerable recognition. A *Taicheng*, as a medical officer, had the opportunity to mingle with upper-class society. Practising medicine and selling drugs, allowed him to amass substantial wealth, affording luxurious gardens and keeping concubines, all without question. *Zhao Taicheng Jia* features a joined roof (*Gou lian da ding*, 勾连搭顶), a design that not only symbolises sophistication but also expands the interior space. Now, if we look beyond the pharmacy in the full panorama view on the left page, we see that this pharmacy is not an isolated store. Its neighbour appears to be *Zhao Taicheng*'s private mansion, with the pharmacy located at the edge of the residence's main gate and to the left of the front courtyard. His private mansion is quite impressive, with at least three courtyards. In the second courtyard, a grand chair and a calligraphy screen are visible in the hall (reminiscent of the tarp on the tandem cart that was once hung in such halls). Overall, the location of the pharmacy is precisely what is known as the wealth position, as *Feng shui* claimed in ancient China.

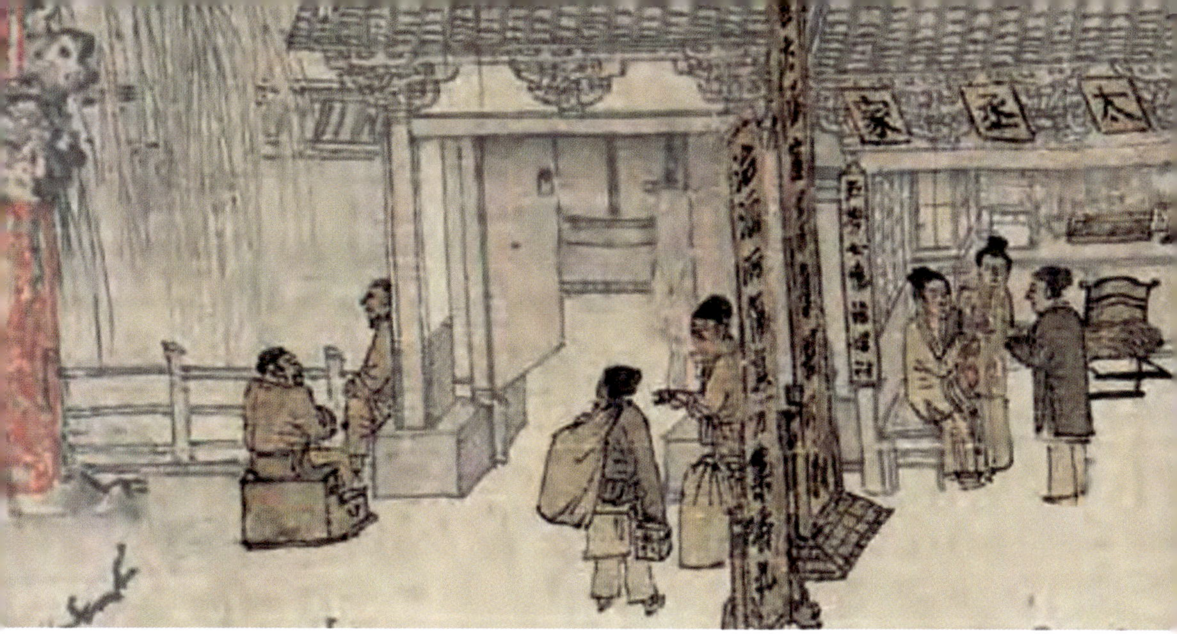

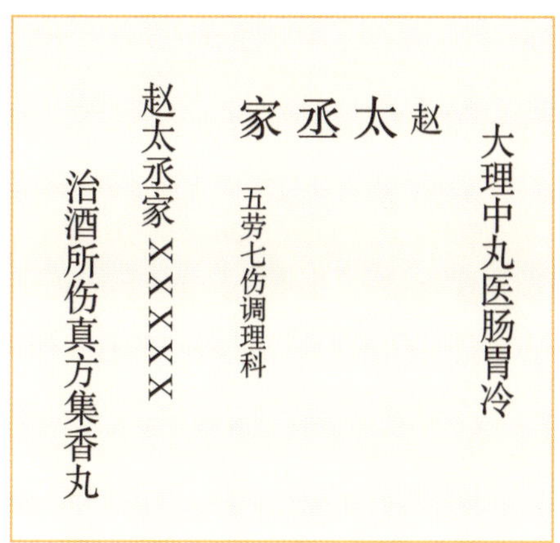

Layout plan of an advertising slogan

Zhao Taicheng clearly had a knack for advertising, evident in the several signs he erected at the entrance. The largest signboard is taller than the roof, thus requiring a solid base made from trapezoidal stone or brick. The other two are slightly shorter, with wooden *Ruyi*-shaped bases that are lighter and easier to move. As we discussed earlier regarding urban management in Bianjing and the issue of street encroachment, *Zhao Taicheng*'s store was

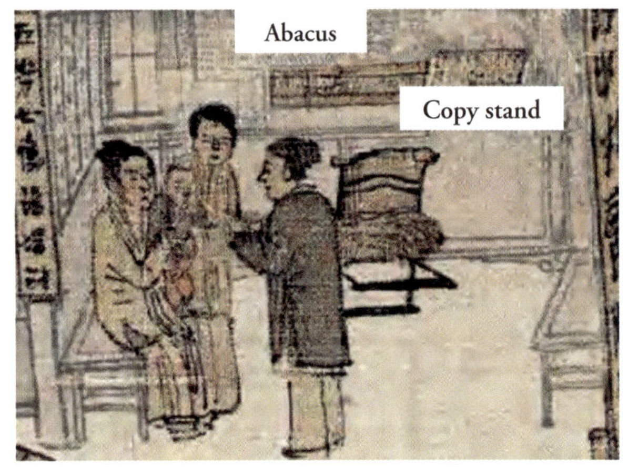

no exception. The outermost signboard encroaches on the street, just a few steps away from the centre of the street. Not only a physician, *Zhao Taicheng* was also a master of advertising. His slogans are concise and to the point (see the illustration on this page; some characters are guessed due to damage, provided here for reference only). Look, the first four characters on the most eye-catching signboard, standing prominently by the street, read: '治酒所伤 (*Zhi jiu suo shang*, treating alcohol-related injuries)'. Throughout the painting, we've seen numerous taverns and bars. The Song people loved drinking so much that alcohol-related health issues were relatively common. Therefore, this signboard gets straight to the point and addresses a prevalent problem of the time. Moreover, I suspect that this sign, '治酒所伤' might also serve as Zhang Zeduan's reminder and suggestion to the emperor. The harm of excessive drinking is not limited to individuals; the indulgence in entertainment and the numbing of will symbolised by excessive drinking can also harm society and the country. The signboards also mention '五劳七伤 (*Wu lao qi shang*, five strains and seven injuries)' ①, as well as '集香丸 (*Ji xiang wan*)' and '理中丸 (*Li zhong wan*)', which are the names of traditional Chinese medicine formulas from *Yu Yao Yuan Fang* (《御药院方》) ② and *Taiping Huimin Heji Ju Fang* (《太平惠民和剂局方》, *Prescriptions of the Bureau of Taiping People's Welfare Pharmacy*) ③, probably used to treat digestive disorders, loss of appetite and other spleen and stomach ailments.

In the picture above, a woman – likely a mother – sits on a stool holding a child, while another woman, possibly a maid, stands by their side. A physician in front of them might be *Zhao Taicheng* himself. He appears to be taking the pulse of the child by holding his hand. Please notice the vivid expressions of the three adults: the mother is stern and anxious, the maid looks deeply concerned and the doctor, with a pleasant and confident demeanour, exudes a reassuring presence. It must be said that Zhang Zeduan's skill in capturing facial expressions is remarkably high.

① 'Five Strains (*Wu lao*, 五劳)' refers to the damage of the five organs: heart, liver, spleen, lung and kidney. 'Seven Injuries (*Qi shang*, 七伤)' refers to the following: overeating harms the spleen, excessive anger disrupts the liver, heavy lifting or prolonged sitting on damp ground harms the kidneys, drinking cold beverages harms the lungs, sorrow and grief affect the heart, exposure to harsh weather conditions harms the body and fear or shock impacts the mind.

② *Yu Yao Yuan* (御药院): Established in the third year of the Zhidao era (997) during the reign of Emperor Taizong of the Song Dynasty, it was the imperial pharmacy in the palace. One of its responsibilities was to secretly prepare medicines for the emperor and the court. *Yu Yao Yuan Fang* (《御药院方》) is China's first collection of secret prescriptions for royal use.

③ *Taiping Huimin Heji Ju Fang* (《太平惠民和剂局方》, *Prescriptions of the Bureau of Taiping People's Welfare Pharmacy*) was first published after 1078. It was a prescription book used by the pharmacy bureau under the Imperial Medical Bureau of the Song Dynasty. Initially known as *Tai Yi Ju Fang* (《太医局方》), it was revised and reissued multiple times, with changes in the title and volumes. During the Chongning era (1102–1106) of Emperor Huizong of the Song Dynasty, the pharmacy bureau drafted standards, known as *He Ji Ju Fang* (《和剂局方》). During the Daguan era (1107–1110), it was proofread by the medical official, Chen Cheng, and others. After the Southern Song Dynasty moved the capital in the eighteenth year of the Shaoxing era (1148), the pharmacy bureau was renamed *Taiping Huimin Ju* (太平惠民局), and *He Ji Ju Fang* was accordingly renamed *Taiping Huimin Heji Ju Fang* (《太平惠民和剂局方》).

Now, let's take a look at a few items inside the room: an exquisite armchair, which seems to be covered with some sort of cushion. On the counter, there are two objects. One resembles an abacus (although abacuses are only documented in the Yuan Dynasty), and the other slightly resembles a computer monitor. Ah, of course, that's not possible; it should be a copying stand.

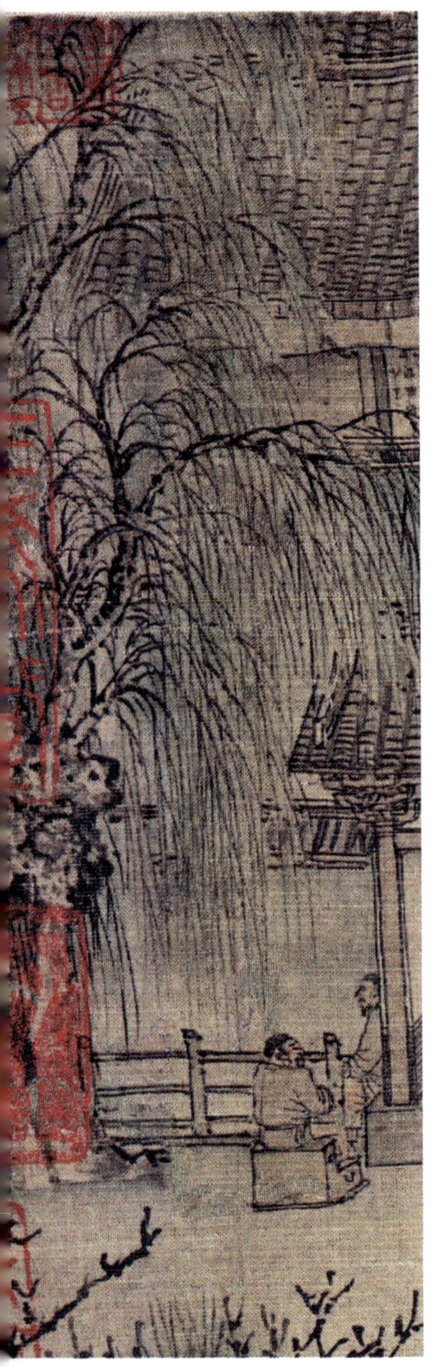

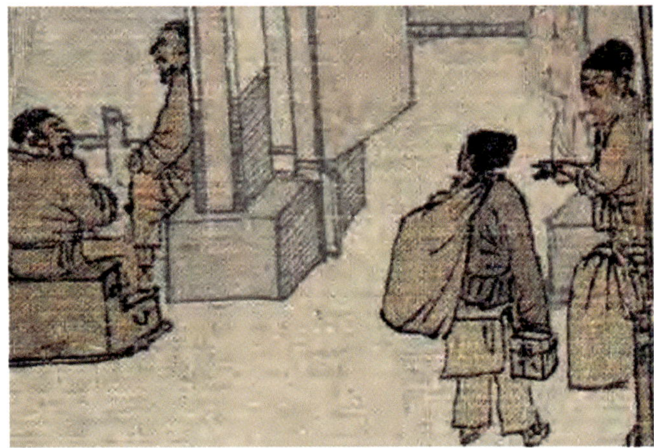

In front of *Zhao Taicheng*'s private mansion sit two men. One person has his right leg crossed over his left, hands clasping his knee – a posture that carries a certain comfort, evoking an indescribable feel of modernity. The other sits on a mounting stone, which was set up in ancient times by affluent households for the convenience of mounting horses. These two figures, one looking backwards and the other forwards, may not be a coincidence but rather a signal of the scroll's ending. It leaves us with lingering interest and endless reflection.

Beyond these figures, a tall, vigorous, ancient willow tree is another signal of the scroll's ending. What's particularly noteworthy is that it is not the common drought-tolerant willow most frequently depicted throughout the scroll, but rather a gracefully weeping willow. 'Among willows, the weeping variety is most valuable.' Its presence seems to hint that beyond this point lies the imperial palace, a place to be seen from a distance but not approached. However, for this book, I would prefer to let these two seemingly insignificant figures mark the conclusion.

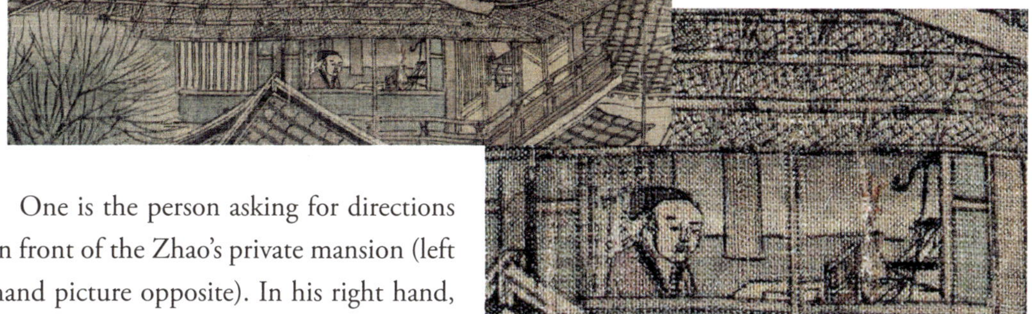

One is the person asking for directions in front of the Zhao's private mansion (left hand picture opposite). In his right hand, he carries a small box, with a large bundle slung over his shoulder. The bundle is so large that it makes him appear diminutive, almost as small as the gift box hidden behind him. Compared to the city gate, this is but a minor entrance; yet, relative to the man himself, it appears as an unfathomably grand gateway. At this moment, he stands at the doorway, alone, timid and bewildered, uncertain whether he will enter or depart. And here, abruptly, the bustling journey of *Along the River During the Qingming Festival* comes to an end. However, as we look back upon the entire scroll, we must not forget the scholar residing in his rented room. Immersed in his books amidst simple furnishings and a plain lifestyle, he finds contentment in his solitude. You see, the artist did paint his eyes – focused and joyful. At the end, we see a hesitant silhouette, but in our hearts, we are left with this determined countenance. How wonderful! At that time, the streets were bustling and the dazzling *Sun Yang Zheng Dian* is just across from him. Near *Wang Yuan Wai* homestay, a group of scholars gather, eagerly enquiring about their futures. Yet, here in his room, it is so tranquil. He does not dwell on fate, but sits upright, absorbed in the book before him. His upright posture is striking, perhaps the most pronounced in the entire scroll. I believe his posture speaks volumes – he may very well be Zhang Zeduan himself, and this 'self-portrait' is his profound legacy to future generations of scholars.

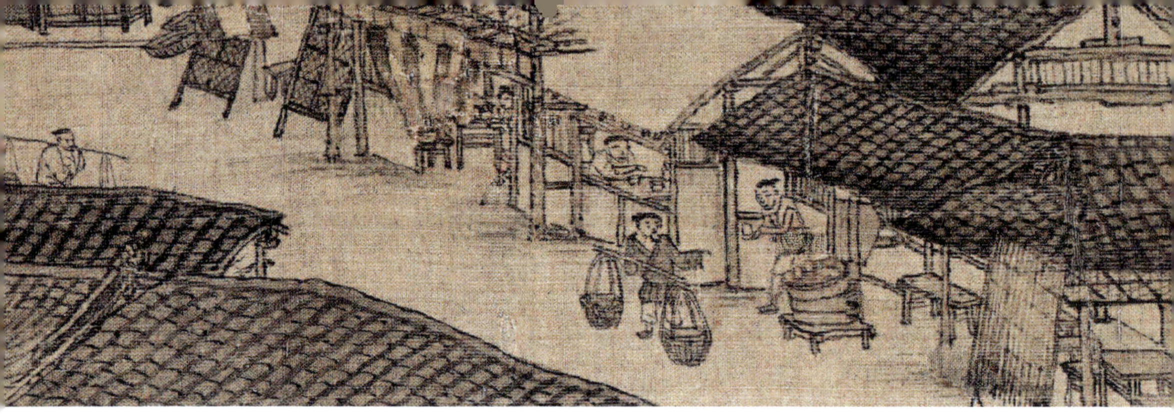

CHAPTER III

Q&A: More Questions from Readers

My dear readers, we have just fully appreciated the entire scroll of *Along the River During the Qingming Festival*. I am thrilled that we've been together until now! During the reading, I hope you've experienced that the more thoroughly we read ancient paintings, the more fascinating they become. Indeed, please remember: in-depth reading is the fundamental method to truly understand Chinese paintings. It also means that you may have more questions than those who just take a look at the paintings. I understand this well, as I have the same experience while my reading. However, the questions that arise from in-depth reading are different from the confusion born out of ignorance or superficial glances. Rather, our questions carry a hint of secret joy, one that only those who are with us can truly get.

Since last year, I have been teaching Chinese painting classes to overseas Chinese students. They raise questions after class, and I answer them all. In this chapter, I will share with you some of our Q&As about *Along the River During the Qingming Festival*. Of course, these Q&As do not mark the end of enquiries; on the contrary, they are just the beginning, encouraging my dear readers to raise even more questions.

If you have any questions, please feel free to reach out using the contact information on the next page. I believe that the Q&A between us will transform this book into an 'infinite book of sand', with no end to its pages. Our shared curiosity, attention to detail and profound love for classical aesthetics will become the strongest spiritual adhesive, ultimately enabling us to learn more about this painting.

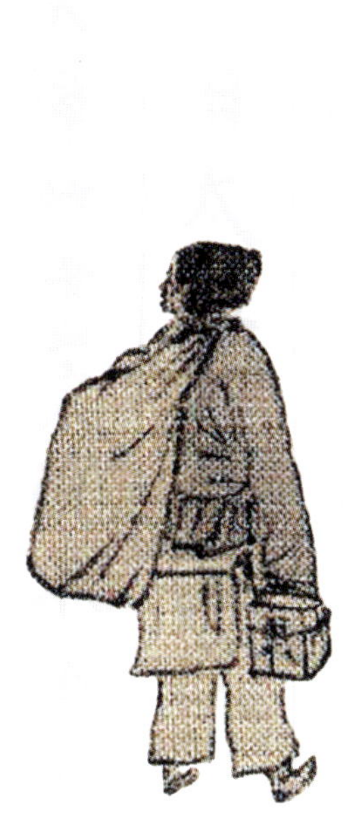

1. How long did it take to paint *Along the River During the Qingming Festival*?

Q: Given so many figures and details in *Along the River During the Qingming Festival,* how long did it take Zhang Zeduan to paint the entire scroll?

A: There are no records of when *Along the River During the Qingming Festival* was painted or how long it took to paint. As a result, we can only speculate based on our experience and other available information.

Some scholars believe that it would have taken at least a year. But if you ask me, I think even this estimate seems overly optimistic; it likely took no less than two to three years.

In addition to our subjective speculations, a piece of historical record offers us further insight. According to the archives from the Imperial Household Department in the Qing Dynasty (*Collected Files of the Workshop in the Hall of Moral Cultivation*, Volume 53, Page 221), court artist, Feng Ning, was commissioned to replicate *An Era in Jinling* on the eighth day of the first lunar month in the 57th year of the Qianlong Emperor's reign (1792). He completed the work in the 59th year of the Qianlong Emperor's reign (1794) in November, taking nearly two years. The scroll measures 35 centimetres in height and 1,050 centimetres in width. Painting a 10-metre-long scroll in two years is considered quite fast. In comparison, *Along the River During the Qingming Festival* measures 24.8 centimetres in height and 528 centimetres in width. Based on this information, we can make a more reliable estimate.

It is also worth noting that the painting of

Contact me with more questions:
① Email: tianyubin@vip.126.com
② Wechat: iyihua
③ Wechat QR code:

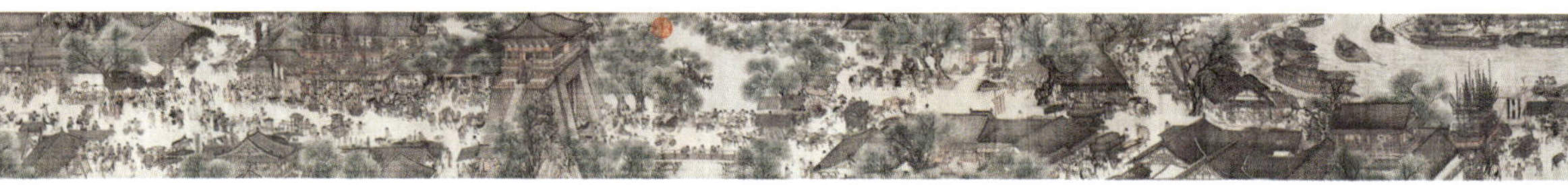

monumental scrolls like *Along the River During the Qingming Festival*, *An Era in Jinling* and *A Thousand Li of Rivers and Mountains* must be supported by the imperial family. And this is another crucial factor that influenced the time required to paint.

2. Is the existing *Along the River During the Qingming Festival* actually complete or not?

Q: Why are the scenes inside the city so short, while the scenes outside are so long?

A: That's a great question. Many people feel that the scenes inside the city are too brief, ending abruptly without much to see, which leads to a speculation that *Along the River During the Qingming Festival* might be a fragment, perhaps shortened over time. Painters from the Ming and Qing Dynasty also held this belief, often extending their copies all the way to the imperial palace. However, from an artistic perspective, I believe that

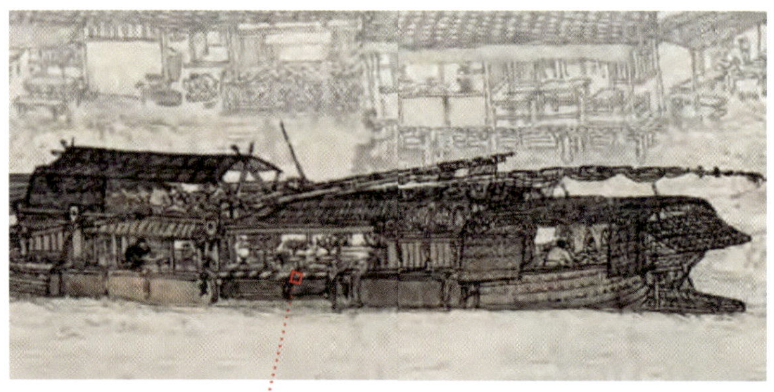

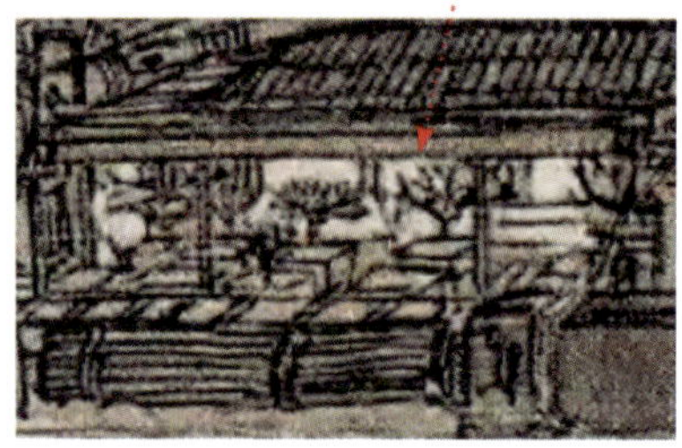

any additions made by imitators to the original Song Dynasty version, as later copies did, is like 'adding feet to a snake' – it diminishes the artistic quality significantly. In my view, the focal point of *Along the River During the Qingming Festival* is

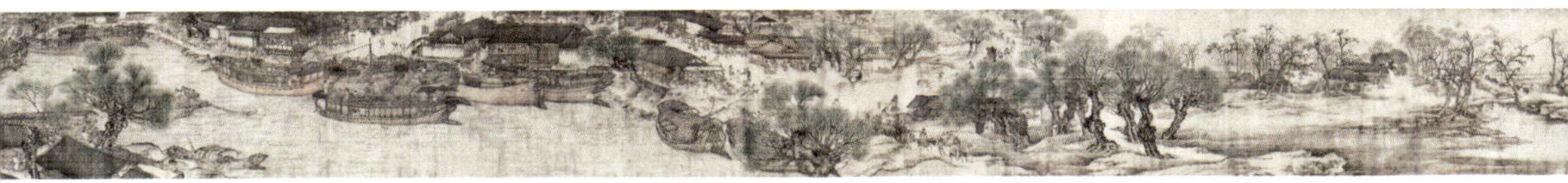

the Rainbow Bridge, instead of the city gate. In fact, with the Rainbow Bridge as the centre, the composition is nearly symmetrical, achieving a perfect balance. The scroll starts with a young boy and a small donkey and ends with a figure seen from behind and a drooping willow tree, infusing the work with a profound literary sensibility. While seemingly casual and understated, it is actually imbued with endless charm and elegance – the mark of a true master.

3. Metropolis in the Song Dynasty: Luoyang, Hangzhou and Nanjing

Q: Besides Bianjing, were there any other metropolises in the Song Dynasty?

A: Yes, there were. For example, Luoyang. Luoyang is the western capital of the Northern Song Dynasty ①. At that time, officials enjoyed gathering in Luoyang and preferred to live there after retirement, making it a cultural and political sub-centre of the Northern Song. Luoyang is also famous for its peonies. The people in Luoyang had such a deep affection for flowers that even the poor wore flowers and drank wine for pleasure. Unfortunately, Emperor Huizong of Song took a liking to peonies in Luoyang and had them transported to Bianjing to adorn his imperial gardens, almost leaving Luoyang without flowers ②. In the illustration on the left, there appear to be some flower-like objects in the large boat's cabin, which might have been the peonies transported from Luoyang and other places.

① The Northern Song Dynasty implemented a four-capital system: The Eastern Capital was the primary capital, located in Bianliang, hence also called Bianjing. The Western Capital was Luoyang. The Southern Capital was not the modern-day Nanjing, but was situated in present-day Shangqiu, where Emperor Taizu of the Song Dynasty rose to power. The Northern Capital was located in present-day Daming, Hebei Province.

② Northern Song scholar, Shao Bowen, a native of Luoyang, wrote in his *The Records of the Experience and Knowledge of Shao Bowen* (Volume 17): the people in his hometown also had a deep love for flowers. And there were many gardens and flower markets. 'Even the poor wore flowers and drank wine for pleasure,' he noted. However, during the Zhenghe era of Emperor Huizong's reign, he passed through Luoyang and found that the gardens and flower markets were gone. He was told, 'Before the flowers bloom, people are sent to guard them. As soon as they bloom, they are uprooted and transported to the capital. The names of the garden owners are registered, and they must annually provide flowers like paying taxes. Thus, the traditions of flowers in Luoyang were abandoned.'

Lin'an (present-day Hangzhou), the Southern Song capital, was also a bustling metropolis. *Scenic Attractions of West Lake* possibly depicts a panoramic view of West Lake during the Southern Song Dynasty. In the previous chapter, when we look at the 'fire lookout towers', we referenced a section of this painting. Now, let me show you another intriguing detail... If we take another close look at the picture below, we will notice the character '解 (*Jie*)' near the fire lookout tower (indicated by the red arrow)! Do you remember the '*Jie pu*' in *Along the River During the Qingming Festival*? The difference here is that the character '解 (*Jie*)' is much larger, and the curtain on which it is written is almost the size of a door curtain. Some believe that this character '解 (*Jie*)' is written on the wall.

Attributed to) *Scenic Attractions of West Lake* (Part), from the Southern Song Dynasty in the collection of Freer Gallery of Art

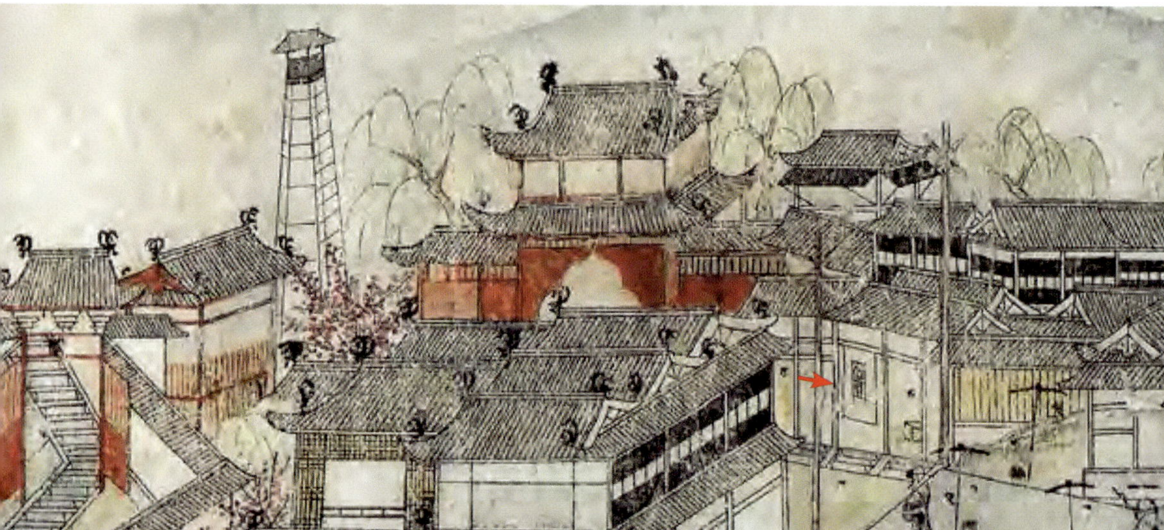

But that is incorrect, as the door curtain is right in front of the entrance steps. Peering through the side door without a curtain, we can see a square stool inside. Considering the high-ranking official building nearby, this '*Jie pu*' might be an affiliated institution of the government office, possibly handling matters related to the imperial examinations. In any case, it is quite interesting to compare this with the one in *Along the River During the Qingming Festival.*

Nanjing was also a bustling metropolis during the Song Dynasty. The Song Dynasty court painting *An Era in Jinling* depicts the state of Jinling (an ancient name for Nanjing) during that period. Compared to *Along the River During the Qingming Festival*, which portrays normal life in the Central Plains, *An Era in Jinling* could be considered as its Jiangnan version. The similarities are so striking that some scholars even speculate that *An Era in Jinling* might be a variant of *Along the River During the Qingming Festival.*

Given its close connection to *Along the River During the Qingming Festival, An Era in Jinling* is undoubtedly a precious artifact, right? Unfortunately, while the original Song Dynasty court version was still extant at least until the Qianlong reign of the Qing Dynasty, it was somehow lost later on. Fortunately, Emperor Qianlong of the Qing Dynasty commissioned several court painters to create replicas of *An Era in Jinling* and, as a result, we still have access to three surviving copies. The first replica was completed by a painter named Xie Sui in the 52nd year of Qianlong's reign (1787). The second was completed by another painter, Yang Dazhang in the 56th year of the Qianlong's reign (1791). Both painters directly replicated the original Song Dynasty court version. Later, the painter Feng Ning was commissioned to create a replica based on Yang Dazhang's version – a replica of another replica.

In the previous chapter, we referenced the barbican from *An Era in Jinling.* Now, let's read a few more scenes from the painting.

The top picture on page 189 depicts a rural household in the suburbs. The mother is cooking, the grandmother is looking after the child, and the man is sweeping the yard. A slender dog has returned home and an ox stands idly by. At that moment, the stove fire is burning brightly, and the child talks to his mother. On the table, there are bowls, jars and a pot. Inside the room, there is a bed with a pillow on it.

The picture in the middle also portrays another heart-warming family scene. The man

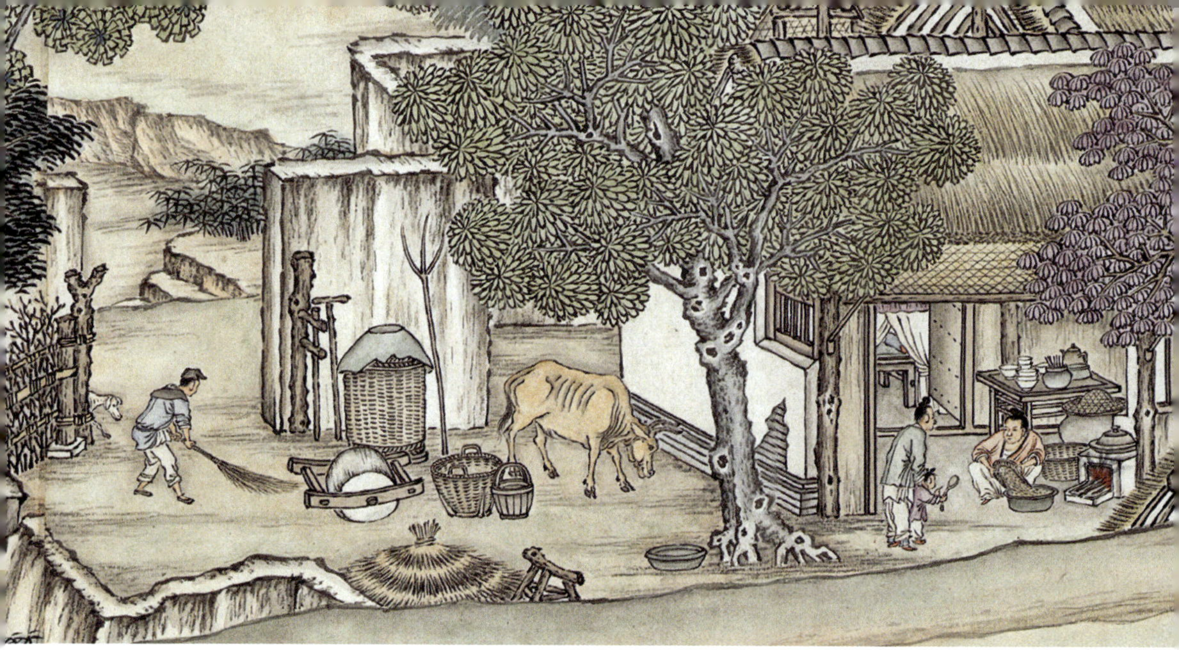

ABOVE: *An Era in Jinling* (Part), Xie Sui, the Qing Dynasty in the collection of the National Palace Museum, Taipei

RIGHT: *An Era in Jinling* (Part), Xie Sui, the Qing Dynasty in the collection of the National Palace Museum, Taipei

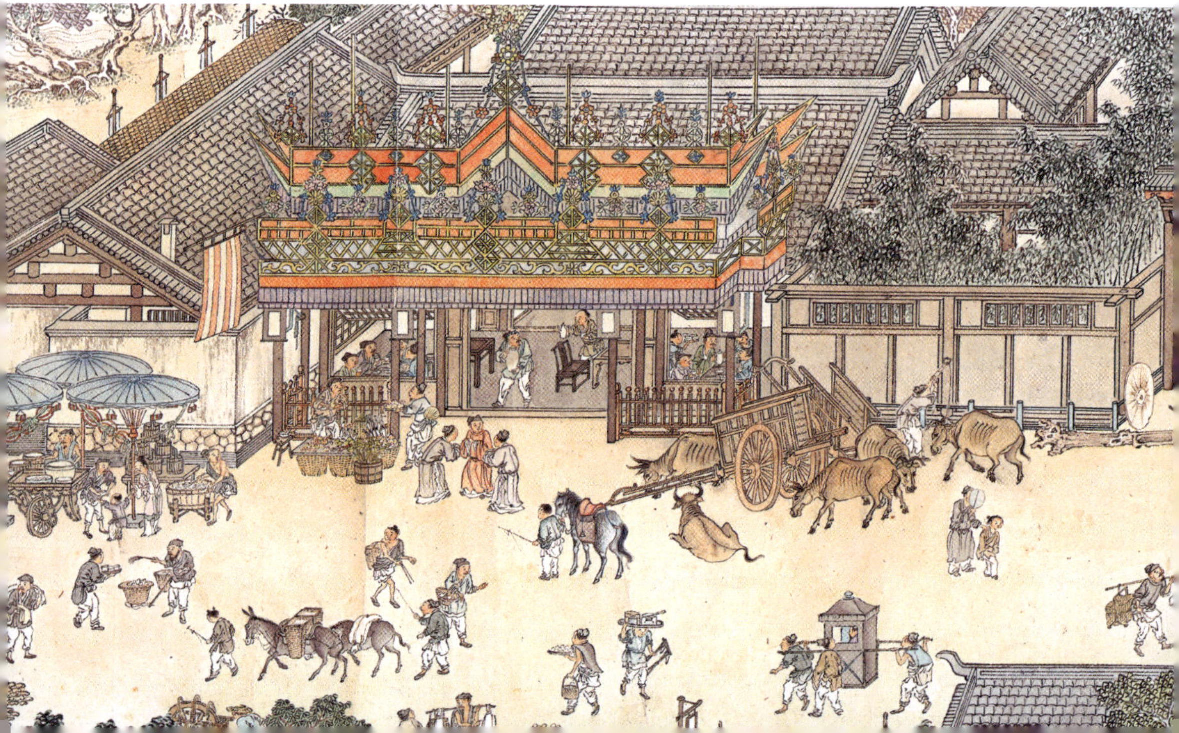

BELOW: *An Era in Jinling* (Part), Feng Ning, the Qing Dynastyin the private collection

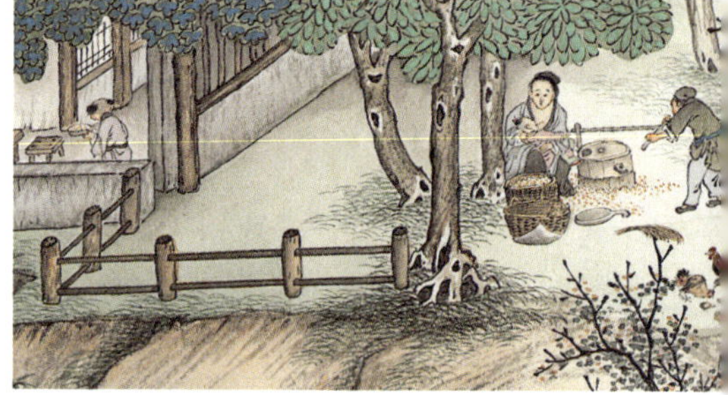

is pushing a millstone, while the mother sits nursing her infant. The eldest son is carrying things into the house. A rooster, a hen and their chicks are pecking at food.

The picture below left depicts the *Cai lou huan men* inside the city. In front of the entrance, a sedan chair is passing by (indicated by the red arrow), with a man inside. In the Northern Song scholar's view, it was considered inhumane for a man to have sedan bearers carry him around. Nearby, a person is holding a fan to cover his face (indicated by the blue arrow) – although no one is actually looking at him, so there's no need for him to do so. Perhaps the Qing Dynasty artists who replicated the Song painting no longer fully understood the behaviour of covering one's face practised in the Song Dynasty.

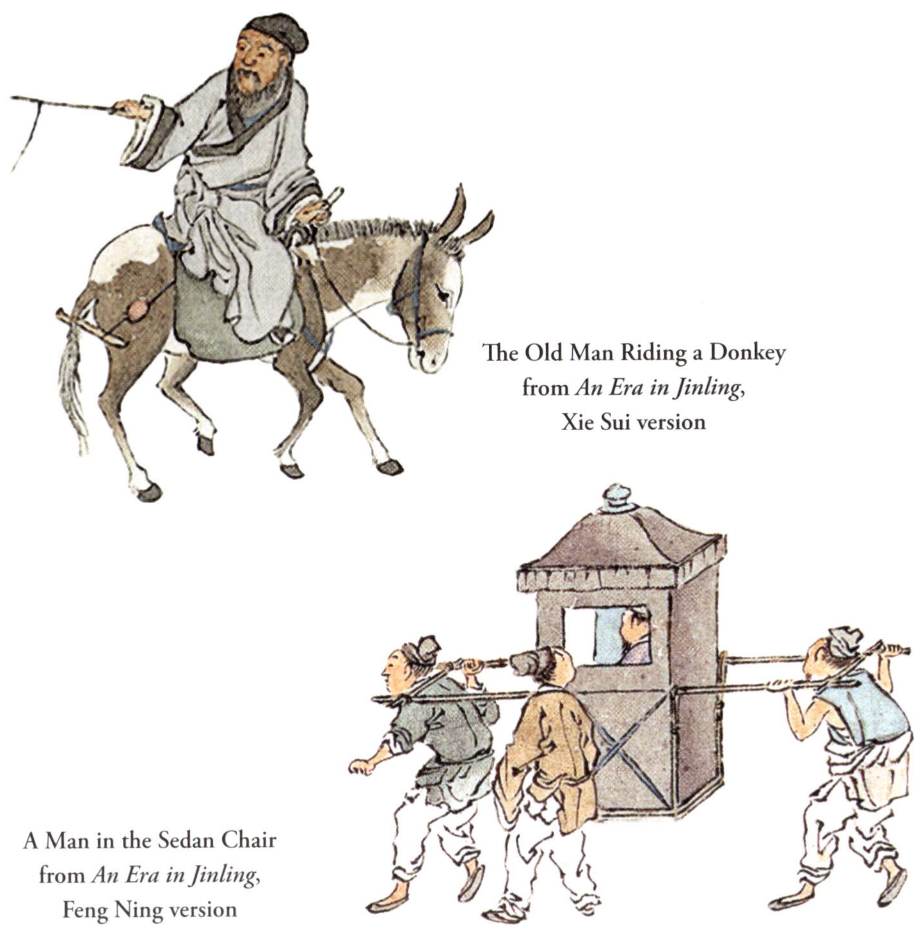

The Old Man Riding a Donkey from *An Era in Jinling*, Xie Sui version

A Man in the Sedan Chair from *An Era in Jinling*, Feng Ning version

元代三跋 Third *Ba* in the Yuan Dynasty

明代六跋 |Sixth *Ba* in the Ming Dynasty

《清明上河图》跋文全貌

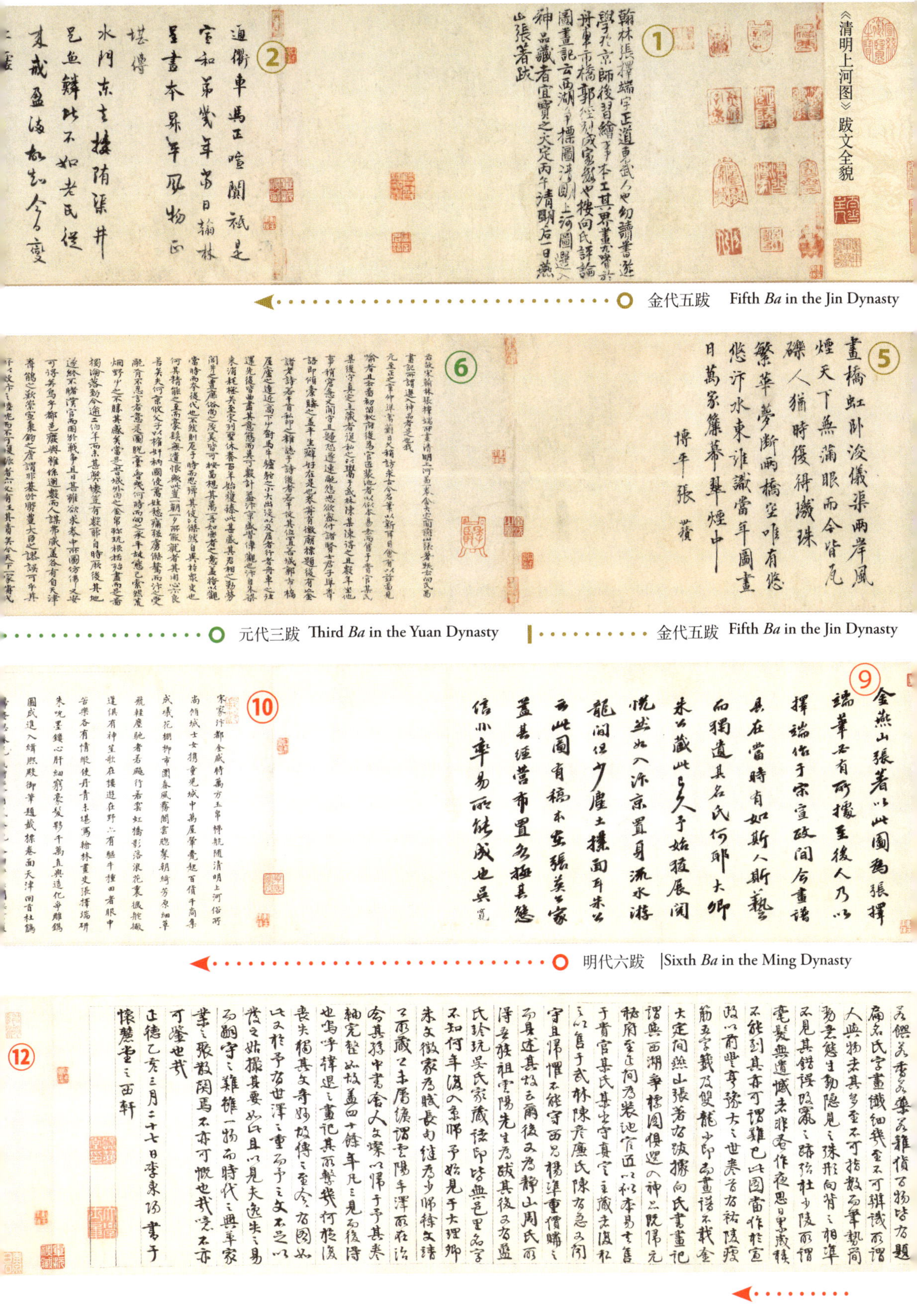
《清明上河图》跋文全貌
①
②
金代五跋 Fifth Ba in the Jin Dynasty
⑤
⑥
元代三跋 Third Ba in the Yuan Dynasty
金代五跋 Fifth Ba in the Jin Dynasty
⑨
⑩
明代六跋 |Sixth Ba in the Ming Dynasty
⑫

4. A brief reading of the *Bas* on *Along the River During the Qingming Festival*

Q: Apart from Zhang Zhu's *Ti ba*, are there any other *Ti ba*s on *Along the River During the Qingming Festival*?

A: The texts written at the beginning or end of a book, calligraphy, or painting are called *Ti ba* (题跋, preface and postscript). More specifically, *Ti ba* are a combination of *Ti* (题, preface) and *Ba* (跋, postscript), with the text at the beginning called *Ti* and the text at the end called *Ba*. The content is often related to the process of creating the book or painting, as well as its evaluations, appreciations and verification. There are a total of fourteen existing *Ba*s on *Along the River During the Qingming Festival*: five from the Jin Dynasty, three from the Yuan Dynasty, and six from the Ming Dynasty. The *Ba* by Zhang Zhu of the Jin Dynasty is the first one and can be considered the most important. Historical records about Zhang Zeduan are scarce, and it is only through Zhang Zhu's *Ba* that later generations have been able to identify Zhang Zeduan as the artist of *Along the River During the Qingming Festival* and gain a general understanding of his life.

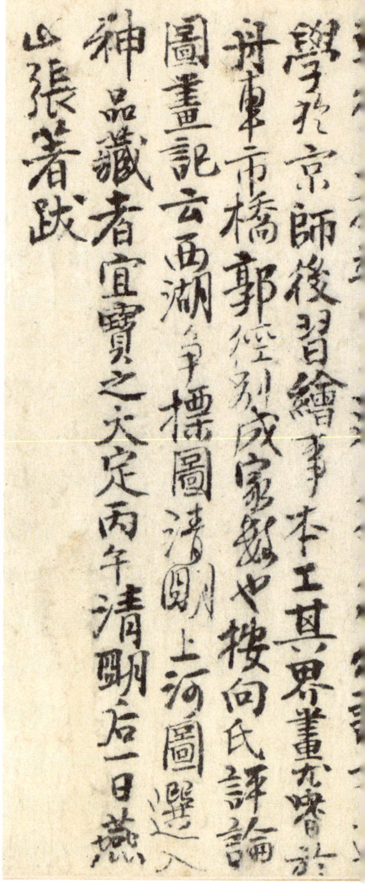
學於京師後習繪事本工其界畫尤嗜於
舟車市橋郭徑別成家數也按向氏評論
圖畫記云西湖爭標圖清明上河圖選入
神品藏者宜寶之大定丙午清明後一日燕
山張著跋

The previous two pages present the full view of the *Ba*s, which are so long (much longer than the painting itself) that they are displayed in four sections. Here is a brief introduction to the *Ba*s.

The five *Ba*s from the Jin Dynasty can be categorised into two types and three groups. The two types are: Zhang Zhu's *Ba*, which forms a category of its own, providing a general introduction to Zhang Zeduan's life, characteristics and works, and advising collectors to cherish the painting as a treasure. The other four *Ba*s are the second type, which, apart from speculating on the depicted locations, also mention the reasons for the fall of the country and express a sense of lament. As for the three groups, Zhang Zhu's *Ba* at the beginning and Zhang Shiji's at the end, each forming a group of their own, and the three people in the middle – Zhang Gongyao, Li Quan and Wang Jian – forming a group. These three were friends, and they likely held a scholars' gathering near Bianjing sometime between 1186 and 1190, during which they wrote their poems as *Bas* in succession.

Hanlin scholar Zhang Zeduan, courtesy name Zhengdao, was a native of Dongwu. In his youth, he read books and pursued his study in the capital. Later, he practised the art of painting. He was originally skilled in *Jie hua*, and was particularly fond of boats, carriages, markets, bridges and village paths, establishing his own distinctive style. According to the *Xiangshi Pinglun Tuhua Ji* (《向氏评论图画记》, *Xiang's Commentaries on Paintings*), *Dragon Boat Racing on the West Lake* and *Along the River During the Qingming Festival* were selected as masterpieces. Collectors should treasure them. Inscribed by Zhang Zhu of Yanshan on the day after Qingming Festival in the bingwu year of the Dading period.

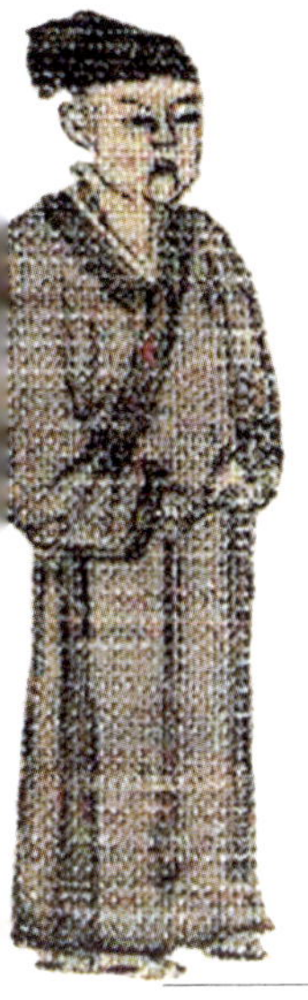

Among them, Zhang Gongyao's grandfather, Zhang Xiaochun, was a minister of the Northern Song Dynasty and once governed Taiyuan. Li Quan's father, Li Qiong, also persisted in resisting the Jin invaders in his early years. However, both of them later surrendered to the Jin Dynasty, with the former becoming the left prime minister of the Bianjing Administration and the latter becoming a general in the Jin army. Their descendants, Zhang Gongyao and Li Quan respectively, also became officials of the Jin Dynasty. It is worth mentioning that Li Quan's teacher, Liu Zhan, had another student named Xin Qiji ①.

How serious am I? I'm the best representative of the 'problem-seeking school'.

① Xin Qiji: A renowned general of the Southern Song Dynasty and a leading figure of the Bold and Unconstrained School of *Ci*, he rebelled against the Jurchen Jin Dynasty throughout his life.

Understanding the identity and experiences of the author of a *Ti Ba* is beneficial for interpreting their *Ba*s. For instance, Zhang Gongyao and Li Quan were both descendants of the Northern Song Dynasty. When they saw the bustling scenes of Bianjing in *Along the River During the Qingming Festival*, and then compared it to the ruins and rubble of the former capital, they couldn't help but feel a sense of melancholy and dismay.

Now, let's turn our attention to the Yuan Dynasty.

There are three *Ba*s from the Yuan Dynasty. As the writers of these *Ba*s lived in an era far from the Northern Song Dynasty, they were less emotionally attached compared to those from the Jin Dynasty, allowing them to focus more on the painting's meanings. Yang Zhun, the first one, believed that Zhang Zeduan likely intended to depict the prosperity of his time to glorify it for future generations, or perhaps he had an extraordinary pursuit in technique. Thus, this dedication exhausted his mind and energy, striving for perfection without leaving any regrets. Although

Then, I'm the representative of the 'spectacle-seeking school'.

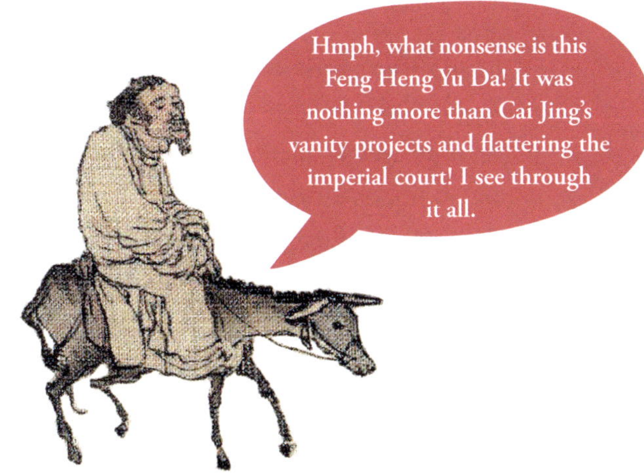

Yang Zhun's understanding was relatively superficial, he was the first to speculate on Zhang Zeduan's motivation for painting. Following his line of thought, by the time of the third *Ba* of the Yuan Dynasty, Li Qi's understanding had deepened significantly. Li Qi had served as a local official, and this experience allowed him to see the problems revealed in *Along the River During the Qingming Festival* from an administrator's perspective, such as the laxity of soldiers, the poor city defences and the chaos in traffic, etc. These issues were undoubtedly highly sensitive in the minds of officials and were easily recognised as unusual. Li Qi also made a comparison, suggesting that it would be better to view *Along the River During the Qingming Festival* together with *Against Luxurious Ease Tu* (《无逸图》). *Against Luxurious Ease Tu* originates from *Shangshu: Against Luxurious Ease* (《尚书 · 无逸图》), which was used to admonish emperors against indulgence and laziness. In Li Qi's view, *Along the River During the Qingming Festival* (hereafter referred to as *Qingming* Scroll) may have served a similar purpose.

Given that Li Qi served as an official during the Yuan Dynasty, he later fled to the mountains amid the chaos in Jiangnan at the end of the Yuan period. Upon hearing of the defeat of the Yuan army, he was often so distressed that he could not eat and wept bitterly. After the establishment of the Ming Dynasty, he remained loyal to the Yuan, adopting the sobriquet 'Old Man of Unwavering Heart' and refused to serve the Ming court. Later, in his twilight years, he was injured in a military upheaval and passed away in his seventies. His *Ba* was written in the 25th year of the Zhizheng era (1365) during the reign of Emperor Shun of Yuan, by which time he was already a weathered old man who had experienced much in life.

There are six extant *Ba*s from the Ming Dynasty, which can be divided into two schools of thought: one that revels in the bustling scenes and another that seeks out problems. Let us take one example from each school as representative.

Let's first discuss the representative of the 'problem-seeking school', Li Dongyang. He was the Minister of Rites and the Grand Secretary of Pavilion of the Imperial Library. Among the six *Bas* from the Ming Dynasty, five individuals wrote them, with Li Dongyang alone contributing two. His *Bas* were written in the 5th year of the Hongzhi era (1492) during the reign of Emperor Xiaozong of Ming and the 10th year of the Zhengde era (1515) during the reign of Emperor Wuzong of Ming, respectively. Li Dongyang was the fifth-generation grandson of Li Qi, which is why he mentions in his *Ba*, 'The ancestral calligraphy of Master Xiqu is here'. Xiqu was Li Qi's courtesy name. Li Dongyang was an official known for his empathy towards the people and his courage to remonstrate with the emperor. Thus, he was highly sensitive to the latent concerns in *Along the River During the Qingming Festival*, saying, 'Alone, from worry and joy, I can sense the rise and fall.' Interestingly, probably inspired by his ancestor Li Qi's idea of viewing the *Qingming* Scroll alongside *Against Luxurious Ease Tu,* he thought of comparing it with *Liu Min Tu* (《流民图》, Zheng Xia). *Liu Min Tu* depicts events from the reign of Emperor Shenzong of the Northern Song Dynasty. At that time, there was a minor official named Zheng Xia who, in order to oppose Wang Anshi's reforms, had someone paint *Liu Min Tu* based on the scenes of disaster victims fleeing famine that he had witnessed, and presented it to Emperor Shenzong. In Li Dongyang's view, *Along the River During the Qingming Festival* also served a similar purpose. Additionally, he mentioned *Feng Heng Yu Da* (丰亨豫大, peace and prosperity)①, which refers to the flatulent promises made by the traitorous minister Cai Jing to Emperor Huizong of Song, claiming that it was a time of great peace and prosperity that the emperor should indulge in pleasures, thus accelerating the downfall of the Northern Song Dynasty. In his subsequent *Ba*, Li Dongyang further pointed out that the *Qingming* scroll was created during the period when Emperor Huizong and his court were engrossed in the concept of *Feng Heng Yu Da.* He also noted the presence of Emperor Huizong's 'slender gold script five-character title and double dragon seals' at the beginning of the scroll.

Feng Bao, a famous eunuch of the Ming Dynasty, represents the 'spectacle-seeking school'. Lacking experience in civilian life, he viewed the painting merely as a lively spectacle, and thus felt only refreshing and delightful. Moreover, Feng Bao's *Ba* is dated to the 6th year of the Wanli era (1578), indicating that the *Qingming* scroll had already been stored in the Ming imperial collection by that time. When exactly was it stored in the palace? It was in the 44th year of the Jiajing era (1565), when it was confiscated from the home of the treacherous councillor, Yan Song.

After Feng Bao, there was another one named Ru Shou (some say he was a monk from the early Qing Dynasty), and with his *Ba*, all the *Ba*s were complete.

① From *History of Song*, Volume 126, Part one of *Treatise on Food and Money*: 'After Emperor Huizong ascended the throne, Cai Jing promoted the concept of *Feng Heng Yu Da*, imposing harsh taxes and heavy levies to satisfy desires, thus hastening the downfall and defeat.' The reign of Emperor Huizong bears some resemblance to the late Ming period, as both were characterised by extravagance and indulgence on one hand and severe crises on the other. Consequently, opinions on *Along the River During the Qingming Festival* among Ming scholars were also diverged into two extremes: some saw prosperity, while others sensed impending troubles.

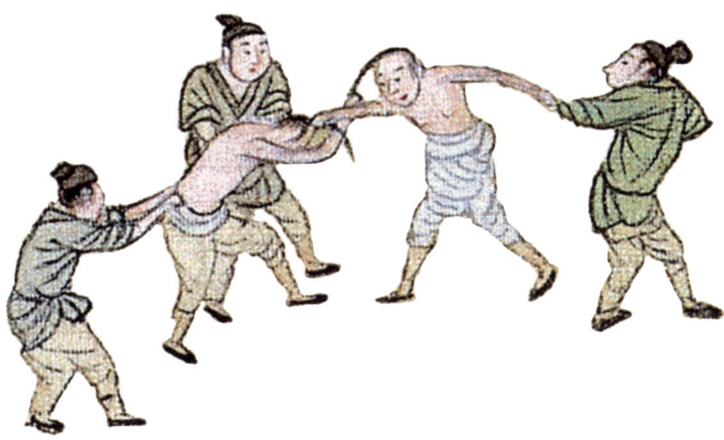

5. The circulation of *Along the River During the Qingming Festival* after the Ming Dynasty

Q: The *Bas* on *Along the River During the Qingming Festival* end in the late Ming period. What was the collection situation during the Qing Dynasty? Why didn't Emperor Qianlong, known for his obsessive stamping, leave his mark on the painting?

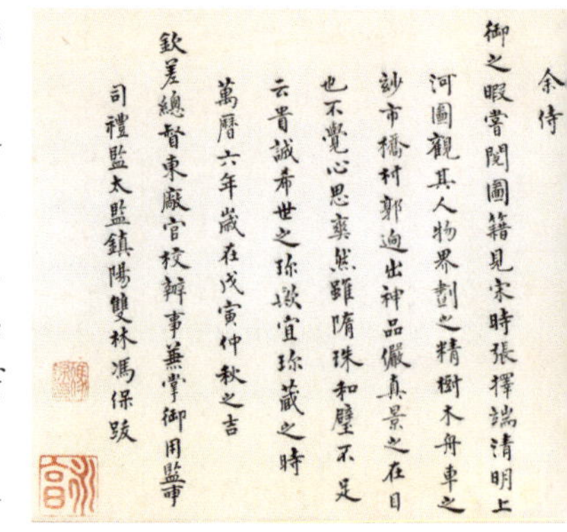
余侍
御之暇嘗閱圖籍見宋時張擇端清明上
河圖觀其人物界劃之精樹木舟車之
妙市橋村郭迥出神品儼真景之在目
也不覺心思爽然雖隋珠和璧不足
云貴誠希世之珍歟宜珍藏之時
萬曆六年歲在戊寅仲秋之吉
欽差總督東廠官校辦事兼掌御用監事
司禮監太監鎮陽雙林馮保跋

A: The story begins with the eunuch Feng Bao – not only did he inscribe the painting, but also stamped his seals. Look at the pictures on the right; he stamped four seals, two of which bear the characters 永享 (*Yong Xiang*). One seal, in particular, reads 冯永享收藏书画记 (Record of Feng Yongxiang's Collection of Calligraphy and Paintings). If this painting were still in the imperial palace, how would he dare to stamp such a seal? Therefore, he must have stolen *Along the River During the Qingming Festival* for himself. Later, the *Qingming* Scroll was no longer in Feng Bao's possession, allowing civilians like Ru Shou the opportunity to write *Bas*. During the Qing Dynasty, the *Qingming* Scroll was once in the hands of Lu Feichi and Bi Yuan. The former had served as the chief editor of the *Complete Library of the Four Treasuries* (《四库全书》), while the latter held the position of Governor-General of Hunan and Hubei. Both were corrupt officials with considerable wealth, enabling them to collect artworks. However, both had their properties confiscated after their deaths. In October of the 4th year of the Jiaqing era (1799) of the Qing Dynasty, the *Qingming* Scroll was in the Jiaqing imperial collection from Bi Yuan's hand and remained there until the end of the Qing Dynasty.

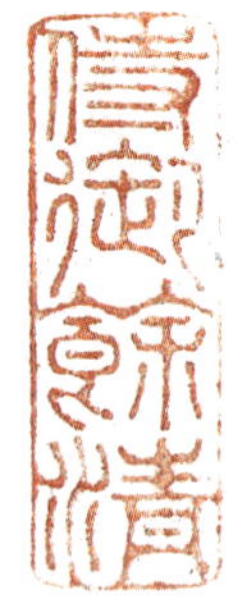

Shi Yu Yu Qing

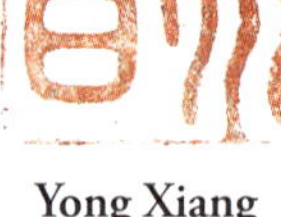

Yong Xiang

Feng Bao

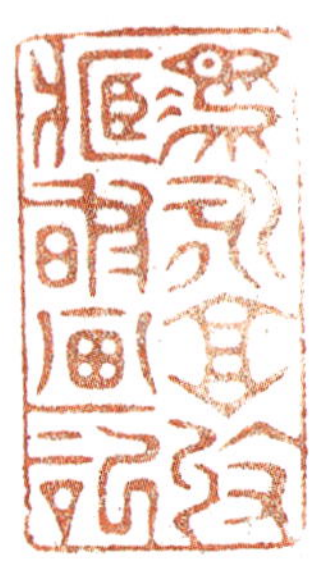

Record of Feng Yongxiang's Collectio of Calligraphy and Paintings

Emperor Qianlong passed away on the third day of the

first lunar month of the fourth year of the Jiaqing reign, so he never had the opportunity to stamp or inscribe on *Along the River During the Qingming Festival.*

In 1911, the Xinhai Revolution overthrew the Qing Dynasty. The deposed Qing Emperor Puyi had someone secretly take *Along the River During the Qingming Festival* out of the palace, and it was later hidden in the Imperial Palace of Manchukuo in Changchun. In August 1945, when Japan surrendered and Puyi fled in panic, the *Qingming* Scroll he carried was lost. After some time, it resurfaced in the collection of the Northeast Museum (now the Liaoning Provincial Museum) in 1950. And it was returned to the Palace Museum at the end of 1953, where it remains to this day.

6. *The* well-documented legacy *of Along the River During the Qingming Festival*

Q: What does 'well-documented legacy' mean?

A: 'Well-documented legacy' (传承有绪, some write '绪' as '序') refers to the traceable history of ownership of an ancient painting or calligraphy. In other words, it means that we can ascertain who has collected it throughout history, with verified key points of its transmission to the present day. Thus, the likelihood that the work is authentic is greatly increased. For this reason, a 'well-documented legacy' is considered one of the important criteria for authenticating paintings and calligraphy. However, it should be noted that a well-documented legacy does not absolutely guarantee authenticity, and there are rare exceptions. Therefore, the determination of authenticity also requires a comprehensive judgement based on various aspects, such as brushwork style, seals and inscriptions, materials and mounting.

7. *Along the River During the Qingming Festival* and *Jie hua*

Q: Some say *Along the River During the Qingming Festival* is a representative work of *Jie hua*. Can you discuss its artistic features in this regard?

A: Generally speaking, *Jie hua* is a painting technique that draws precise lines by a *Jie bi* and a straight-edge ruler. However, the question remains: why are such tools necessary for drawing lines? The answer is, of course, to achieve a strict precision. Then why is such precision necessary? Because when depicting palaces, wooden structures and similar structures, accuracy is essential.

Is there anything wrong with painting precisely? Of course not. However, some people believe that *Jie hua,* which is done by measuring with a ruler, results in rigid lines without any vitality – they even look down upon *Jie hua* and its painters. This view is quite narrow-minded, don't you think? Precision and vitality aren't necessarily contradictory. Zhang Zhu said that Zhang Zeduan was skilled in *Jie hua* and even established his own school. He found that Zhang Zeduan could not only accurately paint boats, carriages and buildings, but also capture the personality and spirit of figures, thus saying that he established his own school. The term 'school' here refers to a distinct style of academic or artistic skills. It is important to note that even when painting architecture, Zhang Zeduan did not always use a ruler. He used tools to draw large structures, but for small houses, he painted freehand. Moreover, please do not mistakenly believe that *Jie hua* only involves straight lines. Painters must also possess a strong understanding of architectural construction, be able to calculate proportions and scales, comprehend the principles of one-point perspective drawing and depict a clear sense of three-dimensionality with distinct foreground and background elements. From this, we can also conclude that the general statement that Chinese ancient paintings prioritise expression over realism is not entirely accurate.

8. Comparison of Different Versions of *Along the River During the Qingming Festival*

Q: Why are some ancient paintings also called *Along the River During the Qingming Festival*, but look very different from Zhang Zeduan's version?

A: *Along the River During the Qingming Festival* is a great masterpiece of realism in genre painting in Chinese art history. Attracted by it, many copies ① appeared in later generations. These later versions are not completely faithful to the original work, and some even have significant alterations. So, if you have seen other versions, you would notice that they differ greatly from Zhang Zeduan's original work. Let's compare the version by Qiu Ying from the late Ming Dynasty (referred to as the 'Ming version') and the version collaboratively painted by five court painters, including Chen Mei, in the early Qianlong period of the Qing Dynasty (referred to as the 'Qing version') with Zhang Zeduan's original work (referred to as the 'Song version').

① Let's briefly explain the differences between *Lin*(临), *Mo*(摹) and *Fang*(仿). *Lin*: This technique involves placing the original painting beside you and recreating it by closely observing and following the original. *Mo*: This technique involves placing a translucent paper over the original painting and tracing it stroke by stroke directly onto the overlay. Both *Lin* and *Mo* aim to achieve a close resemblance to the original work, with greater similarity being better. (Some people sign the original artist's name on their own copies, passing them off as genuine works, which are called 'forgeries'.) *Fang*: Unlike *Lin* and *Mo*, this technique focuses not on the exact replication but on imitating the brushwork and style of the original. Therefore, at first glance, some *Fang* works may differ greatly from the original work, yet they still maintain a clear stylistic connection to the original.

There are three major differences between the Song, Ming, and Qing versions:

First, the tone is different. The Song version begins with a donkey caravan carrying charcoal, traversing a misty forest path, giving an impression of desolation and silence. The subsequent 'startled horse' scene sets the tense tone for the entire scroll. In contrast, the Ming and Qing versions start with leisurely scenes of cattle herding. In the Ming version, the shepherd boy is even playing a flute, depicting an idyllic pastoral scene. Moving forward, both the Ming and Qing versions feature scenes of watching operas and wedding processions, setting a harmonious, lively and festive tone for the entire scroll.

Second, the perspective is different. The Song version adopts a scholar's perspective, where the artist pays close attention to the inner world and personalities of the figures. Even a small child can evoke emotion in the viewer, and even a figure seen from behind can stir feelings. The Ming version, however, employs a secular perspective, capturing worldly pleasures through a merchant's eye, catering to those buyers who pursue wealth and enjoy bustling scenes. The Qing version, commissioned for the newly enthroned Qianlong Emperor, adopts a grand, almost imperial, perspective, emphasising auspiciousness and imperial majesty.

Third, the theme is different. Upon close reading of the Song version, it is not difficult to sense Zhang Zeduan's responsible and heartfelt scholar spirit. The Ming version, on the other hand, caters to secular tastes, while the Qing version satisfies the emperor.

The bottom picture opposite shows the Rainbow Bridge in the Ming version, while

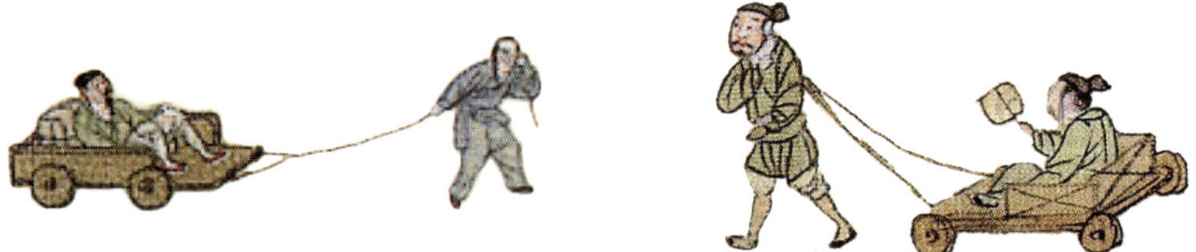

the one above shows it in the Qing version. Both are stone bridges, considerably more solid than the wooden bridge in the Song version. In terms of the proportion between the boats and the bridge, the bridge in the Ming version is quite large but appears modest, giving a sense of humble life. In contrast, the bridge in the Qing version feels grand and magnificent, with a sweeping presence.

Regarding the interaction between the boats and the bridges, there is no conflict at all: the arch in the Ming version is very large, allowing boats to pass through easily. In the Qing version, the boats are very large, but the masts have already been lowered, ensuring smooth passage. However, an odd detail in the Qing version is the presence of two people inexplicably standing outside the railing atop the bridge. Perhaps the Qing court painters were trying to imitate the person throwing a rope in the Song version, but it turned out to be neither fish nor fowl.

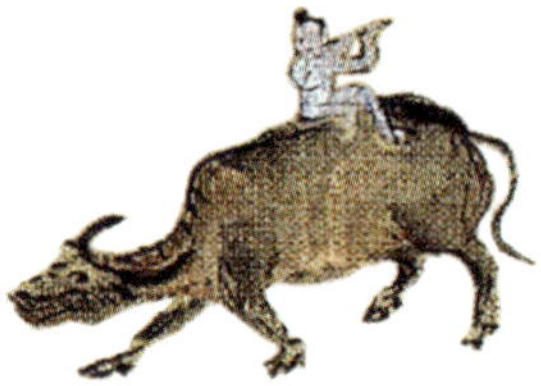

Ming version

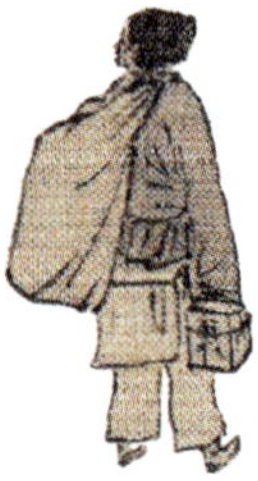

Qing version

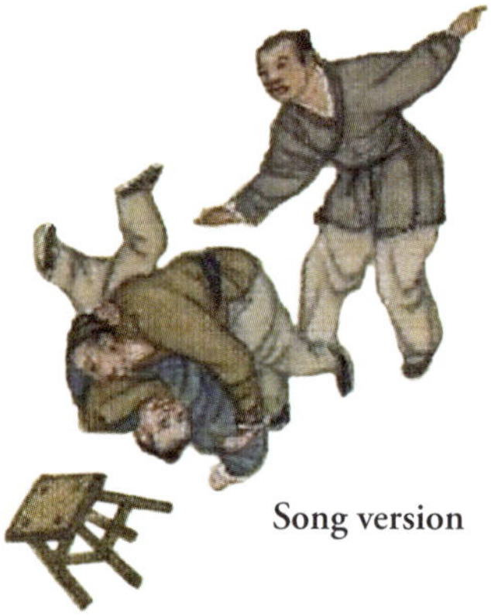

Song version

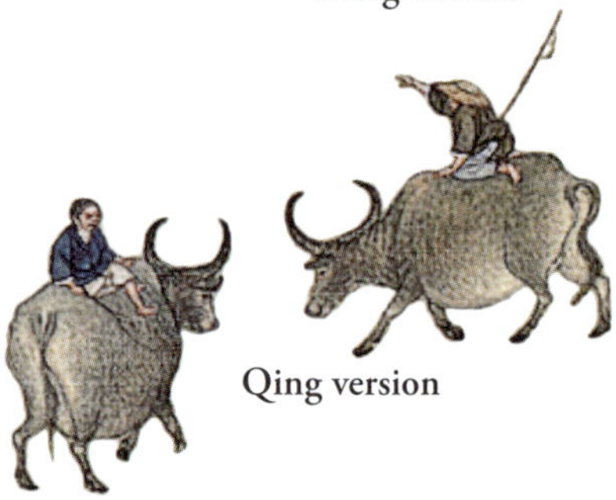

Qing version

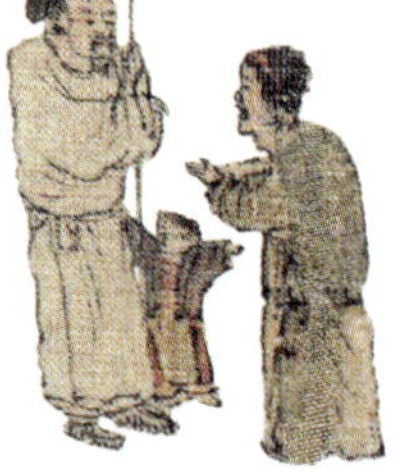

Qing version

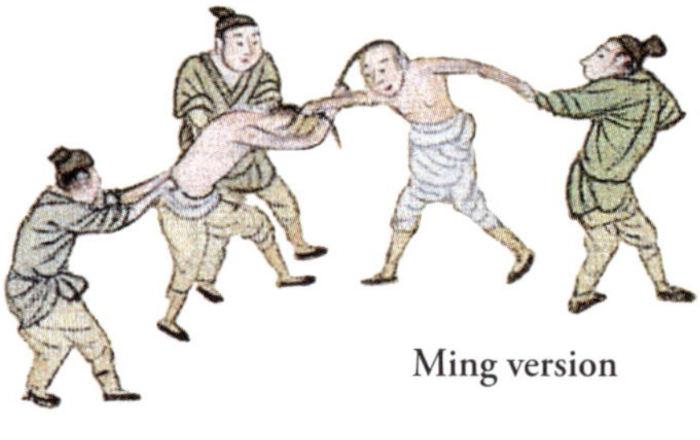

Ming version

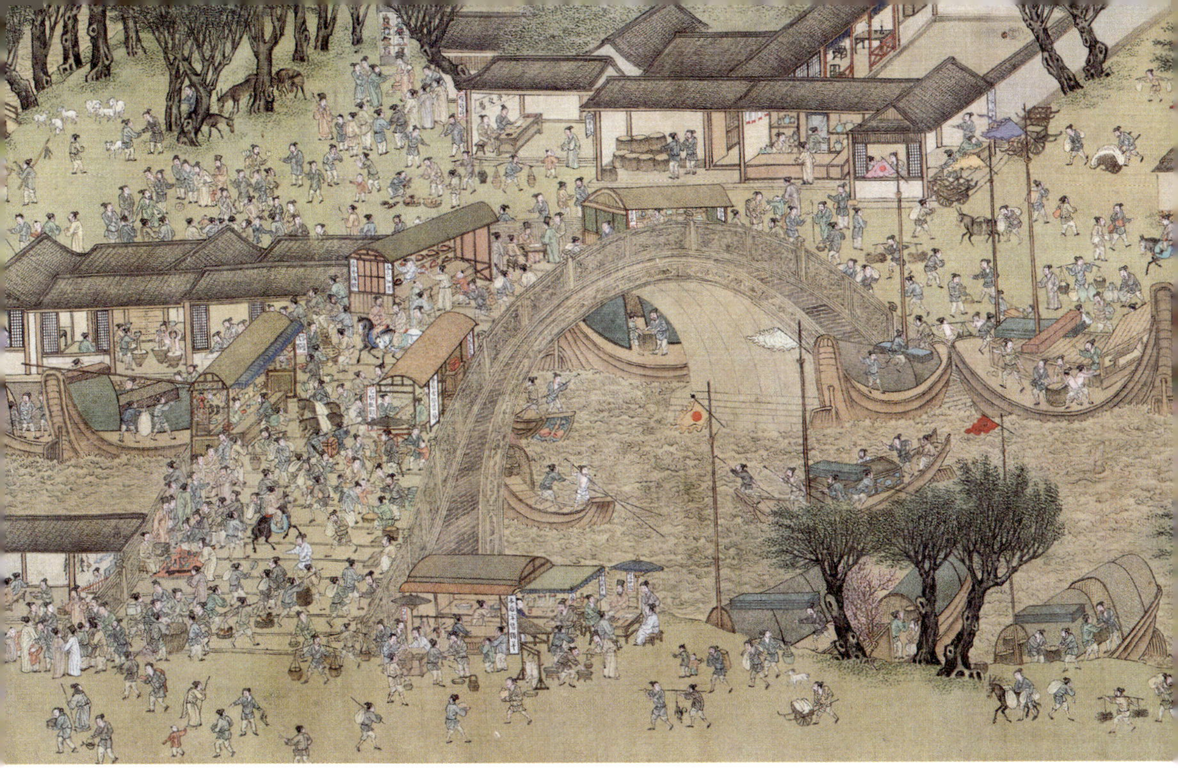

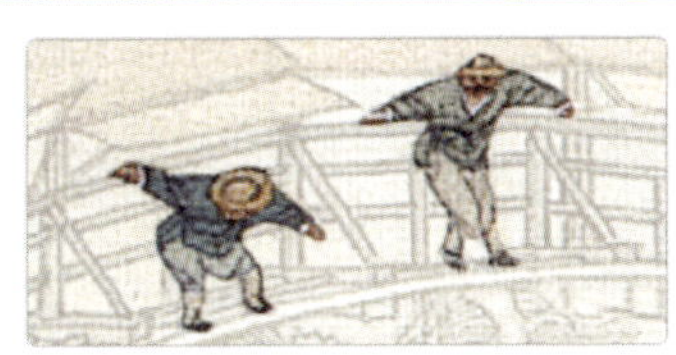

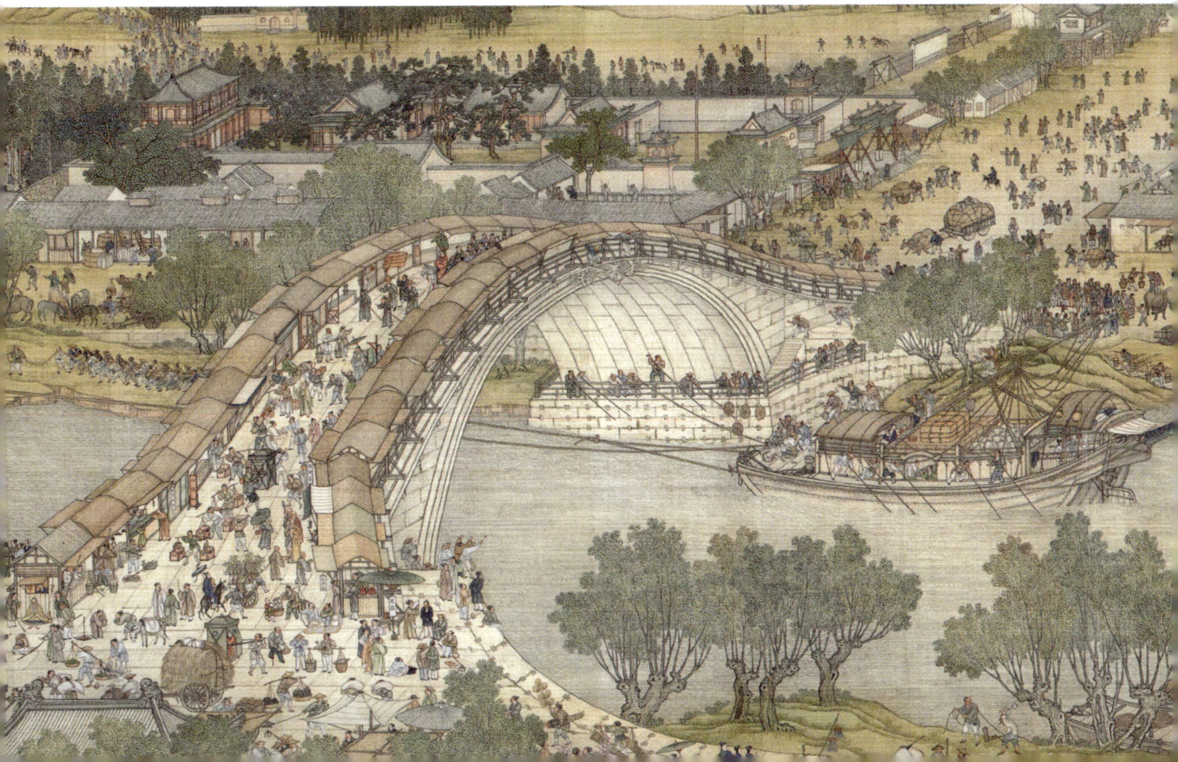

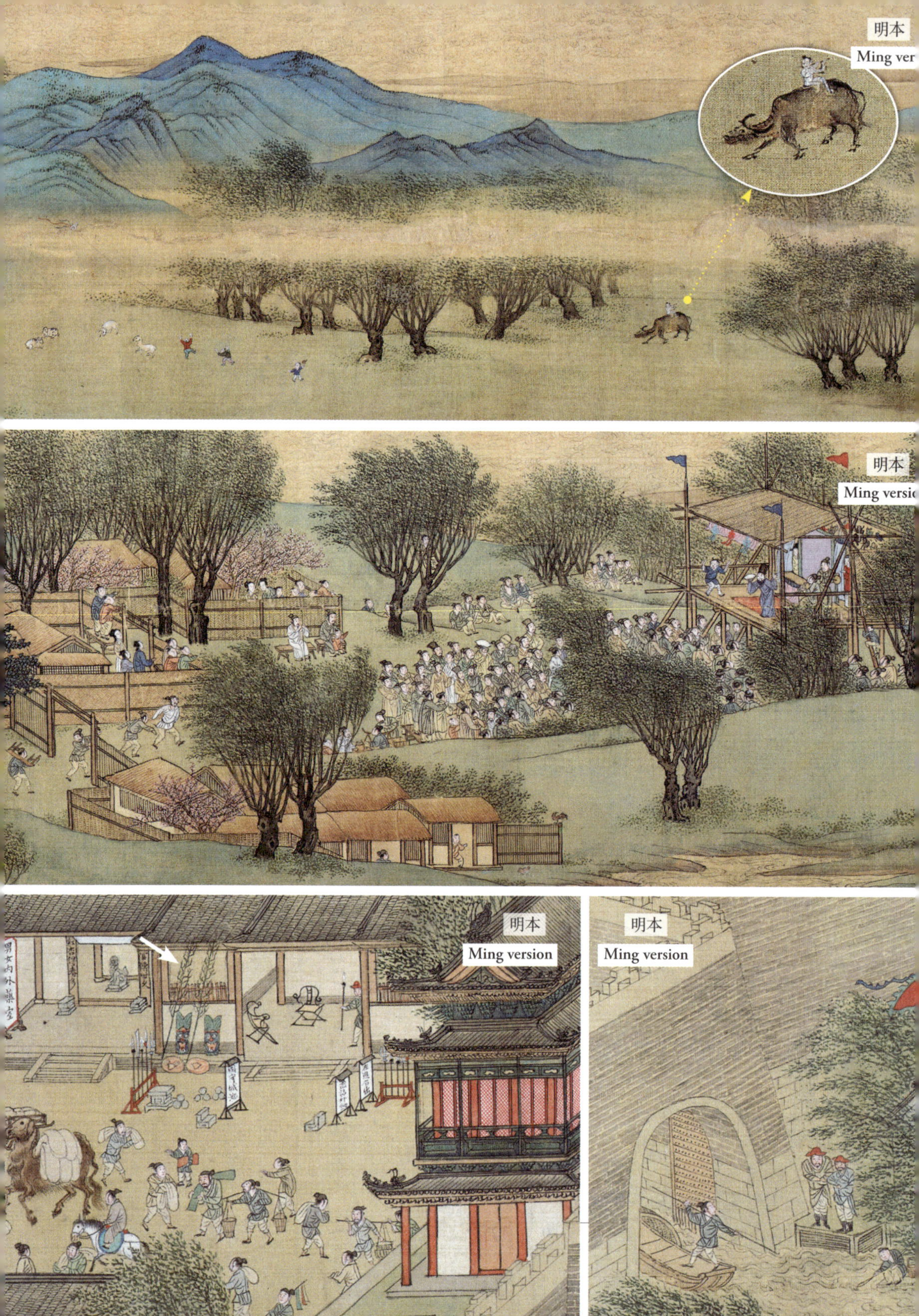
明本
Ming ver
明本
Ming versi
明本
Ming version
明本
Ming version

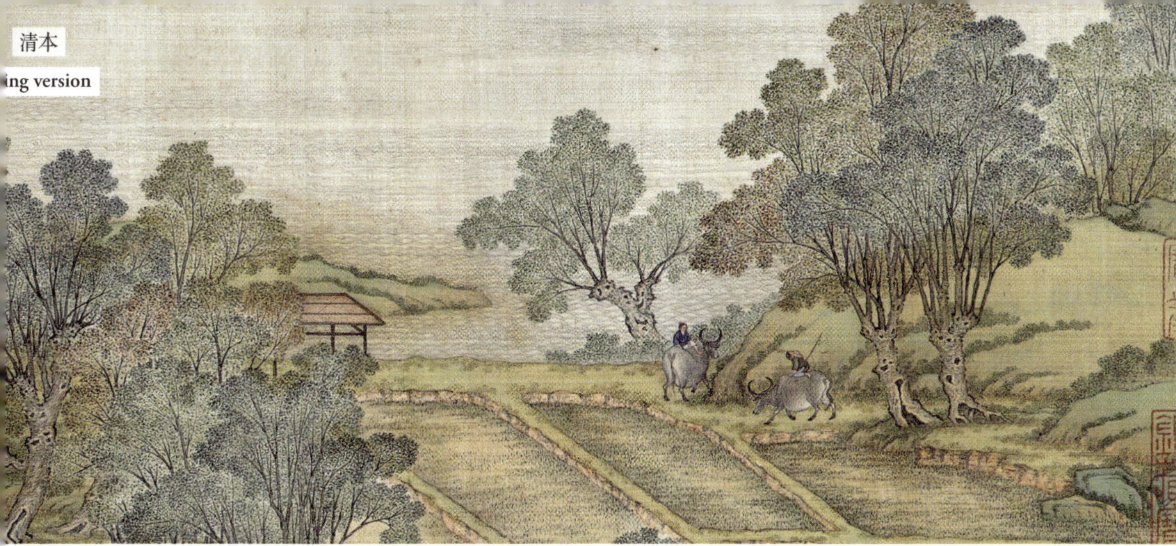

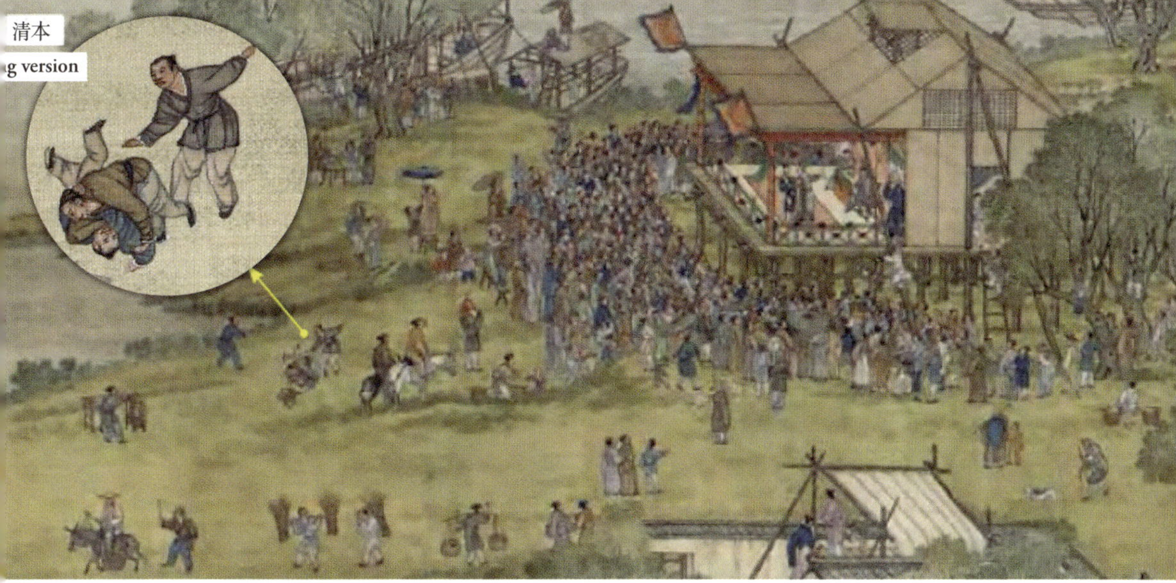

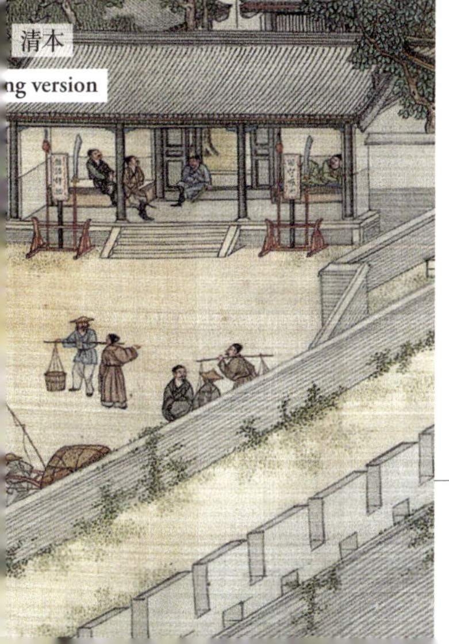

The two pictures on the top of this page and the left page are the cattle herding and opera-watching scenes mentioned earlier in the Ming and Qing versions.

The beginning of the Ming and Qing versions features a broad vision, undulating hills, gentle running water, cultivated field, lush foliage and leisurely cattle herding. It creates an almost idyllic pastoral scene, starkly contrasting with the Song version which focuses on the necessities of civilian life, such as fuel.

Both the Ming and Qing versions begin with a wedding procession, but this does not imply that the Qingming Festival was an auspicious day for marriage in ancient China. The 'wedding procession' in *Along the River During the Qingming Festival* is just a symbol of good fortune, intended to counteract any negative emotions the term 'Qingming' might evoke. It guides our readers to interpret the painting's theme as one of 'peace and prosperity'. Watching operas is another such symbol. Only when people are well-fed and content can they have the leisure to watch operas. Among the people, some climb trees, some stand on stools, some overturn buckets and stand on the bottom, some perch on the boat's canopies and some women even climb onto their rooftops... Although there is no profound meaning, each one is a small delight, a testament to the vibrancy of daily life. There are also people fighting (perhaps for a better view), but it does not imply problems with public security; it is merely to amuse our readers. In reality, both the Ming and Qing versions place great emphasis on city defence and security, as the safety of the city is paramount to putting the wealthy and the emperor at ease. As for the minor squabbles among the lower classes, they are but a trivial matter, inconsequential to the rich and powerful.

There are no city defences in the Song version, but they are quite emphasised in the Ming and Qing versions. In the Ming version, as soon as one enters the city gate, there is a city defence garrison, with signs that read '左进右出 (Enter on the left, exit on the right)', '盘诘奸细 (Interrogate spies)', and '固守城池 (Secure the city)'. There are weapon racks and cannonballs on the ground, and shields and *Lang Xian* (狼筅, indicated by the white arrow in the picture on the left bottom of the previous page, a weapon invented by the famous anti-Japanese general Qi Jiguang) against the wall, and soldiers standing guard with spears. Even the water gate on the side of the city gate is also guarded by two soldiers. In the Qing version, there is also a city defence institution at the city gate, with two signs also reading '盘诘奸细 (Interrogate spies)', and '固守城池 (Secure the city)'. Comparing the Ming and Qing versions with the Song version, it is clear that the lack of city defences in the Song version is absolutely no small matter!

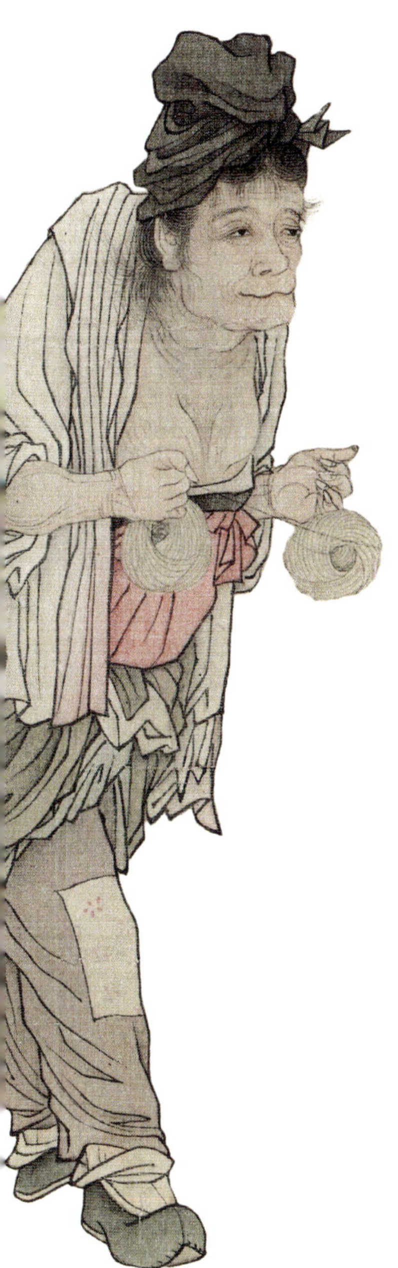

The old woman in *Spinning Wheel*, ang Juzheng, Northern Song Dynasty

9. How to further understand the real life in the Song Dynasty?

Q: Is *Along the River During the Qingming Festival* the best representation of the livelihood of the Song Dynasty? Was their real life like this?

A: Of course, it is! *Along the River During the Qingming Festival* is an incredibly detailed, vivid and exquisite depiction of the streets and activities of people in Bianjing during the late Northern Song Dynasty. It is undoubtedly a representative work that showcases the everyday life of the common people at that time. However, regarding whether the real life in the Song Dynasty was exactly like this, it's more accurate to say that the painting partially reflects the social life during a specific period. On the one hand, it portrays the bustling and lively atmosphere of the streets with great authenticity. On the other hand, it does not depict private residences or provide meticulous details. Consequently, it offers limited insight into the nuances of private life.

Besides the renowned scroll of *Along the River During the Qingming Festival*, there are other significant 'small paintings' that are also worth reading. These works provide additional insights into the real life in the Song Dynasty. For example: *Watergate Gristmill* (《闸口盘车图》, Anonymous, the Five Dynasties to Song Dynasty) , *Spinning Wheel* (《纺车图》,Wang Juzheng, Northern Song Dynasty), *Ren Wu Ce* (《人物册》, Anonymous, Song Dynasty), *The Moxa Treatment* (《炙艾图》 Li Tang, Southern Song Dynasty), *Gengzhi Tu* (*Pictures of Tilling and Weaving*, 《耕织图》, Lou Shou, Southern Song Dynasty, Cheng Qi copy in Yuan Dynasty), *The Process of Making Silk* (《蚕织图》, Liang

Kai, Southern Song Dynasty), *The Peddler* (《货郎图》, Li Song, Southern Song Dynasty), *Gristmill* (《盘车图》, Anonymous, Southern Song Dynasty) and *Shui Cun Lou Ge Tu* (《水村楼阁图》, Anonymous, Southern Song Dynasty). Additionally, murals also provide valuable visual records of the time, such as the Northern Song murals at Kaihua Temple in Gaoping, Shanxi. In short, these 'small paintings' are like fragments of the era. Each piece contributes to a larger puzzle, offering a more comprehensive understanding of life in the Song Dynasty. By immersing ourselves in these visual narratives, we cultivate a deeper empathy for the experiences of those who lived then, enriching our understanding of history and the human experience.

Below, I present a few of these paintings.

The left picture below depicts a scholar in his white robe returning home. He holds a bamboo staff, followed by a boy carrying a *Qin*. At this moment, he can already see the gate of his courtyard. A woman, upon seeing him from an upstairs window, hurries

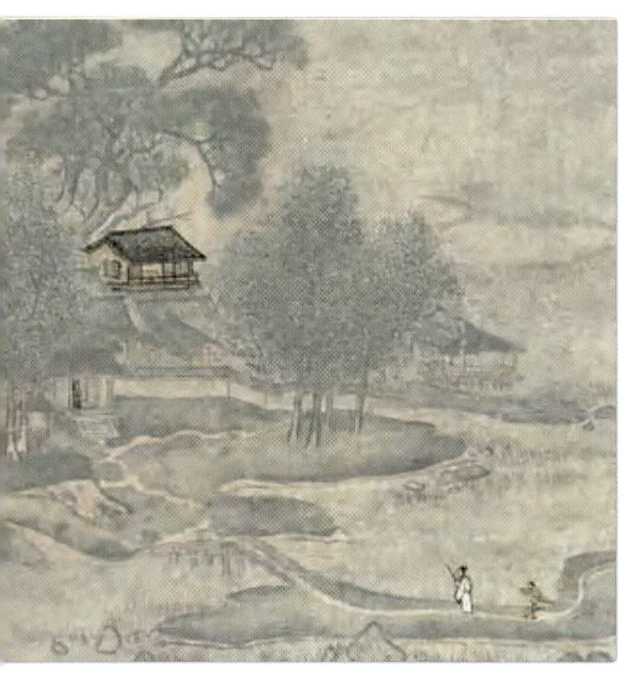

Shui Cun Lou Ge Tu (Part), Anonymous, Southern Song Dynasty, in the collection of the Palace Museum, Beijing

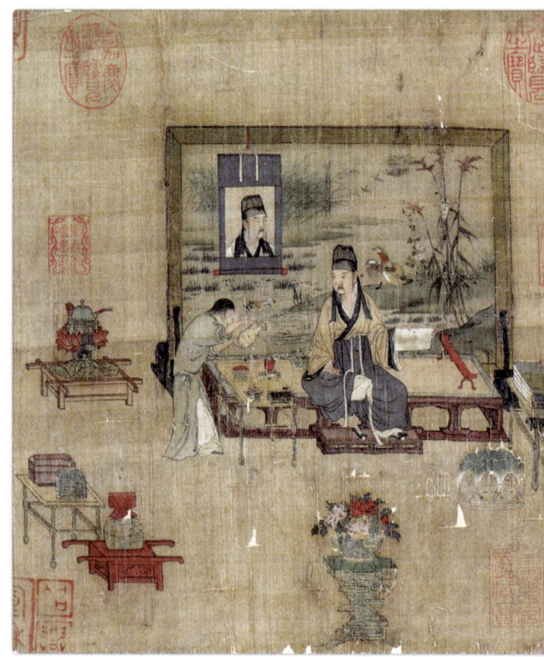

Ren Wu Ce, Anonymous, Northern Song Dyna

downstairs to the door, eagerly awaiting him. Although the figures are small, the scene is filled with deep emotion. This perfectly illustrates one of the ideal lifestyles of scholars in the Song Dynasty.

The picture bottom left on the opposite page is *Ren Wu Ce,* a Northern Song Dynasty work. Yes, the painting is simply named *Ren Wu Ce,* or at most, *Wu Kuan Ren Wu Tu* (《无款人物图》), because it lacks even the artist's signature. It was likely painted in the early to middle period of Emperor Huizong's reign, perhaps around the same time as *Along the River During the Qingming Festival.* The protagonist of the painting is a Song Dynasty scholar. Behind him, his own portrait hangs on a folding screen, and the furnishings in the room are all exquisite, reflecting his taste and lifestyle. In *Along the River During the Qingming Festival*, there are some officials and scholars walking along the bustling streets. *Ren Wu Ce*, in contrast, can help us imagine what they might be like at home. Of course,

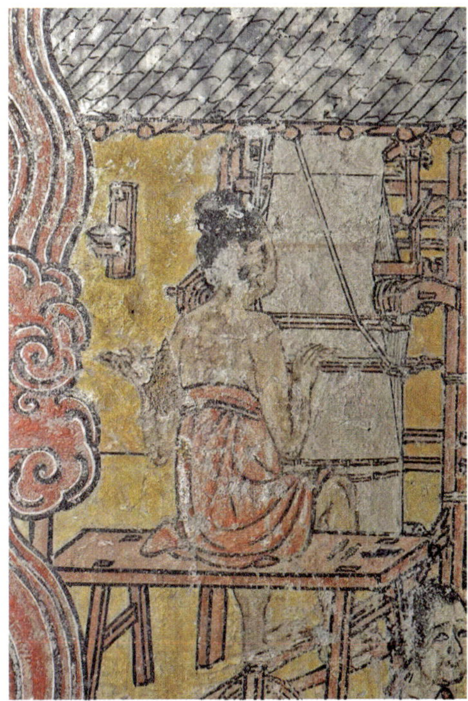

***Guan Zhi Tu*, murals at Kaihua Temple in Gaoping, Shanxi**

while this painting represents the dream of many scholars at the time, their actual lives may have differed.

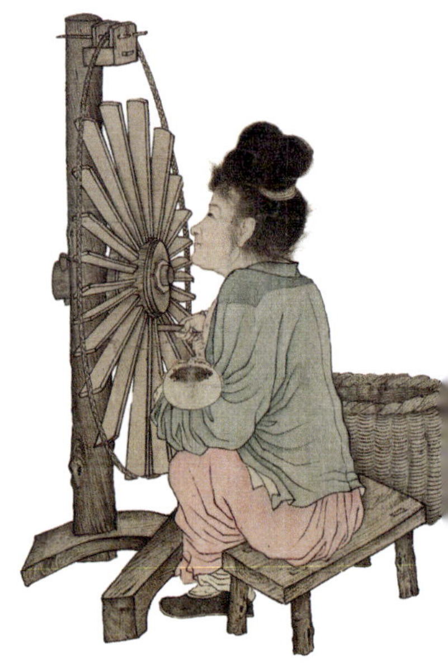

On page 211 is the Northern Song Dynasty mural *Guan Zhi Tu* (《观织图》, observing the weaving). According to the painter's inscription on the wall, it was completed by the painter Guo Fa around the third year of the Shaosheng era (1096) during Emperor Zhezong's reign. The depiction of the weaving machine is remarkably precise, with clear mechanical structures, making it an invaluable visual resource for ancient vertical looms. This type of loom employs foot pedals to control the heddle, raising and lowering the warp threads to weave plain fabrics. The weaver in the picture is not wearing any upper garments, and much of her legs are exposed, revealing the typical attire of working women in ancient times and the arduousness of weaving. To the left of her head, there is an oil lamp on

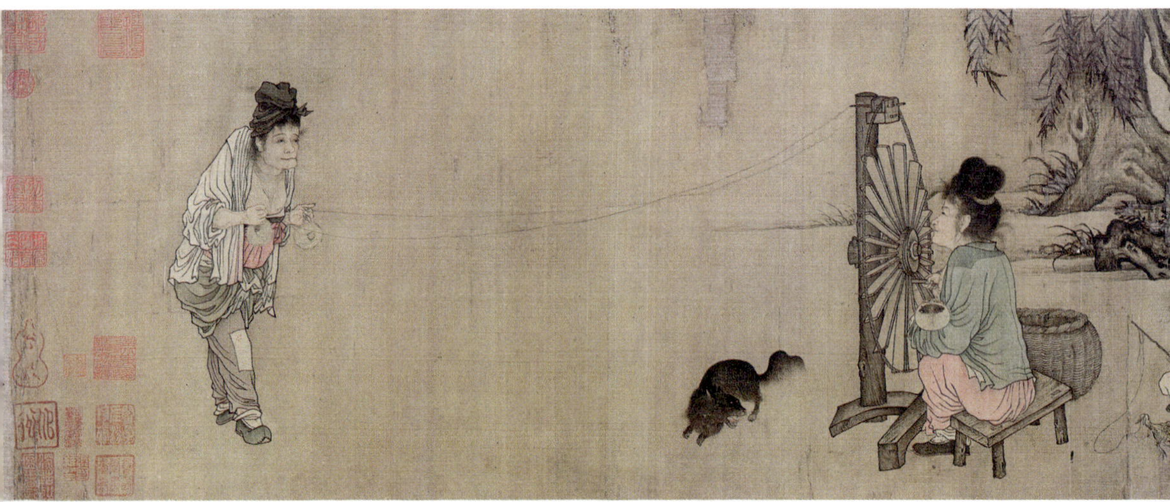

Spinning Wheel **(Part), Wang Juzheng, Northern Song Dynasty**
ink and colour on silk, 26.1 cm × 69.2 cm,
in the collection of the Palace Museum, Beijing

the wall, indicating that she works day and night. Murals also provide significant visual documentations for understanding the real lives of ancient people.

The picture on the bottom of the opposite page is the previously mentioned Northern Song Dynasty painting *Spinning Wheel*. The mother is nursing her baby while simultaneously operating the spinning wheel. Across from her sits an elderly woman, her gaunt chest exposed, holding two balls of thread in front of her breasts. The hemp thread dangles and sways, being drawn onto the spindle as the mother turns the wheel. In the previous large picture of the elderly woman, some readers may have noticed a patch on her knee, adorned with a plum blossom. This detail, a glimmer of beauty amidst the realities of poverty, is particularly striking. Do you remember the beginning of *Along the River During the Qingming Festival*? In the courtyard of a farmhouse, there was the silhouette of a woman. At the time, we couldn't discern the details, but this *Spinning Wheel* can provide a close-up, enriching our understanding of that farmhouse and its inhabitants. Many women in the Song Dynasty likely lived this way – spinning, feeding pigs, nursing their children. Their lives, though seemingly mundane and repetitive, were undoubtedly punctuated by moments of quiet joy and beauty, symbolised here by the delicate red blossom.

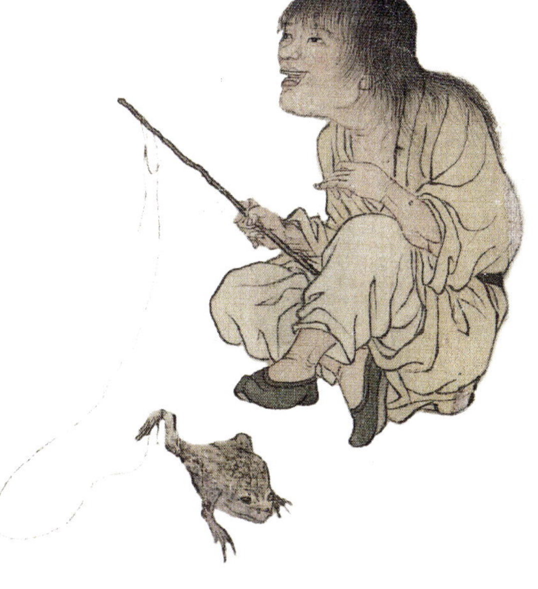

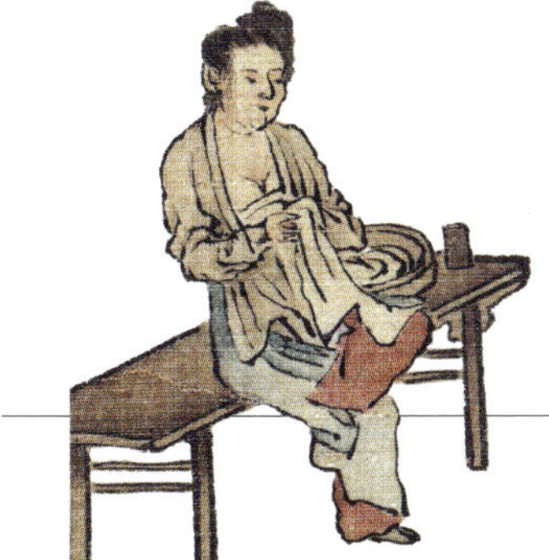

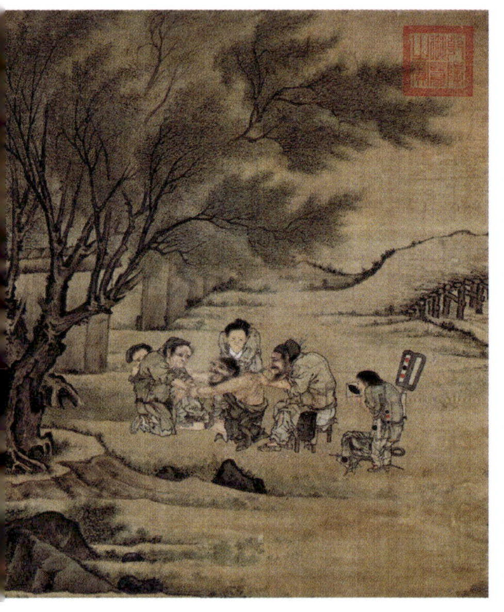

The Moxa Treatment, **Li Tang, Southern Song Dynasty ink and colour on silk, 68.8 cm × 58.7 cm, in the collection of the National Palace Museum, Taipei**

The Moxa Treatment is a genre painting, surviving approximately 900 years, that offers a glimpse into Song Dynasty medical practices. The scene depicts a doctor performing moxibustion to his patient. In the painting, the person with his mouth wide open, crying out in pain, is the patient. The doctor, with his left hand supporting the patient's shoulder, uses tweezers by his right hand to apply the moxa. The two red spots are the ignited moxa. Moxa is typically conical in shape, pointed at the top and flat at the base, made from moxa wool which is processed from mugwort leaves. Mugwort, known for its antibacterial and antiviral properties, has a long history in traditional Chinese herbal medicine to prevent plagues. During the Dragon Boat Festival, people would hang mugwort leaves on their doors to ward off poison and evil spirits in ancient times. Upon another closer look, the clothes of the figures in the painting are all patched, some with patches layered upon patches, even the doctor, whose pants have a large hole. Yet, he seems indifferent to it. We can compare this painting with the *Zhao Taicheng Jia* pharmacy in *Along the River During the Qingming Festival*, to understand that the medical conditions for the common people in the Song Dynasty were quite rudimentary. Moreover, the living conditions of doctors in the village were totally different from those of high-ranking physicians in the capital city.

The pictures on this page are both from *The Process of Making Silk*, Liang Kai, Southern Song Dynasty (in the collection of Cleveland Museum of Art, USA).

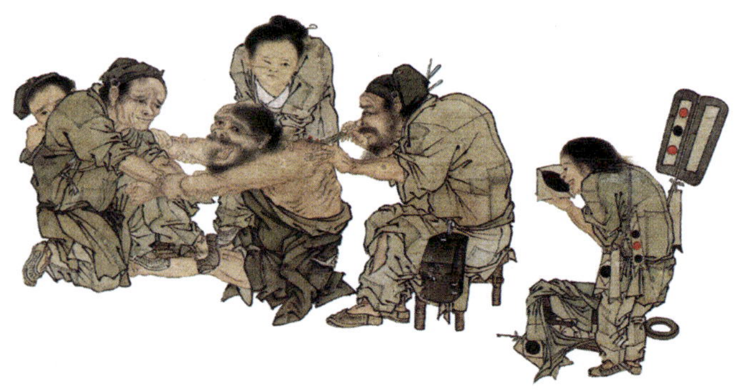